BLOOD OF REVOLUTION

ALSO BY ERIK DURSCHMIED

The Hinge Factor
The Weather Factor

FROM THE
REIGN OF
TERROR TO
THE ARAB
SPRING

BLOOD OF

REVOLUTION

ERIK DURSCHMIED

ARCADE PUBLISHING • NEW YORK

Dedicated to those, who, in large measure and small,
gave of themselves to help others.

First published as *Whipser of the Blade* in Great Britain in 2001 by Hodder & Stoughton, A Division of Hodder Headline

Arcade Publishing books may be purchased in bulk at special discounts for sales promotion, corporate gifts, fund-raising, or educational purposes. Special editions can also be created to specifications. For details, contact the Special Sales Department, Arcade Publishing, 307 West 36th Street, 11th Floor, New York, NY 10018 or arcade@skyhorsepublishing.com.

Arcade Publishing® is a registered trademark of Skyhorse Publishing, Inc.®, a Delaware corporation.

Visit our website at www.arcadepub.com.

10 9 8 7 6 5 4 3 2 1

Designed by Palimpsest Book Production Limited, Polmont, Stirlingshire, England

Library of Congress Cataloging-in-Publication Data is available on file.

ISBN: 978-1-61145-791-9

Printed in the United States of America

Of the great men of this world
we declaim heroic songs
how, rising up like stars
they fall like stars . . .

Bertolt Brecht, *Ballad of the Waterwheel*

Contents

List of Illustrations

Preface to the Second Edition

The story of an overturned apple cart . . .

It started in the most unlikely place for the most unlikely reason.

It was on a Tuesday, the 14th of July, 1789, when a young student climbed on a bistro table, waved a flag, and roused the burghers of Paris to storm the Bastille. So it happened on another Tuesday, 17 December 2010, this time in a dusty town on the edge of the Sahara. Only that young man's revolutionary flag was an apple cart, and the reason for his protest was a shakedown by government officials.

Around 10:30 that morning, in the Tunisian provincial town of Sidi Bouzid, two policemen and their chief, the forty-five-year-old female official Faida Hamdi, walked up to a twenty-six-year-old street vendor, Mohammed Bouazizi, who eked out a meager living selling fresh produce from his wooden pushcart. She demanded to see his vendor's permit (which, according to local law, isn't required). Bouazizi couldn't produce one. The policewoman harassed him; not satisfied accepting the ten dinar fine (about $7.00, his day's take), she demanded a bribe. Bouazizi did not have the money to give and it came to a scream-up.

In the resulting confusion, bystanders stated that Hamdi slapped the vendor in the face and screamed insults at him about his father and the chastity of his sister. She went on to confiscate Mohammed's most precious possession, his scale. Her escorts pushed away his cart with the produce he had purchased on credit. Bouazizi, robbed of his wares, ran to the town hall to complain to the local governor, who refused to see him. In utter desperation, Bouazizi went to a nearby gas station, where he bought a small plastic can filled with gasoline. With it he went back to the governor's office and stood in front of the building.

'How do you expect me to make a living and feed my family?' he yelled at the figure of the town's chief official looking down at him from behind a closed window.

It was now 11:30 a.m. Less than an hour had passed since the initial shakedown. A small crowd had gathered, watching the unfolding scene. Suddenly it happened—so quick that nobody had time to prevent the tragedy. The young vegetable vendor doused himself with gasoline, struck a match, and set himself on fire. In the ensuing confusion, with people rushing about and screaming for help, someone came running out of city hall with a bucket, trying to extinguish the flames with water, which made it only worse. Bystanders carried the badly burned Bouazizi to a car and rushed him to a first-aid station.

The horror of Bouazizi's self-immolation spread like wildfire. By the time the local governor finally decided to intervene it was too late. From the surrounding streets poured the enraged townspeople, chanting anti-government slogans. The town center burst into flames; official cars were overturned and set on fire and the city hall's windows smashed. And while Bouazizi agonized in a hospital, the anti-government rioting spread across the country until it reached the nation's capital. Where a week before a local governor would not see him, the Tunisian president Zine el Abidine Ben Ali, a dictator who during his twenty-three years in power had stolen over a billion dollars from his country's coffers, made a pilgrimage to the dying Bouazizi's bedside. A futile gesture.

On 4 January 2011, Mohammed Bouazizi died. The following day, a crowd in the thousands attended his funeral, chanting: 'Mohammed, we will avenge you. We weep for you today. Now we will make those who caused your death weep.' They made good on their promise. The same day, Tunisia erupted in flames.

Nine days later, President Abidine Ben Ali fled for his life.

A young man's call to do away with greed and corruption kindled a revolutionary fire that quickly got out of control. The story of his act, fed by cell phone, the internet, and social media to other countries, struck the spark to an *Arab Spring*, which quickly engulfed the entire Arab crescent. On one side stood senile and corrupt potentates, out of touch with modern realities; while facing them, a new generation, media savvy and politically creative, determined to create conditions for a democratic future. Using the latest technological improvements at their disposal, they spoke out against a corrupt political system. Once the flame was lit, no despotic ruler could extinguish it. From Tunis to Damascus, Tripoli to Cairo and Sana'a, massive crowds brought down entrenched political structures. Tunisia's corrupt president Abidine Ben Ali fled into exile, Libya's extravagant dictator Muammar Gadaffi was lynched by a mob, Egypt's president Hosni Mubarak was arrested, tried, and convicted, Syria burst into flames, and Yemeni president Ali Abdullah Saleh's thirty-three-year dictatorial rule was ended.

Courage is necessary for real change. The first of the *'heroic martyrs of a new Middle Eastern revolution'* was a simple vegetable vendor, proving that civilian airliners aren't required to make a revolution's flaming sword.

An apple cart, overturned, will do.

Erik Durschmied
January 2013

Preface to the First Edition

Many years ago I set out to discover the meaning of the word revolutionary. Young and filled with boundless ambition to score a big scoop, I met the Latino Robin Hood, Fidel Castro of *el revolución tropical*. He too was young, driven by a contagious fever to fight for the betterment of his people.

One evening in the rugged mountains of Cuba, Castro stared at me as he took the cigar from his mouth to ask: 'Tell me, *periodista*, what do *you* think of our *revolución*?'

'Well, since you ask, I find being a revolutionary can be outright dangerous.'

He answered without the slightest hesitation: 'Plain living can be dangerous. When there is injustice you cannot just sit by and do nothing about it. *Libertad o muerte*.' Was that really the only choice?

'And should things turn out . . .' I was at a loss as to how to say it – in failure. He gave me a hard look.

'If I join a funeral, I march all the way to the cemetery.'

Comandante Fidel Castro was my first contact with a revolutionary. But not my last. Some revolutionaries I met in person, others I read about. I was never a judge, only a spectator to decisive if bloody episodes on the stage of human tragedy. It is up to history to pass its final judgment on the giants of revolution and their deeds, the great men who rose like stars and fell like stars.

* * *

There have been insurrections that have changed the course of history, and represent a momentous watershed. Revolutionary earthquakes that shook the world. Afterwards, our planet was no longer the same. Royalists and revolutionaries have left us their written testaments, which express their political views. Contemporaries of these events generated a flood of documents; their accounts, however, are no longer open to scrutiny. As in most crucial periods of human history, dates are the only certainty – we know for a fact that the people of Paris stormed the Bastille on 14 July 1789. This fact belongs to history; for the rest we can only approximate to the truth.

The list of those to whom I am indebted for advice and historical information is almost as large as the scope of the events I describe. On contemporary events I gratefully acknowledge the help offered by eyewitnesses by allowing me access to their stories and observations. In most cases their names have been withheld at their own request. Many held different views from my own, but contributed greatly to my understanding of the times. My thanks to them all.

I make no claim to compete with the experts, or to have reached a conclusive verdict which only history itself can provide. If anything, it is my curiosity, my amazement, or my naivety that is reflected in these pages.

The research on events in France was done in the voluminous archives of the Ville de Paris. Andreas Hofer and Pancho Villa were researched during trips to their respective countries. For the chapter on Red October, I have been able to draw on the inestimable help of a Russian source with recent access to archival KGB files. The material on the fall of the Kaiser came from Germany's Historic Institute. Operation Walküre involved my own family. I based my account of the Tokyo insurrection on the tales of survivors, and of Che's tragic saga on personal observations. Iranian acquaintances contributed their stories on my various stays in Iran before, during, and after the revolution, including interviews with the shah and the Ayatollah Khomeini.

I wish to thank my literary agent, Luigi Bonomi, for his valuable advice, and my UK publisher, Roland Philipps and his editorial staff, for their patience. Lest I forget, my thanks to my grandsons William, thirteen, and Alexander, five, without whose valuable help this book could have been finished a year sooner.

Erik Durschmied
Domaine de Valensole, July 2000

Prologue

The king must die . . .

King Louis XVI of France inherited not only a great empire but also a bloody revolution. When he asked, 'Was revolution unavoidable?' the answer he received was unequivocal: 'You brought it on yourself.' Throughout history it has been the weakness of those in power, men who failed when the situation called for strong, even brutal measures, that allowed the barbarous to take charge.

'The king must die so that *la patrie* [the country] can live!'

With a single phrase, Maximilien Robespierre – someone never crippled by scruples – sealed the sovereign's fate. Before the French Convention reached a decisive vote, Victorien Vergniaud, leader of the Girondin faction, challenged Robespierre, the Jacobin: 'Kill a king and you will take on the whole world. It will cost lives.'

Robespierre, whose convictions bordered on dogmatism, retorted: 'How many men will it take and how many lives will it cost? How many? One? A hundred? A thousand? Lives will be lost. If you haven't got the courage to back up your convictions, then let us know now . . .'

A whirlwind of violence swept across the country. In the beginning, it was the will of God that France should be shrouded in darkness, and then, on the third day, rise from the ashes.

*   *   *

Genius, courage and creativity are powerful forces. But so is evil. Every century produces its amazing cast of characters, a wealth of heroes and villains who, with their exceptional deeds, leave an indelible mark on history. Some acquired their role through birthright; others arrived unexpectedly on the world stage. Many inspired the masses with a phrase, while others frightened them with a single word. For both, their words carried more power than the might of the great armies that opposed them, whose commanders often found themselves on the losing side. Their tenacity was overpowering; they changed the tide of history; their spirit not only transformed their own nation but also influenced great portions of the globe. Most of them fought for freedom and common decency in the face of destructive forces. These men held the promise of a new era; they broke the classical moulds of society and established new ones. Their heroic sacrifice inspired countless others to live a different life.

Others again brought with them darkness, the piercing of hearts and the crushing of bones. Among them were those who set out to kill their class enemies not for what they did but for what they were. They lived by their motto: 'History will absolve me,' and used evil as a powerful source to fulfil some biblical prophecy. Their willingness to kill without mercy required a whole new thinking process about good and evil. Until at last others stood up to the terror and fought for the survival of the human spirit.

The resolve of these 'heroes' was reflected in their character; they saved their own people when they were enveloped in darkness and helped restore their country's promise. Many of them did not live to see the full realisation of their dreams, but their legacy continued with the starkness of a Sophoclean tragedy or the complexity of a Shakespearean play. These were not ordinary people; their lives were what dramas are made of. They became the sacred warriors, fighting their way to the heart of the cyclone. They were sometimes wrong but often right and they set a shining example of ideals to emulate. Most cared little who laid wreaths on their graves or who spat on their memory. Nor were they all sacrificial martyrs whose principal thoughts and actions were guided by such noble issues as defending the rights of man, fighting the corruption of power, leading a nation to freedom of thought, or improving overall social well-being.

Who then had more impact, the heroes or the villains? Both depended on the other. Threats produced resolve and terror brought forth unexpected courage. All of them, good and evil, imagined that their creation would last for ever. Nothing lasts that long. History is littered with figures from a heroic past who follow in each other's footsteps, sometimes for centuries, only to end up as fugitives in their own countries.

Potentates and dictators spent years piling up the explosive powder. But it only took one day to set it off. Unrest always was – and still is – a phenomenon that can only be defeated by better ideas, by persuasion, and by the conditions that sparked it. Disunity was the 'little people's' curse. Yet the people did not remain in such chaos for ever; from revolution a new order emerged which was able to mobilise the vast potentials of the masses. An insurrection's best asset is the fire in the bellies of its men and women, and empty promises cannot extinguish that fire. There must be popular unrest behind even the smallest revolt, and there must also be a charismatic leader who carries in him the spirit and the imagination that can change the world. He gathers up the inflammable tinder before he releases a torrent of critical energy. *Revolution!*

Revolution is born of hope and its philosophy is formally optimistic. But poets and dreamers cannot make a revolution. A people, neglected, oppressed, wronged, must ally their discontent to that of political enthusiasts. Those who pretend to lead uprisings are unable to admit that they are spontaneous, as all true revolutions are. They fight for the right to differ; they struggle against a complex of betrayals and lies, for something called 'the truth' – only to find that there is no such thing as a truth with which a rational society knows how to act.

Revolution is convulsion, which overturns the existing order by violence. It brings on a reign of terror: not only the drama of the block or the bullet, nor the heightened struggle for power among the great of the new order, nor the tension of civil war, but the eternal tragedy of the many little lives invaded by heroic concerns which are ordinarily not theirs at all. The terror touches everyone with an obsessive power and, during a reign of terror, political indifference becomes impossible.

Revolution is always made in the name of freedom; it is directed against the tyranny of the few for the rule of the many. Revolution is accompanied by clearly defined demands for the abolition of poverty and an equal sharing of wealth. But what do these revolutions really change? Some institutions and some laws are indeed altered. But not everything is changed, because the revolutionaries learn to copy their predecessors. Man simply cannot stand the strain of a prolonged effort to live in accordance with high ideals.

Revolutions are waged and decided in the minds of individuals; their cutting edge is words, not swords. An insurrection creates its own momentum, which again dictates its strategy. The vehicle used by revolutionary leaders never varies. It is to mobilise mass support for their aims. This concept is as old as revolution itself. Danton and Robespierre used their bourgeoisie to kill a king; Trotsky and Lenin unleashed the proletariat on a hapless tsar; and the shah failed because Iran's population favoured Allah over King Mammon.

This is the story of legendary revolutions and men whose lives had but a single, dominating purpose. It is a tale of monarchs born to rule, and those who took that birthright from them, of weak men on the throne and strong men who did not shy from extreme measures to usurp power. All were heroes, just as all were pariahs of history, torn between the demands of their conscience and their belief in an ideal. Fanaticism was their original sin and many left in their wake destruction and death. How did they justify their actions, which brought turmoil, terror and bloodshed? Some did it to foster new ideas and change society; others acted for personal gain or from motives of revenge. Others, observing them from the sidelines, called it treason, whilst others cheered it as heroism and a personal sacrifice in the advance of the human condition. In contrast to the monarchs they faced, who were spineless and incapable of ordering a harsh solution at the crucial moment, the revolutionaries used intelligence, stamina, and panache – provided that someone stood by to help them set aside their moral principles and quash their conscience. Only a few could ever achieve this. Those who came out victorious went on to smite the 'enemies of the revolution', to annihilate political opposition, and to transform their freedom movement into an instrument of oppression. Progressive revolutionaries soon turned themselves into conservative dictators. Absolute authority provided them with the illusion that they possessed something close to eternal power. Through indifference, impunity and flattery, those around dictators allow them to believe themselves freed from any constraint, law, or morality. Blinded by the footlights on a stage of public adoration, such men lost all sense of conscience and confused notoriety with fame. Personal power based on terror was also what led most of them to their untimely deaths – devoured by the violence they helped to create.

Insurrection, revolt, revolution: they were the catalyst for a parade of tragic figures who rushed, with eyes wide open, to a violent end. But their spirit carried on. Our present world of social order and democratic rule does not have meaning

if we do not understand what happened in the past. A
king's head tumbled to the will of a revolutionary, before
the revolutionary fell victim to his own rebellion. King or
rebel, their demise came with bewildering speed. Because –
when the blade falls, it comes down fast.

1

10 August 1792

'Le jour de gloire est arrivé'

Le jour de gloire est arrivé.
The day of glory has arrived.
'La Marseillaise'

L'audace, encore l'audace, toujours l'audace.
Boldness, more boldness, forever boldness.
Georges Jacques Danton, 1792

The tocsin shook the citizens of Paris from their sleep. '*Allons, enfants de la patrie . . .*'

It was followed by the boom of a gun. '*Aux armes, citoyens!*'

It was shortly past midnight, on 10 August 1792. The king had been sleeping fitfully after a pleasant meal. Suddenly an explosion shook him. Like a sleepwalker the king stumbled from his bed, a fat man in a dark-red dressing gown with his wig awry. His fat lips trembled. He was lost in the confusion of interrupted sleep and frightening noises.

'Louis, what is going on?' demanded the queen, clutching her nightgown anxiously around her. The tocsin kept on ringing.

The Duc de La Rochefoucauld charged into the room. The king looked startled: 'What is it? *Une révolte?*'

'*Non, sire, c'est une révolution!* It's a revolution!'

'I rule with my arse in the saddle and my pistol in my hand,' announced the first of the Bourbon line, Henri IV, on the day of his coronation in 1572. Here was a monarch who drank more beer than ten of his soldiers, who led them into battle from the front, and who spent his time when he was not at war with one of his sixty-four mistresses. Henri IV, King of France and Navarre, was no doubt one of the most colourful monarchs in European history. He was not an intellectual, but a man of action, and his court became a cross between a cavalry barrack and a whorehouse. Henri de Navarre was without doubt the most popular of all French kings, someone whose dream was that every one of his subjects would be able to have a chicken in his Sunday pot.

The next in the Bourbon line was Louis XIII, married to Anne d'Autriche. The papal nuncio told him that Heaven (and Catholic France) needed an heir, and the young king fulfilled his marital duties. But when it came to ruling a kingdom, he was too young and unsure. He was fortunate to meet in Armand de Plessis a man better known in history as Cardinal Richelieu. By the time Richelieu died in 1642 he had transformed France into the greatest kingdom in Europe. On 14 May 1643, the day the forty-one-year-old Louis XIII lay dying, he asked for his son to be brought to his bedside. 'What do you call yourself, my son?' There was nothing timid about the child's reply: 'Louis XIV.'

This, the most glamorous of all French sovereigns, adopted the sun as his emblem, and declared: '*L'état c'est moi!* I am the state.' And he added: 'War, if necessity demands it, is a just act not only permitted, but commanded to kings. It is a grave error to think that one can reach the same aims by weaker means.' How the history of France, and probably that of Europe, would have been different, had the future Louis XVI listened to the dictum of his illustrious ancestor.

Louis XV's reign was a time of great refinement but also of considerable conflict. His flagrant lifestyle, as much as his futile wars, depleted the treasury. He lost Canada, the Ohio Valley, and Louisiana to the British. France fell into a rapid decline. Conflict grew from within, fed by a generation of great French philosophers, whose thinking was to touch the entire world. Voltaire and Montesquieu, who were liberally inclined, wanted the monarchy to accept a new form of society. The sarcastic Beaumarchais expected little of social reforms. The extremists, Diderot and Rousseau, loudly voiced their doubts that society would find by itself the strength to force reform; rebels against dogmatism and martyrs to free thought and opinion, they predicted that change would have to be imposed by an example from the outside.

It was not long in coming. In North America a conflict broke out between the colonists and the crown. Europe waited for events to duplicate those taking place across the Atlantic. If citizens in Boston and Philadelphia could find happiness by applying the principles of the French thinkers, why continue to support old monarchical idols? In 1774, Louis XV lay dying. His son, an overweight, sixteen-year-old dumpling of a dauphin, was married to Archduchess Maria Antonia of Austria, a capricious fifteen-year-old blonde. Their heritage was a kingdom on the verge of bankruptcy. The old king's dying words were an ominous prediction: '*Après moi le déluge* – After me the flood.'

The fat boy and the blonde girl ascended the throne as King Louis XVI and Queen Marie-Antoinette. Their lives were a truly Shakespearean tragedy. Louis indulged in gluttony, and spent most of his time as monarch in a private workshop behind his official reception room. His pet project was fixing clocks and locks. The mercurial Marie-Antoinette loved dancing and gambling. She referred to her husband as '*le pauvre garçon* – the poor boy', a comment on his poor performance – or lack of it – in the nuptial bed. Her life was that of a flirt, and her adventures included the tall and mysterious Count Fersen, a colonel in the Royal Swedish Regiment. Rumours spread of her revels on black satin sheets, turning her into a modern-day Messalina. Sleazy drawings of her were passed around in bars. Her reputation for frivolity, extravagance, and duplicity earned her the sobriquet *l'Autrichienne* (the Austrian) or *l'autre chienne* (the other bitch-dog), and she was so hated by 'her people' that she became a liability that was to lead her to the guillotine.

The king's first venture into war was against his country's perennial enemy, England, when he lent his support to the rebellious colonists of Virginia. In 1779, 7,500 French troops under the command of Rochambeau and the nineteen-year-old Marquis de Lafayette forced General Cornwallis to surrender at Yorktown. The War of American Independence was a costly affair to the tune of 2 billion *livres*. Jacques Necker, a pot-bellied Swiss banker, was appointed director of finances. In his *Compte rendu au Roi* (fiscal account), Necker humbly pointed out that France faced bankruptcy. The country entered a period of depression, but in no way did the court diminish its outrageous lifestyle. This situation prompted demands by the bourgeoisie for amendment of the existing tax laws. The court looked for a scapegoat. The capable Necker was fired and replaced by the incompetent Charles Calonne, whose policy, that 'a man who borrows must appear to be rich' pleased the king.

As if Louis' marital problems were not enough, the episode of the Diamond Necklace brought the country to boiling point. A jeweller had shown the queen a necklace of exquisite beauty, but it was too extravagant for her purse. The Countess de la Motte-Valois had slipped into the bed of the forty-four-year-old Cardinal Louis de Rohan, a foppish man whose the ambition was to be another Cardinal Richelieu.

She persuaded Rohan to purchase the necklace and offer it to the queen, with whom she told the credulous Rohan, she had some influence. On a moonless night in the park of Versailles, a veiled prostitute with a striking resemblance to the queen met the cardinal and presented him with a rose. The cardinal was overjoyed at this apparent token of favour. He agreed to the payment terms for the jewels, took possession of them and handed them to the countess who would convey his humble offering to her 'intimate friend' the queen. In a burlesque scene of 'Now you see it, now you don't', the countess passed the diamonds to her husband, who left for London where he sold the stones. The jeweller waited for a week before demanding payment from none other than the queen. The king was outraged, Countess de la Motte-Valois was branded as a thief, and the Cardinal de Rohan was banned from Paris. Yet the damage was done and the odium stuck to Marie Antoinette who became known as '*la Reine Deficit*', dipping her hands into state funds while the people of Paris starved. (Napoleon considered the affair of the Rohan necklace as key to the revolution.)

An event, overlooked since it took place across the border, provided another stepping stone towards the French Revolution. The despotism of the Stadholder of Holland, Prince William V, had so frustrated the merchants and burghers that they kicked him out. In 1786, he returned to power on the back of the English fleet. For once, the French managed to benefit from the tense political situation in Holland. The Marquis de Rayneval, dispatched to the Netherlands by Louis, was shocked by what he discovered. 'The fervour of the Patriot Party has made terrifying progress and if it is not stopped, it is to be feared that it may cause an explosion that will have incalculable consequences.' Lack of assistance from Paris brought a quick end to the Dutch Barbacan Uprising of 1787. As a result, the beaten Dutch revolutionaries fled to

France and brought with them their revolutionary ideas and their radical ardour.

The following year two more calamities befell the kingdom: a disastrous harvest and the coldest winter in living memory. With diminished food stocks and a reeling economy, France was headed for a time of deprivation and discontent. The critical question was whether the French would stoically endure the hardship, as they had so many times before, or would strike out in anger against the old political order. While the court was left to ponder this question but did nothing to relieve the suffering of the people, the population of Paris ate cats and rats. Thousands perished during the terrible winter of 1788. With famine crippling its cities, and its finances in a shambles, France drifted into 1789. The catastrophic situation forced the king into a desperate step. He called for a meeting of the États Généraux (the States General) for 4 May 1789. The assembly was made up of 270 nobles of the high aristocracy, or the First Estate, who by their birthright did not have to pay tax. Also present were 291 clergy, or the Second Estate, who benefited equally from a tax-exempt existence. The last group was the Tiers État, or Third Estate, whose 578 deputies were selected from the grand and petit bourgeoisie. This group had to carry the entire financial burden of France. The question of an 'abolition of privileges' was the crucial point on the agenda; a priest of the low clergy, the Abbé Sieyès, had posed the question: 'What is the Third Estate? *Everything*! What has it been up to now on the political level? *Nothing*! What does it ask for? To be *something*!' The benches of the great hall in Versailles were crowded: the nobility were decked out in silks, albeit rather worn at the cuffs; the clergy were dressed in black, with a sprinkling of crimson or purple; and the bourgeoisie wore rather plain if not drab attire. The nobility received a shock when the king's first cousin, the Duc d'Orléans, and the Count Gabriel Honoré de Mirabeau joined the bench of the Third Estate.

No man worked harder and more thanklessly to save the kingdom from itself than Mirabeau. His personality was impressive; he was the single most powerful force to dare to challenge the king. He initiated a series of events that were to lead to the French Revolution. The nobility loathed him because he had deserted his class; the bourgeoisie mistrusted him because he was of noble birth; and the king thought of Mirabeau as a *chien enragé* (mad dog). Everyone had him wrong. Mirabeau was deeply concerned to uphold order, but not to uphold *l'ancien régime*, the old order of privileges. He remained a royalist at heart, but could not tolerate the idea of saying yes to a hopelessly weak king. 'The monarchy is the only anchor of hope that can preserve this nation from foundering on the rocks,' he stressed over and over again. 'But, mark my words, the king and the queen will lose – and the enraged populace will fight over their corpses.'

Mirabeau could feel the coming thunder. Power no longer lay with an impoverished aristocracy; the wealth of the country had changed hands and so had the balance of power. Gold was stuffed under the mattresses of the bourgeoisie – and there were 26 million of them. The grand bourgeoisie controlled the nation's money through the banks. The petit bourgeoisie provided trade and the social infrastructure. Wig makers and brewers sent their sons to the schools of the Latin Quarter. They graduated as doctors, lawyers, and teachers. The children of the revolution were recruited from the *basoche*, the legal profession; these bourgeois delegates could read and write, but most important, they could talk.

One segment of society was absent, the 'little people'. It was this unrepresented class, once roused by unscrupulous agitators for their own purpose, who demonstrated an implacable hatred of church and nobility, which led to the infamous excesses of the revolution.

In May 1789, control was with the bourgeoisie. The aristocracy and the clergy did not see it that way; firmness had worked in their favour so far and they dug in their heels. If one thing is certain, firmness cannot work for ever. On 23 June 1789 the delicate balance was upset. Members of the Third Estate found the doors of their meeting hall barred to them. With Count Mirabeau in the lead, they marched as one body to the nearby Jeu de Paume (indoor tennis court) where they swore their famous *Sermon de Jeu de Paume* or Tennis Court Oath, 'not to leave the premises before having provided a constitution for France'. With this step they declared themselves as the only legal National Constituent Assembly, or Convention.[1] When the king heard of it, he quickly dispatched his master of ceremony to order the unconstitutional assembly to dissolve. Count Mirabeau stared down the king's envoy and thundered his famous reply: 'Tell those who have sent you that we are here by the will of the people, and that we shall only depart at the point of bayonets!' The monarch had not studied how revolutions begin, nor how a chain of misunderstandings can throw out all counsel for moderation, leading to excesses that can make nations shudder. He only shrugged his shoulders: 'If they don't want to leave, let them be!'

Mirabeau alone realised that if France was to be saved, then it would only be by the formation of a constitutional monarchy. (Its collapse proved to be incomparably more dramatic.) His resolution laid the foundation for the event to come 'The National Convention declares that the person of any delegate is inviolable, and that all those who dare to persecute a delegate, no matter who shall give the order, is considered a traitor to the nation and guilty of a capital crime.'

Mirabeau, the greatest realist on the doctrines of the French Revolution, urged his king to lead the way for change, not combat it. 'Sire,' he argued, 'the very idea of monarchy is not incompatible with revolution. Sire, abolish the privileges,

---

[1] Named after the English National Convention.

modernise the state, and Your Majesty will come out stronger than ever before.' How different history would have been had Louis listened to the wise prophet. Instead he foolishly ordered 30,000 troops to march on Paris. This shocked its citizens into action. Barricades went up and Camille Desmoulins, a firebrand law student, exhorted the citizens to take muskets and powder from the towers of the Bastille. After some shots were fired which hurt nobody, the thirty-two prison guards put down their arms. An enraged mob stormed the towers, decapitated the governor, and paraded his head on a pike. Violence stalked the streets that day, 14 July 1789. The rest is history. With the fall of the Bastille, symbol of the *ancien régime*, ended the old order of monarchical privilege.[2] Paris was in the grip of anarchy: armed gangs marched on the residences of the wealthy and burned them down; churches were ransacked and heads of religious statues knocked off; serfs armed with pitchforks and sickles massacred the nobility and burned their châteaux. The Comte d'Artois (the future Charles X) fled France, followed by the Ducs de Berry, Angoulême, Condé, Enghien, and 20,000 aristocrats.

Six months later, 26 August 1789 brought the outstanding achievement of the revolution: the Declaration of the Rights of Man, based largely on the wording of the Bill of Rights of Virginia. When 5,000 women marched on Versailles two months later, demanding bread, Marie-Antoinette was misquoted as saying: 'Why don't they eat brioche (cake)?' To calm that mob, the king acceded to the women's demand that he accompany them back to Paris. For all practical purposes, the king had become the prisoner of the revolution. From now on, his power was whatever the people were willing to grant him.

At this crucial juncture a man appeared on the political scene who fanned the 'little people's' fury. Jean-Paul Marat

---

[2] A fitting parallel to the symbolism of the fall of the Bastille is the fall of the Berlin Wall, exactly 200 years later, in 1989.

was a Swiss doctor and a part-time journalist. 'A rabid cellar rat, who came into the daylight when the sewers failed and then devoured everything in his way, was the typical representative of the rabble from taverns and bordellos, and whose existence had always been underground, living by robbery and murder' was how a German revolutionary described *l'ami du peuple* – the Friend of the People. In his first newspaper edition of the same name, Marat set the tone by launching into a scathing attack against Louis XVI: 'a weakling without soul, unworthy to sit on the throne, a weathervane deftly manipulated by his courtesans, a tyrant pushed to crime. One whose conduct had always been a web of inconsequence and horror, a despot who washes his hands in the blood of the people, a monster who conspires against public *liberté* and who must be considered a criminal in the eyes of justice.' Such phrases inflamed the 'little people', the manual labourers who toiled for their masters, and even lived alongside them. Cities were not divided into rich and poor quarters; people of all classes lived together in the same houses in the same narrow lanes. According to their *arrondissement* (district), they were grouped into sections, but they had nothing in common with the proletariat of the Industrial Age.

Mirabeau died on 2 April 1791: 'I leave you with a hopeless and cruel thought. Unless you stop the excesses, they will lead on to tragedy, from single murder to massacre, from the fall of a king to the fall of a country.' With Mirabeau's death, the king lost all hope of regaining his throne. He decided on escape. At midnight on 20 June 1791, a man dressed in a long cape led a woman holding the hand of a little girl and two other women to a carriage. A tall coachman stood by to help them into the cab. The man was Louis, the woman Marie-Antoinette, the 'girl' was the Dauphin Louis-Charles, and the coachman was Marie-Antoinette's lover, the Swedish Count Fersen. A travelling coach awaited them on the outskirts of Paris – painted in bright yellow and bearing the royal crest! Only hours from the border, Fersen took a wrong turn and had to double back; they asked a local boy for directions, and the king slipped a coin into the boy's hand, a gold *louis d'or*! The boy ran to alert the local revolutionary committee.

On the bridge at Verennes the royal escape came to an end. 'Halt, who goes?'

The queen snapped: 'Madame Korff, on her way to Frankfurt.'

Monsieur Saussé deputy mayor of Varennes, replied: 'The difficulties of the road are enough to ask you to leave the coach. I offer you my house for the night.'

The leader of the armed group was the local postmaster, Drouet: 'How come a special detachment of dragoons awaits you on the other side of the river? You must come out immediately, or we will fire on you.'

The queen, followed by the king, stepped from the coach. 'You are the king!' Drouet yelled. 'I recognise you!'

'So if you recognise me, why don't you show the necessary respect to your sovereign?' Instead of being shown respect, the king was locked up in a room in a nearby house.

Saussé dispatched an urgent call to nearby villages: 'Come with your guns, we have caught the king.'

Marie-Antoinette pleaded with the wife of the mayor: 'Madame Saussé, think what I feel for the king and my children. A queen of France will owe you her eternal gratitude.'

'You think of the king and I think of Monsieur Saussé.'

The royal family was escorted back to Paris. On the way their coach was stoned, and on their inglorious return to Paris, Louis saw his effigy dangling from a lamp-post. This was enough for Marie-Antoinette to express her fears that someone was out to have them murdered. 'The escape was the road to shame or to the executioner. There is but one way to flee from the throne, and that is abdication,' wrote Lamartine, 'and Louis did not abdicate. From now on, he became nothing but a traitor to the revolution and a marionette in the hands of its leaders.'

On 17 July 1791, a group of radical republicans, led by Marat, gathered on the Champs de Mars.[3] He declared the king to be redundant, but his timing was wrong; France was not yet ready to become a republic. General Lafayette ordered his National Guard to fire into the crowd. Fifty were killed. The Convention split into two camps: the Girondins represented the well-off bourgeoisie, and the extremist Jacobins the 'little people'. Both parties forced the king to underwrite the new constitution. Louis now became a simple representative, a fatal error that the bourgeoisie was to regret. The person of the king had been the only constitutional instrument that could stand up to the extremists and now the bourgeoisie opened the door to raging madmen willing to use mob brutality. A new set of characters entered the public stage.

The following year was a year of decision. On 20 April 1792, France declared war on the Hapsburg monarchy. In July, the Duke of Brunswick stormed into France at the head of a powerful army of 75,000 and stated his intention to reinstall the French monarch to his rightful position. This sealed the king's fate. Although it took another six months, the process was irreversible. A certain Georges-Jacques Danton, member of the Jacobin Club, meticulously planned the assault. Danton, without doubt the most brilliant of all revolutionary orators, came from a small French town. He studied law and was appointed a lawyer in the King's Council. He took no part in the events of July 1789, but became active in 1791 when he founded the Cordeliers Club, the forerunner to the Jacobins. Following the events of August 1792, he was appointed minister of justice, and as such, called

---

[3] Now the site of the Eiffel Tower.

into being the Revolutionary Tribunal, a bloodstained court that was to become the institutional arm of the Terror. With Danton's connivance, trouble began. For days now, hysterical rumours had been spreading that thousands of the king's loyal troops were marching on the city and that the section committees would provide every *citoyen* with a weapon to fight to the death. '*Liberté ou la mort!* Liberty or death!' the tocsin kept insisting, joined by the bells of the sixty churches across the city. '*Aux armes, citoyens!* Citizens, take up your arms!' From the street came the babble of voices, urging every able-bodied man and woman to join and resist the devilish plot hatched by a king, and his bitch of a queen. '*Formez les bataillons!* Fall into your battalions!' The leaders of the revolution had vowed to fight from section to section, lane to lane, house to house. *Aux barricades!* To the barricades! The masses poured into the centre of the city. Someone in the crowd started the first note of a newly composed revolutionary song ... '*Allons, enfants de la patrie, le jour de gloire est arrivée* ... – come, children of the motherland, the day of glory is here ...'

The extremists had finally channelled their disciplined skills into the realisation of their revolutionary ends. Gangs of radical Jacobins had already overpowered the guards at the Hôtel de Ville (city hall) and established an Insurrection Commune. Their plan was to overthrow the Convention and seize national power, but first they had to do away with the constitutional king. When the Jacobins' *coup d'état* took place at city hall, the man who was most on their minds was asleep in his bed in the Tuileries, peacefully ignorant. The queen, her ladies-in-waiting, and her best friend, the Princesse de Lamballe, were still up, playing cards. The hallways of the great palace were dark and silent. Only an occasional flicker from a candle showed the presence of several old nobles who patrolled the hallways, armed with little more than parade swords, hardly effective against the bayonets and halberds that were in the hands of the raging mob. Outside were stationed 900 Swiss mercenaries to defend the Tuileries gardens.

When news spread that 'something was going to happen to the king', and that accounts were to be settled, the frightened burghers barred their doors and locked their shutters. By morning the lanes were filled with Marat's Communards while the Convention sat in utter confusion in the Manège (riding academy) near the Tuileries, a series of buildings surrounded by a high wrought-iron fence. Red-coated Swiss Guards stood calmly on the monumental staircase that led into the palace. Facing them was the 'spearhead of the revo-lution', more than 500 Marseillais with one bronze cannon. National Guardsmen had been rushed in to reinforce the Swiss, when suddenly they switched sides, dragging with them their twelve pieces of artillery. This encouraged the mob to rush the iron grille, just as the royal family with their attendants stepped outside the palace. The crowd jeered 'Death to the tyrant!' and threw rocks in their direction. The king waved, the mob surged forward, and in the press people were crushed against the fence before it gave way to allow waves of howling, halberd-swinging *sans-culottes*[4] into the palace forecourt. Some Swiss Guards whisked off the king and his entourage to seek refuge among the scared deputies of the Convention. The king shouted the order to his Swiss Guards to defend the building, a command that led to the drama. The Swiss Colonel Durler ordered his companies to ward off the crowd and the red-coated Swiss raised their muskets. A woman screamed, '*Vive la République!* Long live the republic!' The mob swept forward and seized five Swiss soldiers who were dragged off, disarmed, and hacked to death. The Swiss company commanders de Castlebourg and Zusler yelled: '*Feuer!*' Hundreds of musket balls tore

---

[4] The term means literally 'without underpants', a reference to the aristocratic silk breeches (or *culottes*) which were not worn by the mob.

into the tightly massed crowd, only paces away. The effect was shattering; bodies were heaped shoulder high in front of the Swiss Guards and the rest of the Communards fled in disorder. The guns of the renegade National Guard boomed in response, but the gunners' aim was atrocious. They missed the square formations of the Swiss Guards and their lethal shot cut swathes through the madly fleeing masses, adding to the general panic and confusion. The Swiss kept up their deadly fire, and the company of Count Salis brought forward a cannon which fired after the fleeing *sans-culottes*. The crowd was caught in a murderous cross-fire; hundreds more died in the next few minutes, torn apart in a concentrated hail of cannon balls and grapeshot. The courtyard was now clear of the mob and the Swiss had reformed into lines, ready to give chase.

The king and his family members were sitting in the Manège, when Deputy Chabot declared that the queen's presence was unconstitutional and that she must be removed from the assembly. The royal family was herded into a side chamber. In the confinement of this small space, the booming cannons sounded even more terrifying to them and the king trembled when he heard the crash of muskets and guns. 'Our children are being put to death,' he lamented. 'We must put a stop to it.' The king, thoroughly shaken, reached the most disastrous decision of his life. As Mirabeau had predicted, Louis was an irresolute, impotent ruler who had never learned the dictum of his illustrious forebear, Louis XIV: 'War, if necessity demands it, is a just act not only permitted, but commanded to kings. It is a grave error to think that one can reach the same aims by weaker means.' Whatever authority had been left with him, it died the instant that he asked Monsieur d'Hervilly to carry his order to the colonel of his Swiss Guard to put down their arms. This compounded the tragedy. Colonel Durler refused to believe that the king could have issued such an insane command.

He rushed to the Manège to confront Louis. They were the same age, but that is where all comparison ended. Something in the arrogant way this Swiss held himself, and the insolent stare from his heavy-lidded eyes, frightened the king. 'Your Majesty, the day is ours. The rabble is on the run. We must vigorously pursue them!'

Louis' mind was blocked, his face frozen in silence. That old, familiar fear was in him. He clenched his fists to stop himself from shaking and tried to speak, but no sound came out. Clearly the thunder of the guns had unhinged him.

'Sire, are we to chase the rabble?' These words were pronounced in a chilly voice.

Louis was caught in the predicament of those who cannot decide once pressure becomes unbearable. He told himself that life on the street, with its hugely visible tragedies, was more real, more human, and more merciful than the life he himself had known in Versailles. The storming of the Tuileries was as pathetic as thousands of broken lives could make it. Before his mind passed Paris, its people, and the reality of its life. He tried to get a grip on himself, tried to focus his mind and would have traded his soul for a few moments of calm.

A voice interrupted his reverie: 'It is a question of minutes, perhaps seconds. I must have your reply.' King and colonel stared at each other. 'This challenge must not be ignored. Your Majesty must act!'

It was now that the king had to step forward and give proof that he was more than just a capable mender of clocks. At the most decisive moment of his life, the power of will failed him. He said: 'If the price of greatness is to be wrong every time, then I am incapable of the task.' In that instant he showed that he was unworthy to be a king. He had spent most of his life sleeping, eating, drinking, urinating, blowing his nose, and fixing clocks and watches. A cardboard cut-out of a monarch, whose thinking was not an activity, but a passivity. The minutes were ticking away, and with them, monarchical rule.

Colonel Durler snapped: '*Par Dieu, lève toi et agis comme un roi!* Get up and act like a king!'

The king's face was ashen. He covered it with his hands and moaned: 'Does everything have to end in blood?' And then the moment was gone. Did it hinge upon the unstoppable march of history or upon the fatal weakness of one man? Faced with the threat of rebellion and death, he failed to act. A few hundred had been killed – but he could have saved his kingdom. Instead, he led thousands to the revolutionary executioner. 'Our wish is for you to lay down your arms. We do not wish brave men to perish.'

'Then, I must insist that you put your order in writing.'

And the king wrote: 'We order Our Swiss to put down their arms immediately and withdraw to their barracks. (Signed) Louis.'

The colonel snatched the order from the king's trembling hands and looked at him in disgust. 'You have just signed the death warrant of my brave Swiss *and of your monarchy*.'

The Swiss were well-trained soldiers who could do nothing but obey and stack their weapons. No sooner had they disarmed themselves than a blood-crazed mob butchered the helpless mercenaries. In total, 786 Swiss soldiers, including their twenty-six officers, paid with their lives for the weakness of the king.[5] When all the Swiss were dead, the mob rushed into the king's residence to continue the slaughter. Every nobleman, gardener, or groom had his throat slit or was thrown from a window. One woman who escaped the horror, Madame Campan, was forced to recite 'The Nation For Ever'. Other ladies of the court were chased into the open, stripped of their clothes and disembowelled. Their heads were impaled on pikes and proudly paraded through the streets. The few

---

[5] In Luzern, a monument was erected to their heroic stand, a gigantic sleeping lion with a lance through its side, clutching the royal arms.

who managed to escape through a secret passageway were cornered in the Rue de l'Échelle. The men were bludgeoned or skewered, and the women were raped before being brutally murdered. By order of the Jacobins, the corpses were left rotting for days to make Parisians fear the power of the extremists.

When the news of the massacres reached the Convention, the extreme Jacobins shouted down the moderate Girondins. Marie-Antoinette clutched her son to her chest and burst into tears. The king sat in his deputy box, a disinterested spectator to the ranting of deputies. 'What you're doing here is not very constitutional,' was all he had to say. Nobody listened to him any longer. The insurrectionists thought nothing of using lies, deception, and terror to goad the crowd into such a furore that their *sans-culottes* were prepared to rush headlong into musket fire in order to butcher the hated nobility and then parade their cut-off heads on pikes. 'Had Louis taken a firm stand and come out on his horse to direct operations that day at the Tuileries, assuredly victory would have been his.' The author of this comment was Napoleon.

On 21 September 1792, Louis XVI became the first king of France to be deposed by his own subjects. The Convention abolished the monarchy and established the First Republic, with its motto: *Liberté, Égalité, Fraternité* – Liberty, Equality, Brotherhood. A few weeks later, the royal family was locked up in the sinister Temple, a square dungeon built 500 years earlier by the Knights Templar. The first man to meet them was Antoine Simon, a cobbler by profession and a revolution-ary by vocation, who herded them into their 'royal quarters' with a single dirty, flea-infested bedstead. Marie-Antoinette put her little boy – heir to a throne that no longer existed – in the bed and she herself slept on the floor. The situation improved once the family was permitted to purchase some basic furniture. Once a day they were allowed to walk in the small garden where the guards had ample opportunity to talk loudly about their fate. This was how the king found out that one of his loyal supporters, the editor of the *Gazette de Paris*, had been guillotined.

The demise of the constitutional monarchy led to the dictatorship of the Commune. Its evil star, Jean-Paul Marat, prophet of *égalité*, used the mob as his instrument to make the old aristocracy and the ruling bourgeoisie pay the political price of a bloody revolution. He schemed to seize ultimate control through the world's first 'dictatorship of the proletariat', by whatever means necessary. But Danton was quicker off the mark when he took over the Paris City Council. When the militia's commander Mandat refused to obey anyone but the elected leaders of the commune, Danton's men shot him and dumped his corpse in the Seine. With this act of opportunism Danton opened for himself a path to dictatorial power, and he became undisputed leader of the Executive Revolutionary Council. His only mistake was that, in contrast to Robespierre, who made sure of killing off his rivals, Danton remained loyal to his supporters and handed out fat appointments to his friends.

Events overtook the revolution. The north-west was in open revolt; Marseilles rose in protest against the rule of Paris; the people of Lyons executed their revolutionary city council; the citizens of Bordeaux marched on Paris; and the major port of Toulon was handed over to the British without a shot being fired The greatest danger came from the Duke of Brunswick who advanced on the capital with a powerful Prussian army. France found itself at the edge of an abyss. An explosion of nationalistic fervour concentrated the resolute will of the entire nation to rush to the defence of their *patrie*. But it was left to Georges Danton to raise emotions to fever pitch and pull down the barriers of restraint with his immortal slogan: '*L'audace, encore l'audace, toujours l'audace!* Boldness, more boldness, forever boldness!' Like Joan of Arc he gave his nation *l'espérance* – hope. Roger de Lisle wrote a song for the Marseilles volunteers marching to the front; thereby the song became known as 'La Marseillaise'. To save the republic, Danton was not averse to carnage; if proof were needed, his complicity in the September massacres showed it.

The call for the September massacres was launched by an article in Marat's L'ami du peuple. On 2 September 1792, three carts carrying twenty-four clergymen were stopped at the Abbey of St Germain des Prés.[6] They were surrounded by a gang of *sans-culottes*, a band of ruffians who had set out to commit murder. Before the revolution, some of them had been parishioners of the ascetic priest who now climbed from the cart to calm the crowd. What he said is not recorded.[7] One of the cart's escorts pulled out his sabre and hacked down the priest. The mob pulled the others from the carts and trampled them to death. Frenzy took hold of them. In the nearby Carmelite Convent 150 clergymen waited for the outcome of their trial. The rabble climbed over the vine-covered fence and began to slaughter them with clubs, pikes, and axes. Priests lay with their skulls smashed in the halls and dormitories, even inside the chapel.[8] As so frequently happens when a crowd goes wild, there is always one who shouts louder and thereby appoints himself as their leader. A sinister character, Citizen Maillard, set up a table in the hallway and presided over an instant court. Every surviving priest was dragged before this judge, condemned, and butchered in the most savage manner. In all 119 priests died in this way and their bodies were thrown into a well.[9]

From the Carmes, the *sans-culottes* returned to the Abbey

---

[6] Today this is the centre of Parisian artistic life.
[7] In some records it states that he cried out: 'Have mercy!'
[8] From the memoirs of Abbé Sicard, the only known survivor.
[9] In 1860, during the restoration of the convent, their skeletons were discovered.

of St Germain, plundered its vast library and threw the invaluable works onto a giant bonfire,[10] because they considered learning as the root of their misery. Three hundred more prisoners were brought before Citizen Maillard's hanging justice. The shrieks of their victims mingled with the chortle of the mob. Their harpy spouses cheered the butchers on: '*Vasy, coupe sa gorge* . . . Go on, slit his throat.' The sexual overtones of the massacre became overt when the mob broke into homes along the Rue de Seine and raped the bourgeois women.[11] Similar scenes took place inside the Conciergerie and the Châtelet prison. That night, over a thousand were savagely put to death.

Their most notable victim was the beautiful Princesse de Lamballe, who was dragged from her cell, tied to a bench, and made to confess that she was the queen's lover. Dozens of grimy men then raped her and forced her to walk barefoot across the mutilated corpses in the courtyard, before a *sans-culotte* hacked off her head. A hairdresser's apprentice combed the Princess's blood-streaked hair, before her head was paraded on a pike outside the Temple prison 'so that *l'Autrichienne* can recognise her lover'.

The mob did the killing, but mobs rarely bear all the guilt. They may be considered guilty, just as is the lever of the guillotine. But a lever does not kill. It only releases the blade. If not directly present at the murders, Danton, as minister of justice, was certainly kept informed of the rampage. He did nothing to prevent the slaughter by using his instrument of power.

That horror helped to drive on the armies of the Duke of Brunswick. Nothing could stop them until Frenchmen from all walks of life, roused by Danton's fiery speeches, joined up. They came from the farms and from the cities. Even the

[10] Hitler's Kristallnacht of 1938, and Nazi ritual book burnings, were a pale copy.
[11] From the account of a contemporary eyewitness, Philippe Maurice.

royal officer corps offered its experience to this first people's army. This was no longer a monarchy that stood in danger, but the sacred honour of *la France*. Under the command of Generals Dumoriez and Kellermann, the nation's soldiers marched behind their revolutionary banners to a windmill near Valmy to face the Prussian army. Kellermann lifted up his hat on the tip of his sabre and at his signal the cannons thundered. The Duke of Brunswick looked at the revolutionary artillery and declared: '*Hier schlagen wir nicht* – here we do not deliver battle.' French élan had stopped a professional army and in doing so had dispelled once and for all the false belief in the inferiority of one composed of civilians. With this amazing victory France was delivered from foreign intervention. Two days later, on 22 September 1792, France proclaimed itself a republic. Now Danton and his Jacobins could turn their full attention on the problems at home. The fate of the ex-king was high on their list. But the mind of at least one revolutionary, Robespierre, was fixed on his nemesis, Danton.

'*L'homme est né libre, et partout il est dans les fers . . .* Man is born free and everywhere he is in chains.' The hollow-cheeked man in the blue silk waistcoat was an ardent admirer of the revolutionary philosopher Jean-Jacques Rousseau. Slowly, Robespierre put down the book and leaned back deep in thought.

It had been a miserable morning, that distant winter's day in Paris, when the headmaster of the Collège de Clermont ordered the class into the cobblestoned courtyard. For hours he kept the boys shivering in rain and freezing cold because Louis XVI, king of France, was expected to pass by the front gate. What was he like, their king and the symbol of unchallenged power, wondered a skinny teenager from Arras, a bright and diligent student who lacked the financial means of his fellow pupils, who were scions of the nobility. Now he stood in the courtyard, with aching calves and water dripping down his back. *Discipline and obedience!* Not only the credo of a boys' school but of a whole country. After an interminable wait, a splendid yellow coach made its appearance at the top of the narrow cobblestoned street. It was drawn by four matching horses and surrounded by armed outriders. The boys never saw the face of their king, only a white-gloved hand waving from behind a passing window. They were on their way back to their classroom, shaking themselves like wet poodles and discussing the omnipotence of royalty, when the headmaster called them back into the courtyard. Another cart had made its appearance. There was nothing splendid about this one, drawn by a tired old mare. A figure stood in it, clad in a shirt which clung wetly to his body, with his hands tied behind his back. 'The tumbril of Monsieur de Paris,'[12] warned their teacher.' 'Let this be a lesson to you. Never rebel against your sovereign.' Not here, not in the *Royaume de France* – somewhere else, perhaps! Like the thirteen English colonies of America. There they had dared to say no to their monarch. They had it easy, separated from their royal sovereign by a wide ocean, not like here, where there were only a few leagues along a straight road from Paris to Versailles. As the cart rolled past the grid of the gate, the eyes of the boy met those of the condemned man. These were eyes of despair and hopelessness. One of the many disinherited, deprived of his civic right to stand up against injustice. It was a moment the boy was never to forget . . .

Robespierre shook himself from his reverie and picked up his book. 'Divine Rousseau,' he mused, 'you've taught me to appreciate the dignity of human nature.' To him, Rousseau's philosophy was the closest thing to religion. Like Rousseau, messiah of change, Robespierre thought of himself as a virtuous presence between the mob's vice and

---

[12] The official title of the public executioner of Paris, a certain Charles Henri Sanson.

bourgeois corruption. His idol had stressed the value of virtue, a byword that was to haunt France. 'Terror without Virtue is bloody. Virtue without Terror is impotent.' Thus terror became virtue, decided Maximilien Robespierre.

On the day that the citizens of Paris stormed the Bastille, that immortal 14 July 1789, he was virtually unknown. A deputy from the north, who never smiled but would spend hours putting on his silk costume and powdering his hair, Robespierre voted against censorship, against the death penalty, and against war, yet it was he who signed all these decrees into power. He was neither a hypocrite, as some of his detractors tried to make him, nor a political opportunist, but a true believer, which made him more terrifying than a hypocrite. He joined a small group of intellectuals who talked revolution in the chapel of an abandoned Jacobin convent. In the beginning they called themselves Friends of the Constitution, before they became notorious as the Jacobins. Robespierre had no use for carousing, nor did he join in the excesses perpetrated in the name of the revolution by this new social phenomenon called 'the mob' – Marat's Communards. This lunatic fringe, made up of the dregs of society, had nothing in common with the proletariat of later date; their philosophy was not based on 'you starving working masses, rise from slumber', but on a 'kill those who have it, and take it from them'. Sewer rats all, who had not participated in the revolution, but certainly benefited from it. He knew only too well that masses do not make a revolution, only leaders do. Mobs serve a useful purpose: they can be manipulated to fulfil a political need as a pressure group for demonstrations or sporadic bouts of terrorism, a technique quite cleverly exploited by Marat. Let them yell and make themselves feel important, or have them invade the Convention en masse and drown debate of an issue with their screams, which could then be interpreted as 'the will of the people'.

Robespierre loathed Marat. This clever 'friend of the

people' had turned his populist *sans-culottes* into a formidable political weapon, since these collaborators of evil had much to gain at the expense of their victims. Contrary to other revolutionary leaders, Marat was a philosopher-killer who held in complete contempt all the principles that served other men as ideals. Marat was a problem that could be taken care of.

But Robespierre was haunted by his envy of another man, Georges-Jacques Danton. In August 1792 this virile, brilliant orator was appointed minister of justice at the age of thirty-two. Jealousy over his rival's exceptional abilities and energy ate at Robespierre's heart. They were equal in age (Robespierre was born in 1758, Danton in 1759); their revolutionary views were similar – but never their personalities. Danton was stocky and spoke in a stentorian voice; he loved publicity and his skills as an orator could be favourably compared with those of Cicero.[13] Robespierre was fine-boned with a pallid complexion; he nervously chewed his fingernails and spoke in a nasal tone. He shied away from the centre stage, operating from the shadows. Danton was a bon vivant who loved his wife, good food, and boisterous company. Robespierre detested Danton's virility. His own existence was that of a hermit; he locked himself away with his books and thoughts in a small apartment in the Rue St Honoré.[14] Both men held dreams of a New France, but while Robespierre reflected the pure philosophy of Rousseau and saw as his prime mission the introduction of a reign of virtue, Danton thought nothing of Robespierre's moral restraints and certainly said so. One day in the Convention, as Robespierre went on endlessly about virtue, Danton bellowed: 'Virtue is what I practise in bed with my wife!' Robespierre suffered nightmares; he even referred to his rival as 'a rotten idol,

---

[13] Danton's quotes fill volumes, and his sayings are still immortalised on monuments.

[14] The Duplay house where he lived was torn down by Napoleon.

putrid with corruption'. The wish to do away with Danton grew daily stronger and drove him to an act of duplicity. During these days of anguish he met the young man who was to play such an important role during his days of tyranny, Louis-Antoine de Saint-Just.[15]

In this undergrowth of revolutionary dogmas, a dense and dangerous jungle, it took great gifts and skills to succeed and to survive. Saint-Just was someone who could think on his feet, cut down an opponent with his acid tongue, and handle a crowd. Elected as the people's delegate from Soissons,[16] this twenty-five-year-old, 'as beautiful as an angel', earned his sobriquet not for his physical beauty. Saint-Just, the 'Angel of Death', was an unconditional fanatic: 'Those who lead revolutions, those who wish to do well, must never sleep – except in their graves!' If Robespierre showed some human failings, Saint-Just was an impassioned reptile feeding on blood. Or was he the one with revolutionary pureness in his heart? That is Saint-Just's enigma. His version of Utopia was a place where men served only two principal functions, either as farmers (to feed the nation) or as soldiers (to defend the nation); where children were taken from their parents at a tender age, stuck in an institution, and pressed through a revolutionary mould into an army of robots.[17] He never mentioned women since he did not even recognise their very existence. These two conspired to bring down Georges Danton.

For the trial of the king, Danton could count on support from the majority of the deputies. It called for a ruse; the king's passion for working on clocks was helped by a professional locksmith, François Gamain. Danton told Gamain that the king had betrayed him, and that his life was forfeited,

---

[15] Saint-Just was born in 1767 at Decize. His parents' house still stands in the village of Blérancourt.

[16] He won by a slender majority of 349 votes.

[17] The 'army of robots' were brilliantly portrayed in Fritz Lang's film, *Metropolis*.

unless ... 'The safe, where is it?' A frightened Gamain led him to a hidden strongbox, which netted 627 secret documents. With these, Danton had the means of bringing a charge of high treason against the monarch. In the Convention, Antoine Saint-Just, as cold and cynical as he was ruthless, declared: 'We are not here to judge a king but to fight him. In the eighteenth century we are less advanced than in the time of Caesar – there the tyrant was killed in the Senate without further formalities by twenty-three stabs from daggers and without any other law than that imposed by the freedom of Rome. So be it here. I demand the king be put to death without trial!' The call of the Jacobins was out in the open: to obtain power, the king had to die! The Convention baulked at this demand. Deputy Chambon was sent to the Temple: 'The Convention charges me to inform you: Louis Capet is to be arraigned ...' Louis was pushed from the room and led into the courtyard. From a small window a queen watched and a child cried. The Dauphin was only seven and did not understand.

'Louis Capet, the French nation accuses you ...' With that phrase the king's trial opened on 26 December 1792. The king was charged with a series of crimes that he knew, as did his accusers, he had never been party to.

'I don't recognise this court. You cannot try a king.'

'We can, and we will. You, not we, are on trial.'

'For what?' asked the deposed king.

'For your life!'

The king sat down and listened with dignified resignation. The public prosecutor Fouquier-Tinville waved a sheaf of papers. 'Citizens, I have here some documents which prove without a doubt that the accused is guilty.'

Two lawyers, Tronchet and de Malesherbes,[18] were appointed

---

[18] Tronchet survived and became a supreme judge. De Malesherbes went to the guillotine.

as legal assistance and were allowed to discuss defence strategy with the ex-monarch. They knew that his chances were slim. The debate on the verdict turned into a heated discussion over three questions:

1. Is Louis Capet guilty as charged?
2. Must the sentence be submitted to a popular vote?
3. If found guilty, what should be the sentence? Detention, deportation or death?

The moderate Girondins fought the extremist Jacobins and their 'Death to the tyrant!' Their 'Angel of Death' spoke: 'Louis fought against his people and he was brought down. He looked upon his own *citoyens* as his slaves. He alone is guilty of the events at the Bastille, and at the Tuileries. Which foreign enemy has done us more harm, I ask?' He paused for a moment before adding in the ice-cold tone typical of him: 'The nation demands his death!'

Thomas Paine, an English revolutionary invited to the proceedings to give them a shred of credibility, wrote a suggestion on a piece of paper and handed it to the Convention president: 'Deport the king to the Americas.' Paine's proposal was not taken into consideration.

'Give us the head of that fat pig,' yelled Marat's mob from the gallery. Danton argued forcibly for the supreme penalty, Saint-Just threatened the deputies; only Robespierre stood by and observed. Marat was high on his list; he had to be put down – and without mercy. A vote was called and for a long time, the ayes and nays hung in the balance. Until the cousin of the king, who now called himself Philippe Égalité, stood up: 'I vote death!' His ballot was the deciding vote. Death to the king by five votes![19] Lazare Carnot, head of the Executive,

[19] It was afterwards established that thirteen votes were illegal; some voters were not even inscribed on the list, and one was too young: Saint-Just, who was still under the permitted voting age.

wept as he signed the decree. A reprieve was rejected. The public executioner, Charles Henri Sanson, known only as Monsieur de Paris, was ordered to prepare for an execution. Monsieur Sanson, a totally apolitical man who prided himself on a 'job well done', was not paid for taking sides. He never asked questions; he would cut off anyone's head, from thief to king.

The last attempt to plead for the monarch's life was made by a well-known actress from the Théâtre Français, Mademoiselle Fleury. She pushed her way into Marat's flat, which was decorated only with a poster on which were written two words: *La Mort*. Death!

'I beg you to show mercy for the king.'

'What do you dare to say? Don't speak so loud that others can hear you, or your blasphemy will be punished with your own death.'

'Oh Marat, I am not afraid. It is you I pity, to see you take the slippery road of blood, and I want to stop you.'

'I don't deny it, it was Louis who helped us make the revolution. Now we have to defend it with all our might.'

'Marat, how many tears, how much blood, before we find our way back to unity and love? For this, you will have to cut off many heads.'

'So be it. Where gangrene has set in, you have to slice off the limb to save the body. We sow in blood and tears so that those after us can reap joy.'

'That is something for the distant future.'

'Strong men can wait.'

Mademoiselle Fleury knew that she had failed.

Louis' cell door burst open and in walked twelve men of the Convention's Executive. The sentence was read out, but the king showed no emotion. An Irish priest, Edgeworth of Firmont, stayed with the condemned man. The king sat down to a late supper; his only remark was that they had taken away his knife for cutting the meat. 'Do they think me such a coward as to take my own life?' Later, the king asked to see his family. First to enter the room was the queen, holding their seven-year-old son by the hand. She was followed by the king's sisters. For once, the jailer showed a shred of decency by closing the door to allow them their final moment of privacy. The princesses cried, the queen tried to keep some composure; only the dauphin seemed unaffected, his youth sparing him the truth of the tragedy. The king and queen took their son by the hand. 'I shall see you tomorrow morning,' promised the king.

'You promise, *cher papa*?'

'I promise,' he replied, and then he whispered to Marie-Antoinette: '*Adieu.*'

Louis placed his personal belongings on the mantelpiece, his snuffbox, his watch, and his spectacles. He then called for the Abbé Edgeworth. He even helped dress the small dining table as an altar and knelt while the priest gave him Holy Communion. Somewhere in the city a cock crowed. Louis groped his way to the mirror. What stared at him was a grey-haired wrinkled face, eyes streaked with veins of red and two deep creases in the middle of his forehead. He checked his watch. Three o'clock. Another five hours. A flock of pigeons flew past the prisoner's barred window. The dawn on 21 January 1793 broke on a bitterly cold day and the streets of Paris were deserted. The *citoyens* had been ordered to remain indoors behind closed shutters. Cannons were placed on every bridge, on every square, and thousands of guards lined every foot of the route. The guillotine stood on the Place de la Révolution (today's Place de la Concorde), between the gate to the Tuileries gardens and the base of a monument that had once held the equestrian statue of Louis XV. The executioner and his assistants made their final preparations. At 8.30 a.m. the bolt on the door to the king's chamber slid back. Three men entered the room. Two were defrocked priests, Pierre

Bernard and Jacques Roux, members of the extremists in the Convention, who had demanded the dubious honour of leading the king to his death. The 'third' was General Santerre, the commander of the National Guard.

Louis tried to hand Roux a roll with his will. 'Would you please hand this to the queen?'

'My job is to lead you to the scaffold, not to run your errands,' scoffed Roux.

General Santerre took the paper. 'I'll see to it,' he said with a dark look at Roux.

Valet Cléry held out the king's overcoat but he said: 'We shall have no need for it.' The king turned towards the general: 'We are ready. Let us go.'

In the black carriage with its curtains drawn, Abbé Edgeworth handed the king his breviary, which Louis began to read. The horses' hooves clattered through the canyons of the deserted streets, across the Place de Grève, along the Rue St Honoré, and into the Place de la Révolution, towards a huge plaster statue of *la Liberté*. It was here that several months later the Passionara of the Revolution, Madame Roland, on her way to the guillotine, looked up to the statue and remarked: 'Oh Liberty, what crimes they commit in your name!' Twelve hundred soldiers with fixed bayonets surrounded the machine of Dr Guillotin. It had been constructed by a Parisian piano maker and the king had helped to improve it by suggesting a triangular blade to provide a cleaner cut. Beyond the mass of armed men stood the black carriage of Philippe Égalité whose ignoble betrayal had led to the death sentence of his cousin. Within nine months he too would climb up the ladder for a date with the executioner.

'General, if We're not mistaken, We have reached Our destination.' The king left out the word 'final'. Without flinching he looked up at the sinister instrument, took off his jacket, and loosened the buttons on the neck of his shirt. Not a sound was heard on the tightly packed square, not one of the thousands moved; the only noise was the neighing of horses and the scraping of hooves on cobblestones. A drum began its roll, joined by another and another, until hundreds of drums rattled. Sanson's helper took the king by the elbows and pulled them back to tie his arms. 'You're not binding Our arms. We shall not allow you.' The assistants were confused. Sanson made a sign and Louis knew it was useless to resist. He put his hands behind his back and an assistant slipped a thin cord over his wrists. Slowly he climbed up the ladder. On the platform, the Abbé Edgeworth made the sign of the cross over the condemned king's head. The drum roll increased into an ear-splitting crescendo.

Louis turned to the drummers: '*Arrêtez vous!* Stop!'

General Santerre countermanded the order: '*Continuez!* Go on!'

The drumbeat continued. The king faced the crowd: 'As the Lord is my witness, I am innocent of all the crimes laid to my charge . . .' But the roll of a hundred drums drowned his words; only an Irish priest heard his justification. Sanson's assistants grabbed Louis under the arms and fastened him upright to the freshly scrubbed wooden plank. The abbé prayed: 'Son of Saint Louis, rise to Heaven.' An assistant pushed the plank forward and it fell into a horizontal position. The hangman's son took the king's head and pushed it into the groove. With a clank the wooden headlock snapped into position. Sanson reached for the lever. There was a moment's hesitation as Monsieur de Paris looked at General Santerre who responded: 'Monsieur, do your duty!' The lever went down, the rope slackened . . . For an instant the shiny blade hung suspended and glinted evilly in the sun. Then the heavy weight of sharpened steel crashed down, cutting through bone and flesh. A cannon fired. An aide-de-camp, Captain le Gros, picked up the head from the basket and held it aloft for everyone to see. A roar went up: '*Vive la République!* Long live the Republic!' The Bourbon king was dead.[20]

Beyond France's borders, reaction to the regicide was one of appalled disbelief. But apart from recalling their ambassadors (those who still had any in Paris), the foreign monarchs did nothing. In France there prevailed a mixture of jubilation and shame. *Le Véridique* newspaper wrote: 'The death of Louis XVI has created one more saint.' Indeed, Louis XVI had tried to satisfy everybody, but had sadly failed. Marie-Antoinette found out about the execution of her husband the next morning when a prison guard cynically called her 'the Widow Capet'. She must be strong, never forgetting that she still was a queen. She saw to it that her little boy brushed away his tears. 'A king never weeps,' she said, and raised her sobbing son to his feet. Then she knelt down to salute him as the new King of France, Louis XVII.

'*Le roi est mort, vive le roi.* The king is dead, long live the king.'

The aftermath was as one would expect. Anything connected with royalty was torn down; statues were toppled and tombs desecrated; the embalmed hearts of great kings were sold at public auction. Everyone remotely connected with the royal family was rounded up and sent to the scaffold. Philippe Égalité's last word was: '*Merde!*' Madame du Barry, the mistress of Louis XV, screamed for mercy. The lawyer who had dared to defend the king died gallantly, together with his children and grandchildren. The king's sister, Elisabeth, was beheaded and her corpse thrown naked into a lime pit.

The three principles of the French Revolution: *liberté, égalité, fraternité*, in fact the very idea of political freedom, was dead. While *égalité* stood for the destruction of ancient

---

[20] His body was immediately dumped in a pit of quicklime in the Madeleine graveyard. Twenty-two years later, his remains were recovered and given a decent burial.

privileges and *fraternité* for a new national unity, *liberté* was
trampled underfoot. Revolutionary tribunals condemned and
the executioner did his work, feeding ever more victims
to his voracious guillotine. France became a giant prison
and its population lived under the permanent threat of the
falling blade. The war with Austria had reached a stalemate.
Citizen Louis-Antoine Saint-Just (he had quietly dropped the
noble *de*), elected to the Committee for Public Safety, was
dispatched as its representative to the Revolutionary Armies
of the Rhine and of the North. The liaison between Paris
and their forces had become so bad that General Dumoriez,
the commander of the northern armies and the victor of
Valmy, was left for ten days in ignorance that England had
entered the war against France. (After secret negotiations,
Dumoriez deserted to the Austrians. His defection was to
spell disaster for his friend Danton.)

'The military techniques of the monarchy are obsolete,'
declared Saint-Just.

> '*La République Française* receives nothing but lead from
> its enemies, and will return only lead. The power of the
> Revolution is with its people and lies in their conquests.
> Our Republic has already its political character, now
> this must translate into a military system to smite our
> enemies. To achieve it, we cannot accept anything but
> unlimited war. Our destiny is to change the face of
> Europe. We shall not rest until all nations are free,
> because their liberty guarantees our own freedom. There
> exist three infamies on this earth: kings; to obey these
> kings; and to lay down our arms as long as there is still
> a master and a slave.

Saint-Just was able to communicate his intransigence to the
troops and instil in the armies of the republic that irresistible
enthusiasm and élan that was to lead them to victory. This

twenty-five-year-old created the essential climate in the art of modern warfare: the offensive spirit or *attaque à l'outrance*. On the political stage, Saint-Just drove his revolutionary zeal to absurd lengths. Before the Committee for Public Safety he justified his line of thought: 'What constitutes a republic is the total annihilation of all those who oppose it. In this we must remain inflexible. We must punish traitors and all those who show no enthusiasm towards our cause. *This Republic owes the good citizens its protection. To the bad ones it owes only death.*' This assertion was to become the guiding directive of the Terror. He pronounced his famous phrase, so frequently repeated by dictators around the world: 'Let our cemeteries overflow, not our prisons.'

Monsieur de Paris was kept busy. A common belief that the public executioner was the high priest of death was deeply anchored within the ordinary people. Nobody dared to speak to him; nobody came near his family. His bread was laid upside down at the bakery so that nobody took it by mistake. His trade was exercised in the centre of town, in a public square. In revolutionary Paris this was the Place de la Révolution. Its size allowed the greatest possible number of people to attend the morbid spectacle, in order to prevent future crimes. But the aristocrats who were guillotined were not criminals, nor were they common thieves, nor had they ever committed murder, like the octogenarian Madame la Maréchale de Noailles. While these wretched souls were transported towards the ghastly instrument, *saltimbanques* (street jugglers) amused the crowd with mock executions; bistros with a view on the guillotine did a brisk business with soups and beer. It became a familiar sound, the executioner's bell on the tumbril carrying the hapless condemned, sitting listless on the planks, no longer noticing what went on around them. They were already dead. Once the carts reached the guillotine, some people had to be dragged up the stairs, whilst others mounted them with quiet dignity. The executioner's assistants blindfolded them – not so that those condemned could not watch their final moment, but for the same reason that spies had their eyes bound before being shot: nobody wants to stare into the victim's eyes. Some went quietly to their death, whilst others cursed their judges before the blade fell and silenced their curses. 'Terror will not cease to be the order of the day until the last enemies of the republic have perished.' Thus the aristocracy of France met their doom; over 3,000 went to the guillotine.

Yet, from all this inhumane slaughter, one victim stands out. On 16 October 1793, nine months after her husband, Queen Marie-Antoinette took her last ride through the streets of Paris. Down the same streets that she had travelled in a gilded carriage on the day she had made her triumphant entry into Paris as the young bride of a future king, twenty-three years later an ex-queen rode in the tumbril used for criminals on the way to their place of punishment. The very crowd that had once spread rose petals before her carriage and enthusiastically cheered the beautiful young princess, now threw curses at a tired old woman with short grey hair peeking from beneath a cap, dressed in a thin, white sheath, and wrapped in an old shawl to keep out the chill. Her hands were tied behind her back. *'Mort à l'Autrichienne!* Death to the Austrian Woman!' That day, the French Revolution reached indeed the depths of infamy. 'This was not regicide, it was much worse than that.' These were the words of Napoleon.

The start of the Terror can be dated: 13 July 1793. Or, to be more precise, it began at ten-thirty that morning, when the twenty-four-year-old pious daughter of a Norman nobleman, Charlotte Corday d'Armont, walked calmly into Jean-Paul Marat's house and plunged a bread knife into his chest while he soaked in a medicinal bath. Before her execution, Charlotte Corday confided in a friend that some higher being had ordained her to rid the world of the Anti-Christ. Who was the higher being that whispered in her ear? Was it God, was it a royalist, or was it perhaps one of Robespierre's disguised envoys? Marat was a pustule that needed lancing.

To this end, Robespierre aligned himself with Danton in what was a most unnatural alliance, because Danton who described Robespierre as a 'virtuous eunuch' was driven by the same ambition and was not loath to use any means to achieve it. Danton was neither prophet nor priest, and he loved only one thing: power! Thus Robespierre connived with the devil himself to oust Marat, a fire-breathing madman and prophet of *égalité*. His bathtub execution unleashed a populist fury against the moderates. Over the preceding years, his vitriolic messages in his *L'ami du peuple* had been responsible for many of the massacres perpetrated by the Paris mob. A month before his death, he had brought about the fall of the powerful Girondin party when he incited his Communards to break into the National Convention and evict twenty-two deputies at the point of their bayonets. With Marat out of the way, the road to dictatorial power lay open for the two radical protagonists who were to symbolise the Great Terror: Danton and Robespierre. Given the dissimilarities in their character and line of thinking, it was obvious that one of them had to go.

For months, Robespierre had sought to bring the Jacobin faction firmly into his grip. But on the day that Marat fell victim to his own class hatred, Danton quickly stepped into the vacuum. The nation was in the throes of chaos and anarchy, and needed a strong man. The Terror began with the elected representatives of the people guillotining each other. The first ones to be put aside were the Girondins. For over a year they had controlled the Convention, thriving on intrigue and endorsing revolt; yet, when it came to the crunch, they were too squeamish to shed blood. The Jacobins had no such scruples. Twenty-nine Girondins were arrested at the point of bayonets, accused of anti-revolutionary crimes, and twenty-nine lost their heads, including their leaders, Vernigaud, Ducos, and Brissot.

Vernigaud tried to excuse his weakness: 'We have erred in time when we tried to achieve freedom for all. Let us not take the future with us into death, and let us grant this nation some hope.'

Ducos: 'And what will we do tomorrow at this time?'

Brissot: 'We shall finally sleep in peace.'

Perhaps they did, but their country did not. In the course of one year, the Dictatorship of the Mountain (the Jacobins) led the nation into a reckless war. The situation became desperate. The south-west joined the west of France in open rebellion. Some ousted Girondins managed to raise an army in Normandy to march on Paris. Corsica rose under the leadership of Paoli. The Prussians concentrated their armies on Mainz and the Austrians took Valenciennes. The English landed at Dunkirk and the Spaniards invaded Roussillon. The old pre-revolutionary generals were executed for 'lack of zeal', and young men took their place. In December 1793, General Dugommier took Toulon from the British, Kleber beat the Chouans at Cholet, Marceau defeated the Whites (the royalists) at Le Mans, and in the north, Jourdan defeated the Austrians at Wattignies. These victorious generals were less than thirty years of age.

In Paris, people cheered and waved flags. The minds of the two great protagonists were not concerned with grappling with external dangers, but with the struggle for power that was taking shape in the Convention. Sure as day follows night, two utterly ruthless, power-mad individuals were headed on a collision course. Just as Danton relied for his strength on the people of the city sections, or communes, Robespierre based his on the Jacobin Club and the powerful Committee for Public Safety (Comité du Salut Publique). With this committee as his tool he began to dig Danton's grave. This time Robespierre proved more efficient. Since he could hardly get Danton on an anti-revolutionary charge, he had to build a different case. In a rehearsal for Danton's arrest, his supporters were rounded up, charged with immoral acts, and sent to the guillotine. This 'immorality issue' led to the next step. With the help of Saint-Just, the paragon of virtue began to concoct charges: 'Danton surrounds himself with immoral elements. How can any man, so alien to ethics, be entrusted to lead the fight for *liberté?*'

Friends begged Danton to counter-attack or flee the country. He rejected their suggestion with a typical Dantonesque reply: 'I do not carry *la patrie* on the soles of my feet.'

Saint-Just fired the first shot. He demanded that the Committee for Public Safety (whose decisive power can be compared to that of the US Senate) order the arrest of one Georges-Jacques Danton on charges of high treason, having aided and abetted the enemies of the republic. He claimed that Danton had connived in the defection of General Dumoriez to the Austrians. Of the committee's twenty members, only two dared to refuse Saint-Just's demand; it was a brave but foolhardy act that led them to the guillotine.

They came for Danton in the middle of the night. When he heard their footsteps in the courtyard, he kissed his wife Louise goodbye. Paris was in uproar over the arrest of its most outspoken revolutionary and of his friend, Camille Desmoulins, the daring young man who had exhorted the Parisians to storm the Bastille five years before. With Danton's arrest, his supporters were leaderless and were easily put down by the authoritarian order of Robespierre and his Committee for Public Safety. As for the tame delegates of the Convention, they cowered under the dual threat of Robespierre and Saint-Just. Only two deputies, Legendre and Tallien, dared to speak up (the same Tallien who was later to play a vital role); their warning was met by an embarrassed silence. If only a fraction of the deputes had acted that morning, most of their own heads would have remained anchored to their necks over the next three months.

Saint-Just read out the accusation:

'Citizens, a vile plot to overthrow the republic by the émigrés of Coblence[21] has been discovered. Worse still, they are being aided from the very bosom of this assembly, [thereby cleverly connecting General Dumoriez' defection with Danton.] Such conspiracy must never again touch our holy endeavour. We must make certain that amongst us no one will remain but true patriots. We cannot build a republic on consideration, but only on fierce rigour and utmost inflexibility against those who have betrayed us. I say, all criminals, whatever their present position, must be punished.'

His speech carried the overtone of the whisper of a blade.

For Danton's trial, the conspirators employed as their willing tool the man who had hunted the king and queen to their deaths, the revolutionary prosecutor, Antoine Fouquier-Tinville. As could be expected, Danton did not take the trumped-up charges lying down. 'I, Danton, will now unmask a dictatorship that is revealing its existence . . .' The court president rang his bell to cut him off, but Danton's bellowing voice carried over it and right out into the street, to the immense crowd that had gathered in front of the building. 'I demand my accuser to come forward. Let him show himself.' Danton was still under the impression that he was up against Saint-Just. 'You, Saint-Just, will answer for your slander . . .'[22] At Danton's challenging words, the audience burst into thundering applause.

---

21 This goes to show how weak these accusations were. Danton was in fact the one who had sent the king to his death. Coblence was at the hub of royalist-activity.
22 Detailed accounts of the period show that Danton still did not realise who the actual villain was.

'Danton, speak in a manner the people will understand,' interrupted Prosecutor Fouquier-Tinville.

Danton pointed with his outstretched index finger to the crowd. 'Ask them. Ask the people. They understand me.' His words were greeted by more supportive applause. 'People of France, judge me after I have revealed everything to you . . .'

At this point Fouquier-Tinville panicked. He knew that Danton would indeed be naming names, and that the anti-Dantonian conspiracy was in danger of losing out to this orator with the stentorian voice. Danton was simply too brilliant and had to be muzzled. '*Citoyen le président,*' the prosecutor yelled, waving his arms like windmills to attract the court's attention. Contrary to any existing law he demanded that the tribunal's president suspend the proceedings. Equally apprehensive at the turn of events, Saint-Just had already slipped away to confer with his mentor.

Faced with imminent disaster, Saint-Just and Robespierre conspired to strip away even the illusion of a fair trial by designing a law so nefarious that it has remained as a milestone to injustice. When the full dimension of their plot was finally exposed, its villainy was to be remembered as an even greater betrayal than the terror of the guillotine itself. Saint-Just rushed back to harangue the Convention: 'Citizens, you have just escaped a grave danger. No further proof is needed; the resistance and vile accusations brought forth by the accused [Danton] against the elected representatives of this nation is enough to show his guilt.' He then forced upon the cowering deputies a motion known to posterity as the Law of 22 Prairial (10 June), a decree that remains unique in the annals of jurisprudence. It refused the accused his basic right to a defence since it stipulated that *accusation is tantamount to conviction.* When this new law was read out by the court president, Danton realised he had lost. Only then did he recognise the identity of his nemesis, lurking in the shadows. Over the bell of the tribunal president, Danton's voice bellowed: 'Accursed Robespierre, as sure as I shall die this day, you too will follow me to the guillotine!'

That night, Robespierre addressed the members of the Jacobin Club to justify his unjust law: 'Danton was the most dangerous of all enemies of *la patrie*, promising our patriots fidelity while burying their trust in intrigue and conspiracies. The word "virtue" made him laugh. Our Revolutionary Tribunal has been instituted to *help* the revolution, not *slow it up* with vociferous defence tactics. Those who go before it are guilty of only one crime, that of high treason. There is only one punishment, death.'

Paris hummed with morbid agitation: '*Grand gibier ce soir*' – big game tonight,' and crowds gathered around the machine of Dr Guillotin. To the very end, Danton remained what he had always been, audacious and insolent. On his final journey, in Monsieur Sanson's tumbril, he noticed a pretty girl in tears: 'A pity I can't leave my prick to that eunuch Robespierre.' The carts carrying Danton and Desmoulins came to a halt before the two wooden uprights. The machine's blade reflected the evening sun, slanting low across the Elysian Fields (Champs Élysées). Next to it stood the oversized plaster statue of *la Liberté*. As Danton took a last look at the monument that he himself had helped to put there, he shook his head in despair. Without a moment's hesitation he climbed the steep ladder to the elevated platform. Perhaps, for a moment, his thoughts drifted to Louis XVI and Marie-Antonette whom he had dispatched to this murderous machine. From the top of the platform he looked down on the silent multitude, held at bay by the bayonets of the Garde Républicaine. Danton turned to Monsieur Sanson, the only man in the country not to be addressed as *citoyen*. 'Show my head to the people. It's well worth it.' The blade came down.

The Terror that followed Danton's death lasted for sixteen

weeks – four months of indiscriminate bloodshed and fear, of accusations and condemnations. With unmerciful logic, Robespierre the theologian lawyer made death his political system. Until Danton's fall, only 116 had been beheaded; afterwards 3,000 were guillotined. A meticulous record of all executions was kept daily, but it does not take into account the murders of many thousands that were committed in the outlying provinces and towns, such as Nantes and Lyons. The first to go were politicians who guillotined each other to escape the guillotine themselves. From then on, death carts in ever increasing numbers delivered a daily menu. (Outside food stands, next to the dishes they offered, was the list of the day's victims, called a 'menu'.) Men of great learning, such as Antoine-Laurent de Lavoisier, father of modern chemistry, inventor of the chemical vocabulary and metric system, were sentenced with a simple phrase: 'The republic does not need scientists.' Another victim was the great mathematician and philosopher, the Marquis de Condorcet who suffered the same fate. André Chenier, a liberal poet, was arrested in a case of mistaken identity. The sentence was intended for his brother. But one was as good as the other: 'We've got him, we haven't got his brother,' and the fact of his arrest alone was enough to send him to the guillotine. Frequently the butchery was as gratuitous as it was haphazard. The widow Mayet was put to death in a batch of fifty simply because someone had denounced her as Madame de Maillet (both were pronounced the same), a lady of the aristocracy. Fouquier-Tinville overruled her plea of innocence with the phrase: 'Since she's already here we might as well execute her too.' A similar fate befell a certain Madame Quetier, a housewife who berated her husband over money for a new *rouet* (spinning wheel) and was beheaded for praising the *roi* (king).

The Conciergerie became their final stop before the guillotine. To cope with the many prisoners, a fenced-in courtyard was

used as a holding area. Inside the stonewalled prison the
situation was almost indescribable.[23] Hundreds were thrust
together into airless dungeons, with neither toilet facilities
nor sufficient water. 'You don't need it, you're going to die,'
laughed their jailers. Prisoners fought each other for sleeping
space; aristocratic women huddled next to guttersnipes, sharing their fleas and their smells. Thieves stripped the nobility of
their shirts and shoes. But what made it most unbearable was
the gripping fear of uncertainty, waiting day by day for their
name to be called. Survival under such circumstances became
a logical improbability. For many it came almost as a relief
once their name was finally pronounced. Then they knew that
their mental torture was finally over, that they were on the list
for the day. Prison goodbyes were always dramatic; husbands
were separated from wives, mothers torn from their children.
The trials led to a huge increase in bureaucratic activity,
the taking down of names, making records of confiscated
belongings. The condemned were allowed to keep one pair
of shoes and an outer garment. Human vultures surrounding
the common grave stripped them even of that and sold
'ladies' shirts' on the black market. Robespierre, who disliked
being an involuntary spectator of the daily procession of
death carts passing by his window, ordered the guillotine
to be moved to the Place du Trône (now the Place de la
Nation).

The City of Light had its lights turned out. Fun and life had
deserted Paris. Culture died on its feet; plays by the 'royalist'
Molière and Voltaire's satiric pieces were either banned or
altered to project a revolutionary message. People took refuge
in the bottle; a drunk managed to slip inside the courtroom.
'*Vive le Roi*,' he yelled and jumped to his death from the
gallery. The most abject of all creatures were the *tricoteuses*
(the knitting women) who sat around the guillotine knitting

23 There are few actual accounts since very few prisoners lived to tell the story.

and cheering as heads tumbled into the basket.[24] Death kindled a sexual frenzy, which they spent afterwards in bouts of unbridled lust. A new must-attend function was the Fraternal Supper, which everyone in their *arrondissement* had to attend and supply with food. If they did not bring enough, they would offend the presiding Jacobin block warden; if they brought too much they would be accused of hoarding. They had to fling their arms around each other and sing joyously as if in a Munich beer hall, all under the watchful eyes of Robespierre's informers.

'Power corrupts, and absolute power corrupts absolutely.' The 'Incorruptible' Robespierre's three months in power can be explained with this single phrase. The Committee of Public Safety, his instrument for the Terror, fell into disarray. Two of the committee's foremost members, Saint-Just and Carnot, were at loggerheads. Two others, Collot d'Herbois and Billaud-Varenne, conspired behind the scenes. Robespierre benefited from their division to make himself undisputed dictator. He used Saint-Just and another acolyte, the cripple Couthon, to prepare his next round for the guillotine. It became known as 'the list'.

The *enragés*, the insolent *sans-culottes*, posed a menace for anyone in authority. Weak in numbers, their basic strategy was provocation. Even after Jacques Roux, their messiah, chose to kill himself rather than to mount the steps of the guillotine, his followers continued to be so troublesome and disruptive that *l'Incorruptible* had no choice but to act. The discovery of a spy of Robespierre's among them started the rumour of a blacklist. Once the idea of a list had been planted in their minds, suspicion grew – and not only among the *enragés*. The strain on Robespierre began to tell, and his nerves started to fray. All it needed was one devilish clever

[24] From a description by the Abbé Carrichon of the Duchess of Noailles' execution.

man to upset the tyrant. Such a man arrived in Paris the day after Danton's death.

Little is known about Joseph Fouché, one of the most fascinating figures of the revolution. Intrigue was his very existence. In large part he was just as responsible for the death of Louis XVI as for the fall of Napoleon. He was a master-juggler of the power politics of six consecutive governments, from royalty to republic, from tyranny to empire and back to royalty, betraying everyone to whom he had ever promised loyalty. When Napoleon confronted him: 'Ah, Fouché, was it not you who voted the death of your king?'[25] his minister, ennobled to the title of Duc d'Otrante, replied: 'That is so, Sire, and it was the first service I did for Your Majesty.'

Fouché observed the power struggle between Danton and Robespierre from the safe distance of Lyons. For months, this city on the Rhône had been in open revolt against the dictates of the Parisian Jacobins, and Fouché had been ordered to supervise its suppression. In the winter of 1793, thousands of Lyonnais were brought outside the city gates and put to death by cannon fire. Their bodies were tossed into the Rhône to float downstream as a dire warning The town's centre was razed with a deadly logic: 'Nothing but the use of fire can give full expression to the omnipotency of the People.'[26]

For a cold-blooded schemer such as Fouché, talk about human virtue was an old wives' tale. That is why the Committee of Public Safety had appointed him and Collot d'Herbois to oversee the application of the 'omnipotency of the People'. Fouché despised Robespierre. With the execution of Danton, whose principal thoughts he shared, Fouché knew he would be next on the death list. His time to strike had come. The day that he returned from Paris, he vanished from public

[25] The final vote on Louis XVI's death sentence had to be proclaimed in a loud voice by every deputy. This was to separate publicly the doves (royalists) from the hawks (republicans).
[26] Edouard Herriot, *Lyon n'est plus*.

view to operate diligently from behind the scenes. With the utmost skill he employed his master weapons: the unexpected and intrigue.

Robespierre received his initial shock when he found out that Joseph Fouché had forged alliances to get himself elected president of the Jacobins Club. Robespierre cursed himself; he had greatly underestimated the reach of this potential adversary. First he had Fouché chased from the Jacobins; next he called for a *Fête d'Être Suprême* (Festival of the Supreme Being) over which he presided, not as the head of his bloodstained Committee of Public Safety,[27] but in his new role as dictator. Great festivities were held in the Tuileries gardens. Robespierre ascended a pyramid to the cheers of a demented crowd. Alone and conspicuous, he stood at the summit as the festivity's high priest. He did not adhere to the ancient wisdom that 'He who sticks out his head above the rest is liable to get it chopped off.' In a symbolism so unique to revolutionary times, he set fire to a figure representing Insincerity. The crowd broke out in 'oohs' and 'aahs' when from its ashes rose a new statue, that of Wisdom and Virtue.[28] This event was to be the coronation of a tyrant. One month later he was dead.

When Robespierre passed the Law of 22 Prairial he also put the seal on his own tyranny. This ignominious law stipulated that: 'No accused shall have his case put aside until the Committee of Public Safety and the General Security Committee *have examined the case*.' A decision as to who should face accusation was thus left to the two committees. Since Robespierre controlled both bodies, he was not only safe from prosecution, but could also decide the outcome of trials. This grim threat to their personal safety was not

---

[27] The festival was also the only day in his bloody reign when the guillotine was not used.

[28] The painter David, who went on to become Napoleon's court artist, designed the statues.

lost on the deputies; nobody was certain that he was not the next on 'the list'. This fear played into Fouché's hand. By exploiting it, he united those who had been hostile to each other. The key to his scheme lay with two men, Collot d'Herbois and Billaud-Varennes, members of the Committee of Public Safety. He took a gamble when he argued: 'When you deliver my head to Robespierre, who will be there to protect yours?' Once they joined in his conspiracy, they could never go back. Time was running out; Robespierre had pronounced an ominous threat in the Jacobins Club: 'All good citizens must be on guard against intrigues.' His accent was on the 'all'. The confrontation was about to begin.

Robespierre and Saint-Just worked through the night on a list of deputies who were to be dispatched to the guillotine. Robespierre organised a contingent from the Paris Commune to occupy the galleries and shout in his support. But Robespierre was no Marat; even the Communards had had enough of a Terror that struck out indiscriminately. The story of the widow Mayet had made the rounds. Many of the 'little people' were no longer in support of the dictator. Fouché was not the only one active. Lazare Carnot, head of military affairs in the Committee of Public Safety, countered Robespierre's rallying cry to the Commune by putting the National Guard on standby. As an added precaution he put his own men in charge of arms and munitions stores. This sabre-rattling fooled no one, since the battle was not to be fought with powder and bayonets; the bloodletting would be done with words on the Convention floor.

On 26 July 1794, a capacity crowd packed the galleries. It was another day that promised the hunt for big game. Gossip was rife among the frightened deputies. Fouché's conspirators circulated to fan the rumours of 'the list' and stir up fears. Robespierre stepped up to the rostrum dressed in a robin-blue silk coat and yellow breeches. Deathly silence descended when he raised his hands and began to speak.

'Loyal men have nothing to fear. But for those whose conspiracy reaches into the Committee of Public Safety and into the General Security Committee, those traitors must be recognised and punished.' He finished by saying: 'You must be informed that within this body exists a league of scoundrels who fight our public virtue.' He then called for the arrest of 'all conspirators'. He did not give names – insinuation had always been enough to achieve his ends. But this time it proved his fatal flaw, since it united all those who feared for their lives. (It was certain that his list contained the names of Fouché, Billaud, Collot, Tallien, Carnot, and Barras.) The snake had spoken and the members of the Convention were mesmerised by its fangs.

All but one, Bourdon de l'Oise, who had been told by Fouché that his name was on the list. 'Citizen Maximilien, you have put forward a grave accusation which must be clarified.' Robespierre stared, speechless. Someone had dared to stand up and demand justification! Before he was given the chance to respond, Cambon, the head of the Finance Committee and a Fouché man, bounced up and rushed to the rostrum, blocking out the daintier Robespierre. 'I shall not be dishonoured,' he cried,' 'I will speak in the name of France. It is time to tell the truth: *there is one man who stifles the Convention.*' To lend added impact to his accusation, Cambon stepped slightly to the side so that all could get a good look at the man in the robin-blue coat, before he declared in a booming voice: 'That man is Robespierre!' It was as if an icy gust had swept across the floor and the galleries, freezing everyone into silence. Billaud-Varrennes jumped onto his wooden bench to point an outstretched arm at a slightly shaken Robespierre: 'Yes! His mask must be torn away! As a member of the Committee of Public Safety, I don't wish to become a partner to his crimes.'

It was left to Deputy Panis to bring the assembly to boiling point. He stood up, and almost like some schoolboy, said:

'The Citizen Robespierre has said that he has drawn up *a list* . . .'

'*The list! The list!*' howled the deputies. 'Name those whom you accuse!'

Robespierre was taken by surprise, searching for words: 'I . . . I listen only to my call of duty . . .'

His words were drowned by an uproar. The five o'clock bell saved Robespierre and the first round ended without a clear winner. The exhausted dictator went home to sleep, while candles continued to burn in the rooms of the Committee of Public Safety. Saint-Just was hard at work, planning the decisive showdown which he knew the morning must bring.

The 9th Thermidor of Year II (27 July 1794) promised to be hot and humid; heavy clouds hovered over Paris. Long before the session opened the floor and galleries of the Convention were filled to overflow with deputies, journalists and supporters; the noisy and the curious had joined the throng. Fouché had inserted his own ace card. He connived to nominate Collot d'Herbois as president for the day's meeting. Robespierre, accompanied by Saint-Just and Couthon, entered the Assembly to the cheers from the Mountain. (This was a reference to the seating arrangements: the liberals were on the ground floor, or the Plain, the extremist Jacobins were on a balustrade, known as the Mountain). He waved benignly, certain of his forthcoming triumph, and installed himself on a bench in the middle of the Plain to gain added support from the hesitant moderates. His plan called for careful timing. Saint-Just was to perform a 'warm-up' before Robespierre himself launched into his attack against Fouché and his conspiracy.

From that moment on, events unravelled at lightning speed. Saint-Just advanced to the rostrum, but before he was able to utter a word, Tallien yelled: 'I demand to be heard!' Saint-Just was taken aback by the interruption. When he recovered his voice, Convention President Collot d'Herbois cut him off with his bell. Unceremoniously, the big Tallien shoved Saint-Just from the podium and bellowed: 'I demand that the curtain is lifted.' Tallien's fellow conspirators now rose and repeated: 'Tear away the curtain!' Before Saint-Just was given a chance to speak, Billaud-Varennes had taken Tallien's place. He pointed towards Robespierre: 'This man is planning to murder the Convention!'

'*À bas le tyran!* Down with the tyrant!' screamed the group of well-organised Fouché supporters, which led to confusion on the Mountain and timid support from the Plain. Fouché's surprise act had shown that there was after all a chance to save their necks. The drifters, those who would always vote whichever way the political wind blew, joined in the 'Down with the tyrant' chorus. Robespierre was stunned; his hands clenched and unclenched. He looked on helpless as his alliances came undone; to save their heads, some Jacobins had begun to switch camp. Tallien pulled out a dagger, which he wielded theatrically above his head. '*À bas le tyran!*'

Robespierre jumped to his feet and made for the rostrum, but was restrained by a wall of Fouché's conspirators. When he called out, his voice was drowned by the president's bell. The hall exploded into bedlam. The deputies yelled, those in the galleries yelled and stamped their feet, the president roared and rang his bell. The stomping of feet grew into a roll, the roll became a syncopated clapping of hands and a cry: '*À bas le tyran!*' With laboured breath and bluish lips, Robespierre kept repeating his desperate plea: 'Let me speak,' and 'Hear me,' but his voice did not carry over the uproar. Collot's bell finally took effect and the noise abated. Robespierre, who always weighed his words with great care, was outraged by the turn of events. The last words he would ever speak in front of the assembly were: '*Donnez moi la parole, Président des Assassins* – Let me speak, President of Assassins.' This insult, calling the Convention a group of assassins, was answered by a single voice which cut like a foghorn through the din: 'Assassin yourself. The ghosts of Danton and Desmoulins haunt you!'

Tallien called out: 'This monster has insulted the People's Convention.'

'*À bas le tyran!*'

Louchet, another deputy, climbed on his bench, waved his hands to calm the crowd, and then spoke the words that nobody had dared to utter but which everyone longed to hear: 'I demand the arrest of Robespierre!'

'Arrest him!' The roar came from the Plain and from the Mountain. In a thin ruse to show supposed legality for the arrest by a calling for a vote, the president found so many hands raised that it made a count unnecessary. There were no abstentions; even Robespierre's Jacobins had abandoned their leader. Deep night touched the 'Incorruptible' in the middle of the day; his eyes stared unbelievingly at approaching death. The noise rose; Collot d'Herbois frantically rang his bell: 'I order the immediate arrest of those accused of treason: Robespierre, Saint-Just, Couthon . . .' A tyrant had been brought down.

The tension that gripped the Convention quickly communicated itself to the communes of Paris. Loyal Jacobins dispatched messengers to the sections to assemble 'a posse of strong men and women' on the Place de la Maison-Commune. Supported by the cannons of the National Guard, they would soon take care of that rebellious Convention. Their leader, François Hanriot, general of the Paris National Guard, was a habitual drunkard and braggart. He began his 'military career' as the valet of a royalist officer before becoming Marat's hatchet man. At Marat's behest in June 1793, he had raised a mob to storm the Convention, oust the Girondins, and install the Jacobins. A few days later, Marat was dead and Hanriot quickly switched allegiance to Robespierre, who appointed him head of the National Guard. The night before the 9th Thermidor, he had assured Robespierre that he would line up his guns on the Convention 'and blast those traitors to hell.'

What next took place can only be explained in terms of the sacrosanct nature of that French institution, the evening meal. In the midst of this momentous upheaval, the Convention took a two-hour dinner break! Paris's mayor, Fleuriot, a stout Robespierre follower, exploited the two-hour recess to gather a force of thousands of his armed supporters in front of the capital's City Hall. The leader of the masses, Commander Hanriot was utterly drunk and incapable of a coherent word. He jumped on a horse and galloped off, madly howling and swinging his sabre, to the Tuileries, where he was unceremoniously pulled from his horse, trussed up, and dumped into a storage room.

When Fleuriot heard about his guard commander's arrest he proved that he too was no military strategist. Instead of ordering a force to save Robespierre, Fleuriot dispatched 200 armed Communards to the Convention to liberate the drunkard. The deputies had now returned from their supper and clashed with Fleuriot's rabble. Nobody was seriously hurt, but it was enough to demonstrate the power of the Paris mob. The inebriated Hanriot was brought in triumph to City Hall, where his gunners had placed their thirty-two pieces; apart from that, they showed no initiative whatsoever. During these crucial hours, Robespierre's supporters held a crushing superiority in cannons – a trump card that would certainly have decided the issue if they could have found a military commander to take charge, because Hanriot had once again slipped away to the Auberge du Cheval-Vert.

For the deputies, this dangerous situation had to be speedily remedied, especially since those guarding Robespierre were terrified by the gathering mob and had let him go. They therefore issued a decree that was to tilt the balance. The Convention declared Robespierre an outlaw; this meant that anyone who came to his assistance would face automatic arrest and execution without trial. The Conventionist Paul Barras was put in charge of carrying out the decision. The first message was sent to City Hall to summon Fleuriot to appear before the Convention. 'I shall come,' the mayor declared, 'and I will bring the people with me.' But other messengers fared better: of the forty-eight communes, only thirteen answered the call by Fleuriot to defend City Hall, while twenty-seven watched the outcome from the sidelines. When other section leaders noticed a change in the tide, they declared in favour of the Convention. While the delegates were still unsure of the result and lived in constant terror of the Paris mob, that mob shuffled aimlessly about and waited for an order. Meanwhile, the weather changed and heavy thunderclouds gathered over the city.

But where was Robespierre? In his greatest crisis he too was overcome by the lassitude that had already doomed the king. During these vital hours of jostling and manoeuvring, the tyrant who had always profited from the failures of his opponents was frozen with shock. While his supporters waited for him at the Hôtel de Ville, a frightened, confused Robespierre refused to leave his Left Bank sanctuary. A crowd without a leader is a chicken without a head. They began to drink heavily and fights broke out as the news spread that the *arrondissements* were switching sides. More precious hours were wasted before Robespierre, Saint-Just, and Couthon arrived at the Hôtel de Ville to join Fleuriot and Hanriot (who had been dragged from his tavern). Once again on this fateful day, Robespierre's luck ran out. This time the weather intervened. A thunderstorm of such fury burst over the city that the great Talleyrand immortalised it with: 'Rain is counter-revolutionary!' It drenched the mob and sent them scurrying for the nearest bistro. Outside it rained and inside they drank. The square was empty.

It was at that point that Barras and fifty gendarmes

showed up. The violence of what next took place can only be explained when seen in relation to the pitiless terror that Robespierre had wielded over the city and the nation. Now he was to be repaid in kind. He and his confederates were gathered in a room on the first floor of the Hôtel de Ville – The door burst open, a shot rang out, and a pistol ball shattered Robespierre's jaw.[29] The dictator's head fell onto the document he had just signed, which ordered the militia – one of whom had just shot him – to rush to his assistance.[30]

Augustin Robespierre, his brother, made for an open window and threw himself into the courtyard, breaking many bones in the process but he was alive.

Joseph Lebas pulled a pistol from his belt. Saint-Just begged him: 'Shoot me first, *mon frère.*'

'*Pauvre con* (stupid oaf), I have more important things to do,' said Lebas. He raised the gun to his head and blew out his brains. The cripple Couthon hid under a table; militiamen found him and flung him down the staircase. The drunken Hanriot stumbled out of a window and came to a soft landing in a dungheap where he slept off his stupor until a gendarme heard him snoring. Bayonets prodded Hanriot awake and he received a beating so severe that it knocked out one of his eyes.

At first light on the 10th Thermidor (28 July 1794) the men who had held France in the grip of the Terror were but a sad collection of shattered limbs and blood-smeared faces. The mob sensed a new wind and quickly switched sides. At the Convention, Barras made a theatrical entry with the cry: 'The traitor Robespierre is outside,' words of deliverance that had the delegates bursting into cheers. Their president proclaimed:

---

[29] The gendarme Merda claimed that he had fired the shot, but it was never proved.

[30] This blood-spattered document, as well as the table on which Robespierre was laid, is in the Musée Carnavalet in Paris.

'His place is not before this august body, but on the Place de la Révolution.' His declaration met with an ovation; for this occasion, the guillotine would be brought back to the Place de la Concorde.

A severely wounded Robespierre was dragged in, fastened to a board, with his arms dangling over the sides and his knuckles scraping across the cobblestones. At the Committee for Public Safety, the traitor Robespierre was placed on the same table from which the dictator Robespierre had wielded ultimate power. Crowds filed past a sorry sight. His shattered chin was bound up with a blood-soaked rag, his silk stockings hung down over his ankles, his robin-blue silk coat was splattered with blood. Those who yesterday had hailed him as the 'Incorruptible' cursed him today as the 'ogre.' An old man who had lost his son to the Terror looked down at the broken figure. 'Yes, Robespierre, there is a God.'

At noon, Robespierre and his twenty-two accomplices were hauled before the Revolutionary Tribunal. Due to the law he himself had instigated to silence Danton, the public prosecutor Fouquier-Tinville (whose days were numbered) had only to read out their names to condemn every single one to the guillotine. 'The accused will stand up. Couthon, Fleuriot, Hanriot, Robespierre, Saint-Just . . .' Those who could not stand were roughly pulled to their feet by gendarmes. Late in the afternoon, the twenty-three were loaded onto three carts. In the first tumbril rode Saint-Just, still impeccably dressed in fawn-coloured breeches and a white shirt, erect like a beacon in a sea of slavering Jacobins. However much the Parisians hated this cold and merciless figure, he went to his death with an air of nobility. He had not uttered a word in his defence. Chateaubriand paid him a tribute: 'Only silence is great, the rest is weakness.'

Gendarmes had to carry Robespierre to the second cart and made him sit on a plank. This was Fouché's way of demonstrating to the people that it was indeed Robespierre who was going to his death. In the last cart lay the manure-caked Hanriot. Beside him cowered Couthon, crying out his innocence. The procession took the well-trodden route Parisians had dubbed the Via Dolorosa.[31] At the Duplay house, from where Robespierre had conspired against so many of his rivals,[32] the horrid *tricoteuses* danced a *ronde* around the condemned. A bereaved woman screamed: 'Satan, the curse of all mothers be upon your head!' Thousands had gathered on the Place de la Révolution to witness the end of a tyrant. Above them loomed Robespierre's own tool of terror, *la guillotine*. One by one, the Jacobins were herded up to face Monsieur Sanson. Only Saint-Just kept his dignity and mounted the ladder to face death with that ice-cold insensibility that had made him the most enigmatic character of the revolution. The others had to be bundled onto the bloodstained board. The twenty-first on the day's 'menu' was *l'Incorruptible*, Maximilien Robespierre. A hush fell over the square, men took a whiter grip on their canes, and women crossed themselves: 'Here goes the devil.' All stares were fixed on an elevated platform and a gleaming blade. Robespierre's broken body was dragged up the ladder, his feet banging hard on each step. From his bandaged face his eyes could be seen, staring at a leaden sky. If he was not unconscious, he was beyond caring. His knees sagged and they let him lie there, symbol of a fallen tyrant, before they lashed him to the board. An assistant tore off the blood-soaked bandage from his shattered jaw. Robespierre screamed out in pain. Sanson gave a brief nod . . . The board tilted forward so that it came to rest between the two oaken uprights . . . A dull thud as the wooden neck-clamp dropped into place . . . A moment's hesitation . . . Total silence . . . Sanson pulled the lever and

[31] This ran from the main gate of the Conciergerie, across the Seine on the Pont Neuf, along the Rue St Honoré to the Place de la Concorde.

[32] Fearing his arrest, Robespierre moved into the house at 398 Rue St Honoré, on 17 July 1791. Today this building is the Café le Robespierre.

the blade fell. Everyone heard its whisper. A sigh went across the Place de la Révolution. A tyrant had entered the hell of history.

The dictator who had thought himself infallible was swept away by a barracks coup; it came with stunning speed. In the Paris of the revolution, he who lived by bluster was undone by it. The skill that made the 'Incorruptible' brilliant in opposition and cunning in insurrection was not suited for enduring leadership. He overlooked the fact that a republic, with its conflicting forces was more in need of legality than a monarchy. The terror he had unleashed finally claimed him.

The Terror's last victim was a ten-year-old boy, condemned to a slow death. His suffering finally ended on 8 June 1795. That day, the uncrowned King Louis XVII died officially in the Temple.

But why 'died officially'? No account of the tragedy would be complete without the 'Enigma of the Temple'. What was the real identity of the boy who died in that prison? If it was the dauphin, then it might have been more humane to put this poor child out of his misery together with his mother, than to allow him to suffer agonies for two years.

In spring 2000, a positive DNA match was made from a lock of the Queen's hair and a sliver of the boy's heart. It was indeed Louis XVII, the Queen's son.

The mystery concerns principally five persons. A ten-year-old phantom king; his jailer, Simon the cobbler; Robespierre; and two Jacobins, Hébert and Chaumette, who entered the queen's chamber in the Temple and took the child from her. Torn from the arms of his mother, he was locked up in a tiny, rat-infested cell without a toilet but with a board nailed across the window to keep out the daylight. He was beaten by his jailers when he refused to sing bawdy songs, given only black soup to eat, and left to sleep in his own excrement. Simon the cobbler turned a bright and gay child into a dumb creature that would never speak again.

In 1819, an old woman, Simon the cobbler's wife, came forward and demanded money for a story. According to her, Chaumette, with the help of Simon and Hébert, had spirited the boy out of the Temple and replaced him with a sick child. Hébert and Chaumette were arrested on charges 'of helping to re-establish the monarchy'; and their accusation carried an even stranger phrase: '. . . and of facilitating the dauphin's escape.'

During the night of 8 June 1795 the boy died. Dr Pelletan, a neighbourhood physician, performed an autopsy on a kitchen table in the prison ante-room. While nobody was paying any attention, he wrapped the child's heart in a handkerchief and slipped it into his pocket, before stitching up the body. This heart was to become the focus of mystery and passion. The doctor kept it in a jar of alcohol, but failed to notice that the liquid had evaporated and the heart dried up. His assistant, who died shortly afterwards, stole the jar but his widow returned it to Dr Pelletan. Years later, the doctor offered it to the restored king and the dead boy's uncle, Louis XVIII, but the king refused it. Dr Pelletan then gave it into the safe keeping of the Archbishop of Paris. During the Revolution of 1830, the archbishop's palace was ransacked and a royalist, Lescroart, tried to save the relic. He was caught by a national guardsman who roughed him up; the glass urn crashed to the pavement but the heart was recovered from among the shards of glass. It was moved to the cathedral of Saint-Denis, the burial site of French royalty. Eventually, forty pretenders presented themselves and claimed to be Louis-Charles de Bourbon. Most were locked up for fraud.

This poor little boy who died was indeed the king, and

he suffered the infamy of a child's martyrdom because the revolution trembled at the idea that he could once more become a king.

A child died, a little boy who whispered: '*Toujours seul* – always alone while my mother is in the other tower.' A child who was never told that his mother had been executed.

And then . . .

The Terror died with Robespierre, a Terror that was inexcusable. He alone was not responsible for the excesses that were committed in the name of an ideal, Virtue. There was, first of all, a king who paid the price of his kingdom's moral and economic bankruptcy. His reversals of fortune and fatal character flaws took on the elements of a Rabelaisian tragedy, and reached their nadir with his indecisiveness when faced by a rabid street mob. Weak by nature, he refused to sacrifice a few in order to save the whole and thereby set the tragedy in motion. Because of him, much blood was spilled. This, the French never forgave him.

And there were the revolutionaries. Marat, one of history's pariahs, motivated by a patriotic belief that only blood can cleanse, who created a new class of citizen – the People's Commune. Danton, the reckless and ambitious 'ultra', who justified his acts of regicide with the need to bolster a fragile revolution. With one phrase he exhorted a nation to expunge the shame of defeat only to fall victim to an ambitious, jealous villain. Saint-Just, that enigmatic, dispassionate archangel of the guillotine, who wished to fill the cemeteries and not the prisons. His wish was to be granted. Finally Robespierre, guided by the virtue of some obscure Supreme Being, who justified his malice with an ideal. On the whole his terror was less efficient, less effectively absolute than that practised by more recent governments.

The French Revolution wrote *finis* to the age of medieval monarchical structure in Europe. Its stigmata have remained as symbols of every subsequent revolution. It invented the purges of an entire class of society; it brought into being the people's courts, trials without defence, and executions without trials[33] and all the other apparatus that we call a totalitarian regime. There were also many positive aspects. The Committee of Public Safety fulfilled its function. Carnot's conscription raised an army of a million men, formed it into a capable fighting machine, and developed the first modern arms industry to mass-produce the musket. Saint-Just rallied the morale of the Rhine Army to defeat the Prussians and the Austrians. These victories saved the young republic and placed the most powerful monarchies of Europe in danger of collapsing like a house of cards. New republics grew out of this confusion. It precipitated the first truly global conflict, the Napoleonic Wars, involving the huge armies of the European superpowers, and it set the stage for British dominance of the seas.

History tends to castigate Marat, to overlook Saint-Just, and to idealise the impure Danton over the 'Incorruptible' Robespierre. 'Heaven has provided me with a passion for liberty,' he used to say, 'and it is for me to draw with my heart's blood the road to happiness and liberty for the people.' With a reign of terror he wanted to assure a reign of virtue, and attain happiness through violence. Where the king was troubled by the thought of causing bloodshed, he marched boldly ahead. Until the day that some of those he terrified rebelled. For it has been proved throughout the ages that man can tolerate only so much interference with the routines of his daily existence.

[33] The Terror cost the lives of 16,594.

One after the other, the great French revolutionaries fell victim to their own vanity. When they climbed too high, their heads were chopped off.

In the end, 'The revolution devoured its children'.[34]

Interlude
1794–1809

The First French Republic lasted seven years. With Robespierre and the Great Terror out of the way, the deputies started on their favourite pastime, bickering. In 1799, the flickering flame of the revolution was put out with a whiff of gunpowder by a young artillery genius, General Napoleon Bonaparte.

Napoleon's interests were diametrically opposed to those of the revolutionary. He was not interested in the good of all, but proved himself a megalomaniac dictator, concerned only with personal power. 'Power is my mistress,' he declared. 'I've worked too hard at her conquest to let anyone take her from me.' To this purpose, he used any and all means to achieve it; he crushed his political opposition; he dealt with the survivors from the revolutionary period by exiling them into the countryside; he made corporals into kings, and kings into outcasts; he instituted reforms tailored to increase his repressive grip, first on France, later across an entire continent. He even used religion, flatly stating: 'Society cannot exist without inequality, therefore we need religion so that we can state: "*It is God's will.*"' By his instructions, a new constitution was written, 'to uphold the

---

[34] The original phrase was spoken by the French revolutionary, Pierre Victorien Vergniaud, a Girondin who perished on the guillotine in 1793: 'The revolution, like Saturn, devours its children.'

revolutionary values of *égalité* and *fraternité*.' His repressive
police methods conveniently overlooked the third principle
of his revolutionary forebears, *la liberté*.

Many of his social reforms have survived the centuries.
Undoubtedly his greatest achievement was a codified civil
law which became known as the Code Napoleon and is still
in use today. He put his country on a solid financial basis by
instituting the Banque de France, and created a fair taxation
system. His cultural ambassadors roamed the world (and
stole the treasures displayed today in the Louvre). His first
years in power were a dazzling success. This triumph, and his
adulation by the masses, went to his head. He was too young,
too ambitious, and too convinced of his unique role in history
to rest on his laurels. France was too narrow for his ambition;
he strove to become the unique ruler of a United Europe. And
thus, he went on to smash all the armies of Europe in one
brilliant strategic manoeuvre after another. In less than ten
years, the penniless Corsican had raised himself to be equal
in rank with the Emperor of the (almost) thousand-year-old
Hapsburgian Holy Roman Empire and the Tsar of All the
Russias.

The danger posed by Napoleon's naked ambitions towards
further expansionism – he even dreamed of a new world
empire based on France's possession of Louisiana – and his
unquestionable military skills, led to war. On 2 December
1805, an ineptly led Austro-Russian army suffered a crushing
defeat at Austerlitz. At the apex of his military glory, no
general could match his genius and no power dared to
challenge the might of his armies. Generals surrendered at the
mere sight of him, emperors and kings buckled before him. He
even forced the Hapsburg ruler to dismantle the 844-year-old
Holy Roman Empire. In order to fracture German unity, the
principalities of Wuerttemberg and Bavaria were elevated
into kingdoms by Napoleon's grace. His peace dictate of
1806 held another clause: to protect his Cis-Alpine flank,

Napoleon handed the king of Bavaria the title to an Austrian province, the Tyrol.

Napoleon seemed invincible. And yet, at the height of his glory came a serious challenge from a most unexpected source. It was a relatively minor affair, but Napoleon committed the capital sin of creating a martyr and thereby united Germany against him.

2

13 August 1809

'Månder, s'ischt Zeit'

Månder, s'ischt Zeit!
Men, the time is now!
Call-up by Andreas Hofer, 9 April 1809

'*Himmelvåtter, s'ischt de Sturmglocken.* Good Lord, it's the storm-bells.'

'Do you have to go to war?' asked his wife. 'Take good care of yourself.'

'That's in God's hands,' said the farmer and ran down into the valley. What started as a tiny brook soon became a rushing torrent of warriors headed for a conflict.

'*Månder, s'ischt Zeit!* Men, the time is now!' For many centuries this phrase called Tyrol's men to arms. This time was now. Men gathered to form into volunteer companies, and companies formed into a *Haufen*.[1] And *Haufens* climbed the steep slopes and sang: '*Wir sind die heil'ge G'meind, und steh'n in Christi Huld* . . . – We are the holy community and Christ is with us.' They piled up boulders and hid behind rocks. There they waited for the enemy who had to pass

---

[1] *Himmelvåtter* means 'Heavenly Father'. *Haufen* is a 'heap' or 'mass', a loosely knit fighting unit of non-officered militia.

this way because it was the only way he could pass – the French and the Bavarians, the troops of Emperor Napoleon, who moved along the narrow defile.

The soldiers from the fertile plains of France felt as if they were descending towards the centre of the earth, penetrating deeper into a dark, hostile universe of steep ravines, dense forests, and raging torrents. Previous rockslides had partially blocked the passes. French units had gone this way before. They were presented with visible proof of a previous ill-fated French attempt to force this passage – rocks littered the valley floor, but also bones, and shreds of faded uniforms. What they feared most was piled up above their heads; murderous rock avalanches. They knew that behind every one of them sat a rebel with his axe, ready to cut the rope.

General Bisson's orders had been clear; he was 'to frustrate rebel attacks, suppress insurgency, and keep communication open across the vital mountain pass'. He surveyed the scene. Before him the dark gorge with its boiling waters seemed utterly hostile, but where was the enemy? He noticed a silhouette on the edge of the cliff above. The man stared down at the French column and raised his arm as in some final salute to those who were lost.

The French general cupped his hands to call: '*Qui es tu?*'. As the man did not reply, he tried again, this time in broken German: '*Wer seid ihr?*' he yelled.

And a deep voice re-echoed from the cliffs: '*I bin der Hofer Andrä.*' Andreas Hofer, the famous innkeeper!

The bearded man took off his wide-brimmed hat and waved it in the air. A volley rang out, its echo bouncing from cliff to cliff. General Bisson knew that his only hope for survival was to order what none of the emperor's generals had ever dared to order before. Retreat! Even for that it was too late. Death came crashing over the cliffs. Huge boulders buried the Frenchmen and Bavarians. They were allies: they fought together, and they died together. There were no cries or moans from the wounded. There were no wounded. There was only silence, eternal silence. The Tyroleans had shown that their particular style of fighting was ultimately suited for the terrain. Napoleon had feared it when he predicted: 'I do not wish to become embroiled in mountain warfare.'

As a revolutionary, Andreas Hofer is the exception. An uneducated innkeeper leading a peasant rabble against the greatest military genius and army the world had ever seen. And why? All to keep an autocratic kaiser on his throne!

'*Für Gott, Kaiser and unser Tiroler Land!* For God, Kaiser and our Tyrolean Land!'

Three hundred years earlier, the Tyroleans had been granted the special right to bear arms. Such a privilege created a special kind of man, stubborn, undisciplined, and proud. Villages were organised into *Schützenverbaende* and the greatest annual competition was the Tyrolean shoot-out. For that, everyone practised hard with his *Stutzen*[2] – by poaching game, their most popular pastime. In case of danger, the *Schützenverbaende* were formed into units of a hundred men. It was up to every valley to elect its own captain; this was usually the village innkeeper, since local meetings took place near his wine barrels around the warm, tiled chimney. Local militia units held an indisputable advantage: they knew each other and their terrain. Most of all, they had a valid reason to turn into furious mountain fighters since they were protecting their families and homesteads. Their fighting spirit made up for any technical shortcoming when facing a trained military force. Throughout history such volunteer units had proved their value as a formidable defence against foreign invaders. Tyrol was a natural fortress of steep mountains, rising sharply from the upper Italian plains and ending in the Danube valley

---

[2] A Stutzen was a muzzle-loader, which had the advantage of being shorter than the military flintlock and therefore easier to use in guerrilla warfare. The Stutzen was the forerunner of the cavalry carbine.

of Bavaria. Its only access was over the Brenner Pass. Ancient Romans had recognised the Tyrol's strategic importance and had built a road, which snaked along passages which had been cut by nature's forces through Alpine rock. Whoever controlled the pass controlled Tyrol.

In 1767, a son was born to the *Sandwirt*[3] of St Leonhard. The boy was brought up to be God-fearing, a trend that the Tyroleans called *Einheit von Denken und Glauben* (unity of thought and faith). Travellers, stopping off for the night at his inn, provided a general outlook on the new revolutionary fever that had broken out in parts of Europe. Hofer truly believed that revolution was the Anti-Christ in person. The villagers elected the twenty-four-year-old Andreas Hofer as their deputy to the Tiroler Landtag[4] where he learned that the French Convention had declared war on Austria in April 1792. How could this possibly concern the people of the Tyrol, he asked himself. Paris was caught in the grip of Robespierre's Terror and the Tyrol was far off the beaten track used by armies! If the French wanted to take their war to Austria, they had to do so either by passing through Bavaria or by taking the southern route through upper Italy, but certainly not by crossing a series of 10,000-foot snow-capped mountains!

That logic held until a rising military star made his foray into the Po Valley and defeated a vastly superior Austrian force. General Bonaparte's[5] intention was to thrust into the soft underbelly of the arch-enemy Austria by way of the north Italian plains, while another French force advanced down the Danube Valley towards Vienna. To join these two

---

[3] Sandwirt was the name of the inn. It was quite common to address a man by his title rather than his name.
[4] Tyrol had its own parliament, or *Landtag*. It is interesting to note that the Tyroleans feared more from the policy of centralisation in Vienna than from any external (foreign) invader.
[5] His personal behaviour, depicted in a famous painting in the Louvre, made him a national hero.

forces called for a south–north passage. There was only one possible way – through the Tyrol.

When Hofer took command, his fighters were more like a herd of wild mountain goats. They had followed the call of the tocsin, they had their *Stutzen* and their dry powder; the rest would follow naturally. The first major engagement between the well-trained French and Hofer's stubborn *Schützenverbaende* proved a near-run thing. The Tyroleans were inferior in number. When everything seemed lost, Andreas Hofer proved his mettle: he stood like a rock while cannon shot fell all about him. To the soldiers of France/ *la grande nation* it came as a shock that these irregulars were made of sterner stuff than the average Austrian soldiery, recruited from all over the vast Hapsburg empire and ready to desert at the earliest given opportunity. These mountaineers were *citoyens* fighting for a holy cause. It convinced the French that they were facing a population who didn't care much for the revolutionary principles of *liberté* and *égalité*; on the contrary, these rural heathens believed only in *Gott und Kaiser*, and considered French liberalism with its progressive ideas as a deadly sin. Thus, the war in the mountains of Tyrol turned quickly from a conflict of revolution versus monarchical feudalism into the struggle of a national patriotic movement. And with it, the *Sandwirt*, Andreas Hofer, took a definite stand. The Tyrol was his universe. He was no longer an innkeeper, but a true patriot, one whose values of fatherland carried over family. The first battles taught Hofer that the Tyroleans would be victorious as long as they stuck to their mountainous environment and used the surprise element of ambush. As for his personal safety: '*Das Schicksal waltet!* Destiny rules!' The deity would decide whether he would ever again walk across his fields.

The youngest brother of the Austrian emperor, Archduke Johann, recognised the Tyrol's strategic importance and the fact that local *Schützenkompanien* were better suited to defend their land than any imperial army directed from Vienna. On a summer's day in 1804, the archduke had visited the Passei Valley. 'As I rode past the Sandwirt Inn, I noticed a big man with a black beard. He didn't bow like the others and his eyes were knowing and unblinking.'[6] Archduke Johann knew that Hofer was no firebrand of the likes of Danton, but a solid, if charismatic, Tyrolean peasant with patriotic beliefs. In secret talks, they worked out detailed plans for a *Tiroler Erhebung* or Tyrolean uprising. It was not a spontaneous act by a people who had been deprived of their religious rights but rather a carefully planned politico-military action guided by the imperial court in Vienna. In the euphoria after Austria's victory over Napoleon at Aspern-Lobau, Emperor Franz I signed the edict called the Wolkersdorf Billett: 'My Tyroleans, herewith I do solemnly declare that I will never sign a peace treaty which does not for ever tie Tyrol to My Monarchy.' On 6 July 1809, Napoleon avenged his defeat at Aspern with a crushing victory at Wagram, and the Austrian emperor sued for peace. Article 4 specified: *Austrian troops are to leave the Tyrol immediately*. The Hapsburg emperor had gone back on his promise to his faithful Tyroleans, and history took its course.

Freed from his Austrian nemesis, Napoleon decided to crush, once and for all, every rebellion throughout his *grande empire*. The Tyrol headed the list. He ordered Lefebvre: '*Maréchal, soyez terrible et sans pitié* – be terrible and without pity.' He added an order, unique in its brutality for a man who, until then, had avoided a scorched earth policy: 'My command to you is that you burn down six towns, and drown the land in blood, unless the Tyroleans hand over 18,000 muskets.' With this instruction, Napoleon finally showed his real face. Commanding a force of 30,000 French,

6 From the memoirs of Archduke Johann.

Bavarians, and Saxons, Marshal Lefebvre entered Innsbruck on 13 August 1809.

That day has gone down in the annals of the Napoleonic Wars. Early that morning priests celebrated mass for the men of Tyrol about to go into battle. Hofer met with his commanders. 'Are you all together, Tyroleans? So, let's get going. You've heard mass, you've had your schnapps, so, in God's name, *gemma Franzos'n schiass'n* – let's go and shoot French!' With such simple words they headed into the biggest battle of their lives.

By the time he and his many thousands of armed peasants reached the Bergisel crest, a crisp mountain sky heralded a brilliant day. His beloved Innsbruck lay like some toy city below him and the battleground spread out like a living map. The enemy had prepared a solid defence. Hofer looked on the most frightening sight he had ever witnessed, an array of perfectly lined up forces, the greatest host that had ever invaded his land. There were the long lines of infantry, their fixed bayonets glinting in the sun's early rays. Placed before them were the big French guns, the terrifying bronze 'Napoleons' with their crews and their neat pyramids of cannon ball. On the flanks were regiments of *chevau-légers* (light horsemen), and, as shock troops, with their polished metal breastplates gleaming like mirrors, was Napoleon's most fearsome weapon, the elite *cuirassiers de la garde*, his pampered boys. What could he, the *Herr Oberkommandant*, put up against such array of well-trained, disciplined power? An unruly bunch of peasants, half of them armed with clubs and pitchforks, the other half without shoes.

The attack started from the Inn Valley and flowed down the mountain slopes. In the face of the French artillery, the Tyroleans showed no fear and acted more like disciplined soldiers than berserk savages. All had their own reason for being there; but their collective destiny was to fight the foreigner who was a grave peril to their church and their faith. They honoured their God with blood, either their own or that of their foe. They attacked with musket and sabres, axes and clubs, and died valiantly. Hofer was in the midst of the fiercest slaughter, oblivious to the immediate danger, as if the carnage had nothing to do with him. In the most important battle of his life, he bore himself nobly and was just what the Tyroleans needed most, a picture of assurance. 'Tyroleans,' he yelled, 'up and at them.'

They ran and they stumbled. They took advantage of every dip, every hedge, and every copse of trees. Wives and daughters, as hardy as their men, reloaded muskets and carried the wounded from the firing line. A swift manoeuvre by fifteen *Schützen* companies drove the French into the River Inn, while on the open plain, the Tyroleans suffered a severe setback when a charge by dragoons hacked them to pieces. A furious counter-attack by Friar Haspinger stabilised the situation, before misfortune befell his *Haufen*. In the open field a canister barrage (small balls inside a canister fired from a cannon) from the artillery decimated them. The Bavarians charged and the Bavarians died. Groups of Tyroleans crawled towards Lefebvre's formations, using paths and gullies as cover. From a hundred positions they cut down the perfectly aligned regiments, or waited until a French line had fired before jumping up to engage the enemy in hand-to-hand combat.

Both sides took heavy losses and, for a long time, the battle proved indecisive. Suddenly, a breach opened in Hofer's centre. Only his personal courage stopped his fleeing Tyroleans. He ducked the bayonet thrust of a French guardsman, grabbed his adversary by the chest, kicked him in the groin, and, as the Frenchman doubled up in pain, clubbed him with the butt of his Stutzen. Friar Haspinger raised his crucifix, cursed the revolutionary French as the Antichrist, and stormed ahead of his men in a final, desperate push against the weakened Bavarian flank. The Tyroleans came on, yelling, howling, brandishing sickles and pitchforks, and were speared by Bavarian bayonets. When all seemed lost, a fresh *Haufen* showed up. Their flanking attack led to a rout of Lefebvre's columns. Another *Haufen* caught Lefebvre's army from the rear. Hofer waved his hat, and threw every available man against the Bavarian position. The approaches to Innsbruck were littered with bodies. Pockets of resistance formed around a chapel here, a fortified farmhouse there, but the battle had been decided. It was dark when the fighting came to an end. It had lasted twelve hours.

Hofer was acclaimed by his troops. He knelt down, pointed towards the heavens, and replied with the immortal phrase:

'*I nit, oes a nit, der da drobn!* Not me, not you, only the *One* above!'

The *Regent von Tirol* (the land's regent), as his people called Hofer, was betrayed. The Austrian emperor signed a peace treaty, in which he abandoned the Tyrol. From Bavaria, Salzburg, and Italy, Napoleon dispatched a great army to crush the rebellion. On All Saint's Day, 1 November 1809, Hofer embarked on one final battle. His men fought on even when hope had died. Andreas Hofer looked on helplessly as his dream for a Tyrol free of foreign oppression came to an end. The French campaign turned into a manhunt, conducted ruthlessly and with great treachery. Any captured guerrilla leader was immediately executed. Napoleon's orders were to hang them. Hofer, the most wanted of all, had vanished and a reward of 1,500 gulden was offered for his capture – dead or alive.

In the High Alps, the autumn that had sown so much sorrow was over. Frosty nights foretold colder times ahead. From the pools in the pastures, ice reached out from all sides. The mountain winter was near. In the winding valleys frost already ruled. The last of Hofer's faithful gathered to confer on a plan of escape. One reached inside his shirt and brought out a torn and bloodstained Tyrolean flag. Its tattered condition seemed to be the symbol of themselves. Most of his loyal followers made it to safety before the first snows, but not Hofer. He decided to go back home. He hid out on the Pfandleralm, only a few hours' climb from his Sandwirt Inn, carrying within him a great pain. On Christmas Day 1809 his wife came with his son. Being reunited with his family gave him renewed hope, for his loved ones, and for Tyrol. He had done the right thing by not running away, of that he was now certain.

In mid-January 1810, as the early winter darkness collected beneath the forest's eaves, a man climbed up from the valley. Under cover of the trees, he waited until his patience was rewarded. Silhouetted against the evening sky he saw a dark shape in a wide-brimmed hat. It was Andrä Hofer, of that he was sure. The *Sandwirt* stood silent in the clear mountain air, took off his hat and clutched it in his fist. That hat had once been his crown; it represented what had passed from him, the power that was no more. He had served his emperor well, commanded a popular force, and defeated the famous generals.

It was a sad day for Tyrol, that dawn they came for Hofer. The man who kept that assignation with him was a farmer, Franz Raffl, who had denounced Hofer's presence to the French. For 1,500 shekels, a Tyrolean had betrayed another Tyrolean. Not long afterwards, the 'Judas of Tyrol' was found hanging from a tree. The official verdict was suicide, although nobody ever believed in official verdicts. Hofer was locked up in an iron cage. Groups of villagers with tears in their eyes silently lined the road along which he passed. A child ran up to his cage and reached through the bars to hand him a bunch of dried flowers from the mountains. Edelweiss, pure and white as the virgin snow, a show of love for which he smiled gratefully. No, his Tyroleans had not forsaken him, nor would his emperor. Kaiser Franz would never let him die. He had a final glimpse of the snow-covered mountain peaks before they led him into the black-walled fortress of Mantua.

At last he began to grasp the situation into which his own masters had driven him. Archduke Johann had gone to see Count Metternich, the true ruler of Austria. Metternich schemed to destroy Napoleon. Austria needed time to rebuild its army and to form alliances. To gain this time, Andreas Hofer was the prize. For him there was no solution, there would be no reprieve; he was the forgotten hostage, a pawn on the chessboard of two emperors. The governor of Mantua, General Pierre François Bisson, had just been handed a personal dispatch from his emperor: *Give the order to constitute a court martial and have him shot. All this to be an affair of twenty-four hours. Napoleon.* Bisson admired his brave adversary, but he could not go against an order by his emperor. However, he would keep up a flimsy pretence of legality and provide him with a defence counsel, Dottore Joachim Basevi.

The trial opened, the act of accusation was read: *Andreas Hofer, leader of the Tyrolean insurgents, an outlaw who has revolted against his rightful monarch, the King of Bavaria . . .*

'But my monarch is the emperor of Austria . . .'

'Silence,' thundered the judge.

Dottore Basevi called Hofer a misguided victim; the guilty were to be found in Vienna, he claimed. Without discussion and unanimously, the military judges reached their verdict: *In the name of His Majesty, Emperor of France, and according to Article 2 of the edict of 12 November 1809, the accused, Andreas Hofer, is sentenced to death by firing squad. The judgment stands.*

The day of his death, 20 February 1810, broke grey over Mantua. At the sound of footsteps Hofer stood erect. A priest entered his cell, crucifix in one hand, bible in the other. Tears of despair welled up in the eyes of that strong, unbroken man as he finally realised the enormity of his betrayal. While the priest spoke in a soft voice, commending the condemned soul for divine grace, Hofer recalled the sacrifices by his men for *Gott und Kaiser*. He felt frustration, even rage. Brave men dying bravely for a cause, brave men who believed that he could lead them to victory. A simple innkeeper against the most brilliant military mind of the time. An unequal contest. He wrote a last note: 'God's will is that I will change my worldly existence with the eternal. Farewell until we all meet again in the heavens and praise the Lord.'

As he stepped from the prison gate, the sun broke through the clouds. Behind him walked the priest of Santa Barbara, Giovanni Manifesti, who had given Hofer a small wooden cross to comfort him on his final journey. The faces of the other prisoners were pressed against the barred windows. Every one of them, from rebel to common thief, shouted encouragement. Hofer walked through the Porta Ceresa, his head held high and the crucifix clutched in his big fist – a simple cross that was to become a signal of defiance. Throughout Europe, more prints were soon being circulated of the famous drawing, *Andreas Hofer's Execution*,'[7] than of any other rebellious pamphlet. It showed a hero's final walk with his crucifix of faith.

On the glacis outside the fortress, Hofer stood against a granite wall. Twelve grenadiers, wearing crossed white bandoliers over their blue coats and the tall bear hats of *la garde*, stepped forward. The officer offered the condemned man a blindfold. Hofer shook his head. His gaze went straight to the distant snow-capped mountain peaks, sparkling in the early sun. '*I såg leb-wohl mei'm schönen Land Tirol, Dir bleib i ewig treu*. I bid you farewell, my beautiful Tyrol. To you I remain faithful.' Such were the brave man's final words. For an instant, his eyes met those of the officer. The young captain

---

[7] The artist was Johann David Schubert.

straightened his shoulders and saluted, before barking out an order. Six men knelt and six remained standing. The officer raised his sword. '*En joue!* Take aim!' To the roll of a drum the platoon levelled their guns. Andreas Hofer looked straight at them – and yelled: '*Feuer!*' The thunder of twelve muskets reverberated around the stone walls. Hofer slid to the ground. Sergeant Michel Eiffel stepped up to the mortally wounded man. A last shot echoed around the fortress of Mantua. It was heard in the valleys of the Tyrol; it was heard in Austria, and in Germany, and wherever the steel fist of oppression enslaved nations.

And people began to rise up and their stream swelled . . .

And then . . .

The Tyrolean Uprising is no great monument to human rights. Both sides committed atrocities; one on the orders of a conqueror who had a strategic goal, and on the other side they were carried out by peasants who simply knew no better. Nor were its leaders paragons of virtue. Many of the Tyrolean captains were jealous and intriguing. Alcohol played a part. Even Andreas Hofer was known as 'the man with the rosary and the bottle'. He was certainly the best of them, a man of courage and honesty, able to remain calm in a crisis. That he was no military genius hardly mattered; he was a man of the people who spoke to them as their equal, in a language they could understand. An innkeeper, who had garnered his strategic wisdom from the harsh life in the mountains, and who could forge a group of rustic individualists into a coherent force. For these freehold farmers, living in solid stone houses, with plenty of cows in their stables and vineyards and fruit trees filling the wide valley of the Etsch, their rebellion was never motivated by economic necessity or the need for social change. They fought for a common cause – a cause contrary to the new revolutionary notion of *liberté*. Theirs was a holy crusade to *uphold* their traditional ties to the monarchy and to stay true to their ingrained, almost reactionary faith in the Holy Roman Church and its defender, the Austrian emperor.

The Tyrol was a land where each hut became a fortress, each farmer a guerrilla, each innkeeper and priest a commander. They hunted their enemies in the same way that they poached the wild mountain goat: with stealth and from cover. The veterans of Austerlitz and Eylau never understood the Tyroleans' way of fighting; time and again, they would charge with gleaming bayonets men who threw rocks at them from cliff tops. Andreas Hofer was an inspired and God-fearing leader, loyal only to his emperor and his country. His greatness can be found in his maintaining the morale of his rude force in the face of impossible odds. This quiet, humble peasant succeeded in achieving what Austrian and Russian generals had attempted but failed to do. Such a man could not lose – until the day his own side betrayed him. It gives a measure of the man that Napoleon paid him a final tribute; asked what he considered his biggest blunder he said: 'My order for the execution of that Tyrolean peasant. I created a martyr. His death united the people of Central Europe against me.'

Due to the stubbornness with which he stood up for what he believed was right, the myth of the *Tiroler Erhebung* grew and inspired an entire continent. Tyrol's just fight against the 'Corsican's tyranny' turned into Europe's uniting symbol. From this, a new coalition was born. Nations put aside their quarrels and joined forces against the French emperor. Three years after Hofer's martyrdom, Bavaria allied itself with Austria to defeat Napoleon in the Battle of Nations at Leipzig. The following year, the Congress of Vienna reunited the Tyrol with Austria. They are still united today.

All leaders of heroic undertakings, in open revolt against the usurper, willing to sacrifice their lives for the sake of justice and liberty, lay the foundation for a personal myth that will remain theirs for all eternity. Such is the case with the *Sandwirt* from St Leonhard. The first song that every Austrian child is taught is the hymn to the fierce Tyrol and its greatest patriotic hero, Andreas Hofer.

Interlude

1815–1910

The post-Napoleonic world was not to be granted peace. Whilst the Congress of Vienna danced, and Metternich & Co. parcelled out Europe, unrest broke out in a distant land. The revolutionary philosophy of Jean-Jacques Rousseau, the weakening influence of the Catholic Church, and Napoleon's military successes over the crumbling monarchies of Europe – especially the toppling of the royal house of Spain – were to prove of monumental impact in the Hispanic New World. A chance encounter in Venezuela was to change the destiny of a continent.

In 1810 two liberal thinkers met in Caracas. One was the German scientist and explorer, Baron Alexander von Humboldt; the other, a wealthy Venezuelan nobleman, Simón Bolívar. The torch of rebellion was lit. On 19 April 1810, Simón Bolívar set out in his role as liberator of an entire hemisphere by deposing the Spanish governor of Venezuela. In 1829, *el grande liberator*, Simón Bolívar, died a heart-broken man with these prophetic words:

'He who serves a revolution, ploughs the sea.'

In the midst of rebellious activity in Europe, and with North America in the throes of a bloody civil war, the French emperor Napoleon III was busy carving out a colonial empire for France. He began to meddle in overseas affairs, first along Africa's Mediterranean coast, then in Latin America. He dispatched to the Mexican capital a nice, inoffensive Austrian archduke as his puppet, very much against the wishes of the Mexicans. With the final words: 'May my blood flow for the good of this land. *Viva Mexico!*' the Hapsburg Archduke Maximilian, who by the grace of France was Emperor of Mexico for three years, died in front of a seven-man firing squad in Querétaro, Mexico, on 19 June 1867. Benito Juárez, the revolutionary leader, wished to teach the European powers a lesson and remained unresponsive to appeals for clemency. He was sworn in as President of Mexico and for a period of three decades, Mexico prospered. The country looked forward to the twentieth century with a degree of confidence unequalled in any previous period. American money poured in and progress was certain and limitless. Virtue walked with progress. In 1910, the year that a new Latin American rhythm, the tango, made its first appearance in the ballrooms of the world, Mexico's peace was shattered.

'Another one of those silly Latino barrack uprisings,' smiled its unconcerned neighbours. It was more than that, much more. What took place in bitterness and cruelty in this first social upheaval of the new century is almost unmatched in modern times. In a land where death was accepted as an everyday factor, forging a modern nation from a feudal society came at a high price. Not only for Mexico, but for the entire world. Because that 'silly barrack uprising' was to lead the United States into the First World War.

3

18 November 1910

'Viva Mexico!'

Better to die on your feet than live on your knees!
Emiliano Zapata, 1910

At ten minutes past two on the afternoon of 10 April 1919, a
man dressed in a black *charro* suit, theatrically trimmed with
silver coins, over which he wore crossed bandoliers, with his
face shaded by a huge sombrero, rode on a white stallion
through the gate of the Chinameca Hacienda. The courtyard
was lined with a military guard of honour. On a command,
the troops presented their arms. Into the hot desert sky rose
the first note of a bugle call, made famous during Mexico's
war with Texas. *Non pardon* – No forgiveness. The rider
jumped from the saddle to exchange *abrazos* with a colonel.
He then stepped back to salute the guard of honour. The final
note of the bugle call rang out in a long drawn-out, moaning
sound that hung suspended in the air before gradually dying
away. It was the signal. The soldiers suddenly raised their
rifles to their shoulders and fired point-blank at the distin-
guished visitor. Slowly his body dropped to the ground.

Emiliano Zapata, the great Mexican revolutionary, was dead.

*　　*　　*

Many years later, whenever Doroteo Arango stared at his
gun, it reminded him of that night of horror when he was
sixteen. After a day of cutting cane in the fields of the
hacendado (landowner) of Durango,[1] he had returned to
his family hut to find his sister on the floor, her cotton
shift torn open and her eyes swollen. She had been brutally
raped by the *hacendado*'s son. With a soul-tearing howl,
Doroteo stormed from the hut. Then, one moonlit night he
waylaid the rapist. '*Ola, mestizo*,[2] out of my way,' scowled
the young man whose father owned all the land and the *peóns*
(labourers) living on it. He kicked out with his riding boot,
when out of the darkness a pair of thick-muscled arms pulled
him from the horse. He did not even have time to scream
before Doroteo's long-bladed machete cut through gristle and
bone. Doroteo Arango left him to bleed to death by the side
of the road.

It was a ghastly business, unheard of; a serf had dared to kill
his master's son. No need for a court, just swift justice; string
him up and let the crows do the rest – as soon as they caught
that murdering *mestizo*. His 'wanted' poster stared from every
church door throughout the Rio Grande province; a thousand
gold pesos were offered for information leading to his capture,
'dead or alive'. But he was never caught. Doroteo Arango,
vengador (avenger) of his sister's honour, had fled into the
hills where he joined a band of outlaws, robbing landowners
and holding up banks. The teenage fugitive proved to have a
natural talent as a leader of men. With his sad, black eyes,
his droopy moustache, and his short bow-legs, he looked
more like an overweight farmer than a bandit. But then,
appearances can be deceptive. He planned each attack with
the cunning of a coyote, and as his exploits became bolder, so
did his fame – but no longer as Doroteo Arango. The name
by which this man, capable of wild, contradictory impulses,

[1] A village in Mexico's Rio Grande province.
[2] A *mestizo* is half white, half Indian. (Ola, mestizo – hey there, slang).

became a household word to millions around the globe who followed his incredible exploits in newsprint – was Francisco 'Pancho' Villa.

Pancho Villa and Emiliano Zapata epitomised the delirium and savagery that was to sweep Mexico for the next ten years, a decade of murders, executions, and betrayals. Their bouts of violence belong in those categories that abound in all civil wars, and add much to their sinister characters, at a time when crimes are effortlessly committed and completely wanton.

The Mexico of 1910 was a country divided into landowners and serfs. The state was presided over by an unscrupulous dictator, Porfirio Díaz, whose political machine fed on the blood of the underprivileged. After thirty years in absolute power, he chose to ignore the signs of an approaching revolutionary hurricane. The country was bankrupt, its government 'one of administrative prostitution and corruption, and the looting of the exchequer never more complete and shameless'.[3] In 1910, Díaz's mandate ran out and he called for new elections. An anti-Díaz party under Francisco Indalecio Madero opposed him. 'This country is ready for democracy. It is time Díaz relinquished power.' Díaz took this affront as an opportunity to order his opponent's arrest. As a police squad arrived to his house, Madero slipped out the back way and escaped to San Antonio, Texas, from where he issued a call for an armed uprising in his Manifest of San Luis Potosi.

The first shot of the Mexican Revolution was fired on 18 November 1910, during a bungled arrest of one of Madero's sub lieutenants, Aquiles Serdan. It resulted in the deaths of Serdan and the Puebla police chief. Two days later, Madero crossed the Rio Grande into Mexico but failed to raise popular support. But he had rung the bell of revolution. Those who would act as his military leaders had heard

---

[3] Quoted from Luis Lara Pardo, a Mexican historian.

the call. From the mountains of the north and the villages in the south came the men who were to raise the rebellion. From Morelos province appeared the most romanticised and revered figure of all, a slender *indio* with an Asiatic smile and a mandarin moustache. His most fascinating features were his eyes, black and hard as obsidian. Thousands followed his rallying cry: *Better to die on your feet than live on your knees!* This was Emiliano Zapata. And from the north came Pancho Villa, who started on his extraordinary career with a mere fifteen followers. Within weeks, Villa's force swelled to 500 riders. Madero asked him to become his 'General of the Revolution'.

In his first major action, at San Andrés, they overrode the local garrison and Pancho demonstrated his true character; every captured officer was shot out of hand, as were postal inspectors, judges, and sundry Díaz *officiales*. To the ordinary soldier he gave a choice of instant execution or joining his rough-riders. From the very beginning, Villa showed his ferocious racial hatred of anyone 'non-Mexican'. This antipathy was not only directed against the land-owning class, whom he considered as imported Spanish conquistadores, and whom he put into the same category as the American gringos who exploited his country's mineral resources. There were other examples of his cruelty towards foreigners. Following the capture of Torreón, one of his men died after drinking bootleg alcohol. As this happened in a Chinese restaurant, he had all the Chinese manhandled into the open, tied by their pigtails to horses, and dragged along the main street by wildly shouting riders.[4] Despite such gratuitous violence, *El Revolución* gained momentum. 'Red' Lopez, a cattle rustler turned rebel general, attacked Agua Prieta, a town along the Mex–Tex border. Three American spectators, watching from the opposite riverbank, were killed. A fourth, a reporter

---

[4] From an account by Henry Baerlein, an eyewitness.

who helped bring the 'Mexican affair' to the attention of the American public, was wounded. US President William Howard Taft ordered 20,000 troops[5] to the Mexican border. He feared, quite correctly, that the ouster of Díaz would lead to anarchy and, with it, the destruction of American property in Mexico. The move was viewed by nationalists like Pancho Villa as American interference in his country's affairs. The US press published his anti-American outbursts, which only increased America's fascination with the colourful *revolucionario*. A number of *Yanqui* adventurers joined his ranks. One was Sam 'The Fighting Jew' Dreben, a New York stockbroker turned explosives expert who called himself 'Dynamite Devil'. Another was a Texan cowboy who later became a big star of Western movies, Tom Mix.

Other Americans helped the revolution in various ways. A typical episode was the affair of the bronze cannon, a memento of the American Civil War that sat in front of El Paso's city hall. Villa sympathisers pulled the gun from its base, attached it to a motor car, and towed it across the border bridge. It was to play a decisive role in the battle for Ciudad Juárez, a strategic railway junction. Madero, a true politician, lacked the stomach for bloodshed and was ready to abandon the attack when Villa showed up. 'It is shameful to retire without a fight,' declared Pistol Pancho. He dispatched his men along an unguarded irrigation ditch. From there they began to pepper the mud-brick *cuartel* (fortness) and the town houses. When Madero heard the shots he blanched, thinking that his own troops were under attack. He sent one of his lieutenants under a white flag to stop the fighting. He never got far, as Villa's men shot him. Madero was livid, Villa unrepentant: 'Sometimes a civilian chief is unable to see what is obvious to his military subordinates.' At this point a car pulled up, towing El Paso's Civil War cannon. Villa's

---

[5] At the time this represented 25 per cent of all American forces.

first piece of artillery was fired – and missed Ciudad Juárez altogether. The second shot went too high, but it drilled a hole through the town's water tower. The subsequent lack of water was to lead to the federal garrison's surrender. Foreign military observers, watching for the first time a Villa army in combat, were incensed by the lax discipline and unorthodox fighting methods of the *revolucionarios*. Wherever they staged an attack, they moved in and out as they pleased. An unruly lot of swaggering men in white cotton *calzones* (peasants trousers) with no plan and certainly with no co-ordination, who saved their bullets for the mass executions that followed the surrender of a town. When they had had enough of fighting and yelling, they sat down in the shade to eat, drink, or take a nap. This, however, was common sense. While the beleaguered garrison lost their sleep and their morale, the rebels were always fresh. At sundown all firing stopped, since Mexicans never fought in the dark.[6] In Ciudad Juárez, the sly Pancho came up with another refinement to save the lives of his men: he told them to enter the first building in a row of houses, then dynamite their way through the dividing walls right into the centre of town. After two days of fighting, Ciudad Juárez was in the hands of the Villistas. The shooting stopped and the looting began. Villistas strutted around in silk shirts and squeaky new shoes, while *federales* (federal troops) had to bury their dead in a common grave. Madero, who had nothing to do with the victory, made his triumphant entry. The town was swamped with people from both sides of the border. Many Texans took souvenirs with them, including typhus.

The boomerang effect of the fall of Ciudad Juárez can only be measured by its aftermath. The morale of the *federales* collapsed; most towns gave up without a fight. In the liberated areas, Madero sympathisers took over government functions

---

[6] From an account by Timothy Turner, a reporter for the *El Paso Times*.

and Villa's victorious rabble set out on a bloody rampage across the countryside. A huge crowd of Madero supporters gathered on Zocalo Plaza in the nation's capital. Maxim guns, mounted by Díaz's bodyguards on the roof of the National Palace, fired into the throng and killed 200. This bloodbath signalled the end for Dictator Díaz. He fled to Veracruz where he boarded the German steamer *Ypiranga*, a ship soon to gain notoriety for a more sinister reason. Madero installed General de la Barra as his interim president. While the *politicos* in the capital jostled for position, dividing up the spoils and the cushy jobs, Pancho Villa dissolved his forces, retired to Chihuahua, and opened a meat business. Nobody dared to look at the origin of his cattle herds, which were sold across the border in Texas.

Emiliano Zapata proved a serious challenge to the new power clique. General de la Barra dispatched federal troops under General Victoriano Huerta to Morelos province to disarm Zapata's *indios*. Given the ambitions for power of this hard-line general, it was an unwise move and it sent the country up in flames. Madero sincerely thought he could achieve a lasting peace, and he fired Huerta only days before a general election. Madero was elected Mexico's new president. During the inauguration ceremony, Germany's Ambassador Hintze whispered to his American colleague: 'Mark my words, in the end you will have to intervene.' He was to be proved right.

Mexico was not to be granted peace. A ruthless rebel, Pascual Orozco, launched his savage *colorados*[7] on a reign of terror, raping, pillaging, and murdering. An entire Mormon colony fell victim to them. Pancho Villa held no love for Orozco; he closed down his meat business, raised a force of 500, and moved on the town of Parral. He dispatched a messenger to the federal commander. 'If you're loyal to

[7] The Americans called them the 'Red Flaggers', they were an elite riding corp named for their red dusty clothes.

President Madero, come out and receive me. If you're not, come out and fight me. In any case, I'm coming in. (Signed) Pancho Villa.' His threat was enough to open the gates. A gringo in Villa's service, Tom Fountain, was captured by Orozco's *colorados*. Rather than execute him and risk a powerful American protest, Orozco handed Fountain a silver dollar and told him he was free to go and have breakfast. Orozco's officers then lined the sidewalk and used Fountain for target practice. Next, Orozco hijacked a locomotive, stuffed it with dynamite, and sent it hurtling into a *federales* troop train. President Madero was forced to call once more on the services of the hated General Victoriano Huerta, with his short-cropped hair and steel-rimmed glasses, to take charge of his federal troops. With this step, Madero signed his own death warrant.

Victoriano Huerta, an efficient general but otherwise a great villain, went into action. Getting rid of all *revolucionarios*, including those loyal to his president, became his immediate task. He pounced on an unsuspecting Pancho Villa and sentenced him to death on the charge of having stolen a horse. As Pancho Villa was led to a wall,[8] a dispatch rider dashed up to Huerta to deliver a message. It was from President Madero, staying the execution. Villa thus became one of the very few who faced a Mexican firing squad and lived to talk about it. 'As I stood in the square the sergeant of the platoon went up to the wall and made a cross on it with chalk. He then ordered me to stand at the foot of the mark. I could not continue for the tears that choked me. The sergeant pushed me forcibly against the wall. I threw myself to the ground, pretending to beg but only fighting for time. "Why am I being shot?" I screamed. "I served my government well."'

Still suffering from shock, Villa was brought before General

[8] A photograph exists of the scene.

Huerta, who stared at him through his glasses. Pancho asked: 'Why?'

To which Huerta rasped in a nasal tone: 'It's a simple matter of honour.' Gentleman's honour, a white officer chastising a lowly *mestizo*. Without giving his prisoner a further glance, he turned away and ordered Villa shipped off to the military prison in Mexico City.

While General Victoriano Huerta was busy crushing Pascual Orozco and thus became the new strongman of Mexico, Pancho Villa bought the services of a warden to unlock his cell door. On Christmas Day 1912, he boldly walked out of jail, entered a waiting car, and drove out of town. All went well for forty kilometres until they ran into a military roadblock. With the boldness for which he was known, Pancho acted like a rich *hacendado* annoyed over the delay: 'I shall complain about this to your colonel.' Thus Villa bluffed his way past the baffled soldiers. On 2 January 1913, he crossed the American border to seek refuge in a dingy El Paso hotel where he gave interviews to American journalists.

In February 1913, revolution flared anew in the capital. Artillery duels and snipers kept citizens off the streets. President Madero ordered up 4,000 additional troops in the defence of the National Palace. But he picked the wrong commander. General Aureliano Blanquet, a Huerta man, drew his revolver and pointed it at the chest of his president: 'You are my prisoner.' Victoriano Huerta arrived at the palace to send out a telegram: 'Have assumed charge of the government. Madero is my prisoner.' Two cars emerged from the palace gate. In the second car rode the deposed Madero. As the convoy turned the corner, out of view of the assembled photographers, shots were heard. The reporters dashed around the corner to find Madero slumped in his seat. The officer in charge of the escort, Captain Francisco Cardenas, gave a brief statement: 'Madero is dead. They tried to rescue him and he was shot.' Huerta's complicity in the assassination was never proved.

In America, an election had taken place. The liberal US President, Woodrow Wilson, saw in the thirty-nine-year-old Huerta a usurper as well as an assassin of his legally elected president. Wilson was determined to make an example of him to re-establish democratic values throughout Latin America. He did not need to interfere; the governor of Coahuila State, Venustiano Carranza, took over as head of an anti-Huerta movement. Another man who joined the revolutionary cause was a thirty-three-year-old wealthy *hacendado*, Alvaro Obregón, descendant of the famous revolutionary, Miguel Obregón – better known from his Irish rebel days as Michael O'Brien. And back rode Pancho Villa. With just eight supporters he splashed across the Rio Grande. Masses flocked to his magical name, even women. Whenever one of these *soldaderas* lost her man in battle, she wept, then took another man into her bed. In Casas Grandes, Villa fell upon 400 *colorados*, lined them up three deep, and had them shot in rows to save precious bullets. To finance their military operation, Villa's men rustled cattle herds, and exchanged them in Texas for guns and bullets.[9]

Venustiano Carranza, the grandee, offered Pancho Villa, the *mestizo*, an alliance. They met. 'With the first words Carranza spoke to me,' declared Villa afterwards, 'my blood turned to ice. He never looked me in the eye. From the beginning, I knew he was not my ally but my rival.' Villa's army grew; the original eight had become 8,000. When recruiting, he made little distinction between true revolutionaries and mad killers. A notorious example was Villa's railroad specialist, Rodolfo Fierro, a brutal thug. In a single session, he personally executed 300 *colorados* and stopped only long enough to massage his aching trigger finger.

[9] Many Texans benefited from the Mexican Revolution to lay the foundation of their fortunes.

Villa's next target was the town of Torreón, held by 2,000 Huerta *federales* and 3,000 auxiliaries. He captured thirteen cannons, six machine-guns, half a million bullets, an armoured railway train, and two dozen locomotives. The captured officers were lined up and shot. In a gesture that turned him into some sort of Robin Hood, Villa levied a tax on the town's business community – and distributed the money to the poor. His victory at Torreón gave him the means of transporting his army in comfort. His home and his headquarters for his Division of the North became a red-painted railway carriage.[10] Framed by chintz curtains, he received hordes of American newsreel crews who flocked to his camp to film the legendary revolutionary. His 'rolling army' camped on every available space, in and on top of railway coaches. *Soldaderas* baked their men's tortillas over the locomotive's fire. During the day the men put up umbrellas to protect themselves from the sun, and shot at everything within range, from cacti to coyotes. Those who rolled off the coach tops in their sleep (or from an overdose of tequila) had to wait along the track for the following Villa Special.

While this travelling horde made the countryside unsafe, Dictator Huerta was getting desperately short of manpower. His recruiters invented ingenious means to press-gang men into the federal forces. One was to show films 'for men only', then round up the spectators, put them uniforms, and send them against Villa, who was now moving on Ciudad Juárez. He decided to take the border town by ruse, demonstrating his ingenuity and military genius. With two men he rode to a whistle stop along the Chihuahua – Ciudad Juárez line. There he put a gun to the telegrapher's head and ordered him to wire a message to the Juarez' military commander: 'LINE TO CHIHUAHUA DESTROYED. SEND

---

[10] Pancho, notorious for his many marriages, was never far from his latest wife. At one instant there were at least three Señoras Villas living in the same town. When Pancho died, five women claimed to be his legal widow.

IMMEDIATELY REPAIR TRAIN.' When the repair train arrived, another message was dispatched: 'REBELS ON APPROACH. WHAT ARE YOUR NEW ORDERS?' That did it. The train was ordered to return immediately to Ciudad Juárez. Villa stuffed the coaches with his own troops; this Trojan Horse passed the city's defences into the heart of the town. The only serious resistance came from American gamblers in the casino who were relieved of their dollars. Villa captured the city without losing a single man. Huerta officers and officials were executed. To show the Americans across the river that all was well in town, Villa ordered the captured military band to parade along the riverbank, playing the 'Star-Spangled Banner'.[11]

Huerta dispatched his last reserves, but before they had time to deploy, Rodolfo Fierro, Villa's Lieutenant, destroyed a railway bridge. Tierra Blanca (White Sands) was like a stage set from a Hollywood Western: a rail track stretching into the endless desert; a water tower on a railway siding; three houses; a bar with swinging doors; and a few donkeys tied to a telegraph pole. Villa kept his men hidden behind a crescent of shallow dunes. The *federales* acted precisely as Villa had anticipated: they stormed the siding in a concentrated assault. Villa observed them through his binoculars and when his hand came down, guns belched fire. Fountains of desert sand rose. Hordes of madly howling Villistas came out of the dust; entire companies of *federales* threw away their weapons and fled towards their troop train, which was idling on the track. Fierro raced on his horse after the fleeing train. In best Hollywood style he leapt from his horse, jumped from roof to roof until he reached the locomotive, and shot the engineer and fireman. He uncoupled the brake cylinder and brought the carriages to a halt. In a senseless act of brutality Villa's men massacred every single soldier aboard. Before

11 *Collier's Magazine* referred to it as 'Villa's Uprising'.

horrified American journalists, Villa justified the action as a necessity 'to plant such terror in the enemy's heart that others will run away without posing further resistance'. Militarily, his assessment was correct: three days later the Chihuahua garrison surrendered without firing a shot; but in human terms the action was indefensible. The remainder of Huerta's forces swam across the Rio Grande and were interned at Fort Bliss, Texas.

Villa decided to establish Chihuahua as his headquarters. His first action was to kick out the town's Spaniards, whom he associated which all *rico hacendados*, a class he had loathed since his poor childhood years. Two hundred families were forced to cross on foot 500 kilometres of desert. They faced a blistering sun, poisonous snakes, and sharp cacti. Only a few survived this 'death march to Torreón', leaving behind a trail of belongings and bodies.

Villa set up his own press and printed two million 'Villa pesos'. 'Now I have all the money I need,' he bragged to an American reporter showing off boxes stuffed with freshly inked bills. He made his men run the power plant, the flourmill, and the telephone exchange. 'The only thing to do with soldiers in time of peace is make them work,' was his philosophy; 'an idle soldier will always think of war and killing.' Encouraged by the success of his cavalry attack at Tierra Blanca, Pancho spent time forming an elite corps, which he named the *dorados*,[12] a key element in his future victories.

What had been so long expected finally took place. The Mexican Revolution entered the world stage. This was mainly due to ill-advised foreign policy decisions in Washington, which were to push America into the First World War. In a surprise move, US President Woodrow Wilson lifted

[12] So called because of a golden insignia on their stetsons.

the American embargo on arms to Carranza's rebels, and Germany immediately stepped in on the side of President Huerta. The Germans cleverly exploited Wilson's act, presenting it as America's first step to annexing all the land between Texas and Panama in order to achieve direct access to the newly built Panama Canal. This view met a resounding echo throughout Latin America and was to play a decisive role in the politics of the Americas for many years to come. A series of unconnected events brought matters to a climax. From Germany three ships sailed with arms for Mexico's *federales*: the *Ypiranga*, the *Bavaria*, and the *Kronprinzessin Cecilie*. This German arms deal had greater political repercussions, since it provoked the United States into protecting their interests as specified by the Monroe Doctrine. Originally designed to defend the US's Latin American market from English traders, it proscribed non-American powers from intervening in the affairs of the Western Hemisphere.

Pancho Villa was playing beautifully into German hands. William Benton, strong-willed Scotsman and the owner of a Mexican cattle empire, confronted Villa over some stolen herds: 'Take your cattle rustlers and get the hell off my land.' This was not the way to talk to the short-tempered Pancho Villa, who ordered Fierro to shoot Benton. The murder of a British citizen aroused a wave of indignation, and England considered sending her navy. It had the Germans smiling, as the cloud of war began to loom ominously over Europe.

While Villa pushed south, a force headed by Carranza moved on Huerta's *federales* at Tampico, where the ships of the US Navy's Fifth Division under Admiral Henry T. Mayo lay at anchor. Also present was the British ship HMS *Hermione* and the German cruiser *Dresden*. The 'Tampico Incident' was a silly affair made worse by the obstinacy of the American admiral. The crew of a US Navy boat, gone ashore to pick up fuel, was arrested by the *federales*, then quickly released and the appropriate apology sent to the commanding admiral of the US fleet. The intransigent Mayo insisted on having the Star-Spangled Banner raised over Tampico, together with a twenty-one-gun salute. Given the insignificance of the incident, the Mexican commander rightly refused. This incident came to the attention of Washington at the very instant that the US consul in Veracruz reported that the German ship *Ypiranga* was making for port with 200 machine-guns and 15 million cartridges for Huerta's army. In an act reminiscent of British gunboat policy of the nineteenth century, the might of the US navy was called on to stop a merchant vessel. The battleship USS *Utah* intercepted the *Ypiranga*. President Wilson justified this act of piracy with the supposed insult to the American flag at Tampico: 'I have no enthusiasm for war. But I have great enthusiasm for the dignity of the United States.' Neighbouring nations throughout Latin America winced.

On 21 April 1914, 3,000 US Marines waded ashore to seize the custom house and railway station at Veracruz, and Huerta's *federales* had to withdraw. Only the cadets of the naval academy held out and suffered terrible casualties when shelled by the guns of the USS *Prairie*, USS *Chester*, and USS *San Francisco*. The Mexicans lost hundreds of men; American casualties amounted to just nineteen. Huerta's reaction was understandably one of defiance and Latin American newspapers howled: '*VENGENZA!*' Even Carranza, who could only benefit from the American intervention, warned Washington that Mexico did not want to be dragged into an unequal conflict. Villa fumed; he had always hated the gringos and now they had dared to invade *his* country and were meddling in affairs that did not concern them. Nevertheless, Commander Tweedy of HMS *Essex* went to Mexico City to take 800 Americans to safety and President Wilson ordered the mobilisation of the American army! Attacked by the US, harassed by Zapata and Villa, Dictator Huerta was on his way out.

Villa became the man of the hour, the only hope of all those embroiled in an insane fury of fratricidal hatred which had obliterated their past and darkened their future. Villa handed out food to the streams of refugees who had left villages that could no longer offer them food or shelter, let alone security. As always, the civilians suffered most. However hard they tried to avoid taking sides, the beast of war devoured them. If they refused to assist the revolutionaries, they would be liquidated without mercy. And if they did help the *revolucionarios*, then the *federales* would come and exterminate them. The *peóns* were trapped in the wheels of a cog that crushed everything it touched.

Pancho Villa, with his pot-belly and drooping moustache, was at the height of his popularity. He was recognised everywhere and enthusiastically cheered with the now so popular '*Viva Villa*'. This aroused the insane jealousy of Carranza, to a degree matched only by his political ambition. That is why he ordered Villa to hold back from his drive on the nation's capital, as he feared that the *mestizo* would end up in the National Palace and seize the presidency for himself. When an emissary from Carranza delivered this order, it so infuriated Villa that he had two captured Huerta officers brought before him. Calmly he pulled out his pistol, shot them, and left them lying in the sun, just to teach those *politicos* a lesson. Carranza's emissary threw up and Pancho growled: 'You chocolate-drinking politicians want to triumph without remembering the blood-drenched battlefields.' The message was not wasted on Carranza. Angry words travelled along the telegraph wires, culminating in Villa resigning his commission as chief of the Northern Revolutionary Army. General Angeles, Villa's second-in-command, added a note in his own inimitable fashion: 'Señor Carranza, you are a son of a bitch.' Villa's officers revolted and would not accept their general's demotion. With 23,000 men, Pancho stormed into Zacatecas to resupply his army from captured federal stores. [13] Meanwhile, with Villa moving in from the Atlantic in the east and Obregón from the Pacific in the north, Mexico City was caught in a vice. On 17 July 1914, President Huerta fled to Spain on the German cruiser *Dresden*, a few days before 'the lights went out all over Europe'.

On 15 August, General Alvaro Obregón beat Pancho Villa in the race for Mexico City. Now the only non-aligned revolutionary force still to be accounted for was that of Emiliano Zapata. Carranza's soldiers faced Zapata's forces in an uneasy stand-off while Obregón, the shrewdest of the revolutionary generals, met Villa to seduce him back into the Carranza camp and thus protect their revolutionary unity. Villa agreed, on condition that Carranza would call a general election and not run for the post of president. Obregón readily accepted without even checking with Carranza. As they were having lunch together, news arrived that Carranzistas had attacked a Villista column. Pancho went red in the face, seized hold of Obregón, and called for a firing squad. As Villa's men pushed Obregón against the wall, Pancho calmed down and, rather than eliminating his potential rival, he offered Obregón a drink, a gesture he was bitterly to regret. 'The destiny of Mexico is in our hands, yours and mine,' said Pancho. 'I am a simple *peón*, but you are an educated man. So you will become president.' On that they shook hands.

Without Obregón, the revolutionary leaders met at the Convention of Aguascalientes (Hot Springs). They appointed Villa as commander-in-chief of all Convention forces, a step that forced Obregón to join Carranza and declare war on Villa. Pancho Villa would have carried the day, had it not been for another occurrence, which came from an unexpected quarter. President Wilson, hesitant over which side to support, ordered the withdrawal of American troops; Veracruz

[13] At Zacatecas, the British vice-consul was arrested and faced execution, but Villa stopped it.

was delivered into Carranza's hands and gave him a base from which to operate.

Next it was Emiliano Zapata's turn to become hyperactive. His 'little brown men with their cartridge belts around their gaunt bellies' occupied Mexico City, where they knocked politely on doors to ask for food. Villa, not to be outdone, also moved on the city. A historic meeting took place where the two famous revolutionaries met in the rural schoolhouse of Xochimilco outside Mexico City. This closely documented and filmed event took place on 6 December 1914. Tense haggling followed their brotherly *abrazo*, which was resolved when both managed to agree on one point: they would ride side by side into the nation's capital. Afterwards, they left with their armies of 60,000 *Conventionistas* to crush Obregón's and Carranza's *Constitutionalistas*. It was agreed that Villa would drive north towards Veracruz and Zapata south from Puebla. Neither Zapata nor Villa made good on their promises. Both spent the rest of December living it up, Pancho in Mexico City, Zapata in Puebla. Without a fight to keep their men occupied, this time of idleness turned into a period of bickering, arbitrary arrests, and executions. A *Conventionista*, David Berlanga, was having dinner at a restaurant when some Villistas at a nearby table refused to pay their bill. Berlanga paid for them: 'I am a revolutionary who does not want to see the uniform you wear dishonoured.' For this the bloodthirsty Fierro shot Berlanga. Finally Pancho Villa headed north. With the capital undefended, Obregón marched his army of 10,000 into the city. Zapata attacked Obregón's ring of outer defences, blew up the pumping station, and deprived the capital of water. It caused panic and a typhus epidemic scythed through the capital.

Obregón moved against his greater threat, Pancho Villa, who by now had gathered a huge army. His audacity and swiftness had swept him from victory to victory. But in General Alvaro Obregón he had met his match. Villa's advantage in numbers was more than equalled by Obregón's German-supplied machine-guns. Near the town of Celaya, General Obregón and his military adviser, the German Colonel Maximilian Kloss, put up a network of trenches protected by strings of barbed wire, a system that was proving its value on the bloody fields of France. To enhance the rate of killing, Kloss arranged a pattern of interlocking lines of fire, so that an attacking force would have to run the gauntlet of machine-gun bullets. The stage was set for the bloodiest battle on American soil since the American Civil War.

On the morning of 13 April 1915 near Celaya, 25,000 Villistas struck at 15,000 Obregónistas. In a repeat of his proven shock tactics, Villa's elite *dorados* charged between the railway embankment and a dry river bed, a suicidal act in the face of concentrated machine-gun fire. Waves of *dorados* on sturdy mountain horses, their sombreros pulled down over their faces and their sabres high, rode in a re-enactment of the Charge of the Light Brigade into Obregón's staggered defences. The assault was met by the Obregónistas' machine-guns with shattering effect; within minutes the majority of Villa's top regiments lay dead or wounded in the scrub. Those who managed to cross the curtain of bullets became entangled in the barbed wire, where sharpshooters picked them off. The rout of Villa's feared *dorados* was complete. In a single go, Pancho Villa had wasted his crack forces; over a thousand were dead.

After a day of respite, Villa gathered his battered army and planned a new attack, this time employing all of his thirty-four artillery pieces. His bombardment began to creep towards Obregón's position, seeking out the machine-gun nests. Shells from his masterly directed artillery slammed into their targets, throwing up geysers of bodies and barbed wire. The Villistas had learned their lesson and, this time, they advanced doggedly on foot. With their remaining machine-guns, Obregón's men managed to slow down the enemy. The foremost Villistas fell, but others came hurtling forward, regardless of losses in what became a human assault wave. They advanced, darting from bush to bush, through the curtain of steel and fire.

Colonel Kloss was in his observation post, when one of his lookouts pointed to a macabre drama unfolding in front of their trench line. A group of *federales* had been cut off. They were killed as they fled – but not their officer, who judging by his uniform was a colonel. He was surrounded by sombreroed figures who dragged the struggling man back with them. Kloss could do nothing to save him and ordered a machine-gunner to fire on the group. The young man swallowed hard before sending a stream of bullets into the bunched-up enemy, killing them all, including the colonel. It was a mercy killing. The Villistas would have lacerated his soles and sent him walking barefoot through the cactus. They had done it before.

For the Obregónistas the situation became critical, but their general had a final surprise in store. The timely arrival of General Castro's 6,000 federal cavalry had escaped the attention of Villa's scouts. When Castro's riders broke out and stormed across the sand flats, Villa no longer had his *dorados* for a counter-charge. They had been wasted against Obregón's machine-guns. Villa's rout was so complete that he lost thirty of his thirty-four precious guns; over 3,500 men were killed and 8,000 captured. For Obregón it was no time for celebration; Mexicans had died on both sides. That evening, staring down at the many dead who had been gathered in a common grave, General Obregón gave a last salute to the fallen, while Villa collected what was left of his shattered army.

Celaya was the beginning of the end for Pancho Villa. He had to retreat. At León he clashed again with Obregón who had almost won the battle when a shell landed near him; the explosion blew off his left arm. Afraid of a slow death, Obregón tried to shoot himself. Fortunately for Mexico, his pistol was not loaded. He survived and Villa suffered another setback. From now on things moved fast towards an international climax.

Villa led his remaining 6,500 men to the Carranza garrison at Agua Prieta, straddling the US border. Villa controlled the rail lines, so reinforcements could not reach his beleaguered adversary. For Carranza there was but one solution: *pass men and munitions through the territory of the United States*. Once again, Washington bungled. President Wilson recognised Carranza as Mexico's leader and soon Mexican troops were pouring into Agua Prieta, travelling on US rails and pulled by US locomotives. During the battle for the city, Villa's riders were machine-gunned and also blinded by a new invention: searchlights. Villa claimed that the powerful beams came from the American side. That was not correct: the searchlights were inside Mexico – however, the power to operate the searchlights *was* provided from across the border. On the retreat from Agua Prieta, Rodolfo Fierro met his maker when his horse stumbled and threw him into a lake. He was pulled under by his money belt weighted with stolen gold coins.

Villa was livid and blamed his defeat at the American border on 'gringo treachery'. Near Santa Ysabel, seventy Villistas under Colonel Pablo Lopez stopped a train carrying a party of eighteen American mining engineers. 'If you want to watch some fun, watch us kill these gringos,' shouted Villa's colonel to the Mexicans on board. His men took off the train a number of Americans and told them to run. With a '*Viva Villa*' and 'Death to the gringos,' they shot them in the back. Other Americans were forced to climb onto the coach roof and were knocked over like bowling pins. The Villistas overlooked one American, Tom Holmes, who managed to get away and tell American reporters about the massacre. Whether Villa gave the orders or not, the American press now turned their erstwhile hero into a bloodthirsty ogre: 'People who murder in the name of a revolution are nothing but ordinary bandits and must be dealt with accordingly.' The Santa Ysabel incident was followed by uproar along the border towns; Texan crowds had to be turned back by US troops to stop them from going on a rampage across the Rio Grande. The killing of ordinary Mexicans by Texan gunslingers degenerated into organised 'rabbit hunts', bolstered by the knowledge that no Texan jury would ever convict a white man for gunning down a Mexican.

Villa could not get over his Agua Prieta defeat, and his hate for anything which smelled of gringo took such a grip on him that he lost all caution. Given his state of mind and character, this could only lead to tragedy. It did. On 26 February 1916, Villa and some 450 of his followers left their hideout and moved towards the US border. They headed for Columbus, a dreary one-horse town in the middle of the desert, three kilometres north of the Mexican border in the US State of New Mexico. An American miner spotted the long column of Villistas and rode hell-bent into town to sound the warning. Unfortunately, Colonel Slocum, commanding the US 13th Cavalry, had received many such reports and took no additional precautions. At midnight on 9 March 1916, the Villistas cut their way through the border wire and entered the sleepy town. The first raiders stumbled into Fred Griffin, a US private on sentry duty, and killed him. Lientenant Castleman heard the shot and rushed outside in his pyjamas to face a Mexican who fired at him. The lieutenant shot the Mexican, while another American used a baseball bat to kill a Villista. Inside the barracks there was turmoil. 'Fire at will!' yelled Castleman, as he shot a Mexican who rushed at him with a machete. The next thirty minutes turned into a scene from *Gunfight at the OK Corral* with everyone blasting away at everyone else, but mostly at passing shadows. Mrs Castleman hid with her children under the bed. The Castleman car parked in front of the bedroom was later found peppered with nineteen bullet holes.

In the town, Villistas went to rob the bank and the mercantile store. The latter was owned by Sam Revel, who was asleep at the Commercial Hotel. He was pulled from his bed by two Villistas and marched across the main street to open the safe. He was rescued when a soldier fired through a window and picked off the two bandits. During this incident a bullet hit a large drum of gasoline. With a shower of sparks the drum blew apart, setting fire to several buildings. Soon the main street of wooden houses was an inferno. It provided American machine-gunners with target illumination, and their bullets began to find their marks. A troop led by Major Tompkins managed to chase the Villistas across the border. When Villa realised how small this chase party was, he went on the attack and drove Tompkins' men back across the wire.

The telegraph lines hummed across the nation and the following morning, America awoke to the stunning news of the Columbus shoot-out. The US ambassador to Berlin, James Gerard, sent a coded telegram to US Secretary of State Lansing: 'AM CERTAIN, VILLA'S ATTACKS ARE MADE IN GERMANY.' The implication was clear: Germany wanted to keep the United States preoccupied with the Mexican problem and distract them from getting involved in the war that was raging in Europe. If such was their plan, then Germany was devilishly correct in its assessment. American concentration on nearby Mexico blotted out any thought of the far-off battlefields of Flanders. The Columbus Incident induced the American president to order a full-scale reprisal raid, and a fifty-five-year-old general, John J. Pershing, was put in charge. His 2,000-man force was made up of General Custer's old 7th Cavalry, plus a Negro regiment, the 10th Cavalry. The pursuit of Pancho Villa proved a hard task for the ill-prepared Americans. Obstruction from the local population and Carranza's refusal to let Pershing use the

Mexican railway hampered it. The conditions faced by the men of the US Cavalry were appalling: their eyes smarted from the dust whirled up by the columns; their skins crawled with fleas and lice; worst of all there was an insufficient supply of water for man or horse.

There was one remarkable occurrence. A young American lieutenant from Texas, driving his private car through the countryside, had stopped near an abandoned farm. He began to walk towards the buildings when, all of a sudden, the gate burst open and three riders galloped straight for him. The young lieutenant drew his Colt and shot the first man from his saddle. It turned out to be Villa's chief of the *dorados*, General Julio Cardenas. The lieutenant calmly reloaded his pistol and killed the horse of another rider. With Texan chivalry, he waited until the man got up and had time to pull his own gun before killing him. The lieutenant then returned to camp with the three dead Mexicans draped over the hood of his car. His name was George Patton. (Like Patton, many future US generals emerged from the Mexican campaign.)

Pancho Villa proved too fast, always a step ahead of Pershing's cumbersome columns. Only once did he find himself in trouble. Near the town of Guerrero, a bullet pierced his right leg and shattered his shinbone. A unit of the 7th Cavalry under Major Dodd was informed of Villa's attack on Guerrero and set off in pursuit. Two miles out of town, their Indian scout took a wrong turn at a fork in the road and Pancho escaped to his mountain redoubt. That was as close as the Americans ever came to catching him.

In order to settle the international dispute over the *Yanqui* invasion, General Alvaro Obregón met US General Hugh Scott to resolve the situation and get the Americans out of his country. The two men could not agree on anything. In a sharp note to General Pershing, Carranza next demanded that the American general pack up and go home. Advised of the

'Mexican stalemate', the German ambassador to Washington cabled Berlin: 'THE PUNITIVE EXPEDITION AGAINST VILLA WILL LEAD TO A FULL-DRESS INTERVENTION BY THE UNITED STATES.'

America's Mexican expedition ended as a flop, both militarily and diplomatically. But before it was over, an event took place with repercussions far beyond its real meaning. Eighty-four men under Captain Charles T. Boyd approached an American-owned hacienda near Carrizal that was held by Mexican government troops. Captain Boyd foolishly ordered a frontal attack. His troops ran into concentrated machine-gun fire and twelve Americans were killed. This incident brought Mexico and the United States to the edge of war, and led to the fateful Zimmermann telegram.[14]

Arthur Zimmermann, the German foreign minister, invited Mexico to start a war on the United States when he cabled his ambassador in Mexico City:

... WE MAKE MEXICO A PROPOSAL OF ALLIANCE ON THE FOLLOWING BASIS: I. MAKE WAR TOGETHER, 2. MAKE PEACE TOGETHER, 3. GENEROUS FINANCIAL SUPPORT, 4. AND AN UNDERSTANDING ON OUR PART THAT MEXICO IS TO RECONQUER THE LOST TERRITORY IN KANSAS, NEW MEXICO AND ARIZONA.

British Intelligence, which had broken the German secret code, leaked the intercepted message to the American press; the public uproar was beyond imagination. Until that point, despite Germany's unbridled submarine attacks and the sinking of the *Lusitania* (a British ship with US citizens aboard), America had stayed out of the war. But the cable's final phrase, offering three US states to Mexico, goaded the United States into declaring war on Germany on 6 April 1917.

[14] See Barbara Tuchman, *The Zimmerman Telegram*.

Zimmermann's lack of diplomatic finesse and timing could have been hardly worse. His offer arrived on the very day that US troops finally withdrew from Mexican soil, removing the context of intervention. Also, Carranza had no stomach for going to war against his neighbour and he refused Germany's offer. However, it can be claimed with great justification that Pancho Villa was directly responsible for setting in motion the step that brought the US into the First World War.

Carranza's overriding concern for the moment was to settle once and for all the lingering Zapata problem. He sent his army against the guerrilla leader. More crops were burned, more peasant villages levelled, more women and children herded into churches that were then set on fire. Zapata answered in the same coin. *Hacendados* were hanged, factories looted, trains blown up. Carranza was caught in his own trap. Getting rid of this troublesome *indio* would take another two years and a feat of treachery. While the chase for Zapata was in full swing, Carranza appointed Francisco Murguia to give chase to Villa. General 'Pancho' Murguia soon became known as 'Hanging Pancho', since his method was to put a rope around the neck of every Villista he caught, and when he caught someone about whom he had his doubts, he hanged him anyway just to make sure. The two 'Panchos' conducted a campaign unmatched for its violence and carnage. *Non pardon* became a key phrase in both camps, which indiscriminately slaughtered combatants and bystanders alike in ruthless round-ups. The mere suggestion that at one time a person had dared to shout '*Viva Villa*' was enough to have him strung up on the nearest branch. Mexico was drowning in a river of blood. Murguia's principal aim was the destruction of Villa's source of manpower, since anyone over the age of twelve was regarded as a potential terrorist. Throughout the blackened and blasted countryside, thousands of badly decomposed corpses hung from trees. In a tit-for-tat, captured *federales* were cut down with machetes, or forced to run barefoot through razor-sharp cactus and then left for the coyotes to finish them off. Their cadavers were strewn along hedges and fields, headless and disembowelled. At Chihuahua, a group of Villa supporters stumbled into General Murguia. Within minutes, Murguia had every one of the 256 Villistas strung up in bunches on the trees lining the elegant Avenida Cristoforo Colon.

It was at this time that Pancho Villa turned from revolution to banditry. He became his own tax collector and forced gringos, whom he held responsible for his decline, to contribute to his war chest. He began by abducting Frank Knotts, the owner of the Erupción Mining Company, and released him for a ransom of 20,000 gold dollars. Next he raided a Mormon ranch which brought him $20,000 more. He then overran Parral where he hanged the town mayor and his two sons in front of the city hall. The rest of the citizens were given a choice: to come up with $100,000 or die. They paid up. A car dealer, Gabriel Chavez, never forgot his ordeal and was later to play a significant role in the life of the revolutionary. Villa then attacked Ciudad Juárez, and several Americans died when bullets flew across the border. For the last time, American cavalry under Colonel Tompkins took swift action, and by nightfall Villa fled. His final act of brigandry was to hold up a passenger train carrying money. He had the railway guards lined up and he executed them personally, but allowed the passengers to go free. With that, Villa faded from the scene.

The warlord was defeated, but remnants of his gang were still lethal; they lived off the country in a hit-and-run existence. One of these ragtag forces made for villages along the Texas border. As with any routed army in flight, their morale was terrible. Revolutionaries descending on any village were always bad news, but then one couldn't have good days all year round. After ordering the villagers to serve them food, the rebels killed their chickens and ducks and ordered the farmers' wives to cook these on the stoves. Others meanwhile carried off young girls, or raped them in front of their families. Afterwards they helped themselves to sacks of rice and beans. The male population was rounded up and marched off, never to be seen again.

In April 1919, Jesus Guajardo, a Yaqi Indian with the rank of colonel in the *federales*, contacted Emiliano Zapata, offering to defect to his side. To discuss the proposal, Zapata rode to the San Juan Chinameca hacienda, where this meeting was to be held. In the courtyard, Colonel Guajardo's guard of honour raised their rifles in salute, then suddenly levelled their barrels and shot Zapata. Guajardo collected $10,000 blood money and was promoted to general. But the 'Zapata myth' would not die, and even to this day, *indios* in Morelos province refuse to believe that their great hero is really dead. To them, he still rides on his white charger and will soon appear as their saviour.

President Carranza fatally put his signature to Article 27 of a new Mexican constitution, decreeing that only Mexicans by birth or naturalisation had the right to 'develop subsoil wealth' (oil). This authorised the government to expropriate foreign-owned properties. He was now taking on the Americans – and in doing so brought about his own downfall. At home, in the meantime, Alvaro Obregón formed an alliance with army officers and forced Carranza to flee. His train was intercepted and he escaped to a village, San Antonio Tlxancalantongo, where he came across Rodolfo Herrero, a bandit who had promoted himself to general. Herrero led Carranza towards a peasant hut, and told his president with a wicked grin: 'For tonight this will be the National Palace.' Around midnight, armed men burst into the hut and coldly executed the president with three bullets to his chest. Herrero was held accountable for the murder, but the judge of the tribunal was poisoned and Herrero was set free. As interim president there was another Huerta, but no relation to the ousted dictator. General Adolfo de la Huerta was a stout Obregón supporter, who guaranteed room for political movement by making a peaceful settlement with the only remaining threat, the wily Pancho Villa. The once penniless *mestizo* retired to a 25,000-acre estate, Canutillo, near Parral, which the government purchased for him, far from any railhead or major city. As personal protection Villa was allowed to keep fifty *dorados*, while his remaining 800 men were either incorporated into the Mexican army at their given rank, or provided with a suitable homestead.

With Emiliano Zapata and Pancho Villa out of action, the people of Mexico finally gave a sigh of relief. As a peace offering to the *peóns* of Morelos, de la Huerta arrested Zapata's assassin, General Guajardo, and had him publicly executed. After pacifying the country, Adolfo de la Huerta, a sincere and good man, resigned in favour of General Alvaro Obregón,[15] who was to become the new President of Mexico. On 1 December 1920, Obregón was sworn into office. After ten years of savagery, the Mexican Revolution was over.[16]

And then . . .

A new era had begun. With a surge of American investment Mexico rebuilt its destroyed factories and railway lines. Not much was done to repair the devastated countryside or to solve the lingering problem of the Mexican *peón*. People clung to their faith and flocked into the churches to ask for their priest's counsel: the church exerted a vital influence in the

[15] In another reversal, so typical of the Mexican Revolution, Adolfo de la Huerta took up arms against Obregón, but was defeated and fled to California, where he died as a music teacher.
[16] Obregón was assassinated by a mad artist, Leon Toral, on 16 July 1928.

affairs of the country. Old alliances were revived. President Obregón tried to raise his country from the ashes and make his people forget the horrors of the past. His vision was of a different tomorrow and he saw no place for old-fashioned revolutionaries such as Pancho Villa.

This popular figure was safely out of the way in a dusty town miles from anywhere. Parral was a place where time stood still. A rutted main street, lined by sun-baked houses, their wooden shutters badly in need of paint; a few bodegas with an assortment of cowboys, prostitutes, and town drunks. The only bangs came from the exhaust pipes of a few cars, terrifying donkeys tethered to lamp-posts, the same lamp-posts that had served as gallows. In the centre of town was the *cuartel* (barracks) of the *federales* with bored sentries leaning half asleep on the rifles. They had nothing to fear: gone were the *revolucionarios*, Zapata and Villa. The signs of war, however, were present everywhere. Adobe walls carried the pockmarks of the bullets that had ended lives, and at the local newspaper offices there were faded photographs reminding the brave citizens of the horrors of war. For the ordinary *peón* nothing had changed. Their fate was hardly better than it had been before; they lived in huts built from biscuit tins left behind by the US cavalry. The only noticeable change was for the young ones, who now had access to a school, built and paid for by the local celebrity, Francisco Villa. '*Viva Villa*' was still a popular cry, but it was now more of a nuisance than a danger to the authorities. Perhaps it annoyed Obregón, a president who had to vie in popularity with a retired revolutionary, for Pancho Villa was not only rich, he was a celebrity. He became a favourite subject for Hollywood producers; he was showered with presents from American companies who asked for his endorsement of their products, especially automobile makers – because by now, the paunchy Pancho had switched from a pony to the comfort of a motor car.

While the legendary and much publicised *revolucionario* Villa had become the larger-than-life hero of American newspapers and screens, the *bandido* Pancho lost his aura with a section of the Mexican people, to the point where a 'Kill Villa' fund was started. The first to contribute was the Parral car dealer, Gabriel Chavez, the man who had been forced to pay Villa a heavy ransom. He loathed seeing the *bandido* flaunt wealth so evilly obtained, this vile *mestizo* who strutted around town like some noble grandee. Attempts to kill him had failed because Villa was well guarded, until Jesus Salas Barraza took up the challenge. He hired eight gunmen and purchased the gangster's favourite tool, the Thomson sub-machine gun.

To a stranger, the area around Parral appeared to be an inhospitable wasteland, a desolation of enormous skies and limitless horizons, a land condemned each year, each day, to die under a pitiless sun. But this impression was misleading. People lived there, tilling the land, harvesting their fruit trees and, now that peace had returned to the country, living a fairly decent existence, all due to one man who had helped them improve their standard of living.

Set in this wide plain was a cluster of splendid, red-tiled buildings. Spreading trees and a topiary hedge led through an archway into a shaded forecourt. The owner of the hacienda sat mostly on his patio with two dogs at his feet, their tongues lolling. Pancho Villa had gained weight. So much so that the buttons on his jacket must have been sewn on with piano wire to keep them from popping off. He was not a happy man; he hated this feeling of inaction forced on him by his sudden retirement. Perhaps he should stir up a little excitement in his province of Chihuahua, nothing much, mind you, just enough to keep him from getting rusty. The wife of one of his *dorados* had given birth to a son, and on Friday, that holy day of the week, they would baptise the newborn. It was reason enough to celebrate, anything was, anything to rid himself of this gnawing boredom. He would have a great fiesta, with firecrackers and music, an ox turning on the spit, fruit, and tortillas. And plenty of tequila. But first there would be the religious ceremony in Parral's Spanish cathedral. Villa had graciously consented to become the child's godfather. He would be dressed in spotless white and he would leave his pistol behind. A church was no place for a gun, and his fifty *dorados* would be in the cathedral to protect him, having gone ahead to Parral to form the guard of honour.

It was half past eleven, on Friday, 20 July 1923, when Francisco 'Pancho' Villa and his secretary, Miguel Trillo, climbed into the open Dodge. Through his windscreen, partly opaque from the incessant onslaught of sand, the dusty road into town spread like a painting before him. The first houses of Parral came in sight, their windows shuttered to protect the inhabitants from the broiling sun at high noon. The main street was dead; all signs of life had disappeared. There were no women with pots and baskets, sitting under their umbrellas by the side of the road; no men, with their sombreros pulled over their eyes, lounging in the shade of doorways. Only a solitary figure leaning drunkenly against the wooden post of a patio. Pancho leaned out of the car, hanging onto the crown of his sombrero to keep it from blowing off.

The solitary man in the white peasant *calzones* had been posted as lookout. Quite cynically, the signal was for him to shout. '*Viva Villa*' and wave his sombrero. The killers, lurking in the shaded recess of an open window, were all experienced. The man in the open car was still too far away to identify his face hidden below broad-brimmed sombrero. But the light was good and the target was perfectly outlined behind the windscreen. If this was the right man, then . . . Pancho passed by the market place, its stalls shaded by closely interwoven wicker roofing. Nobody there either, how odd.

The town of Parral resembled an open tomb . . . The lookout squinted at the oncoming car. Only when he was absolutely certain would he slowly raised his wide sombrero. From the shock of his dark curly hair ran a driblet of sweat, the sweat of fear. His mouth opened, showing stained, badly formed teeth . . . Perhaps Pancho felt a sense of exposure; something was definitely not right. Why was there only a lone man in a road that should be crowded? For weeks, Pancho had had a nagging suspicion that someone was out there gunning for him.

The target was very close now. The gunmen waited for final confirmation from their lookout . . . The lookout was now sure. '*Viva Villa!*' he yelled at the top of his voice and waved his sombrero enthusiastically. Pancho Villa leaned sideways, and a smile crossed his face. This man was one of his supporters, or perhaps a beggar. For an instant he looked at the brown face with the toothy grin and threw the man a coin. Over the rattling of the motor's exhaust the assassins heard '*Viva Villa!*' A sombrero went into the air. Villa was in the driver's seat! The gunmen flicked off their safety catches . . . The car had almost reached the crossroads. From there, the street to the left led towards the cathedral square. Pancho slowed down to negotiate the sharp turn, when suddenly the characteristic tearing and knocking racket of Thomson sub-machine guns exploded. From the shadow of doorways and windows, eight assassins poured burst after burst into the oncoming car. The windscreen shattered, fine glass fragments shivering in the air. Villa's body was punched back into the seat, struck by seven bullets. He died instantly. The most revered and feared of all Mexican *revolucionarios* was forty-four.

It was never established who masterminded his assassination. The presumed killer, Jesus Salas Barraza, was arrested, brought to trial, and sentenced to twenty years. By presidential decree he was freed after six months, and made colonel.

On his deathbed,[17] Barraza stated: 'I'm not a murderer. I've rid humanity of a monster.' Not even in death did Pancho Villa find peace. His grave was desecrated, his body unearthed, and his head stolen.

The historic importance of men such as Pancho Villa must be measured by the political consequences of their actions. An act of droit de seigneur, the rape of his sister by a drunken *hacendado*, had been the catalyst for a whirlwind of revenge and rebellion against the ruling class of rich landowners and the *jefes politicos* appointed by them. In Francisco 'Pancho' Villa (and Emiliano Zapata), the little people found their hero. They raised him to a pinnacle of power unknown in Latin America since Simón Bolívar. Whatever the methods used by Villa, whatever the horror and cruelty he meted out as 'Pistol Pancho', he changed his country. The pattern of Mexican life that had been the accepted way for centuries was buried for ever. The Columbus Affair was the cause of his downfall, providing his enemies with the silver bullet to gun him down. In a wider sense, Columbus was the apex of his international career, since it gave rise to the break between the United States of America and Germany. There can be no doubt that Villa's border raids pushed America towards unsolicited and unwise military intervention in the affairs of a sovereign neighbour. Without Pancho Villa, American troops would never have crossed the Mexican border to be met by a resounding chorus of '*Yanqui* go home', a chorus that tempted Germany to offer Mexico their military support for a war against the United States. A proposal, so it can be argued, that was the key to America's entry into the First World War.

Pancho Villa: a serf who rebelled against injustice and who went on to become the most enigmatic and controversial figure of the Mexican Revolution. That is no small monument.

---

[17] Barraza died peacefully in 1951.

Interlude
1914–1917

'What if they gave a war and nobody came?' That was the daring question of the great pacifist, Carl Sandburg. Unfortunately, such a question was never posed when the guns of August 1914 began to thunder across Europe, and the world was at war. The armies of the kaiser overran Belgium and slaughtered the Russian bear at Tannenberg. Everywhere the Allies were in retreat and the Germans knocked on the gates of Paris, only thirty kilometres from parading down the Champs Élysées. In a desperate attempt to stop the German steamroller, 2,000 Parisian taxis ferried 50,000 French reservists to the front line. The German advance was brought to a halt and the war turned into a battle of attrition, fought with machine-guns from soggy trenches. Plodding bayonet charges and static artillery duels replaced lightning thrusts.

Nineteen-sixteen was a special year. In February, the German chief-of-staff, General von Falkenhayn, launched a million men against the defences of Verdun. His plan was to lure the French into making massive sacrifices. His plan worked, although his forces suffered just as many casualties as did the French. A million men died and nothing was decided. In Flanders, the English were hardly served better. General Haig attacked the Germans on the Somme. The British foot soldiers advanced across a moonscape of shell craters and knee-deep mud into the mouths of German machine-guns. British losses were staggering. On the first day of this ill-conceived attack, they suffered seven times as many dead as at Waterloo. In the most murderous war the world had ever known both sides were bled white.

It was no different on the Eastern front. Except that here, chiefly one side – Russia – did the dying. German divisions routed Russian battalions; the tsar's army was in headlong flight. Regiments dissolved, widespread rot set in, soldiers threatened to murder their generals, and agitators yelled: 'Peace for the soldiers, ruin to the palaces!' The Russian capital, Petrograd, lived on the edge of a volcano. Profiteering reached new heights: food trains were stopped from reaching the city and their supplies sold on the black market. In July 1917, serious rioting erupted. This time the people shouted: '*Doloi Voiny!* Down with war!' Only swift intervention by loyal Cossacks saved the government.

While millions slaughtered each other on the muddy plains of the Somme and in the cragged Carpathian Mountains, and nations fought for their survival, another relatively minor event took place, but it was to shake the world to its foundations. It began when the German generals tried to find a way out of their disastrous two-front war and came up with a brilliant solution. All it took was a taxi from Zurich to the Swiss–German border, a locomotive to pull a sealed, green-painted railway carriage all the way to the Finland Station in Petrograd – and a Trojan Horse. 'They transported him like a plague bacillus in a test tube,' wrote Winston Churchill. That bacillus was the Bolshevik, Vladimir Ilyich Ulyanov, known to history as Lenin. Nothing could stop him now.

The 'mother of modern revolutions' was already in its planning stages. Two men were principally responsible. One came from Zurich in a sealed railway carriage, courtesy of the Germans' the other arrived from New York by boat. The two had been rivals, serious rivals. Now they were about to unite in a common front. Because, more than anything, lack of a political plan and a co-ordinated leadership had brought every previous Russian revolutionary movement to nothing. The ashes of the July riots were still cooling when, in grey wigs and glued-on moustaches, a dozen Bolsheviks gathered, ready for Black Earth and Red Fire.

4

7 November 1917

'Vsya vlast Sovetam'

Vsya vlast Sovetam.
All power to the Soviet.
Lenin, 7 November 1917

'The truth?' asked the man with the steel-rimmed spectacles and the goatee. A cynical smile crossed his face. 'No! What we must create is an illusion of the truth! Insurrection is an art, and like all arts, it has its laws.'

The clandestine meeting held on 10 October 1917 in Galina Sukhanova's apartment in Karpovka, a fashionable neighbourhood of Petrograd, would have made Brutus, Cassius, and their conspirators look like raw amateurs. The men and women assembled there had one thing in common: they loved to take risks. Furthermore, they were quite willing to achieve their goal by any means necessary without worrying about such minor considerations as widespread bloodshed. The list of the twelve participants, about to light the fuse for an explosion that would go down in history as Red October, was impressive.

Among them were Vladimir Ilyich Ulyanov, a.k.a. Lenin; his wife, Nadezhda Krupskaya, known as 'The Fish' for her bulging eyes; Gregory Radomylsky, a.k.a. Zinoviev, a thirty-two-year-old party organiser; Alexandra Kollontai, an overweight feminist aristocrat; Yakov Sverdlov, the sinister 'Inquisitor' who, within a year, was to order the execution of the tsar and his family; Felix Dzerzhinski, founder of Cheka,[1] the notoriously ruthless secret police; Lev Rosenfeld, a.k.a. Kamenev, a bespectacled intellectual Jew and the first editor of *Pravda*; the ill-tempered mass-liquidator Iosif Vissarionovich Dzhugashvili, a.k.a. Joseph Stalin; and finally, another escapee from Siberia, the thirty-eight-year-old party ideologue and brilliant orator, Leiv Davidovich Bronstein, a.k.a. Leon Trotsky.

To escape the attention of the Okhranka, Russia's secret police, they had travelled across town in an assortment of wigs and false beards. Lenin wore a grey wig that had been made for him by a theatrical designer in Helsinki when he had slipped across the Finnish border aboard a freight train, dressed as a fireman. Now, by candlelight, a decision was debated: *if* – and *when* – to start the uprising. For almost an hour, Lenin discussed the merits of an armed revolution. 'The time is now,' he said. 'The German navy is in open revolt [this was true, but only a minor portion of it], and our sailors will come over to us. After that, the people will come out into the streets and join our insurrection.' It was a daring thought, but utterly suicidal.

Trotsky yelled: 'The people – what people? The proletariat? Don't count on them. Nowhere can we determine the attitude of the working class. What if our uprising alienates the third camp?' He was referring to a group made up of the petit bourgeoisie, shopkeepers, kulaks (land-owning peasants), and minor officials.

Zinoviev, taking into account Trotsky's warning, disagreed with Lenin's overall appreciation of the situation: 'Without

---

[1] Cheka stands for *Chrezvychainaia kommissia po borbe s kontr-revoliutsiei i sabotazhem*, or for short: CH.K.

being sure of the urban middle class, we cannot stake the future of our *world revolution* on armed rebellion.'

Kamenev, frightened by the idea of going out into the streets and perhaps dying, put it in more diplomatic terms: 'It's a gamble, and we have no right to stake the future of our movement on an armed uprising.'

'The hell with the petit bourgeoisie, we'll take care of them,' yelled Felix Dzerzhinski.

If we have more time for senseless discussion, we'll probably make many more mistakes, thought Trotsky. More than anyone else he knew the dictum of Marx: 'The proletariat does not have the right to take power before it is prepared.' And the proletariat was not prepared.

Only the Georgian, Stalin, remained aloof from their heated discussion. He took the temperature of that meeting and waited to find out who would emerge as winner before taking sides.

It was a stalemate. With nerves strained to breaking point, each person in the room was a potential time bomb ready to explode at any moment. A decision had to be reached. Lenin took Trotsky aside. What was discussed between them, what deal was struck, is unknown, but when both men came back into the room, Trotsky had changed his mind. The dawn was about to break over Petrograd when Lenin finally pronounced: 'It is time to move from words to deeds.' He tore a page from a notebook and wrote: 'Armed uprising is inevitable, the time for it has come. The Bolshevik Central Committee orders organisers to be guided by this directive.' This resolution was passed by a vote of ten to two, the two being Kamenev and Zinoviev. Leon Trotsky voted in its favour and suggested that the insurrection should coincide with the forthcoming People's Congress, called for 20 October. When Zinoviev brought vodka to celebrate their decision, Lenin snatched the bottle from the table and, in his squeaky voice, yelled: 'This is a revolution of the

'Aux armes, citoyens . . .'
14th July 1789. The storming of the Bastille sent the signal to the revolution.

'We sow in blood and tears so that those after us can reap joy.'
Jean-Paul Marat, who used the Paris mob to terrorise and whose assassination sparked the terror.

'Virtue is the principle of a government by the people.'
Maximilien Robespierre. The true believer, more terrifying than any hypocrite.

Above left: L'Adieu du roi:
'*I shall see you in the morning.*'
21st January 1793. Louis XVI
to Marie Antoinette and his
son, the dauphin, as he was
led to his execution.

Above right: '*To discourage
other kings.*'
Revolutionary poster with
the head of Louis XVI.

Left: '*He who climbs above
the crowd is bound to lose
his head.*'
28th July 1794. The execution
of Robespierre brought the
Great Terror to an end.

'Give him a fair trial, then shoot him', ordered Napoleon.
20th February 1810. The Tyrolean rebel leader Andreas Hofer
prayed before his execution. The famous engraving by D. Schubert
started the anti-Napoleonic movement throughout Europe.

'Why am I being shot? I served my government well.' 15th November 1912. Pancho Villa faced a firing squad and walked away from it.

'Viva Villa, Viva Zapata.' 6th December 1914. The day they divided Mexico. Pancho Villa (*right*) and Emiliano Zapata (*left*)

Below: 'It is important to win battles in war . . .' 13th April 1915. Pancho Villa's army on the way to face General Obregón at Celaya.

Above: 'They're not worth the bullet!'
In 1917, General Murguia strung up every Villa supporter.

Right: 'His spirit never died.'
Emiliano Zapata.

Above left: 27th February 1917. The year of all revolutions began with the fall of the Tsar.

Above right: 'Power to the Soviet.' 26th October 1917. Leon Trotsky exhorted the virtues of a growing movement from a Petrograd park bench.

Left: 'Comrades, the revolution is achieved.' November 1917. The first Soldier's Soviet meets in Petrograd.

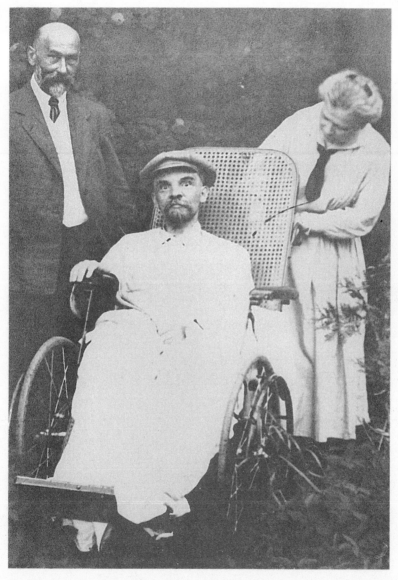

'The revolution does not need historians.'
Autumn 1923. A dying Lenin watched the vicious power struggle
between Trotsky and Stalin for his succession.

Above: 'Long live the Internationale.'
Rosa Luxemburg addressing a crowd at the Congress of
the Internationale, Stuttgart, 1907.

Left: 'The German Army is the German Nation in arms.'
Wilhelm II. German Emperor 1888–1918.

Below: 'Shoot the bastards.'
January 1919. Revolutionaries at Berlin's Brandenburg
Gate during the Spartakus Rebellion.

pure.' The die was cast; now it took only a spark to set it off.

Russia was a barbaric and wild country. The tsar owned the land and the people. 'Russians are arrogant, because they get no education other than in shamelessness and lying; they are always drunk and violent, and incredibly superstitious. It is one of the principles of the tsar to hinder his people from going abroad, lest they should behold the spectacle of liberty elsewhere.'[2] The people lived by a contradiction: being brutes, it took a super-brute to rule them, someone who by sheer force of will and intolerable cruelty compelled his subjects to knuckle down to his dictates. Nothing much had changed over the centuries.

The Romanov dynasty came to power after the death of Ivan the Terrible in 1584. This Rurik tsar had pushed his kingdom's borders across the Ural Mountains into Siberia and had ensured his own permanence on the throne by having put to death every potential male challenger, including his own son. Peter I the Great (1682–1725) declared himself Emperor of all the Russias. The power of the monarch was at its height under Catherine the Great (1762–1796) who usurped the throne from her weak and incompetent husband. Alexander II lost the war against the Turks, but liberated farm workers from their serfdom. A Jewish student, Grinevitsky, threw a bomb into the royal carriage and killed him. This led to a pogrom under Alexander III. Next in line was his son Nicholas, whose childhood was unhappy. His life changed when he married the beautiful Alexandra Feodorovna, a Hessian princess who was therefore dubbed 'The German Woman'. She became the dominant character in the tsar's circle. Alix bore him four daughters, Olga, Tatyana, Maria, and Anastasia, and an heir, the Tsarevich Alexei, who suffered from haemophilia,[3] which

[2] From the memoirs of Kotoshikhin, after his escape from Russia.
[3] The failure of blood to clot.

was at the time an incurable disease. Nicholas's reign began with a drama. At his coronation celebrations a huge crowd gathered on Khodynka Field. As wagons drew up carrying free beer, they pressed forward and a thousand people were trampled to death.

Nicholas was the classic example of a man unequal to his mission, a monarch who was the sole author of his own tragic destiny. His lack of realism and will-power led to the final tragedy; the weakness he displayed caused him to lose respect and confidence. Around the crowned houses of Europe he became known as 'nice Uncle Nicky' and he was just that; a deeply religious but otherwise ineffectual sovereign, who reigned more by proxy than by his own volition. Resisting social reform was possible in a peasant society, but it was no longer feasible in the age of industrialisation. His foreign policy was a disaster. His first military venture ended in a crushing defeat inflicted by the rising power, Japan, in 1905; in the Straits of Tsushima, the cruisers of Japanese Admiral Heihachiro Togo literally blew the imperial Russian fleet out of the water. Russia had to accept a shameful peace that not even the Soviets could swallow when Japan was later on its knees in 1945. This venture cost Russia 400,000 dead. With the debacle of Tsushima, the tsarist regime began to stagger towards its doom.

Russia's military setback brought international humiliation and revolutionary challenge at home. Cracks appeared in the iron shell of Russia's isolationism. Peter the Great had laid down the principal rules: 'Europe is still necessary to us for several decades; after that we will turn our back to it. Quickly take what is ready, what is best, and improve upon it at home.' On this basis, the tsar's policy was governed by a bizarre dualism; a reaching out towards ideas from the outside and an inbred isolationist phobia of ideas from the outside. An example was the railroad, a brilliant Western invention which could serve the vastness of Russia's territory – but with a larger rail gauge than the rest of Europe. The result was that a train from Poland, Austria, or Prussia ran out of rail at the Russian border. In this way Russians were prevented from comparing their happiness or misery with that of other nations, and tsars could paint an image of Russia as God's own paradise.

Excessive and prolonged use of power can blind sovereigns to human dignity, justice, even honour. Tsar Peter and Tsarina Catherine were untouchable deities, who subtly transformed warlords into perfumed courtiers; but the Alexanders and Nicholases showed extraordinary political ineptitude for monarchs of the industrial age. In terms of the gap between the rich elite and the poor working proletariat and rural serfs, Russia was unique. Industrialisation required an unskilled workforce which formed the base of a new proletarian working class. This class suffered cruelly at the hands of factory bosses; their families lived in appalling conditions, in tiny holes in crumbling brick barracks thick with layers of black coal dust, as filthy as they were uninhabitable. An unjust pay scale prompted a timid representative body to defend the workers' rights. Such unions were divided; strikes were put down with utter ruthlessness and demonstrations lacked political muscle as the proletariat did not have the means for effective, collective action. This was an auspicious moment for a man of destiny to step forward, unite the proletariat, and shape not only the destiny of Russia, but the political considerations of all the major powers for a long time to come.

Leiv Davidovich Bronstein grew up speaking better Yiddish than Russian. He went to university in Odessa, fell in love with an opera soprano, and studied theatre, which was his apprenticeship for addressing large crowds. The works of Rousseau and Marx, Nietsche, d'Annunzio, and Zola stimulated his thoughts. 'The spiritual estate of man is so vast in its diversity that we must stand on the shoulders of our great predecessors,' he wrote before he was put on a train to Siberia in 1899. In prison, Leiv Davidovich established a friendly relationship with a simple-minded fur hunter who knew that part of Siberia. In 1902, they managed to escape, the fur hunter leading the way to Irkutsk, the nearest railhead. For the escape, Leiv Davidovich had forged an internal passport. One of his prison guards had been a brutal bully whose name was Trotsky and who hated smart Jews. Bronstein added an irony when in his forged passport he used the name of the brute. From there on, Leiv Davidovich Bronstein became Leon Trotsky. The forgery was good enough to get him past the officials at Irkutsk and onto a ship to London, where he joined up with two revolutionaries, Nadezhda Krupskaya and her husband, Vladimir Ilyich Ulyanov, or Lenin. It certainly was not love at first sight. Trotsky found Lenin's political views morally repulsive. And Lenin viewed Trotsky as a blabbering, four-star son of a bitch.

Lenin, small of stature, and bald with Mongoloid eyes, came from a well-to-do middle-class background. His uncompromising radical views earned him years in tsarist jails. His life changed after he met Georgi Plekhanov, the exiled leader of Russia's Social Democrats, who accused him: 'We show the liberal bourgeoisie our face, you show them your arse.' This led to a split in the party. Plekhanov formed the Mensheviks and Lenin the Bolsheviks. The only opposition party inside Russia were the Social Revolutionaries, a confused group with no clearly defined aims. They were not effective, and yet they grew. To offset their growing influence, the Okhranka had helped to form a Union of Russian Workers, whose leader, Gapon, was an Orthodox priest. After the Russo-Japanese War, the growing unrest in Russia tempted Trotsky to St Petersburg. He formed a Soviet (the Russian word for council). His political career took off on a blank, cold winter's day, 22 January 1905. With growing discontent in the factories, the police ordered Gapon to lead his Workers Union in a public display of loyalty to the tsar. Thousands of workers and their families marched to the Winter Palace, carrying a petition of their grievances to be presented to Tsar Nicholas: 'We, your loyal workers, our children, our wives and our helpless parents are here to seek truth and protection. We are poor, we are oppressed, they laugh at us and do not treat us like human beings, but as slaves. Our patience has reached its limit. For us the moment has come where death is better than continued torment.' This peaceful demonstration, without flags or banners, ran into a solid barrage of soldiers and mounted Cossacks. Suddenly, the soldiers fired point-blank into the massed crowd; they kept on firing for hours and in the massacre over a thousand died. 'This bloodbath was the general rehearsal for our revolution of 1917,' wrote Trotsky. The end result of Bloody Sunday was a strike wave that swept the country. A million workers put down their tools – all without directives from any political organisation. The authorities reacted with utter brutality. Thousands were jammed into trains and shipped off to forced labour camps in Siberia. The 1905 Revolution had been a muddled affair, without planning and without leadership, and the Cossacks drowned it in a sea of blood.

On 4 February the young Socialist Kalyaev threw a bomb at the carriage of the tsar's uncle. All they found of Grand Duke Sergei Alexandrovich was a foot. The regime looked for a scapegoat, and the blame was laid squarely on Jewish revolutionaries. The military and their acolytes launched a terrible pogrom. Ghettoes were burned, houses looted, Jews killed by the frenzied mob. The bomb-thrower never told the court who had pulled the strings.

Trotsky, on Okhranka's list as a narodnik (man of the people), and one of the growing nucleus of intellectuals who went out to teach workers 'the joys of liberation from slavery', was once more on his way to Siberia. As was Vladimir Ilyich Ulyanov, who took on the name of the river that passed near the prison camp, the Lena. But before Trotsky was put on the train, he had his hand in one more event. Graciously, the tsar had agreed to a 'Freedom Manifesto'. For the opportunist Trotsky this was a way to prove his talent as a brilliant orator. He addressed a workers' meeting in Petrograd, waving a paper. 'We have forced this butcher on the throne to grant us liberty. The right to vote, he has promised us. But don't celebrate yet. If the government is sincere in making peace with its people, they must begin to grant amnesty to all our comrades in Siberia.' The crowd went wild: 'Amnesty! Amnesty!' Trotsky held their full attention. 'Workers, our power is in ourselves. We must brandish our swords and defend our liberties. The Freedom Manifesto is nothing but a sheet of paper. Today the tsar gives it to you, and tomorrow he will take it back and tear it into pieces, as I tear this paper-freedom in pieces before your very eyes.' He let shreds of paper flutter over the crowd.[4] The tsar did precisely what Trotsky had predicted. His fear of becoming unpopular with his dominating uncles, cousins, and nephews, and a slowness of political thought led to irresolution. Even at this stage, the Soviet Revolution was not a foregone conclusion, had he acted with vigour. He failed miserably, and his personality became inextricably linked with the journey towards revolution. 'He is a rabbit,' the bourgeoisie sniggered, referring to his lack of personal courage and the increasing political interference of his wife. 'He can only perform in bed, and then only with her permission.'

Trotsky was in the frozen taiga above the Arctic Circle, a thousand miles from the nearest railhead. This time, escape seemed impossible. His guards had not reckoned on the ingenuity of Leon Trotsky; he befriended a habitually drunken Zyrian tribesman who supplied the guards with home-brewed vodka. One evening Trotsky loaded the drunken Zyrian on his reindeer sledge and drove out of

[4] A. Muller, *Gespräche zur Weltgeschichte*.

the gates under a pile of foul-smelling furs. It is difficult to imagine their journey of a thousand miles through the Siberian winter night. They travelled in Arctic darkness while Trotsky kept up his guide's interest by telling him a string of fairy tales. This exercise would prove useful in the future, since he repeated the stories but with a different ending to fit a particular need. After several weeks they reached the railhead of Bogolovsk[5] where Trotsky presented himself as a polar explorer; he was so convincing that the local governor asked him to give a talk to the town's nobility about his adventures. The rest was simple. With real papers, provided for the 'eminent Professor L. Trotsky' by the amiable governor, Leon took the train to Moscow, and from there to London, Berlin, and Vienna, before he settled in Paris. At the outbreak of the First World War he became the correspondent for an underground newspaper, *Slovo*. His acerbic wit got him expelled from France and he took passage to New York, where he was swallowed up in the Jewish ghetto of the Bronx.

In Russia, anarchy raised its ugly head but the tsar was given a temporary reprieve. Supported by a Russian faction, a Serb nationalist organisation assassinated the Austrian archduke in June 1914. In the nationalistic fervour to go to war, children waved flags, women shouted patriotic slogans, and men were mobilised 'in the defence of Holy Mother Russia'. Nicholas took no part in the war other than to arrive at a fateful decision. He ordered his unprepared armies (Rennenkamp's 1st and Samsonov's 2nd Army) into an ill-conceived attack on East Prussia. A deep personal dislike between his two army commanders, and the fact that the Germans were reading Russian orders of battle sent out *en clair*, contributed to Russia's crushing defeat at Tannenberg, where a well-trained, well-equipped army defeated a giant with feet

---

[5] There is no record of what happened to his Zyrian guide.

of clay. Six hundred thousand died in all. General Brusilov's offensive on Austro-Hungarian lines resulted in another million Russian casualties. Troop morale collapsed, the façade of Russian patriotism was wrecked, and the monarchy began to crumble. Had the tsar sued his cousin, the kaiser, for an honourable peace, he could not only have saved both his and his cousin's throne but he could also have made the Great War the shortest major conflict in history. German armies advanced, while the Russians fell back in disorder, taking horrendous losses.

The situation was not helped by the deep chasm that had always existed between the officer class and the peasant soldiery. Officers benefited from frequent leave from the front, to see their wives and sleep with their mistresses, while millions of conscripts were considered as nothing better than 'meat in a battle'. With hunched shoulders and heads down, they had to stand guard in waist-deep mud. They were ordered in waves into the sights of German machine-guns or ended up hanging on barbed wire. Refuseniks were shot without trial. Russian soldiers began to loathe their officers, up the ladder of command from captain to colonel to general, all the way to the tsar and his 'German bitch'. Front-line units turned into rebellious powder kegs with an ever-shortening fuse. Grand Duke Nicholas, commander-in-chief of the army, begged the tsar to distribute land to the soldiers in return for exceptional bravery. The tsar relieved the grand duke of his command. 'We have taken a great step towards Russia's overthrow,' joyfully remarked the German chief-of-staff, General Erich Ludendorff, when he heard about the grand duke's removal. The inept tsar now tried his hand at soldiering, taking sole charge of the war. 'This is her doing,' growled his generals, 'that German woman and her cursed monk will lead us into disaster.' To fight an enemy was one thing, but having to combat one inside your own motherland, at the very moment when national unity was called for: that went beyond the limits.

St Petersburg, rebaptised Petrograd to appease Russians fighting the Germans, was a city that had borrowed its architecture from Rome, its amusements from Paris, and its pretensions from Berlin. It was a place where the cleverest made fortunes and others came to relieve them of their wealth, a city of masks and secrets, seething with enemies both seen and unseen. The highly strung, unbalanced Tsarina Alexandra Feodorovna was preoccupied with the fading health of her haemophilic son Alexei. Nothing helped, neither physicians nor pilgrimages to the holy shrines. Until a Siberian monk arrived on the scene and the tsarina fell under the spell of this cunning *muzhik* (Russian peasant). The charlatan monk Grigori Yefimovich Rasputin claimed that he had received a vision from God and that he could heal her son's illness. With Nicholas at his field headquarters, in Mogilev, decisions of state were left in the hands of the tsarina and her evil spirit, Rasputin. The state appointments they made together were disastrous. In December 1916, the transvestite Prince Felix Yussupov lured Rasputin, a notorious womaniser, to his palace by promising him the favours of his beautiful wife Irina. Yussupov and two accomplices murdered Rasputin; they poisoned him, they shot him, and when the monk still showed signs of life, they dumped him among the ice floes of the Neva. '*Ubili* – they've killed him,' was the jubilant cry as the country celebrated his death as if it were Easter. The tsarina wept bitterly. War was war and uncounted millions had to pay with their lives for the tsar's ineptness – but they were *canaille*, peasants born to die for their tsar. This single death was special to the imperial family.

'Who will now weep for us?' Alix asked pleadingly.

'My love, all of Russia will weep,' replied Nicholas.

He was mistaken: the people's hatred now focused on the tsarina, that 'German bitch'. People damned her as they stamped their feet in the cold waiting in food queues. Soldiers at the front cursed her: 'That bloody German woman is responsible, she doesn't want us to beat her own cousins.' This dangerous rumour soon grew into menacing proportions. Some were shot for spreading defeatist slander. Others took their place.

After three years of a devastating war, with her armies beaten into submission by German artillery, with famine at home, palace intrigues and a shattered economy, Petrograd had become a Rome of the Borgias. Now that Rasputin was out of the way, power reverted to the tsar's uncles, who imposed their will on an impotent parliament, or Duma (assembly). Despite casualty figures in the millions, despite the hungry people in the cities demanding bread, for the ruling clique of Petrograd it was 'business as usual'. The bourgeoisie had learned that an angry proletariat had no power to shake political institutions. But this time it was different. The officer corps was no longer assured of the loyalty of its troops; military commanders had more problems trying to stop soldiers from deserting than fighting the Germans. The Russian army had become a 'militia of peasants', led by subalterns from outside the privileged classes. The question was not, would revolution come – but when it came, whether it would be from the collapse of an incompetent monarchy or from mutiny in the army. At Stavka HQ, officers debated 'the bigger strategy' over candlelit dinners and the tsar took strolls with his dog, while on the front regiment after regiment was sacrificed, left to die in freezing mud. Every morning the dead had to be hacked from the icy quagmire lining their trenches. The front was a picture of decaying dugouts, rotting medical tents, collapsed shelters, and mud. To withdraw would mean admitting failure; the officers therefore ordered their soldiers to stay and to die.

There comes a point when even the most stout-hearted or stupid will object. That point was about reached. All

it took was an organisation to bind people together. The
fire in the betrayed soldiers was stirred by a new brand of
politically trained agitators, who told the troops how the
cats were getting fat and how ambitious politicians and black
marketeers profited from the military disasters. This was no
more than the truth: thousands of miles behind the battle
lines, profiteers stuffed their pockets and went to the ballet
with their dainty mistresses. The credibility of Russia's Prime
Minister, Mikhail Rodzianko, was tarnished by the terrible
losses at the front and by the enfeebled economy at home. No
longer could he deal with the nation's soaring disenchantment
and fiscal anaemia. Conditions were bleak indeed. Out of the
shadows stepped a figure that was destined to preside over
the demise of imperial Russia.

Aleksandr Fyodorovich Kerensky, a flamboyant lawyer, had
spent some months in prison after the revolution of 1905; it
proved a useful sentence as it provided him with the badge of
a Socialist revolutionary, but he considered Marxism as something borrowed from abroad. In a politically smart move,
Kerensky began to co-operate with the Petrograd Soviet of
Workers and Soldiers, which had become the rival assembly
to the Duma, whose deputies prided themselves on representing 'respectable society' and who looked on the Soviet
as an 'unwashed rabble'. This Soviet defended the rights of
factory workers. It had been created by the Socialists – and
not by the Bolsheviks, as was later claimed; it had nothing
to do with an emerging Bolshevism. With this daring step
Kerensky bypassed the stalled negotiations between the elected
representatives of the Duma and the monarch. Astutely,
Kerensky brought the urban proletariat over to his side,
but overlooked a much greater danger: he was providing
a platform for the grievances of the urban working class
and also activating the disheartened peasant soldiers at the
front. It is the final irony that Lenin and Trotsky, two
enigmatic men who were to shake the world in a manner

neither could have envisaged, took no part in the events of February 1917. At that time, Lenin was living in a walk-up apartment in Zurich and Trotsky was giving lectures in New York on the failure of international Socialism. Contrary to later Soviet propaganda, the Bolsheviks were not responsible for ousting the tsar – as a matter of fact, they hardly existed as a political instrument!

Petrograd, 23 February 1917. It began with a spontaneous demonstration by women workers on the first floor of the Neva Thread Mills. Within the hour it had mushroomed into a shouting mob: '*Doloi Tsarskoi Monarckhy!* Down with the tsarist monarchy!' They linked arms and advanced along Bolshoi Prospect. Cossack units stopped them with sabres and police waded into the crowd with batons. By a miracle, the day ended without deaths or arrests. Fortunately, as the mayor of Petrograd said that evening over champagne at the Astoria: 'My God, imagine what our foreign allies would think of us, had we splashed the snow with the blood of our own people.' In the Duma, Aleksandr Kerensky was shouted down. 'Traitor!' When the assembly had calmed down he pointed out the window. 'You call me a traitor? Are you blind? These women out there, your mothers, your wives, your daughters, for them hunger is their only tsar.'

Three days later, the revolutionary radicals, who now called themselves Bolsheviks, were in a meeting when Okhranka agents burst in to arrest them. But some escaped the police dragnet and rallied a crowd of 200,000 – including, for the first time, soldiers and students. They marched across the bridges over the frozen Neva; to avoid roadblocks, thousands crossed on the ice. Destiny, and the refusal by General Khabalov to fire on them and to break up the ice, was in their favour. Word spread that the soldiers of the Preobrazhenski Regiment were with the people. 'Now even the Turks will have reason to laugh at us,' said old Count Alexei Petrovich. At around 9.30 a.m. he was sitting in the

Astoria lobby, reading his newspaper, when he saw a mob approaching along the boulevard. Then the revolving glass door of the hotel's entrance was smashed in with a rifle butt and someone yelled: 'There's one of them!' The old count was slammed back into his seat by the impact of the bullet. He was the revolution's first victim. Another mob rushed towards Znamenskaya Square and the Nicolaev Railway Station, where they ran into machine-gun fire. On Nevsky Prospect, a mob was mowed down by the Pavlovsky Regiment. The crowd collected their martyrs and carried the blood-splattered corpses through the streets of Petrograd. A battalion received an order to fire on them; instead, the soldiers turned on their commander, Colonel Eksten, and hacked him to death. More troops, who were there to protect the city from riots, joined the insurgents. At Tsarskoe Selo, the tsar's residence fifteen miles from Petrograd, the Romanov girls looked through their frosted windows on a peaceful park covered in snow. While bloodshed erupted in the city, the imperial family was out of touch with the explosive situation, as was Tsar Nicholas hundreds of miles away in Mogilev.

That night the telegraph lines hummed from Petrograd to centres across Russia. Rioting spread to Moscow where a crowd pulled down the giant statue of Tsar Alexander III, and then cheered when children peed on its crowned head, lying broken in the gutter. In Petrograd, the disorders began to take on serious proportions. Armed gangs roamed the streets, smashing shop windows and helping themselves to luxury goods; the bar of the Astoria was emptied of its vodka. Along Nevsky Prospect a hysterical mob chased after a cavalry officer and lynched him. The garrison of the Peter and Paul fortress released all their prisoners. By 1.30 p.m. most army units had gone over to the revolution. Commandeered taxis raced along fashionable boulevards, loaded down with rioters who waved their rifles and yelled from the top of their voices: '*Svoboda! Svoboda!* Freedom!' The Duma was in a state of

shock; a new panic erupted every thirty seconds. Some ministers begged the revolutionaries for protection from the street
mob. Mikhail Rodzianko, as head of the government, ordered
General Khabalov to re-establish order by whatever means
necessary. The general replied that he had no more troops
he could trust. Rodzianko cabled the tsar in Mogilev:

'SITUATION SERIOUS. MUST FORM NEW GOVERNMENT IMMEDI-
ATELY. RODZIANKO.'

Too late, Rodzianko was out and Kerensky, the Menshevik,
was in. Kerensky, with his hand stuck inside his coat like an
imitation Napoleon, Kerensky who could talk the hind legs
off a donkey, that same Kerensky had to act quickly. By
playing along with the Workers Soviet – in his bourgeois
mind a disgusting rabble who smelled of garlic and belched
out *Svoboda* – he had woken a dragon and now the monster
had to be destroyed. Without representation in the Duma,
getting the members to agree to a political settlement could
be tricky. The Soviet had already issued Order No. 1, telling
the soldiers to ignore their officers and ordering them to
form revolutionary councils, elect committees, and only obey
orders from the Soldiers Soviet. Kerensky and his fellow
liberals had opened Pandora's box and let its evils out.
Suddenly it was no longer the bourgeoisie who controlled
events, but the voice of the streets. The sacred halls of the
Duma had taken on the aspect of a railway station waiting
room on the wrong side of the Urals. The common man had
entered the sacred hall and brought with him his arms, his
sweat, and his disorder. A few deputies cowered in a distant
corner. Kerensky managed to fight his way to the speaker's
podium and played his trump card: he threatened to resign
unless all political exiles were returned from Siberia, a move
that he knew would earn him cheers from the Workers and
Soldiers Soviet. He became the man of the hour when he
offered to form a Provisional Government of Salvation. To
make this possible, the tsar had to go!

The person so much on the mind of the new strongman had boarded his imperial train to rush him from Mogilev to the side of his beleaguered family. In doing so, he isolated himself from both his army and his government. There was neither telephone nor telegraph on the train, and the stations along the way were in the hands of the revolutionaries – as were the switching controls. And so the tsar set out on a journey that meandered up and down the Russian countryside. He called on General Nicolai Ruzski, commander of the northern armies. The general was non-committal when he should not have been. (Eventually, the Bolsheviks captured and shot him.) While the imperial train crawled along at a snail's pace and rebels changed the points making it steam around in circles, His Imperial Highness was left in total ignorance of the political situation. It came as complete surprise to him when he was handed a telegram which suggested his immediate abdication:

'DEMANDS FOR AN ABDICATION IN FAVOUR OF YOUR SON ARE HARDENING.'

An alternative was that 'the old despot who brought the country to utter ruin would be deposed by force'. A delegation selected by Kerensky was dispatched to intercept the tsar's train and to prevent Nicholas from reaching loyal army units.

Pskov, 2 March 1917. Nicholas's nightmare voyage was quickly coming to an end. That evening he sat down in his carriage and wrote in his diary: 'All around me is treason, cowardice and falsehood.' Railroad workers had disconnected his coach and he passed the night in an unheated compartment. He woke to the sound of a whistle of a train steaming into Pskov Station. Two men got off: Vasily Shulgin, a monarchist deputy turned Kerenskyite, and Alexander Gruchkov, another deputy who was appalled by the insurrection. They were faced with an impossible task: the only way to save Russia from total anarchy was for Nicholas to go. Contrary to Kerensky's directives, Gruchkov and Shulgin knew that the country couldn't exist without a tsar – Nicholas had to make room for his son Alexei. That needed the tsar's agreement; only he could now save Russia.

The tsar, dressed in a grey Circassian long-coat, stepped out and simply nodded to the delegation. The three sat down around a table in the parlour car. Tea was served, that sacred ceremony that neither war nor revolution could extinguish. The parliamentarians outlined the critical situation, and begged the tsar to abdicate in favour of his son. The tsar looked dismayed. 'I shall give some thought to your demand.'

Gruchkov rubbed his hands together nervously: 'Your Majesty, for this there is no more time.'

'You cannot expect me to take an immediate decision.'

Shulgin: 'I'm afraid we must insist.'

It was now 1 p.m. on 2 March 1917 (15 March, according to the Gregorian calendar). Nicholas retired to his private car from where he sent a telegram to Rodzianko (since he did not recognise Kerensky) in which he agreed to the formation of a new government under Prince Grigori Lvov. Inside the coach, Gruchkov turned to Shulgin whose face showed the stress he was under. 'What does he care – he has been abdicating ever since he's become tsar. All he can think of is his own family.'

Nicholas returned, his face pale, but he seemed calm. Perhaps he had still not grasped the seriousness of the situation.

'Sire, you must act, time is running out.'

'Do you think it could have been avoided?' asked the tsar.

The parliamentarians looked at each other, stunned! A true monarch, who could still count on a vast number of loyal troops who were well trained and equipped, superior to anything the rabble could put up . . . Another tsar would have ordered his units to put down the mutiny, hang the mutineers, and re-establish order. Of course, blood would be spilled – it was unavoidable in order to save the country.

It called for a hard man to make a hard choice. And now this despicable weakling was asking whether it could have been avoided!

'A few years ago, yes; a few months ago, maybe; but not today,' replied Shulgin.

Just before 3 p.m. the Hughes telegraph spilled out Petrograd's reply: 'THE TSAR MUST GO. KERENSKY.' For Nicholas it meant the end. His conscience would not allow him to admit that he hated himself for his failure to make hard and fast decisions. He hoped that with his sacrifice he could save his beloved country from further bloodshed. Back in his private coach, he picked up a silver-framed photograph of his family and studied it for a long time. He was so lucky; he had his pretty daughters, just like the girls one meets at an English tennis party. He sighed and called his secretary to dictate a letter of abdication:

> . . . In these decisive days in the life of Russia, We thought it Our duty of conscience to facilitate for Our people the closest union possible and a consolidation of all national forces for the speedy attainment of victory. In agreement with the Imperial Duma We thought it well to renounce the Throne of the Russian Empire and to lay down Our supreme power . . . May the Lord God help Russia!
> (Signed): Nicholas. 2 March 1917, 3.05 p.m.

It can be said that in the final moment of his reign Nicholas showed more energy than he did while ruling the empire. 'There must be another tsar, there has always been a tsar, and there always will be one,' he said as he handed over his message to be telegraphed to Petrograd. But even with his last act he committed an error. Instead of handing the throne to Alexei, who was innocent, Nicholas abdicated in favour of his brother, the Grand Duke Mikhail. The tsar had wasted his last chance; Gruchkov and Shulgin had lost, and with them, Russia. 'God protect Mother Russia,' said a dejected Shulgin. Kerensky would have none of it: no more tsars! Within the hour he forced Grand Duke Mikhail to sign a denouncement manifesto: ' . . . I ask all citizens of the Russian State to obey the Provisional Government which has formed and been invested with complete power . . . (Signed): Mikhail.'

With the Romanovs' abdication, a relative calm returned. Relative – because much worse was yet to come, but that was no longer of the tsar's making. Nicholas returned to Tsarskoe Selo to his family and a life of imprisonment, surrounded by hostile guards. With all his political acumen, Kerensky failed to see the looming danger to his bourgeois dictatorship. 'I'm not going to die like Marat in his bathtub,' he said, carried along on a wave of power. He was more preoccupied with the spectre of a monarchist-renaissance than the increasing threat from the Bolshevik ultras. Kerensky and the Duma replaced the Imperial Presence as the controlling body of Russia. This parliament was made up of several major parties, the Octobrists (landowners), Cadets (Constitutional Democrats), Social Revolutionaries (with a terrorist tradition), and Mensheviks (a splinter group from the Social Democrats). Sitting on their left was a minute representation from a new political formation: the Bolsheviks, an extremist offshoot from the Social Democrats, prepared to resort to any kind of violence in order to gain power and willing to sign an armistice with Germany. That is why they were also called the defeatists.

By June the city was flooded with thousands of deserters shouting 'Doloi Voiny! . . . Down with the war!' In no time, everyone yelled 'Doloi Voiny!'; striking workers from Vyborg factories, mutinous sailors from Kronstadt naval base, entire regiments refusing to go to the front all yelled 'Down with the war!' Rebellious units occupied the railway stations; roadblocks closed the bridges across the Neva. Shooting broke out between Cossacks and armed gangs. But the rebellion lacked either unified leadership or a spokesman to incite the *seryi liud* (commoners) to join in. Supported by loyal units, the Provisional Government put down the July uprising. Kerensky had bought time. But the problem did not go away; it went underground, while hunger invaded the cities, profiteering reached new heights, and more soldiers died at the front. Russia waited for someone to take up the torch.

In New York, few had taken notice of the smooth-talking Jewish immigrant until he began writing in *Novy Mir*, an émigré paper. His circle of action widened; he gave lectures about the growing power of the proletariat. His exposés produced the same impact as a stone thrown into 'a puddle of pompous frogs'. Trotsky became despondent over the mental quality and courage of American socialists. Labour leaders shunned 'the Jewish upstart who wants to muzzle in on our turf'. Cartoons appeared in local papers of Leon Trotsky as the very caricature of the revolutionary: a heavy shock of curly hair the colour of painted cast iron; a prominent nose; protruding, fat lips framed by a black moustache and goatee; and thick, steel-rimmed glasses. Until the national press discovered that this fast-talking stranger was magnetic and irresistible, and that his quotes made for excellent copy. 'Europe is a powder keg ready for social revolution. The Russian proletariat will drop a torch into it. Just to suppose that it will cause no explosion is to go against the laws of historic logic.'

He wanted to be there when the explosion took place. He decided it was time to go, following a lecture, after which a twenty-nine-year-old Bolshevik, Nikolai Bukharin, begged him to renew his contact with the party he had abandoned since his split with Lenin in London. In March 1917, Trotsky sailed from New York aboard the *Christianafjord*. British naval police arrested him in Halifax and put him into a concentration camp for captured German U-boat crews, in order to stop this defeatist on his way to join the Movement for Peace with Germany. Russia was England's valuable ally, pulling many German divisions away from the Western front. In the compound, Trotsky proved so convincing a speaker that he converted the imprisoned sailors to Socialism, much to the annoyance of their Prussian officers. To their immense relief, Trotsky was released and continued his voyage to the farewell cheers of the German sailors.

Another protagonist had also returned to Russia. Nicolai Lenin arrived to a tumultuous welcome by his followers. Standing atop an armoured train at Finland Station in Petrograd, he shouted: 'Long live the worldwide Socialist Revolution!' Kerensky accused Lenin of being an agent provocateur in German pay, since the Germans had delivered him by sealed train to the Russian border in order to foment unrest and pull Russia out of the war. Lenin fled back to Finland and the extremists were again without a leader.

Not for long, however because Trotsky was now back in Russia. Without much ado, he waded into the Duma, ignoring the right-wingers and addressing himself directly to the deputies from the Bolshevik Soviet of soldiers, peasants, and intellectual leftists: 'Don't trust the bourgeoisie, rely only on your own strength.' With Lenin still invisible, Zinoviev and Kamenev at loggerheads, Bukharin too unstable, and that new face, Joseph Stalin, too coarse and callous, Trotsky represented the public image of Bolshevism. The word got around that, as Bolsheviks go, Leon Trotsky was worse than anything the Duma had met so far. He accused Kerensky of leading a government of national treachery, of warmongering for the benefit of profiteers, and of using the bony hand of hunger to suppress the proletariat. Kerensky countered by promising elections, a ploy that was of no use to the Bolsheviks since they could not possibly win an overall majority. Therefore, if an armed coup was the only alternative, it had to take place *before* the elections.

Day after day, Trotsky stood on his favourite park bench and inflamed the masses. 'Who is the root of our misfortunes? The bourgeoisie – think only of the wealth that passes through the hands of these parasites.' The crowd growled in anger. 'Who creates this wealth? Who ploughs the earth, who mines the treasures, who sweats and slaves on the machines?' The growl increased to a jeer. 'Who creates the world they enjoy and feed off?' And the damned of the earth roared: 'Down with the bourgeoisie!' The country reeled on the brink of chaos. Banks closed, wages were paid with worthless paper money, and strikes took on unmanageable proportions. Anarchy raged in the countryside; farmers, armed with pitchforks, ganged up with deserters to kill landowners. The army, sent in to establish order, disobeyed their officers and participated in the looting and killing. Lynch law became the only kind of justice. Disorder spread like a infectious disease; the empire was breaking up into nationalistic splinter groups. The Ukraine, Belorussia, the Baltic States, even Siberia – all demanded their constituent assemblies. Don Cossacks and Mongols, Orthodox and Muslims, Tartars and Jews called for autonomous regions. Kazakhstan organised a Muslim army. Siberian troops ran amok and killed their commanders. The country was ripe for a change.

Beset by internal pressure, Kerensky's phobia of a monarchist revival turned into a fixed obsession. The ousted tsar's continued presence in Tsarskoe Selo had become a major issue in the ongoing struggle between the dual seats of power, the Provisional Government, who tried to calm it, and the Soviet Workers and Soldiers Assembly, who asked for nothing less than the tsar's head. 'Nicholas II has inherited from his ancestors not only a giant empire, but also a revolution. And they did not bequeath to him one characteristic that would have made him capable of governing an empire, or even a province of a country,' was Trotsky's vociferous attack. 'Getting rid of him won't lose us anything, keeping him will bring back the monarchy.'[6]

Foreign pressure was growing. The tsarina was George V's cousin, and the British government watched the precarious situation of Russia's imperial family with concern. They proposed to send a cruiser to Murmansk, and even obtained a promise of safe conduct from the German Kaiser in order to save his cousin Nicky. Kerensky's foreign minister expressed his concern: 'We must get the tsar to safety.' Allowing the tsar to go into foreign exile could spell danger of a monarchist comeback. And while Kerensky hesitated, the English withdrew their offer of asylum. Meanwhile, trainloads of deserters were streaming back from the front. For the Mensheviks, the situation turned from confused to outright dangerous. Kerensky summoned his inner council for advice. 'We must act to appease the workers and soldiers,' they advised. 'Damn the Soviet and their agitating Jew – you'll see, this idiot will hang himself.'

Another added: 'Trotsky has brains and what is more, he represents the uniting element. Throw him a bone, exile him.'

Kerensky looked at them, his mouth agape. 'What, Trotsky?'

'Not Trotsky – the tsar. That should calm that nefarious Jew. After that, strike him down, smash him and his mad dogs.'

Kerensky finally notified the ex-tsar that his government had chosen Tobolsk in Siberia as the monarch's 'temporary residence'. He justified this step with the danger to the tsar's family. 'It's a refuge, not an exile.' He was trying to show an honest face, but his half-truth, more distasteful than a lie, was a political expediency. Tobolsk was miles from anywhere, a sleepy backwater east of the Ural Mountains. The only way to

---

[6] Quoted in Trotsky's *History of the Russian Revolution*.

reach it was by steamer – as long as the river was not frozen, which it was for at least seven months of the year. Kerensky issued strict orders to the train guards to remain on their best behaviour. 'Do not step on people when they are down.' He was to remember his warning.

On 1 August 1917, the family's exit from the palace of Tsarskoe Selo had something of a regal ceremony. At the station, Kerensky bowed stiffly to the tsar. The family entered a railway carriage, and the train with its blinds drawn and marked 'Japanese Red Cross Mission' left for Siberia. Four days later the train crossed the Ural mountain range. From Tyumen, the family boarded the river steamer *Russia*. They remained on deck, admiring the vastness of their country which they had never seen before, its unending forests of pine and birch. When they arrived in Tobolsk, the whole town lined up on the riverbank to stare at them, not hostile, not cheerful, only curious, as if looking at stuffed animals in a museum. The family was put up in Freedom House, formerly the governor's residence, a white, two-storey brick building. To the children, used to the wide spaces of Tsarskoe Selo, it had all the appearance of a prison. Their parents were given a room on the first floor; there was a maid's room for Tsarevich Alexei; and the girls had one room with flowered wallpaper between them. For an illusion of privacy, they curtained themselves off with bed sheets. Hot water was a rarity and had to be shared.

Freedom House was not the Alexander Palace, and Tobolsk was not Petrograd. Here, people ate dried fish, smoked shag rolled in newspaper, and drank vodka greedily from cupped hands. But it was far off the beaten track and produced a false feeling of security. Nicholas never gave up hope that their loyal friends would come soon to deliver them from their Siberian confinement. Then what? Perhaps via the Trans-Siberian Railway to Vladivostok, and from there to Japan. Their movements were not restricted, but without outside help they had no means of making good their escape. Also, the tsarevich's health was rapidly fading. He shrank to a mere skeleton, unable to walk. Dr Botkin, who had faithfully followed the family into exile, could not stop the child from haemorrhaging.

In Siberia, a group of loyal officers were meeting in the temporary HQ of General Koltchak. 'We must liberate His Majesty and form a new monarchy. The troops will do whatever we tell them.'

'Many of my units have been infiltrated by agitators,' said another.

'I think I'd even get to love Kerensky if he were to shoot all those Bolshie troublemakers. There are more than fleas on a dog.'

'Let the Bolsheviks take care of the Mensheviks,' offered Koltchak's chief-of-staff. 'Once Kerensky is out, and the Bolshies take power, they won't last a week.'

Russia marched towards a self-fulfilling prophecy. The news from the front was disheartening, but not due to a renewed German attack. The Germans did not have to move; they simply waited for the Russian army to disintegrate. 'They tell us, we are at war with the Germans,' agitators exclaimed. 'We are at war against the capitalists, and it is no longer up to them to govern us.'

Kerensky helped to contribute to the radicalisation process; with his broken promises he fuelled the explosion throughout Russia for which history would not forgive him. He and his Mensheviks did not see the squalor in the city slums, only a stone's throw away from their splendid residences along the Neva. They failed to recognise the profound change in the people and ignored the fact that these slums had become the ideal breeding grounds for yet another, more terrifying revolution. The bourgeoisie thought that the leftist dogma of 'you starving masses rise from their slumber' was just so much window-dressing. What a silly idea; all masses behaved like sheep! Bolsheviks thought otherwise; with a 'Power to the masses!' they expected to seize centre-stage.

They were to succeed beyond their wildest dreams. In a shouting match on the Duma floor, delegates from the Burzhui majority called Trotsky 'a callous bandit chieftain of a group of hooligans'. He replied: 'We know that this Government of National Treachery prepares to flee and open this city to bourgeois adventurers.' He hid his party's weakness behind a bold phrase: 'The people are with us!' And with that, the sixty-six-member minority of Bolsheviks walked out of the proceedings. 'Good riddance,' shouted the 500 majority delegates. They did not know that Trotsky and his followers were headed straight for the barricades. With the prospect of having to suffer through another terrible winter, the patience of the factory workers snapped. Neglected for too long, Russia's degraded proletariat was about to capture the attention of the Provisional Government, and with it, the world. The Bolsheviks knew that machine-guns in the hands of insubordinate troops spoke a language more persuasive than the empty phrases of parliamentarians. Trotsky began to put into practice his 'illusion of the truth'; he gave the masses what they most wanted to hear: 'Peace to the army, factories to the workers, land to the peasants.' He was cheered and hoisted onto shoulders. A leader figure was born.

Across the Finnish border, Lenin watched Trotsky's ascension with an apprehensive eye. In order to claim his leadership position, he slipped across the Finnish-Russian border. The fateful meeting of the Bolshevik Inner Council or, as it was soon to become known, the Central Committee, took place on 10 October 1917. Fate played into their hands. A German offensive captured the major Baltic port of Reval. The Bolsheviks cleverly pounced on this opportunity. 'Patriotism to the proletarian state is a revolutionary duty, whereas patriotism to the bourgeois state is treachery.' This thinly disguised Bolshevik call to arms resulted in the formation of a Military Revolutionary Committee or *Milrevkom*, which would become the military arm of the October Revolution. Undoubtedly, one of Trotsky's greatest achievements was a series of committees to influence, and control, the masses. 'The Action Committees will help us to pass from spontaneous violence to organised violence.' He recognised that the coming crisis was not a contest for executive power, but a rebellion arising from despair over a murderous war, from famine in the cities, and from the oppression of serfdom. His Action Committees had only to throw out a bridge to the disenchanted, to establish a common ground between the proletariat and the Bolsheviks, who could then channel the frustrations of the masses into a purposeful political direction. The success of the revolution depended on it. For a man so astute, Kerensky got it all wrong – he was worried that a Bolshevik uprising would lead to a monarchist counter-coup. He was confident that he held at his disposal more than enough strength to crush any insurrection.

The October Revolution – or Red October – was an amateurish affair which took everyone by surprise, most of all those who had conspired to make it happen. The Bolsheviks came to power with less than 5 per cent of the garrisoned strength of one key city. That it did succeed was mostly due to two men: Leon Trotsky, and his skill as an orator, and Lenin, whose cold-blooded stand during the crucial hours made all the difference. Their support came from a population that clamoured for food and peace. Military strategy for the planned Bolshevik *coup d'état* had been entrusted to Vladimir Ovsenko. He knew from experience that it was vital to capture the nerve centres of a city, such as transport, newspapers, bridges, and main intersections. He need to control the rail stations and the telephone exchange, electricity plants and water pumping stations, and to take into custody as many members of the cabinet as possible. Everything was planned down to the smallest detail, and special action units were assigned for each designated point. No target was overlooked – except one. For the Smolny Institute, a fancy academy for the daughters of the super-wealthy, he failed to assign a guard. And yet the Smolny was the heart of the entire operation, as it contained the Bolshevik co-ordinating headquarters with all its leaders.

The crucial day, 6 November 1917, began without great furore. Mid-morning, a few dozen workers, directed by professional agitators, came out into the street to protest against the Provincial Government's failure to provide food. Red militants formed strike committees and a few picket lines were set up. A small police detachment arrived on the scene, took one look at the crowd, and decided this was too big to handle. At the Mariinsky Palace, Kerensky announced: 'The Bolsheviks have put out a call for insurrection. Let it be clear that the Provisional Government will defend the people of Petrograd against the mob of the streets.' He telephoned Colonel Vassiliev, commanding the Peter and Paul fortress, and a voice answered: 'This is Blagonravov, head of the Soldiers Soviet. We execute only the orders of the Revolutionary Council.' Blagonravov then trained his eighty Colt machine-guns at the city.

Trotsky climbed onto an equestrian statue of some tsarist general who pointed his sabre towards a distant God, probably imploring his help to deliver him from the pigeons nesting on his head. Trotsky's first words were greeted with whistles, catcalls, and shouts of: 'Bloody Bolshevik!' It is a compliment to Trotsky's great gift that he managed to swing the crowd onto his side. Like Mark Antony's famous speech to Rome's Senate, he began his harangue in a calm tone before building up to a fever pitch.

'When a people has suffered too long, then time has come to say no. And the Russian people have suffered too long. This morning they said no! This morning they have come out

into the streets to demand an end to a murderous war.' The
first yelled: 'He's right! End the war!' Others screamed: 'Shut
up! He is like all the others, full of empty words.' Trotsky
remained undisturbed, thriving on the adrenalin of argument.
'We say, let this war end! Bring back our sons, our loved ones;
bring them back from the blood-soaked trenches before they
are sacrificed! Millions in every part of our Mother Russia
want this, and millions are on our side. Throw out the clique
of warmongers and profiteers, who continue a bloody war
for nothing but personal gain. Never trust what they say, for
no oppressor will ever tell the truth to the oppressed!' How
true a prediction. Trotsky knew that he had scored no small
victory. Perhaps these men and women would not come out
in their support, but they most certainly would not hinder
the struggle.

Curiously, life in the city was going on as if nothing
noteworthy was taking place. Trams worked, electric mar-
quees blinked outside cinemas, and Fjodor Chaliapin was
singing the title role in *Boris Godunov*. On the night of
6–7 November 1917, Petrograd celebrated its final 'Dance
on the Volcano'. The *maradiors* (speculators) enjoyed a spicy
kharcha (sausage) at the Bear Restaurant; high-priced prostitutes strolled with officers on Vosnesensky Prospect; and
an after-opera crowd swilled champagne at the Astoria. That
night, Lenin wrote a final note. 'It is clear to all of us
that everything hangs on a hair, that our order of the day
cannot be solved by committee, but only by armed masses.
In all circumstances, we must overthrow the government this
morning, or risk losing all.' Near midnight, Lenin rose, put
on his coat and cap, and with his friend Rahja stepped out
into the deserted street. Suddenly from around a corner
rode two Cossacks who threatened them with their *nagaika*
(horsewhips) and arrested them. On the inspiration of the
moment, Rahja played drunk and stumbled into a Cossack's
horse; Lenin ducked into a side alley and disappeared into the

safety of darkness. How history could have been changed by two Cossacks. In a few minutes it would be Wednesday, 7 November 1917.[7]

Petrograd woke up to find the streets covered in slush. The seventh of November was Leon Trotsky's birthday; he was thirty-eight today, but nobody brought him a cake. A platoon from the Oranienbaum Regiment entered the Rabochy Put and Soldat printing plants and smashed plates and presses. 'The newspaper must go out,' ordered Trotsky, quite content that the opposition had foolishly launched an assault. This would legalise the Bolsheviks' claim of acting in 'defence against the villainous conspiracy'. To protect the presses, he called on the soldiers of the infiltrated Lithuanian Regiment, while the radio transmitter of the cruiser *Aurora*, in the hands of rebellious sailors, sent out a continuous stream of calls to arms. 'The people's enemies have taken the offensive during the night. Put your units on alert and wait for further instructions from *Milrevkom*.' Red Guards took over the Nicolaev Station and the Potemkin Palace, sailors from the *Aurora* jumped the eleven teenage cadets defending the strategic Nicolaev Bridge.

Lenin was at the Smolny. Kerensky cut the telephone lines into the Smolny and called up his 23rd Don Cossacks. They found the rail lines blocked by derailed wagons. Cut off from all communication lines, Felix Dzerzhinski handed a hastily scribbled paper to two men who happened to be dawdling in the corridor. 'Your signed order to take over the telephone exchange. Re-establish communications.' The two rushed off and presented the paper to the baffled guards at the telephone exchange entrance, before forcing their way into the main operation room with its many hand-operated switchboards. The lines to the Smolny were back in operation. Warsaw Station fell into the hands of the insurgents without a struggle.

[7] According to the old Russian or Julian calendar, this date falls on 25 October, so the events became known as 'Red October'.

Meanwhile, the Smolny Institute – a squat grey building which looked more like a museum than a revolutionary command post – was guarded by one solitary teenage youth. Any group of loyalists could have marched into the building and bagged the entire Bolshevik leadership. It was only a stone's throw from the Central Police Building and yet, nothing happened and no troops appeared.

At the Duma, a Committee for Salvation ordered that the riots be suppressed with the dreaded Bronniviki, armoured cars with mounted machine-guns, the perfect instrument for breaking up demonstrations. Trotsky dispatched a young ensign, Nicolai Krylenko, to stir up trouble among the tank crews. 'The government is in your hands, Great Russia is yours, don't give it back,' Krylenko argued. The tank crews took a vote and decided 'not to give Great Russia back'. Their commander, who pleaded with them to support the legal government, was shot.

Mid-morning, news reached the Smolny that the 5th Motorcycle Battalion of the feared Savage Division was on its way into the city. Sverdlov ordered one of his ablest agitators to stop them. If proof were needed of the power of the word over the force of a gun, it was demonstrated in the next few minutes. With only a few men, Comrade Ordzhonikidze blocked their route and harangued the heavily armed motorcyclists. 'Power has passed to the Soviet. The entire Petrograd garrison has switched over to the revolution. Your intervention will cause only unnecessary bloodshed.' As the motorcycles halted in the outskirts of Petrograd, the Duma doors were flung open and Red Guards entered the sacrosanct hall. A commissar rushed up to the desk of Assembly President Avxentiev: 'This meeting is closed!'

Until now, the *coup d'état* had been accomplished with very little bloodshed. Orders to the Red Guards were to arrest all Kerensky ministers, but that assignment was bungled and not a single top official was detained. Neither were any attempts made to arrest Kerensky, or to occupy his offices at the Winter Palace. Without consulting the Military Revolutionary Council, Lenin drafted a note which was immediately broadcast by the radio transmitter aboard the *Aurora*: 'Citizens of Russia! Power of the state has passed into the hands of the Military Revolutionary Committee, which is at the head of the proletariat.'

The elite Cossacks of the 1st, 4th and 14th Regiments took a vote and decided to remain neutral. When informed of the Cossacks' decision Kerensky handed command to Admiral Verderevski, but Verderevski refused the dubious honour. He sat on the fence, to his own loss. The revolutionaries would soon shoot him off his perch. Trotsky made his way with great difficulty through the milling delegates at the Smolny. 'Comrades!' He had to yell a few times to silence the bedlam. 'Comrades! The Kerensky government no longer exists.' He held up his arms in an attempt to make himself heard over the cheering and pointed towards the door. 'Comrades! Among us on this historic day is Comrade Lenin.' Caps flew into the air as the hall erupted in an ovation. Lenin, small and well shaved, entered the room and climbed on the stage. The hall fell silent.

'Comrades! The Workers and Peasant Revolution, which we of the Bolshevik Party have called for, is achieved. The old government apparatus has been smashed. The bourgeoisie will never be allowed to participate in a government of the Soviet. A new era has come.'

The despondent Kerensky had disappeared. To avoid Russian bloodshed, when pressed by his subordinates for drastic action, he could come to no decision. Kerensky was just another weak man, and with his weakness, Russia was doomed. (In 1970, shortly before his death in New York, Kerensky stated: 'We were too naïve.') Lenin was giving an interview to a friendly foreign journalist, John Reed. 'The old state apparatus is being uprooted and a new machinery created,' he declared, but did not say what or by whom. The entire operation began to look like 'the changing of the guard, but lacking in its military precision'. Gunboats, supposed to bring back the mutinous sailors of the Baltic fleet, never arrived because, on his way to organise it, the Bolshevik Pavel Dybenko's car ran out of petrol.

Lenin ordered a siege of the Winter Palace, a potent symbol like the Berlin Wall so many years later. This monumental, squat building of 1,000 rooms and 2,000 windows was defended by 800 teenage cadets and a women's battalion. The signal for attack was to be by a red light from the Peter and Paul fortress. However, its Soviet commander could not find a red lamp. Eventually his guns fired two shells, which missed the huge structure by several hundred yards, and the guns of the *Aurora* thundered a few rounds in the direction of the palace. As the ship had just completed its repairs and carried no live ammunition, the guns actually fired blanks. Thousands of wildly shooting Red Guards rushed forward. Bullets zinged along corridors, blood flowed down the monumental staircase, holes appeared in oil paintings and mahogany panelling. One final door, and the first Red Guards burst into the Malachite Room. Inkbottles had been spilled on the green carpet; papers littered the floor. Near a large table stood the ministers of Kerensky's Provisional Government. 'In the name of the revolution, you are all under arrest.' The clock on the marble mantelpiece showed 2.10 a.m., 8 November 1917.

'The Winter Palace is ours!' This cry created pandemonium at the Smolny where the Soviet was in session. Over the entrance of the stunningly decorated white and gold ballroom with its plaster cupids and painted ceiling, where noble debutantes were once presented to their equally aristocratic suitors, a strip of red cloth ripped from a ballroom curtain dangled on a broomstick. A blue haze of cigarette smoke pervaded the convention hall, rifles were propped against the wall, and unshaven men in their dirt-stained workman's clothes sat next to soldier-delegates wearing the standard issue peaked caps of the tsar's army. There were delegates from Moscow, the Baltic States, Siberia, and many other parts of the nation. According to a letter from one delegate, they seemed more like a rabble that had crept out of holes and corners than a representation of the Russian people. Everybody claimed for himself the right to speak, and all at the same time. Violent opinions were voiced, some calculated, some spontaneous, all infected by the charged atmosphere. While reformists suggested more modest solutions, the hardcore Bolshevik leadership was for an unrestrained climax to the insurrection. There were premonitions of terror and the dangers of a bloody civil war.

Trotsky called it the most democratic parliament in the history of mankind. Above all, the October Revolution was characterised by this roaring mass of spontaneous committees and assemblies running their own affairs. They installed themselves in classrooms, picked a chairman, and then conducted their business. They had no experience of politics or economics – they knew nothing of revolution and they thought up the most outlandish schemes. In this epoch-making event, many were present at the launching but not many were left at the end.

A grey dawn was rising over Russia. From a distance, Petrograd looked dead. For once, no familiar pall of factory smoke hung over the city. From the top of the Winter Palace fluttered a red flag. Hastily put-up barricades on every major intersection and river crossing stopped all traffic. The worker and soldier brigades marched into a conflict they did not understand, where chaos, violence, and mayhem took the place of the rules of engagement and discipline. 'Many will die very soon,' admitted Trotsky. 'They have no experience and know not what awaits them.'

The majority of citizens looked on and did nothing because

they did not believe that the Bolsheviks could last. At the Smolny everybody awaited the arrival of Lenin, while Trotsky formed a *Soviet Narodnik Komissarov*, a Council of People's Commissars. Its positions were parcelled out: Lenin as chairman, Trotsky in foreign affairs and war, and Stalin in national affairs. This last appointment was a serious mistake, since Trotsky was handing Stalin control over the internal police apparatus. Stalin put Felix Dzerzhinski, a killer loyal only to him, in charge of the Cheka. This man was so paranoid that he ordered the prison guards to change sides of the corridor every two hours, so that they would not get familiar with their prisoners. Kamenev and Zinoviev were relegated to secondary roles. Ryzanov was handed commerce, although he had no previous experience in trading, and Menzhinsky was handed the finance portfolio, because he had been a bank clerk. When a twenty-year-old student stood up to announce that he had written an article about foreign investment, Menzhinsky promptly appointed him director of the State Bank.

The first vote taken by the new Soviet was to abolish the death penalty. The newly elected chairman, Lenin, appeared in a black undertaker's suit with a flowered tie and growled at Trotsky: 'How can you lead a revolution without executions? What other means of repression does this leave at our disposal?' The prison cells changed occupants; Bolsheviks walked out, and the ministers who had ordered their arrest walked in. All that was needed to get a bullet in the neck was to wear a fur coat, the symbol of a profiteer. In a way, Lenin and Trotsky were behaving like cheap Robespierres.

At the Smolny, Lenin announced that he had ordered an immediate cessation of hostilities with the troops of the German kaiser; soldiers flung their caps into the air. 'All private land-ownership is abolished, and without compensation.' This time the cheers came from the peasant delegates. And the sly Trotsky, referring to the disturbing news that Kerensky's Cossacks were marching on the city, quickly added: 'Of course, the lands of the brave Cossacks serving in our revolutionary forces will not be confiscated.' (In fact, these were the first lands to be appropriated by the state.) The delegates voted for the creation of a People's Soviet of one hundred, of which 'only' seventy were Bolsheviks, because it was still too early to push for single-party rule. 'We are for social justice and equality for all.' Soon red flags fluttered everywhere, and the Provisional Government faltered. Lenin and his Red comrades somehow muddled through, although it was more a slinking in through a side door and a slow takeover. 'Power to the Soviet!' was their rallying cry. In Moscow, loyal cadets from the officer training corps stormed the Kremlin. Many people died that day.

At Gatchina, on 11 November, Kerensky finally met up with the Cossack Corps of General Krasnov. By mid-morning, the Don Cossacks had reached Pulkovo Heights, more a hill than a mountain. From there they could have walked into the city and put an end to 'that Bolshevik nuisance'. When cold-blooded action was called for, none was forthcoming. Kerensky was hesitant and refused to give the order for an advance into the city, while Krasnov faced the problem of the low morale of his inactive elite corps. Krasnov ordered an advance, but stopped on the outskirts of the city before hastily thrown-up, flimsy roadblocks. Kerensky was not the man of the hour; Lenin was. He personally supervised what would turn into the crucial show of force. He mobilised everyone at his disposal and sent them 'to the revolutionary front'.

At dawn on 12 November, the decisive battle of the revolution took place. Facing each other were the 700 Cossacks of General Krasnov, well trained and equipped with field artillery. On the other side were 12,000 bayonets in the hands of inexperienced factory workers, four cars with machine-guns, and two small cannons. The first wave of Bolsheviks, about 5,000 strong, advanced slowly in a skirmish line, keeping up a constant fire. They managed to take ten Cossacks as their prisoners. The Bolshevik commander, Pavel Dybenko, decided to extort a quick victory. The prisoners were lined up in plain sight of the Cossack riders and shot, one after the other. It produced an adverse effect. The Cossacks were outraged and charged on their little horses at the Bolshevik lines. They peppered the Red columns, blasted their trucks, and mowed down the men. Their mortar shells hit a pile of ammunition crates, sending zigzagging fireworks into the sky. Groups of terrified Bolsheviks ran, only to be sliced up by vicious Cossack sabres, before the Roughriders from the Don ran into soft, swampy ground. Their horses could no longer advance. Cossacks were horsemen and would not consider anything so base as continuing on foot. They halted, and Kerensky's last counter-offensive fizzled out. It had been too little too late to stop the Bolsheviks. Kerensky fled, and the Bolsheviks took power. Total power.

With the cessation of internal hostilities, the Central Committee ordered the chief of the Russian forces, General Antonin Dukhonin, to propose an immediate ceasefire to the Germans. When Dukhonin refused to betray his country, Lenin put a thirty-two-year-old former schoolteacher and 'revolutionary hero', Ensign Nikolai Krylenko, at the head of Europe's largest armed forces. (He was executed on Stalin's orders in 1938.) Krylenko, a hysteric and soon to be called the 'most repulsive dwarf in Russia', shot the general. Within hours, German and Russian armistice delegates met. As the newly appointed commissar for war, Trotsky headed the Russian delegation. The armistice was signed at the fort of Brest-Litovsk on 3 March 1918. The Russian army dissolved; for them, the war was over. What started now was much worse than anything that had happened to the nation before.

On 6 December 1917, the Bolsheviks declared themselves as the only legal representative body in the country. Their strategy relied on a simple formula: 'Kill the landowners and take away their land.' It was an invitation to murder and pillage, which appealed to the basest instincts. The dispossessed flocked to the Bolshevik movement without having the faintest idea what Bolshevism stood for. The party offered escape. Once in it, they found authority, safety, their own brand of law and order. In the party, a man 'belonged'; his comrades respected him for his courage or his cruelty. Suddenly he was someone important who had found 'his family', and he had to prove his loyalty. His directive was to eliminate the former elite. Trotsky gave these men the signal when he declared: 'There is nothing immoral in the proletariat finishing off the dying class.' The fear and hatred that these killers provoked was very real, although they represented a minute proportion of the population. Night settled over Russia, scores were settled, and people died; shot, bludgeoned, hung, stabbed, burned – slaughtered like cattle. Felix Dzerzhinski, Stalin's brutal henchman, justified the dictatorship of the proletariat: 'We don't need justice, we want to settle accounts.'

Dzerzhinski's notorious Cheka (later the KGB) was the organism for combatting 'counter-revolutionary elements' and it acted as the punitive system of the totalitarian dictatorship, answerable directly to the top leadership of the party. No accurate account exists of how many were tortured, raped, shot. Dzerzhinski, an utterly ruthless man, had appropriated the right to mete out immediate execution without trial. When this was brought up at the supreme council, Lenin refused to discuss the matter. He felt that Dzerzhinski was acting rightly. The Cheka received the official seal of approval when Comrade Sverdlov issued a call for merciless mass terror. This call became known as the Red Terror Decree of 5 September 1918, which stipulated that anyone found, or simply accused of having been, in contact with counter-revolutionaries was to be shot. Dzerzhinski immediately put the decree into action by ordering the execution of 500 hostages.

Suddenly, a new danger loomed from the east in the form of Siberian units loyal to the tsar, promising a revival of the monarchy. This called for the immediate removal of the imperial figurehead, the Romanov tsar.

To the fishermen and fur hunters of Tobolsk, events on the other side of the Urals hardly concerned them. It was winter and it brought Siberian temperatures. News from Petrograd was scarce. They had to depend on a telegraph link which seldom worked once the frost set in, when pylons broke under the weight of snow and metal wires snapped like glass. The imperial family huddled around a metal stove in their living room. The girls occupied their days with needlework; the tsarina read and the tsar took strolls in the woods. On a crisp winter's day, news reached them that Kerensky had been ousted by a group of Bolsheviks under Leon Trotsky and Nicolai Lenin.

The head of the Soviet for the Red Urals, Comrade Sasha Byeloborodov, and the military commissar of the Ural Bolsheviks, 'Filipp' Goloshekhin, heard about a plot to free the tsar. They put the matter of this high-security risk into the hands of his trusted subordinate, Yakov Yurovsky. A secret meeting took place in Moscow to discuss further plans for the tsar. It was decided to send a detachment of 200 armed men to Tobolsk. The man in charge of the unit, Vasily Yakovlev, was told by Sverdlov, Lenin's number two, that the tsar and family had to be brought back to Moscow for increased security. During his briefing, an alternative destination was vaguely discussed should the overall situation become critical: Ekaterinburg.

In Tobolsk, spring was just around the corner. For the first time the imperial family felt the true bite of Bolshevism when Yakovlev arrived from Tyumen, where he was told that White Russian forces under Admiral Koltchak were on their way to deliver the tsar. Yakovlev assured Nicholas that he would be shipped off to Scandinavia. The family was bundled into sledges and the convoy left town at breakneck speed. On 28 April 1918, they reached Tyumen. Yakovlev cabled Sverdlov for instructions, who replied: 'TAKE CARGO TO MOSCOW.' Commissar Sasha Byeloborodov, head of the powerful Ural Soviet, would not hear of relinquishing their 'precious captive'. Nicholas was a pawn in a bargain for increased power. Koltchak's army operated freely in Siberia; the Ukraine had declared its independence on 22 January 1918, followed by Armenia, Azerbaijan, Belorussia, Caucasia, Cossakia, Estonia, Georgia, Latvia, and Lithuania. And so, 'the cargo' never reached Moscow. Its final destination had been changed to 'Red Ekaterinburg' where the family was speedily transferred to the Ipatiev House on Vosnesensky Prospect (Ascension Avenue). Sasha Byeloborodov read out the decree: 'By order of the Central Committee, the former Tsar Nicholas Romanov and his family are transferred to the Ural Soviet and shall henceforth have the status of prisoners.' It was the week of Holy Easter, and Russia was awash with blood. In Ekaterinburg, prisons overflowed and Bolshevik firing squads were ordered to shoot a daily ration of selected prisoners. The cells were permeated by the rancid smells of sweat and fear. Nothing had been decided about their most precious hostage.

Other members of the Romanov family were less fortunate. On 12 June 1918, three Chekists stormed into the Korolev Hotel in Perm. They took Grand Duke Mikhail and his English private secretary, Brian Johnson, to the outskirts of town, where they were shot and thrown down an abandoned mineshaft. The chairman of the Perm Bolsheviks, Myashnikov, who had pulled the trigger, dispatched a telegram to Moscow: 'UNIDENTIFIED MEN DRESSED AS SOLDIERS ABDUCTED MIKHAIL ROMANOV AND HIS SECRETARY. SEARCHES HAVE NOT YIELDED RESULTS. THE MOST ENERGETIC MEASURES ARE BEING TAKEN.'[8]

---

[8] This was revealed in 1965 in a death-bed statement by the second killer, Andrei Markhov.

*   *   *

In their new confines, a one-storey bourgeois residence built
in Russian rococo style, Romanov family ties became stronger
than ever and everyone looked for solace in common prayer.
They erected a small altar and celebrated daily mass. They
were preparing for their 'return to Moscow', but their final
voyage was to be down a much shorter road. To solve the
problem of the imperial family, Commissar Goloshekhin
took a train to Petrograd for a meeting with Chairman
Lenin. Before his arrival, Lenin called a secret meeting of
the Central Committee.

Bukharin: 'The Romanov? You concern yourself about the
life of *one man*?'

Sverdlov: 'It must be legal. He must be charged with
treason . . .'

Lenin needed to feel the pulse of the rest of his committee.
'We must weigh its political consequences carefully . . .'

Trotsky took the bait. 'Why?'

'World opinion . . .'

Trotsky, with a smouldering hatred for the Romanovs
ever since their pogroms in his youth replied: 'We must
put an end to that church babble about the sanctity of
human life!'[9] And so Lenin had his reply from the one who
really counted: Leon Trotsky was with him! It is therefore
clear that it was actually Trotsky who sealed the fate of the
last of the Romanovs when he added: 'The first question to
ask is: what class does the tsar belong in?' One who did
not participate in the heated discussion was the man from
Georgia, Stalin, sitting silently, observing his comrades, and
taking notes about their behaviour for his own future use.
Trotsky was left the final word: 'Once a king is dead, then
there is no way back!'

But what was really decided at this extraordinary meeting,

---

[9] Quoted by M. Latsis, former member of the Cheka board, in *Red Terror*.

nobody knows for certain. Its participants are all dead. No vote was taken and the final decision was left to one man who had a reckless and irrational obsession with doing away with the symbols of Old Russia. Lenin was willing to flout world opinion in the Bolsheviks' quest for absolute power. The drama of the ex-tsar was rushing towards its climax.

A visitor to Ekaterinburg, showcase of Soviet industrial might, originally named in honour of Catherine the Great, will find it a boring industrial site of smokestacks belching their noxious fumes across forests stripped bare by acid rain. But in the hot summer of 1918, it was just a sleepy railway siding on the Trans-Ural Railway, until a single event put it on the map, an event of such infamy that the new regime could not live it down in seventy years of Communist rule. The greatest murder mystery of the century, surrounded by secrecy, myths, and lies. What happened on that hot summer's night in 1918? A vile and stupid deed. An act of cowardice buoyed up by vodka. A crime that proved that hatred did not need an organisation in order to destroy; yet it was the organisation's leaders who ordained it and, by the very act, condemned themselves. Within a short time, most of the executioners were dead, victims of the humiliations they had heaped upon the helpless, victims of others who silenced them to protect a terrible secret. One thing is certain. No act of the Bolsheviks drew more public condemnation than the cold-blooded murder of Tsar Nicholas II, his wife Alexandra Feodorovna, and their children.

Since his arrival at Ekaterinburg, Nicholas's hair had gone white and his eyes had a hopelessly haunted look. He had good reason for despair. His family was now in the hands of the cruel Yakov Yurovsky, whom the tsar called 'the dark man'. The future regicide was the son of a Jewish glazier and a seamstress. He had passed his youth in abject poverty and his family had suffered from hunger. He hated God, the Orthodox Tsar, and his bosses. As chairman of the infamous Revolutionary Tribunal of the Red Urals, he dispatched hundreds to the firing squad. The following incidents give a measure of the man. Whenever the imperial family knelt down for evening prayers, Yurovsky never left the room. On one occasion he allowed a priest in the house to celebrate mass. The presence of the tsar overawed the officiating priest and mistakenly he intoned the psalm: 'Rest in peace with the Saints', which is usually sung only during a funeral. Yurovsky sniggered: 'Good practice.' When he noticed a cross on a thin gold chain which the tsarina had hung over her sick son's bed, he tore it off. Little Alexei was seized with a coughing spell and tears streamed from his eyes. 'Please,' the child pleaded, 'please leave me my cross.' Yurovsky laughed: 'Where you're headed for, you won't need a cross.'

At the end of June 1918, Omsk fell to the White Russian Army and Koltchak advanced from the east on Ekaterinburg. He began his offensive in the hottest days of summer. The Reds fought valiantly, holding their ground to the last bullet. The breakthrough was enough to throw the local Bolshevik Committee into a panic, which led to an argument about the tsar and his family. Goloshekhin arrived back from Moscow and put an end to the suspense; he ordered Yurovsky to search for a suitable burial site, so hidden and so deep that nobody would ever find the Romanovs. 'The family has been evacuated to a safe location,' he was to wire. That safe place would be six feet down. Yakov Yurovsky, accompanied by Pyotr Ermakov, the military commissar for the Issetsk district, and his deputy, the sailor Vaganov, scoured the region for a suitable disposal site. They found one: the Ganina mine in the forest of Koptiaki.

The riddle of the tsar's fate is buried in a three-line telegram. Yurovsky's crucial notes of the telegram were confirmed during the Khrushchev period: EKATERINBURG, 16 JULY 1918. A TELEGRAM HAS ARRIVED CONTAINING THE DECREE TO EXTERMINATE THE ROMANOVS. GOLOSHEKHIN HAS ORDERED THE DECREE TO BE EXECUTED. Whatever cruelty Yurovsky dished out, he was still only a minor cog in a big machine of terror, a sadist who would have never dared to act without strict directives from above. Yurovsky's boss, and the only one from whom he was to take orders, was Comrade 'Filipp' Goloshekhin, and 'Filipp' again waited for the go-ahead from Moscow. It arrived in the form of a message from Zinoviev, a leading member of the Central Committee. This is the wording of that famous telegram:

NO. 14228, 16 JULY, 21.22 P.M.
   TO MOSCOW, THE KREMLIN, SVERDLOV
   COPY TO LENIN
   THE TRIAL AGREED UPON WITH FILIPP [Goloshekhin] DUE TO MILITARY CIRCUMSTANCES CANNOT BEAR DELAY. WE CANNOT WAIT. ON THIS SUBJECT CONTACT EKATERIN-BURG YOURSELF. ZINOVIEV

Who instigated the order for THE TRIAL, code name for murder? Not Zinoviev – he had no anthority for such a step. We must remember that Zinoviev was Lenin's pencil-pusher and that the addition of COPY TO LENIN suggests that it was Lenin himself who asked for a copy of *his own order*. By the address, SVERDLOV, and the wording: WE CANNOT WAIT – CONTACT EKATERINBURG YOURSELF, it becomes clear that it was Sverdlov who passed on the verbal instruction for the family's execution after a lengthy delay. Whom did Sverdlov talk to during these hours? The fact is that this telegram arrived in the Kremlin shortly after 21.22 p.m., or *six hours before* the execution. In other words, if Lenin did not directly order the murder, he certainly knew of the plan and did nothing to stop it!

The callous brutality with which the murder was carried out was certainly of Yurovsky's making. In later years, his savagery was explained away as an act of folly committed by a Jew who was taking revenge for the progroms his people had suffered under the tsar.

The Ipatiev House, 16 July 1918, 8 p.m. It was a stifling hot summer's evening such as only Siberia can produce. The family ate a late supper. Bedridden, Alexei was playing with his favourite toy, a wooden battleship; his sisters sewed before their prayers for the night. Then they all went to bed. They did not know that it was for the last time.

It was 11 p.m. The city of Ekaterinburg crouched in the dark mass of the forest, unaware of the killers who would come at midnight. All was silent inside the Ipatiev House. The irony of it all: it was at the Ipatiev Monastery that the first Romanov, Mikhail, had been anointed with the Russian crown, 304 years before. Now events were about to come full circle. The hallway stank of vodka and stale tobacco. A fly, sluggish in the heat, crawled on the shaven crown of the soldier on guard. He was too tired and too drunk to brush it from his bull-necked head. He burped and took another swig from a bottle before biting off a piece of sausage, heavy with garlic. Then he burped again. From somewhere under the stairs came the laboured snores of a second guard. Earlier that afternoon, the off-duty guards had gone into town to forage for vodka, and ever since then they had been at the bottle. Now they were asleep: the tsar and his family could simply have walked out the front door, and nobody would have stopped them. Nicholas was the last to wash. On his way to his room he looked at the guards Stolov and Proskuryakov oblivious to the world in their filthy tunics. All seemed as usual, and yet tonight something was different. While Bolsheviks such as these two drowned their fear in vodka, the White Army was closing in, that much was certain.

The moment of decision had come, and the ex-tsar must have recognised the pattern of impending tragedy. They had taken from him his empire; now they would take his family and, probably, his life. Yet dying like this might achieve something. The world would awake to the Red Threat and stop the contagious disease of Bolshevism before it had a chance to spread.

The time for the final act had been fixed for midnight. It was well past that hour and Yurovsky waited impatiently. As did Goloshekhin, standing by for his directive from Moscow.

It was 1.30 a.m. Goloshekhin ordered a truck to the Ipatiev House, driven by Sergei Lyukhanov, a trucker from the Verkh-Issetsk factory. The truck reached the Ipatiev House just before 2 a.m. Yurovsky entered the rooms of the imperial family ordering everyone to get dressed and assemble in the courtyard where transport had come to take them away. He explained that anti-revolutionary disturbances had erupted in the town and that their safety could no longer be assured. The tsar picked up his ailing son and carried him in his arms; both were dressed in olive-green soldier's tunics and wore regular issue forage caps from which the insignias had been removed. The tsarina wore a lilac costume; her daughters were in long dark skirts and white blouses. Anastasia carried her little pet dog, Jemmy. Demidova, their chambermaid, clutched a pillow to her bosom.[10] Sewn into it was part of the crown jewels. Stumbling and drunk with sleep, the family was herded across the courtyard. They saw a truck with its motor idling; it reassured them that they were to be taken to the train station. Yurovsky ordered them towards a pair of double doors which led into a dank cellar. Quietly they obeyed and moved down the stairs. The room was narrow, with a vaulted arch on one side and a wooden partition to

---

[10] Demidova was chubby, but the maid who was murdered in the cellar was described as being tall and thin. Therefore, it is not certain that Demidova was actually there that night.

a storage room. When the tsar asked to be allowed to sit down, Yurovsky snapped an order and his deputy, Grigori Nikulin, brought three chairs from upstairs. Yurovsky told the family that their photo was to be taken, and they began to line up.

The scene was indeed like a stage-set for a family photograph. The final one. Framed by the stone arch sat Tsar Nicholas II, ex-Emperor of all the Russias; next to him leaned the ailing Tsarevich Alexei, who threw his father frightened glances and reached for his hand; next to Alexei sat Tsarina Alexandra Feodorovna. She stroked her beloved son's head and murmured calming words into his ear. Behind them, arranged in line, stood their daughters, Olga, Anastasia, Tatyana, and Maria. The family doctor, Dr Botkin, the maid Demidova, and two other servants, the lackey Trupp and the cook Kharitonov, had moved to one side. For several minutes, nothing happened; everything seemed peaceful; but the Romanovs' sense of deliverance was short-lived. Heavy boots tramped down the cellar stairs. Twelve executioners faced the eleven condemned. Nicholas rose, shoulders squared as if about to take a salute by his army, his arm supporting the feeble Tsarevich Alexei. For a sharp-etched moment, the Emperor of all the Russias stood proud and unbroken. Yurovsky took a paper in his hand and began reading the execution order.

> Decree of the Ural Executive Committee of the Soviet of Worker, Peasant and Red Army Deputies. Possessing information that Czechoslovak bands are threatening the people's capital of the Urals, Ekaterinburg, and bearing in mind that the crowned hangman could hide and escape the people's tribunal, the Executive Committee, carrying out the will of the people, has decreed to execute the former tsar, Nicholas Romanov, guilty of countless crimes . . .

The ex-monarch shook his head. 'What? What? Will you repeat it?' he asked.

Yurovsky looked down at his paper, then put it into his pocket. 'In view of the fact that your agents are continuing their attack on Soviet Russia, the People's Committee has decided to shoot you.'

The tsar turned to face his family. 'May the Good Lord have mercy on our souls.'

Pyotr Ermakov pulled his Mauser from a leather holster. But Mikhail Medvedev was faster. The blast from his Browning automatic shook the cellar, a sharp and resonant boom bouncing from the walls. The tsar's body jumped. He uttered no sound as he slid to the stone floor. Shocked by their father's death, the family stared around, pleadingly. 'Oh, my sweet God,' murmured the empress. A shot hit the tsarina. It was the signal for butchery. Like some demonic thunderstorm, an orchestration of screams and shots echoed in the confined room. Revolvers barked, insanely and savagely. A storm of bullets slammed into the imperial family. They were dead before their bodies fell. Pools of fresh blood covered the floor. The shooting stopped as suddenly as it had begun. An exhalation, foul as dragon's breath, hung over the scene, a fog of sulphur and sweetish blood. The killers coughed and their boots slipped in the wetness. Suddenly there was a scream. Demidova, who had been standing to one side, was still alive. 'Use your bayonets,' yelled an agitated Ermakov. The maid was stabbed repeatedly until she lay still. All was over . . . but not quite. A wailing sound echoed through the basement. 'The dog,' yelled the guard Nikulin, 'Anastasia had a little dog.' It was not the dog, but Alexei, the tsarevich. Everyone in the room was shocked to see the boy open his eyes and with his skinny arm reach towards the bloodstained tunic of his father. Grigori Nikulin emptied his entire chamber into the child's head. By having survived his father, if only for moments, Alexei had in fact become the last Tsar of Russia.

The execution commando worked in a frenzy. Andrei Strekotin stripped the women of their jewels, whilst others wrapped the still-warm corpses in pieces of tarpaulin. 'When we laid the lifeless bodies on the stretcher, some of the daughters turned out to be still alive. We couldn't shoot any more, because with the open cellar doors the shots could have been heard. Ermakov took my bayonet from me and began stabbing. When he tried to stab one of the girls, the bayonet wouldn't go through her corset.' This incredible statement by Andrei Strekotin was to lead to the saga of Anastasia's miraculous escape. On the truck's flatbed they covered the Romanov dynasty with a tarpaulin. This was a highly secret operation. Yurovsky was in a great panic and urged the men on, who passed around a bottle of vodka as they worked. (Koltchak's advance guard, the Czech Legion, was by now only miles away, poised to enter Ekaterinburg, which helps to explain their panic.) Ermakov, who was supposed to supervise this part of the operation, had begun to drink heavily. A group under Mikhail Medvedev mopped up the blood from the basement floor. (To remove the incriminating bullet marks entirely, the house was eventually destroyed.) The killer squad dispersed, their part over. Another group was to take care of the disposal of the bodies.

Just before sunrise on 17 July 1918, a lorry sped westwards, its exhaust crackling like gunfire. This angry sound woke up many of the town's people who peered cautiously through the wooden slats of their shutters. They saw several men holding onto the running-boards of a truck, which accelerated past the cracked brick walls of the abandoned Verkh-Issetsk factory and then swung north, across the level crossing of the Trans-Ural rail line. At a storage shed near this railway crossing, the driver Lyukhanov told Yurovsky that he had to stop the truck as its engine was overheating. (This barrier at crossing no. 184 was hand-operated by a man named Lobukin. In April 1919, Lobukin confirmed to Nicolai Sokolov, a White

Russian investigator, the presence of an idling truck near his cabin.) Driver Lyukhanov walked away from the truck, ostensibly 'to fetch water for the radiator'; the guards went behind the shed 'to relieve themselves', but actually to swig from a bottle that one of them had stashed away under his tunic. Ermakov had passed out on top of the bodies, dead drunk. Yurovsky went off in search of his burial detachment which was supposed to meet him at this crossing, but had not as yet materialised. The reason became obvious once he tracked them down: they were all drunk. His search took him half an hour.

What happened in the next hour has become material for mystery books, songs, and films. Because if one of the tsar's daughters did manage to escape, with or without help, or if a switch was made, if . . . if . . . if . . . Then it happened there, at that hut near railway crossing no. 184. It is, however, highly unlikely. The only person who could possibly shed some light on the affair was the barrier-man Lobukin, and if he did know, he took the great secret to his grave.

After a delay of almost an hour the truck moved on. It veered off into the forest, to a clearing known to the local population as the Four Brothers of Koptiaki. In his panic, driver Lyukhanov did not notice a boggy patch on the track and the front wheels got stuck. They were still several hundred metres from the chosen Ganina mineshaft. The bodies were transferred to makeshift stretchers. While they were loading the women on the stretcher, Yurovsky noticed that one girl's corset had been torn open by a bullet and the sparkle of diamonds caught the morning sun. He ordered the girls stripped naked. Eighteen pounds of diamonds and pearls were found sewn into their lining. Yurovsky dispatched the detachment 'to protect the perimeter of the burial site from intruders'. He may have done this because he wanted to recover the diamonds, or perhaps he had suddenly discovered that one or two of the bodies were missing and this would have meant his death sentence. The plausible explanation that he gave his group to send them off was that nobody but those specially cleared were to know the precise site of burial. Only Yurovsky, Ermakov, and Nikulin remained behind, and should something go amiss, they would have to face the same fate as Yurovsky.

In their haste they had forgotten to bring shovels, so they sent Lyukhanov back to town to fetch tools, sulphuric acid, and gasoline. This took some time, and for the rest of the day, they hid out in the woods near the bodies, which they had covered with branches. The next night, they built a pyre made of railroad sleepers that they had found near the abandoned mine, then burned the corpses, and poured acid over the charred bones. Then they dug a round hole, some three feet deep and ten in diameter. There they disposed of the remains. Afterwards they scattered lime and earth over the hole. (Subsequent records made by Yurovsky and Ermakov differed on that. Whilst one said that the corpses were thrown down a mineshaft, the other's story was of burial in a shallow grave. Yurovsky's story of burial has been proved, but does not explain the missing bodies.)

The wind sang mournfully in the tall trees. Behind the ramparts of dark pines and silver poplars, in the bitter, brooding forest, in a shallow, unmarked grave lay the remains of the family of the Tsar of all the Russias. It was as if they had never existed. The killers, and with them all of Russia, walked into a world of infinite darkness.

What next took place has become shrouded in the fog of history. There were no witnesses, at least none who survived for any length of time. Russia's new Red Tsar made sure of it. But even the best-kept secret has its weak spot. A fisherman's wife by the name of Anastasia Zykova had been on her way to town to sell the day's catch. Suddenly, out of the forest galloped two riders. One was a big brute who wore a high-peaked cap with a red star sewn to it. 'Go back where you came from, old woman, just keep on walking and don't look around or I will shoot you.' Before she turned, she saw something big and black coming out of a cloud of dust. It was a truck, which veered off into the forest. The frightened woman ran home and told her husband about the truck. Curiosity got the better of him. The fisherman Zykova, in the company of two more peasants, Nicolas Papin and Pierre Zubritsky, went to take a closer look. They stumbled around the forest near a former mining site and were chased off by one of the guards. Once the Red Guards left the region, farmer Papin went back. This time he took along his son Oleg. They followed deep ruts in the soft ground, which led them to a clearing. There they discovered two piles of ashes and the handle of a hairbrush with the initials A.F. Papin could not read, and was not to know that A.F. stood for Alexandra Feodorovna. But he did recognise something else: engraved over the letters was the imperial crown. The little boy Oleg looked up; he thought he heard a moan. Or was it the wind?

'Don't show this place to anyone, my son, it's haunted by ghosts and evil.'

Down came a red curtain and the mystery was to end there – almost. The place was haunted; nobody dared to go near it, nobody even dared to speak of it. The local fishermen and farmers passed away from old age and the burial site was condemned to oblivion, but for one peasant who had taken his small son Oleg to the clearing and sworn him to secrecy. Sixty-one years later, this Oleg, by now an old man, took two geologists and a local film-maker to the site that he and his father had discovered, so many summers ago.

The Czech Legion of Koltchak's White Russian Army took Ekaterinburg. Yakov Yurovsky made it by the skin of his teeth onto the last train out of town, carrying on him a sealed box with the tsar's personal papers and diaries.[11] His deputy, Grigori Nikulin, escaped in shabby worker's clothes, carrying a canvas bag. It contained the Romanov gems. The White Army found the tsar's prison, the Ipatiev House. They found a pockmarked cellar wall and blood, lots of blood. But no bodies. Their inquiry in the town led to a *tshelovek* (bar waiter) who had overheard one of the Red Guards speak of a mineshaft, the Bolsheviks' favourite type of disposal site. But which one? Open workings were dotted all over the region, many of them flooded.

The execution was confirmed by a copy of a coded telegram:

18 JULY 1918. TO COUNCIL OF PEOPLE'S COMMISSARS PRESIDENT OF THE EXECUTIVE COMMITTEE, COMRADE SVERDLOV THE EXECUTIVE COMMITTEE OF ALAPAYEVSK COMMUNICATES AN ATTACK BY A GANG OF UNKNOWN BANDITS ON THE HOUSE, WHICH HELD AS PRISONERS IGOR CONSTANTINOV,[12] CONSTANTIN CONSTANTINOV, IVAN CONSTANTINOV, SERGEI MIKHAILOVICH AND PALEY. DESPITE THE HEROIC RESISTANCE BY THE GUARDS, ALL PRISONERS WERE ABDUCTED. THERE HAVE BEEN CASUALTIES ON BOTH SIDES. WE ARE CONDUCTING AN INQUIRY. 4853.

The town was scoured for witnesses. One may well imagine the White Army's surprise when they tracked down Proskuryakov, Yakimov, and Letyomin, three of the Red Guards who had been present at the slaughter. All of them had been so drunk that they failed to make their escape in time. The first, Letyomin, was caught because he had attached himself to Anastasia's little dog, Jemmy, and took it to his hut. Thus Jemmy became the only known survivor of the drama.

---

[11] Edvard Radzinsky, *The Last Tsar*.
[12] Code name for Nicholas and family.

All three men talked their heads off, since their fate was a foregone conclusion. What was supposed to be the best-kept secret was speedily revealed.

Fate, and Stalin's secret police, caught up with those who could bear witness to the callous deed, and all were eliminated. Some died right away of 'natural causes', others were rounded up and shot.

Yakov Sverdlov, Lenin's number two, survived the tsar by only a few months.

Pyotr Ermakov, head of the killer detachment, was shot.

Grigori Nikulin, who emptied an entire chamber into the tsarevich, was shot.

Mikhail Medvedev-Kudrin, who claimed to have shot the tsar, was himself shot.

Andrei Strekotin, Alexei Kabanov, and Pavel Medvedev were all shot.

Proskuryakov, Yakimov, and Letyomin were shot.

Six 'Latvian sharpshooters', whose names are unknown, were shot.

The 'Butcher of Sverdlovsk', Yakov Yurovsky, officially 'died of a burst ulcer'.

Commissar 'Filipp' Goloshekhin was shot.

The head of the Ural Soviet, Sasha Byeloborodov, was shot.

Only Sergei Lyukhanov, the man who transported the corpses in the back of his truck, then left his lorry 'to fetch water for the engine', escaped – by remaining on the run. When he died an old man he took with him a great secret.

In utter irony, the town made infamous by the murder was renamed Sverdlovsk as a monument to the man who had butchered the tsar, Yakov Sverdlov. With the demise of Communism, it was the first place to recover its original name, Ekaterinburg.

In 1918, a dissident Socialist Revolutionary woman terrorist,

Fanny Kaplan, shot and seriously wounded Lenin. His health never recovered and he died in 1924. Trotsky, who loved publicity and 'would have willingly died fighting – if there was a big enough audience,'[13] was elbowed aside by the Georgian with the liquid eyes and the cruel mouth, Joseph Stalin. Stalin's Terror began in the late twenties, in what had now become the Soviet Union (the name changed in 1922). His terror was to last for the next thirty-one years during which his sadistic henchmen killed over 20 million Russians.[14] The first to suffer were the land-owning peasants, or kulaks, who were starved to death during the forced introduction of collective farming. Then followed a never-ending string of executions, most of them without trial.

There was a great distinction between the early terror and that of Stalin. Lenin directed his execution orders against a specific class and thus the Russian bourgeoisie ceased to exist, only to be replaced by the party *nomenklatura*, which soon began to act like the tsarist bourgeoisie. Trotsky's target was religion. The state, or the party, was to be the new religion, not the church. Stalin's mania was directed against all those who plotted against him. 'To choose one's victim, to prepare one's plan minutely, to slake an implacable vengeance, and then go to bed – there is nothing sweeter in this world.'[15] For that reason, no one was spared in the days of his Great Terror. It may be seen as ultimate justice that his henchmen were executed by other henchmen who soon thereafter suffered a similar fate. Being a true Bolshevik or, as they were now called, Communist, was never a guarantee of longevity.

Stalin set a process in motion which – once it got going – not even he could stop. High on his hit list were those closest to the seat of power; in other words, closest to him. To his thinking, all were men with sinister intentions ready

---

[13] From an account by Robert Bruce Lockhart, British consul-general.
[14] According to Soviet statistics, based on the Census of January 1959.
[15] Boris Souvarine, *Stalin*.

to destroy his myth. He did not worry about world opinion. The world had ways of shutting its eyes on the ill-fortune of millions. They may have understood the plight of the Russians, but were not especially bothered by a dictator who consolidated his power by piling up corpses. The first wave were party old-timers, such as Kamenev, Zinoviev, and Bukharin. Four NKVD officers shot the trio in a special execution cellar of the NKVD Building on Dzerzhinski Square. A few days later, the executioners were also dead – adhering to Stalin's established policy of no witnesses. 'I prefer people to support me from fear rather than conviction, because conviction can change,' explained Stalin to Genrikh Yagoda, the bloody NKVD psychopath, whom he also had shot. Next was the army. Stalin had the entire general staff executed. The winner took all: control over the party apparatus, over the ethnic regions, over the entire country; even beyond his nation's borders his impact was felt. The increasingly paranoid Stalin suffered from recurring nightmares. There was still one enemy left: Leon Trotsky, who had coined a famous phrase to describe Stalin's rampage: 'The end may justify the means – as long there is something that justifies the end.'

Stalin was a maniacal killer who never forgot the face of an enemy. Especially not one who had once tried to steal his limelight, one whom he only referred to as 'The Yid'. In a Cain-and-Abel syndrome, Stalin and Trotsky shared an equal hunger for ultimate power. To some extent, both believed that a predictable clash between socialism and capitalism would eliminate the capitalist system and lead Communism to world dominance. (As it turned out, the clash was between two similar ideologies, fascism and socialism.)

Trotsky had managed to make his escape from Stalin's Soviet Union across the Turkish border. President Cárdenas of Mexico granted him political asylum in 1937; from there, he intended to cut Stalin down with the weapon he handled so well, the pen. On 20 August 1940, Jaime Ramon Mercader, a KGB agent, planted an ice pick in Trotsky's head.[16]

Trotsky once described Stalin as someone who 'seeks to strike, not at the ideas of his opponent, but at his skull . . .' His prediction came true.

And then . . .

For eighty years, Communism dictated the destinies of half the world's population.

Of the many after-effects of the First World War, the most lasting was the Russian Revolution. Its shock wave spread in ever-widening circles. Coupled with it was the ineptness of the Western democratic powers of the time: England and France were bled white by their casualties and were out of the game, and the American President Wilson proved unwilling to negotiate with Kaiser Wilhelm II. The destruction of Prussia as its eastern bulwark eliminated any arbiter in continental Europe. For the next seventy years, this created global instability, leading to another devastating war and taking the world to the brink of mutual nuclear destruction.

For the people of Russia, the consequences of Red October proved cataclysmic. Christianity was replaced by Communism; its prophet was Karl Marx and his manifesto the new bible. It equated material progress with national happiness and declared the idea of class distinction an outdated notion. The 'dictatorship of the proletariat' (a phrase borrowed from Karl Marx) came into being, and the benevolent autocracy of Nicholas Romanov was replaced by the totalitarian regime of men like Trotsky, Lenin, and Stalin,

[16] Mercader was brought to justice but he never divulged who had ordered him to execute Trotsky. He served twenty years.

where blood and violence became the midwife of history.

Nicholas's weakness brought about his downfall. When firmness was called for, the tsar was unable to use the same savage methods as the men who would kill him without a moment's hesitation. More than his own death, it took the massacre of his teenage daughters to make a stunned world aware of the haunting spectre of a new doctrine, which fed on injustice and terror. As for Kerensky, in the moment of peril he was gripped by the same indecision as the tsar before him. Others, more brutal than he, took power.

'Revolutions are the locomotives of history. Drive them full speed ahead and keep them on the rails,' declared Lenin. Perhaps he could have kept his revolution on the rails, but for that he died too soon. As for Stalin: 'All in all, Stalin was a monster who, while adhering to abstract, absolute and fundamental utopian ideas, in practice had no criterion but success – and this meant violence, and physical extermination.'[17] Stalinism was an aberration, a wilfully achieved distortion of the workers' movement, which led him to power. The masses followed him blindly – Stalin was their father. Blindness is never without complicity; one has to be touched to be manipulated, to serve the lie of which one is the victim. Trotsky was a revolutionary who unceasingly chased respectability, but he became tainted with the guilt and cruelty of his revolutionary times, and frequently acted as if he had to take revenge on all humanity. Altogether, the Bolsheviks had stirred up hope in an oppressed society when they promised a Brave New World. All they delivered was a change in the country's name. Tsarist Russia became the Soviet Union, where the turbines of Communism turned people into parts of a huge machine, where Big Brother watched one and all, and the

[17] Milovan Djilus, *Conversations with Stalin.*

Great Terror of a paranoid, vindictive dictator sent millions to their deaths.

If the proletariat of Russia believed that Red October had lit up their lives with the brilliant sun of history, Trotsky tried to tell them that history progressed mainly via its dark side; for this, his voice was silenced. Never was modern history more obscure than in the Russia of the twentieth century. If one really believes in an ideal, one may well neglect the truths that seem too small and mediocre not to be called derisory. In the Soviet Union, the believers found out that nothing is eternal, neither empire nor society. With the fall of the Berlin Wall[18] their prophet Marx died.

It took eighty years for the murder mystery of the century to be solved. Or was it ever solved? In most other aspects of the repression following Red October, the Soviets' collective evasiveness produced historical dishonesty of astounding magnitude, so why not here? One thing is certain: had the tsar and his family not been liquidated in such a pitiless manner, we might well have forgotten that he ever existed, like the two other great monarchs of that period, Karl I, the last of the Hapsburg emperors, and Kaiser Wilhelm II, the last king of Prussia. With his death, the last Tsar of all the Russias, this weak man who preferred the closeness of his family circle to the burden of public office, made sure that the world remembered the first victim of the Red Terror. A final enigma remains: of the eleven persons who died that night, only nine skeletons were recovered from that shallow grave. The body of Tsarevich Alexei and that of one of the girls are missing. But which one? Even here, the great mystery continues. Tests have shown that it was not Anastasia.

Today, many Russians call the tsar's children the *golubchiki*, the dear little ones. '*Jelaiju tebe vetchnuju jizn.* – I bid you eternal life.'

---

[18] On 9 November 1989.

Interlude

1917–1918

The Great War was reaching its climax. The troops that the Germans had managed to release by manipulating Russia out of the war were kept busy enough by a new foe: the United States of America. The monolith of Prussian militarism was cracking.

Avoiding the death of innocent human beings wholly justifies any change of direction in a civilised society. And *change* was the rule, not the exception. New forces reached for power. The turmoil created by the war – the *Völkerwanderung* (migration of peoples) of whole nations, of peasants exchanging a feudal system for the slavery of the urban proletariat – was bound to result in worldwide unrest. And so it was to be during the waning days of 1918 in Germany. There was no tolerance or justice – which was exactly what Germany, and the rest of Europe, needed most in those unquiet times.

The post-war period provides one of those fascinating historic moments when a flash of lightning suddenly throws the social landscape into sharp relief. It showed just how troubled Europe really was under a system whose political mythology had so few relevant answers to offer a rapidly changing society. While Russia was embroiled in a bloody civil war, strikes broke out in England, France, Austria, and Germany. Initially motivated by economic reasons, the strikes soon took on a distinctly political nature. In Germany, strikes by sailors and workers, which ultimately led to the kaiser's abdication, marked not so much the end of an era as the beginning of a new one. All it took was for someone to band together the various factions solidly to present a single list of demands. Out of the shadows stepped a woman. With fiery language, she challenged the limits of the present and outlined the possibilities of the future.

Of the great men of the world, we declaim heroic songs . . . If it needed proof, then she provided it: that women are not only equal but, in many cases, superior to men.

5

9 January 1919

'Es lebe die Internationale!'

Es lebe die Internationale!
Long live the Internationale!

Freedom is always and exclusively freedom
for the one who thinks differently.
                              Rosa Luxemburg, 1918

'You must stop them, you must stop them!' yelled the kaiser.
In the overcrowded map room, the atmosphere was one of
apprehension and confusion. Everyone's nerves were strained.
Yielding to one's temper in such circumstances was most
unseemly. An expression of impotent despair flickered over
the German kaiser's face. For a long time he remained motion-
less, too bewildered to feel insulted by the haughty tone taken
by the chief-of-staff of his powerful army. The monarch was
drowning in a nightmare; everyone around him appeared mad
and now he himself was behaving like a madman, overcome
by a feeling of indescribable oppression. He had only himself
to blame; it was he who had cast the die.
   '*Verlässt die Kugel erst den Lauf, haelt sie kein Kaiser
Willi auf.* – Once the bullet leaves the barrel, not even
Kaiser Willi can stop it.' Thus chanted the children in the

street, the farmers in their fields, and its meaning terrified diplomats from Whitehall and the Quai d'Orsay all the way to St Petersburg. Wilhelm had unleashed the beast of war when he preferred the 'shock of civilisations' to diplomatic dialogue. The emperor was confused. How could it have come to this? Germany had threatened and 'Germany' meant the 'Prussian general staff'. Austria had mobilised, as had Russia in support of Serbia, but Italy remained neutral. France had already rejected a German ultimatum, and so had the Belgians who would not allow the passage of German troops through their neutral territory. Britain was pulled into the war 'over a scrap of paper', to protect Belgium's neutrality. This time the kaiser had really overstepped the mark. Once this infernal war machine – his Prussian army – was set in motion, the juggernaut of annihilation rolled faster and faster, and no one could stop it. 'You've got to stop them.' This plea was spoken in a whisper, a beseeching appeal addressed to a man with red stripes along the seams of his grey trousers, who squeezed his monocle more forcefully into his eye as he pretended to study a map. The general's voice was metallic: '*Ihre Kaiserliche Majestät*, all has been planned, all has been set in motion, it can no longer be changed.' He pointed to a blue line dividing the large wall-map of Europe: 'The German army has crossed the Rhine.' And so it was that on 3 August 1914, the brake was released on a train of cheering soldiers and it rumbled across the bridge that separated Germany and France.

The royal house of Hohenzollern lasted for 503 years. It rose to prominence in the summer of 1415, and came to an end with the abdication of Kaiser Wilhelm II in the autumn of 1918. It was not so much brilliance as historic good fortune that brought the Hohenzollern to world predominance. What began as a land of swamps and dark forests between the rivers Oder and Elbe, became an imperial powerhouse whose jackboots marched across Europe. One hundred years after the dynasty's foundation, a single event changed not only the destiny of Prussia, but also the world. On the evening before All Saints' Day in 1517, an Augustine monk nailed his defiant denunciation of the hitherto 'untouchable affirmation' of the Catholic Church onto the door of the town church in Wittenberg. His name was Martin Luther. The Markgraf of Brandenburg quickly accepted the new faith, not as a believer but as a shrewd opportunist who saw it as a way to rid himself of the Catholic Hapsburg emperor. The devastating Thirty Years War (1618–48) made the break complete between the Protestant north and the Catholic south. The man who turned Prussia into a major power was *Der Grosse Friedrich* (Frederick the Great). To put a stop to the expansionist ambitions of the Hapsburgs, he initiated a *Füerstenbund*, a prince's club and a thoroughly Machiavellian scheme. It became Frederick the Great's political testament.

Following Napoleon's demise Prussia created the Deutschen Zollverein, a Germanic customs union under the protection of the Prussian king. England ruled the waves and carved out its colonial empire, France rebuilt its military might, and the Austrians were kept busy quashing trouble in Italy and Hungary. The new Prussian King Wilhelm I set the tone in his coronation speech: 'The Prussian army will be the Prussian nation in arms.' He appointed the Iron Man, Count Otto von Bismarck, as chancellor. Bismarck singled out a brilliant young army officer, Count von Moltke, and had him put on the Prussian general staff. In 1864 General Moltke refined his strategy during a brief but successful try-out against Denmark. Bismarck knew only too well that the annexation of Schleswig-Holstein must inevitably lead to war with Austria. He planned it that way and eventually that was what happened. Bismarck's greatest achievement was twofold. First, in line with his single-front strategy, he needed to keep France out of the war against Austria. Second, he had to defeat Austria in a lightning war without humiliating the Hapsburg kaiser, and yet leave the Austrian army sufficiently intact to provide a counterweight against France.

On 3 July 1866, at Koeniggraetz (or Sadowa), luck was with the Prussians. The biggest loser was not the Austrians, but the French emperor, Napoleon III, caught off balance by the rapid success of the Prussian army. Had Prussia lost the day, Prussian jackboots might not have set foot on their road to both world wars. Bismarck's aim was to unite Germany's duchies under Prussia's iron fist. Equally, the sole aim of France was to prevent such a unification from taking place. The Prussians' luck held. In 1870, when it came to the conflict that Bismarck had so cleverly engineered, the French army marched into a trap. The speed with which Prussia's forces had swept away one of the mightiest armies in Europe was almost unprecedented in history. It was also to have grave consequences, as it lured the Prussian High Command into the erroneous belief that France was weak, and would fall just as fast should there ever be another war. On 18 January 1871 the 'Iron Chancellor', Otto von Bismarck, proclaimed Wilhelm I King of Prussia, as Kaiser of Germany. The French launched themselves into a virulent movement of revanchism. As for the rest of Europe, where most of the ruling houses were interrelated by marriage, they continued to go about their business, which was seizing colonies in Africa and Asia. This led to trade rivalry and England began to see its commercial empire threatened.

In 1888, Germany had a new kaiser, Wilhelm II. Shortly after his birth, his mother, the English-born Princess Victoria, wrote to the British monarch: 'Your grandson Wilhelm is extremely lively and up to all kind of tricks.' He certainly was. As Wilhelm II he would have a big crown and an even bigger ego; a boorish autocrat whose ambition outreached his political acumen, a humourless man who demanded blind obedience. He overestimated his intellectual capacity beyond reason, and at no time did his intellect match his political ambitions. His first act was to fire Otto von Bismarck, thereby removing the only man able to defuse the explosive political situation. While Bismarck's greatest aim had always been to keep France and Russia from joining forces, Wilhelm's political bungling so upset his two neighbours that they signed a defensive alliance, followed by their *entente cordiale* with England.

August 1914. From the four corners of Europe, nations marched with gusto into a holocaust. They took up arms 'in the defence of their holy fatherland' – or 'motherland', depending on where they marched from. Germans, Russians, Austrians, Frenchmen, British, Serbs, Turks. All yelled 'Hurrah' and then went to their deaths by bullet, torpedo, or dysentery. The kaiser's aims were to rule the world, but the price was too high, as it condemned Prussia to the slavery of warfare; once Prussia took on the entire world, the resulting conflict would inexorably lead to its own extinction. Prussia's strategy was based on a *Vernichtungsschlacht*, or war of annihilation. So their young men were indoctrinated not only to fight for their country, but to die for it. It was the beginning of a new era, that of the 'supreme sacrifice'. It was a spirit that dominated speeches and newspapers. Suffering casualties was considered a measure of national resolve. Germany's final offensive on the Western front ended in abysmal failure. In August 1918, Allied units brought about a collapse of the German line. The German army lost 1.5 million men defending something that could not be defended. Its patriotic days were long gone and the war had turned into Germany's bloodied, muddied Gethsemane.

The generals blamed their failure on betrayal by the politicians at home. The slaughter on the Western front was just the final show in a sequence of events that neither began nor ended there. More than 150 years earlier, a Prussian junker (member of the aristocratic officer class), Heinrich Dietrich von Bülow, had penned a treatise[1] on the correlation between politics and war. In it he firmly insisted on the need for a single unifying intelligence to lead a warring nation, and stressed that under modern strategic conditions, there could be no separation between politics and war. Kaiser Wilhelm failed abysmally in both these respects. The winter of 1917–18 saw the world to the east of Germany explode in a series of bloody revolutions. That winter also laid bare the political and economic wear and tear of four terrible years of war. The leading Social Democrats were paralysed, and the tired kaiser was too inept to take control. He could see for himself the erratic domestic situation during a visit in 1918 to Kiel. One day there was no bread, but public transport ran. A few days later the bread returned, but the buses stopped. People grumbled, but with no alternative, had to slog on with their miserable daily existence. Posters, glued hastily on house walls, became an everyday occurrence. '*Kaiser raus!* Out with the kaiser!' Groups gathered on street corners, and on the shop floor union agitators grew bolder. 'Always these damn Reds,' said the kaiser. General Hindenburg did not mince his words: 'Majesty, our army is in flight; we must sue for an immediate ceasefire.' At that moment, the kaiser must have known that his role as supreme monarch was rapidly coming to an end. While he was still contemplating his next move, General Ludendorff burst into the room. 'Has a new government been formed?' he cried out.

'I'm not a magician,' yelled the irate Wilhelm.

'Your Majesty, this is not the moment to waste time in discussion. The whole front line will collapse and the enemy will invade our lands.'

On 3 October 1918, the Kaiser chose his cousin Max von Baden as Germany's chancellor. Two days later, US President Wilson's 'fourteen points' were accepted by the Allies as their

[1] *Der Geist des neuer Kriegssystems*, 1799.

basis for the negotiation of an armistice. Wilson demanded 'the destitution of a government, which, until now, has imposed its will on the German people'. Germany did not reply. Ten days later came a clear message from President Wilson: 'We can no longer deal with an autocratic kaiser, we cannot consider a ceasefire. Only a surrender.'

Two major causes led to the German November Revolution of 1918. The first was the setback to the German forces on the Western front. The soldiers were tired of a war that ground on, day after day, and which the newspapers headlined with the famous phrase: '*Im Western nichts Neues.* – All quiet on the Western front.' Second, the refusal by the government to implement social reforms had created a split between the ruling class and the urban proletariat. Germany became a powder keg.

In the forefront of the looming German crisis stood a political organisation known as Spartakus. The base for its foundation was laid down in a series of letters written by a woman whilst in prison for anti-war activities. The name she picked for her movement was symbolically that of another revolutionary who fought against impossible odds, the Roman gladiator Spartacus, a slave who dared to rise in rebellion! He went on to defeat Rome's legions before he was captured and crucified. Her name was Rosa Luxemburg.

Rosa Luxemburg came from Zamoshc in the Polish part of Russia, one of the many Jews from the ghettoes of Eastern Europe. The *Koshere Yatkes* (Street of Jews) was always narrow and rutted. In winter it was glazed over with a sheet of ice; in spring it turned into a sea of mud; in summer the dust choked everyone who lived along it. But living there had one advantage: that was where most synagogues had their *grosse shul* (big school), a centre of intense learning which produced men of great wisdom. Every ten years throughout the Pale,[2]

---

[2] The area of Russia in which Jews were allowed to live.

anti-Semitic riots and pogroms devastated the Jewish community. The worst time was Passover, or Easter. It was a time when the Russian Orthodox priests demanded that every Jew whose house faced a church, brick up his windows. In Polish Russia there was nobody who would protect the Jews. In 1881, Tsar Alexander II was assassinated by a young Jewish terrorist. A terrible period followed and a great number of Jews fled to America or Germany. Among them was the Luxemburg family. They abandoned their business, their house, and all their belongings apart from what they could carry on their backs, and moved to Switzerland.

Rosa's destiny was to become the mastermind and decisive personality of an emerging political organisation, the future Communist Party of Germany (KPD). She was neither ugly nor pretty. Her strength lay in her superior brain, her sharp tongue, and her extraordinary passion, every ounce of which was directed towards the betterment of the proletariat. Personal ties were never a factor in her life. She had only two affairs, one with a young doctor who died in the trenches, the other with the son of her best friend.[3] Men shied away from her, most of them repulsed by her first-rate intellect. Admirers called her the German Danton,[4] critics referred to her scathingly as 'the most destructive influence in our effort to win the war'. In 1889 she received a law degree *cum laude* from the University of Zurich. In 1899 she moved to Berlin and married Gustav Lübeck to obtain German nationality. The opposition papers never let her forget that she was nothing but 'a Polish Jewess'. In 1904 she was sentenced to three months in prison for a derisory remark made in public about His Imperial German Majesty.

Her first major public appearance came in 1907; she addressed the Congress of Socialists, sharply criticising Lenin's formula that social democracy was a Jacobin

---

[3] Dr Hans Diefenbach and Kostja Zetkin respectively.
[4] After the flamboyant hero of the French Revolution.

organisation of the proletariat. The same year she became a
lecturer at the SPD (Socialist Partei Deutschland) University.
From 1912 to 1914 her energies were fully concentrated on
warning people about the looming threat of war. Her warning
cry was taken from Schiller's 'Ode to Joy': '*Alle Menschen
werden Brüder* – All men become brothers.' In 1916, the
Socialists in the Reichstag (German parliament) voted by a
substantial majority to continue the war. Rosa considered
this as a betrayal of the working classes, broke with the
party, and published her views.[5] For making statements
like: 'When we are being asked to wield the murder weapon
against our French brothers, we say: we will not do it,' she
passed most of the war years in prison. When she was
released for a brief period in 1916, she used it to form the
Spartakus Bund.

Her partner was Karl Liebknecht, the scion of an established Socialist family. His father Wilhelm had been a prominent Socialist and member of the Reichstag. In 1875, together
with August Bebel and Ferdinand Lasalle, they had founded
Germany's Socialist Workers Party. Wilhelm Liebknecht was
also the creator of the Socialist newspaper *Vorwärts* (*For-
wards*), which was destined to play a decisive role in the
events of 1919. Young Karl, an insignificant-looking man
wearing thick glasses (a clone of Leon Trotsky), followed in
the footsteps of his father and took up politics. He was elected
to the Reichstag, where he became an outspoken opponent to
Germany's entry into world conflict. He attacked the war in
an illegal leaflet titled 'The principal enemy is inside our own
country', which earned him several years in prison. He was
freed in October 1918, just in time to cause the government
serious trouble.

The Spartakus Bund was made up of a handful of leftist
extremists from within the mother party, the Socialists. All

---

[5] *Junius Brochure.*

had one thing in common: they were against the war. Rosa Luxemburg's focus was on revolutionary action in the fight against war itself. In one of her letters she wrote: 'The anti-militarist action is the most intensive form of class struggle against war and the power structure of capitalism.'[6] For statements like this she was willing to pay a heavy price. Like Liebknecht, she was eventually freed from prison when the masses stormed the jails.

For years, the daily output of the press had been under the tight control of the military, and the shock of learning that Germany was about to face defeat was total. For such an eventuality, Germany was unprepared. With mutinous army units tired of dying for a kaiser unwilling to help their starving families, the fear of a Bolshevik takeover loomed over Germany. From that moment on, the German Revolution became a tight-rope act for gaining the support of the masses, with the radical Socialists and the Spartakists on one side and the centre Socialists in government. To anyone within the German government, one thing was becoming obvious: the kaiser had to go, and with him, the monarchy. However, nobody dared to openly oppose imperial authority.

On 1 November 1918, Prince Max von Baden dispatched his foreign minister to Spa to try to reason with the kaiser, but Wilhelm would not hear of abdication. And then events took a sudden turn for the worse. The focal point of the war shifted back to Germany or more precisely, to Kiel, the home harbour of the German High Seas Fleet. Its 3rd Squadron, comprising the battle cruisers *Bayern*, *König*, *Kronprinz Wilhelm*, *Markgraf*, and *Grosser Kürfuerst*, was being fired up in the Kieler Schillingswharf for a final, all-out sortie against the British fleet. This order was an act of folly amounting to suicide. In Kiel harbour, 25,000 sailors and

---

[6] Quoted in Liebknecht, *Antimilitarismus*.

15,000 Marines were gathered to man the ships. There was a minor mutiny which was suppressed and its leader arrested. The sailors of the cruiser *Markgraf* demanded the immediate release of their comrades. The commander of Kiel ordered all units confined to their barracks and armed the officer corps.

When the sailors refused to obey, the harbour commander ordered a company of Marines to break up the demonstration. A stoker, Karl Artelt, member of the German Workers Rat (equal to the Russian Soviet of October 1917), jumped on a hastily erected barricade and called one: 'We are not here to hurt you!' The Marines subsequently refused to obey their officers. The *Markgraf* was ordered to sail, but the stokers put out the fire under the boilers. More Marines were called up and all but thirteen refused to obey. The *Stadtkommandant*, Admiral Souchon, issued new orders, but never the right ones. Instead of calming the growing insanity, which was heading straight for a massacre, the admiral declared a state of martial law, overlooking the fact that under martial law, violence becomes unavoidable. In anticipation of a sailors' protest march into town, he formed a 'White Guard' made up of untried officer cadets. The operation became a textbook copy of what had taken place in Petrograd.

Everything was in place to set off the final spark and bring the complete imperial power structure crashing down. The 'White Guard' cadets panicked and fired into the mass of slogan-shouting sailors. Thirty-seven were killed. With a shout of '*Es lebe die Internationale!* Long live the Internationale!' the sailors stormed the navy's weapons depot and armed themselves with rifles and machine-guns. In the early hours of 4 November, 260 sailors of the *Grosser Kürfuerst*, led by a stoker named Bodolski, swore a holy oath to avenge the murder of their comrades. The mutineers formed a *Soldatenrat* (soldiers' council), the first of many. The uprising spread like wildfire. By noon, these *Soldatenräte* already boasted 20,000 rifles, as well as most of the heavy ship's artillery, manned by naval gunners who had joined the insurrection. They issued a demand. Article 1: 'Abdication of the Hohenzollern . . .' A call for a general strike went out. Without warning, representatives of the *Soldatenräte* burst into Admiral Souchon's office. The admiral pursed his lips at their demands, but offered to enter into talks with them. He liked to lecture his subordinates, but this time it did not work. The soldiers would no longer listen to his tirades.

'If our request is not granted . . .' announced their leader.

'You threaten me?' rasped Souchon.

One thing was obvious: the time for discussion was over. Prince Heinrich, commander-in-chief of the German Baltic Fleet, escaped with his life by bolting out a back door. A government delegation came from Berlin to reason with the rioters. They could do nothing but watch the rapid contagion of the sailors' revolt. From Kiel it spread to Lübeck, Travemuende, Wilhelmshaven, Brunsbüttel, Bremen, and Hamburg. The rioters needed political direction. When the leader of the Berlin delegation, the Socialist Gustav Noske, saw that nothing could be done to stop the rebellion, he quickly joined it and managed to win the sailors' trust. He was elected head of the *Soldatenräte*, pushed out Admiral Souchon, and appointed himself military governor of Kiel. After this, he formed a provisional government and quickly constituted an 'Iron Brigade' of professional soldiers and anti-Bolsheviks to put down the 'Red sailors' who had elected him.

The main cause for the failure of the Matrosenbewegung of 1918 (sailor's movement) was not a lack of mobilisation of the masses, but the lack of a political leadership, such as Lenin and Trotsky had provided during Red October.

When 9 November 1918 dawned, it was dreary and cold. A

leaden sky hung over Spa, and the bad weather stretched all the way to Berlin where, at 9.15 a.m., a telegram was put onto the desk of the *Reichskanzler*, Prince Max von Baden. It stated categorically: 'THE HIGH COMMAND OF THE ARMED FORCES HAS DECIDED TO INFORM HIS MAJESTY THAT HE CANNOT COUNT ON THE ARMY TO STAND BEHIND HIM IN CASE OF CIVIL WAR.' When the *Reichskanzler* read this message, he burst out: 'That's the end!'

Faced with the explosive situation at home, the kaiser contemplated leading his loyal front-line troops against the rebellious sailors. The ignominy of his fleet's mutiny had wounded him far more than the degradation of defeat in France. He convened the *Kronrat* (crown council) to the Château de la Fraineuse in Spa to discuss 'an operation in the homelands under the leadership of the kaiser'. However, his generals knew that it was too late; the once-proud German army had begun to dissolve. And not only dissolve, but much worse. The victors of Leuthen, Waterloo, and Sedan, steeped in the Prussian tradition of blind obedience towards their war-lord, these same soldiers were now in open revolt, arresting their officers, blocking roads, and cutting communications between the fatherland and the front.

'Majesty, it is no longer a rebellion, it is civil war. The mutineers hold all key bridges across the Rhine. Most of our troops have deserted to the revolutionaries.' To those present it seemed that the kaiser did not grasp the seriousness of the situation.

Finally, General Groener took a deep breath: 'Your Majesty no longer has an army.'

The kaiser advanced on his general and yelled: 'Excellency, I demand your declaration on a piece of paper! I want to read in black and white that the German army will not follow its *Kriegsherr* [warlord]. They have sworn their oath of fidelity to me!'

General Groener looked around the room; he saw only

pale faces. 'Majesty, as it stands now, such an oath is mere fiction.'

The kaiser's world felt apart. He blamed the mutiny, which he saw as an attack on his imperial person, on the Red government in Berlin, those Social Democrats who conspired only at his downfall.

It was at this moment that the phone rang. Berlin was on the line, Prince Max von Baden. The situation in the capital was chaotic: 'This afternoon the workers' and soldiers councils will call out a republic with the Bolshevik Liebknecht as its leader . . . All the troops have gone over to the rebellion . . . Our government is without power . . . We have only three regiments still with us . . .' Moments later, another call announced that these three elite regiments had also defected; that an immense crowd had gathered outside the seat of the *Ministerrat* (council of ministers) in the Wilhelmsstrasse and any moment now they would storm the building.

Five minutes later, Prince Max was again on the phone. 'Your Majesty, a general strike has been called. You must abdicate, or Germany will plunge into a civil war.'

The kaiser refused to reply and put down the receiver. The myopic politician in him still believed that none of this could touch his august person. 'We shall achieve a great victory,' he said to no one in particular, studying a map of military units that no longer existed, or were in open revolt. 'We must put more men in here . . .' Those around him looked at one another in silence.

A few minutes passed, and the phone rang again. It was an outcry of panic from Berlin. 'Your Majesty, it's a matter of minutes. I implore you . . .'

Von Schulenburg answered the phone. 'Such an important step cannot be taken in haste. His Majesty is formulating a note which should be in your hands within thirty minutes.'

' . . . that will be much too late . . .'

Von Schulenburg looked imploringly at his kaiser. A shudder went through his closest followers at the sight of the monarch's nervous state, his twitching mouth and glazed eyes. A low rumble of distant artillery rattled the delicate porcelain cups. Finally the kaiser left the group and walked over to his writing desk. 'I'm about to lose my empire,' Wilhelm kept on muttering, mostly to himself, before he sat down to draft a telegram announcing his decision to give up his title as German kaiser. However, he added as a final stipulation: 'We shall retain the crown as king of Prussia.' His ego would not let him accept a further humiliation. No longer a kaiser, he would still remain a king.

In Berlin the situation had got completely out of hand. With thousands of demonstrators howling for the kaiser's abdication and a seething mob about to wrest control from the legally elected government, an act that would end in great tragedy, it took a bold step to save what was left of Germany from the bitterness of a bloody civil war. Fortunately for the country, a man willing to take such a step was present. Even before the kaiser's telegram landed in Berlin, Max von Baden stepped out on the balcony of the Wilhelmsstrasse. It took him several minutes before he managed to silence the frenzied mob by waving his arms.

'*Seine Kaiserliche Majestät hat abgedankt* – His Imperial Majesty has abdicated . . .'

For a moment the crowd was stunned and remained silent. So Max von Baden repeated his announcement: '*Seine Kaiserliche Majestät hat abgedankt . . .*'

The crowd on the Wilhelmsstrasse went wild and erupted in cheers. The people hugged and kissed each other, yelling: 'Kaiser Willi is gone, the war is over . . .'

To forestall further bloodshed, the chancellor called the *Wolff News Agency* and put out a message for immediate release:

THE GERMAN KAISER AND KING OF PRUSSIA HAS DECIDED
TO RELINQUISH HIS THRONE. THE REICHSKANZLER WILL
REMAIN IN OFFICE UNTIL ANY QUESTION ARISING FROM
THE ABDICATION OF THE KAISER, AND THE REFUTA-
TION OF HIS RIGHTS TO THE THRONE BY THE CROWN
PRINCE OF THE GERMAN EMPIRE AND PRUSSIA, HAS BEEN
SETTLED . . .

Max von Baden knew he had no right to send such a note
without conferring first with his kaiser, but events had left
him with no choice. In Spa it was now 2.30 p.m. The kaiser's
telegram was finally dispatched. A few minutes passed; then a
message arrived from Berlin. It was short and clear and replied
to the kaiser's earlier message:

'TOO LATE, CANNOT BE USED ANY MORE. THE CHANCEL-
LOR HAS ALREADY ADVISED THE COUNTRY THAT KAISER HAS
ABDICATED. PRINCE MAX IS CARETAKER, EBERT IS NEW CHAN-
CELLOR.'

'Treachery!' yelled the kaiser, when a copy of the Baden
telegram reached him. His face was ashen; with great beads
of sweat pouring down his forehead. 'Dastardly high treason!'
He dictated a series of contradictory messages. But it was of
no use. The generals knew that it was out of the question for
the kaiser to remain even as king of Prussia. The Spartakists
of Karl Liebknecht and Rosa Luxemburg had already stormed
the royal palace in Berlin.

The Socialist Party under Friedrich Ebert panicked. The
Reichstag was not united in purpose; many of the Socialists
now moved among the seething mob in its hallways, aligning
themselves with their former enemies, the Spartakists (Communists), who had mined the congressional battlefield with
revolutionary slogans. Inside the noble hall pandemonium
broke out. Philipp Scheidemann, a minor secretary of state
in the cabinet of Max von Baden and a Socialist delegate,
raced up the magnificent staircase of the venerated building,

the staircase reserved for visits by His Imperial Majesty. From its landing he announced in a pompous tone: '*Brüder, das deutsche Volk hat auf der ganzen Linie gesiegt.* – My brothers, the German nation has been victorious.' His statement was followed by a great cheer from the delegates of the left. Scheidemann, caught up in the excitement of the moment, raised his arms and a hush descended on the hall. With a single sentence he catapulted himself into the history books. '*Ich erkläre hiermit die Deutsche Republik*! . . . I hereby proclaim the German Republic!' The members of the Reichstag broke into convulsive cheers, mixed with some cries of abuse. Simple relief that the war was finally coming to an end overwhelmed the majority. The delegates banged their desks and stamped their feet. Those who had formerly been gripped by fear of an autocratic monarch abandoned themselves to an outburst of emotion. '*Lang lebe die Republik Deutschland!* Long live the German Republic!' Those who might still have shown some spark of loyalty to their kaiser only minutes before, now hurriedly abandoned the doomed monarch. After more than five centuries, the Hohenzollern dynasty had been brought down. The German monarchy was history. '*Lang lebe die Republik Deutschland!*'

While these momentous events took place in Berlin, the situation in the kaiser's entourage at Spa was one of utter confusion. They had been informed that the Rhine bridges were under the control of red-flagged soldiers and that all roads to Berlin were blocked by rebellious regiments; that bloody street battles had broken out between police units, loyal to the ruling conservative Socialists; and that not only the progressive Spartakists but all political prisoners had been released, including Rosa Luxemburg. Everyone was fighting for scraps of the Hohenzollern empire; in the Reichstag the Bolsheviks voted for a worker's state *à la Russe*, while the leading Socialists opted for a moderate bourgeois republic.

The German army no longer had a supreme commander. Hindenburg said to the kaiser: 'As a Prussian general I cannot take the responsibility of seeing you arrested by your own troops and dragged before a revolutionary tribunal.' The implication that the kaiser might meet the fate of other deposed rulers was clear. This was no longer a revolt but a revolution.

Wilhelm stood erect, as if staring down from his full height on horseback. His nostrils flared slightly; his cheeks were flushed. His contempt for the troublemakers in his far-off capital was bottomless. So was his irritation over his own inability to prevent his generals from placing him in a ridiculous position. 'Do you really think I'm afraid to stay with my own troops?'

Hindenburg's expression was serious: 'You have no more troops, Majesty. I wish to God it was different.'

Kaiser Wilhelm stood in his favourite pose, straight and tall, his right foot in his highly polished boot slightly forward, as though about to stride on and subdue the world. But something in him had changed. He had finally accepted the situation and now he fell into the same lassitude that had overcome so many leaders in their moment of crisis. He thought of the great days of glory, the splendid parades in Berlin, the visits by crowned heads, the bowing and scraping by his court officials. The drive towards the flag-bedecked parade stand in front of the Siegessäule, Uncle Willi's victory column of 1871; with the wide boulevards lined with flag-waving, cheering Berliners; the precision march-past by his Prussian battalions. It must have dawned on him that he alone was the author of the sacrificial smoke belching from shell craters, the putrefaction of the bodies of men who, as living beings, had sworn eternal loyalty to kaiser and Reich and who then had fought and crouched and prayed and died in open fields and trenches . . . The memories proved too painful. The mantle of night had descended upon his empire. What unending misery he had brought on his people; no nation could survive such devastation. No powerful potentate is immune from his people's fury or the degradation of defeat. Without a further word, Wilhelm II, ex-Kaiser of Germany, walked from the room to inform the crown prince of his intention to go into exile in Holland.

His train steamed out of the darkness of the last day of the war. He ordered it to halt at Liège. Anxiety chilled him more than the cold of the night. For a moment he paused in the doorway of the imperial coach to button up his grey overcoat, as if to wrap himself in a cocoon of security. Only then did he alight from the train. Despite all the uproar in Berlin, Liège was a dead city at this time of the night. His aide, Sigurd von Ilsemann, had to borrow a petrol lamp from the stationmaster to light the kaiser across the rail yard and out of the station. For the first time in his life, the German kaiser stood alone on a deserted street, with no crowds to cheer him.

Two limousines drew up. Wilhelm got into the back of the second car and was handed a loaded rifle. Travelling through the centre of Liège, the kaiser saw a town like all the others that his victorious armies had moved through. Walls pockmarked with bullet holes, chimneys sticking up like tombstones from the rubble of collapsed factories. Between the ruins there were some hastily erected cemeteries with row upon row of white crosses, all bearing witness to the hot summer days of August 1914. Only four years ago? – Yes, only four years, which had changed the world and brought death to millions. Then they were out of the town, the headlights playing ghost-like up the long, straight road north. After a bend in the road, the two-car convoy reached a hamlet and a narrow wooden bridge. Suddenly in front of their cars loomed figures pointing rifles. A roadblock. The lead vehicle screeched to a halt and steel-helmeted men in field-grey encircled the cars. Fortunately it was a unit that still showed obedience to a general, so von Falkenburg managed to talk his way through.

Another hour went by. The two cars finally reached a double string of barbed wire, which stretched away into the distance. On the far side lay neutral Holland. In the headlights appeared another barrier, guarded by men from the Bavarian Landwehr. The kaiser's hopes sank when he saw a red flag tied to a pole that was stuck in the ground. In the light of a trench searchlight which blinded both drivers, the soldiers aimed their rifles at the cars. In contrast to the previous roadblock, these men took a great interest in the convoy, especially when one of them discovered traces of the imperial crest on a car door. A *Feldwebel* (sergeant) walked forward with a pistol in his hand. He was at most twenty-four but looked more like fifty, with a weathered face and hands red from hard work. His fist rested firmly on the butt of his gun. '*Das sind Offiziere*' (these officers, cowardly deserters) said one of his men a broad Bavarian accent, '*feige Ausreisser* – cowardly deserters,' and his trigger finger tightened while his pistol pointed straight at von Falkenburg's head. The sergeant waved him off and stuck his head through the car window. '*Wohin willst Du?* Where are you headed for?' No saluting, no 'Herr General', just the familiar 'Du' used among common soldiers.

In the second car, the kaiser's knuckles were white around his rifle. He breathed heavily; anticipation of what lay ahead made him twitch nervously. Would they dare to lay hands on the sacrosanct person of their kaiser? Their silence was more disturbing than if they had yelled in fury.

'What will they do with us?' he whispered in a voice that struggled for control.

'Let's hope that common sense will prevail,' hissed Ilsemann on the edge of panic, his brisk coolness gone.

More soldiers came up from behind, cutting off all possible retreat. Wilhelm knew that he was lost. Sitting there trapped, he saw a nightmare reaching its conclusion, and he himself was solely responsible. Defeat seeped through him. Any moment now, the sergeant would recognise the face that had stared from a thousand photographs and banknotes. Before the sergeant was given a chance to identify the occupants of the second car, General von Falkenburg leaped from the lead vehicle. His red stripes showed up clearly in the bright lights. He barked an order: '*Was soll denn das?* – What is the meaning of this?'

His authoritarian voice did the trick. The soldiers who had encircled his vehicle did not at first know how to react, until the sergeant slowly brought up his hand and saluted his superior officer who snapped at him: 'General von Falkenburg in urgent matters on his way to Holland.' It was a daring bluff, but the general counted on the blind obedience that was ingrained in every German soldier. And he was proved absolutely right. Sergeant Alois Mittermaier of the 193rd Bayrischen Landwehr Battalion, a soldier who had gone through hell for four long years and with the thousand-yard stare of hopelessness of the common soldier, snapped his heels and brought his hand to his *Stahlhelm*. '*Jawohl!* This way, Herr General.' This was a command of followed by '*Schranken auf*' to raise the barrier. The sergeant seemed to understand the general's urgency; he had heard on the grapevine of the imminent signing of an armistice and he took the occupants of the cars for the German delegation: 'These are our parliamentarians.'

General von Falkenburg jumped onto the running-board of the lead car. 'Quickly now, across the border,' he hissed to the driver, 'and whatever happens, don't stop.' The kaiser was still in the grip of confusion and shock and did not know what had just taken place. He only sensed his car accelerating past the steel-helmeted men in grey. The striped beam was raised, Wilhelm II turned in his seat, and a Bavarian sergeant saluted the passing cars. It was the German kaiser's final salute from a German soldier.

At 11 a.m. on the eleventh day of the eleventh month, in

the year of Our Lord 1918, the guns fell silent and the dying stopped. Wherever Germans met, they always asked the same question: how could a nation, victorious in a hundred battles, lose the war? The answer had been supplied a century before, by Napoleon: 'In the face of an overwhelming superiority, one can win many battles, but never a war.'

There still remained the problem of the political legacy within Germany. It was plain that the great powers who had fought together to bring down the kaiser never spared a thought for the dragon's teeth they had sown with their demand for an unconditional surrender. They had shamed a proud nation and in doing so they created a monster. But that would come later. What counted now was that the guns had finally stopped and the terrible war was over, but not the bloodshed: a new war loomed in Germany where the working class had arms as well as the rebellious soldiers. The struggle for power made civil war inevitable. In a war, the decisive factors are known; in civil strife, it is not always the largest party that carries the biggest stick. It is then that moral and intellectual factors play a much larger role than they do in war, when the foundation of society are destroyed and the response of the masses can be full of surprises.

On 9 November, in the first issue of their newssheet, *Die Rote Fahne* (*The Red Flag*), the editorial by Karl Liebknecht stated: 'Workers, soldiers. Your hour has come . . . *Es lebe die Internationale!* Long live the Internationale! The Spartakus Bund.' The article specified a number of points: do away with dynasties; form soldier councils; and, critically: make contact with the Russian workers' proletariat. The article achieved its desired shock effect. From that moment on, Karl Liebknecht and Rosa Luxemburg spoke from street balconies, on factory floors, in public squares, even in army barracks. Thousands cheered their rousing speeches. On 22 December 1918, a special session was called for the seven members of the Directive Committee of the Spartakus Bund. The time had come to decide on a permanent title for their newly formed party. The name Spartakus was a good-symbol of defiance, but not appropriate for a permanent political formation. Rosa Luxemburg's choice was Socialistische Partei (Socialist Party), but Liebknecht and three other committee members voted for Kommunistische Partei Deutschland (the German Communist Party).[7] With unerring clarity, Rosa Luxemburg foresaw the problem that the name would create and warned that it was blatantly connected with Lenin's government in Russia.

This battle over a name was not merely symbolic; it contained a slow-burning fuse, which was to explode into their faces. The founding congress of the new KPD party was convened, made up of eighty three members of the Spartakus Bund, twenty-nine Radical Socialists, and three members of the Red Soldiers Council. The Bolshevik Karl Radek shocked the assembly when he presented the condescending greetings of the Russian Bolshevik Party. Their reply was: 'We are Germans, not Russians.' With that, the delegates got up to leave the hall. To forestall disaster, Rosa jumped up and raced to the speaker's podium. She managed to calm the delegates when she began to speak about '*our* programme and *Germany*'s political situation'. Her speech became the highlight of the founding ceremony when she stressed the importance of gaining the support of the proletarian masses: the workers, peasants, and soldiers back from the war. 'The fight for socialism is only feasible through their support. We have to fight capitalism from inside the factory and the countryside. Socialism cannot be made by decree. Where capitalism has forged the chain of oppression, that is where the chain must be broken. What is our weapon to achieve this? *The strike!* The economic phase must be moved into the

---

[7] It was the first time the name Communist was used for a party, and preceded the Soviet version by two decades.

forefront of our struggle.' Then she made it quite clear that she was not about to follow the example set by the Bolsheviks in Russia. 'The revolution led by our comrades in Russia was different; they did not face the same problems we have to face. Our struggle is, and must remain, German. Our party must remain German.'

This speech was to be her public swansong. She worked hard, writing articles, chairing meetings, bullying politicians and party hacks. Rosa proved herself a powerhouse of forcefulness with great strength of nerves; it seemed as if her years in jail had stored up surplus energy in this diminutive woman. But all this confidence was only on the outside: after each public appearance she was plagued more and more by headaches and bouts of vomiting. She spent New Year's Eve with Karl Liebknecht, who for once provided amusing company. In the first days of January 1919, Rosa often walked the streets to feel the pulse of the crowd, both as a participant and a spectator. All too soon she realised that the majority of them did not understand what *revolution* stood for.

For the first time, the three main radical groups united and formed a Revolutionary Council, but the council was unclear about its role in the struggle to gain proletarian power. They counted on the armed support of a section of the Volksmarine Division under its commander Dorrenbach. According to that former seaman, all troops, including those garrisoned on the outskirts of Berlin, were ready to join together and bring down the Socialist government. Dorrenbach's assessment proved foolishly optimistic. Rosa's thinking was along more political lines; she considered that eventually a push by the masses, which could be organised, directed, and its energy funnelled, would in itself be enough to win. But she was equally convinced that the time for an uprising, if necessary supported by bullets and bayonets, had not yet come. The best they could hope for was to take power in Berlin. They were presented with a real dilemma: her new party possessed neither the numbers necessary for such a gigantic venture, nor the means to win the masses over to their side. But Rosa had no choice other than to stay with the revolutionary elements and partake in their victory, or their loss. Mathilde Jacobs, her companion, wrote: 'I live with Rosa, and fetch her every night from the station. Her face is etched with deep lines; she is tired and overworked, but quickly recovers when I feed her a cup of chocolate, a rare delicacy these days which we get from our Bolshevik comrades at the Russian embassy.' It led to the story that most of the funds for the purchase of weapons came from Russia via the Bolshevik ambassador in Berlin, Joffe.[8]

The events in Berlin of January 1919 were provoked by a series of unconnected incidents. Chancellor Friedrich Ebert had called a general election for 19 January. A police commissioner was forced to step aside. Massive demonstrations by striking workers flooded the streets of Berlin. In a counterweight to the striking workers, ultra-republican militia, recently returned from the slaughter on the Western front and well versed in killing, banded together under the overall command of General von Luettwitz. They called themselves the Freikorps. The budding Communist Party was drawn into the maelstrom by radical extremists. If there was open strife, the revolutionaries, who were all lumped together as Spartakists, would have to face the guns of the republican Freikorps. While all this manoeuvring was taking place, the Centrist Socialists and Chancellor Ebert hesitated until things finally got completely out of hand.

Emil Eichhorn, the police chief of Berlin, had once worked for a Russian news agency and the newspaper *Vorwärts* dubbed him a Bolshevik agent. What began as a series of articles turned into the Eichhorn Incident. *Die Rote Fahne* reacted: 'With the attack on the police chief, an attack has been launched against the German revolutionary movement.

[8] E. Bernstein, *Die Deutsche Revolution*.

Out into the streets for a powerful demonstration of the people's will . . .' It was all that was needed to bring the kettle to the boil.

'Spartakus Week' began on 5 January 1919. *Die Rote Fahne* published Rosa Luxemburg's call for civil disobedience. In the biggest demonstration the German capital had ever witnessed, it brought out hundreds of thousands into the streets. The MSPD (the Centre Socialists) tried to resolve the tension in a peaceful manner, but the KPD, under the signature of Rosa Luxemburg, issued another order: *'Don't talk! Don't negotiate! Act!'* Some groups stormed the building of *Vorwärts* and printed their own newspaper, which demanded the removal of the 'traitors Ebert and Scheidemann – if necessary by force!' That same afternoon, blinded by the massive turnout to their strike call, the Revolutionary Council decided to bring down the government by open rebellion. This was despite their uncertainty about their military arm, the Volksmarine Division, which had given no assurances that it would join the insurrection. The council's plan was betrayed, allowing Chancellor Fritz Ebert to act, and this time with vigour. Troops loyal to the government moved on Berlin. The Spartakists refused to abandon their plan for an armed *coup d'état*. Guns were made ready and the fighters moved to the barricades.

Rosa Luxemburg wrote a frantic note to stop them, arguing that 'the most elementary rules of revolutionary action are being disregarded'. Even Karl Radek, the Bolshevik extremist who never shied away from aggressive action, demanded that they 'stop this foolishness'. The tripartite Revolutionary Council would not listen, and Rosa Luxemburg was left with no other choice than to join in the rebellion. Her reason was simple: she knew that one could not manipulate a mass of people into a situation, and the next day, manipulate the same mass out of it again. The fatal order went out to the Spartakus cadres: 'We shall fight shoulder to shoulder with our revolutionary brothers whenever a revolutionary action is launched.' Now blood would flow and nothing could stop it.

Little is known of Rosa Luxemburg's moves or her whereabouts in the bloody days that followed. Berlin was too busy trying to stay alive to notice a tiny woman with her hair in a chignon. From the moment that events were set in motion, Rosa Luxemburg became a disconnected spectator, observing from the sidelines a *Götterdämmerung* (twilight of the gods) of all she had ever believed in. It is not certain whether she was aware of the mortal danger that she was in from her equally radical antagonists, the Prussian junkers, or whether she simply chose to ignore it. On 11 January she wrote a letter to her closest friend, Clara Zetkin: '*Many of our brave boys have died. For today I have to say goodbye.*' It was her testament.

Following the bloodless takeover of *Vorwärts*, the Revolutionary Council called a vote for a violent insurrection, a proposal that was carried by a majority. Machine-guns began to echo in the canyons of Berlin's thoroughfares. The problem with this Revolutionary Council was its abject incompetence. On 6 January it issued a proclamation, ending with: 'The undersigned Council has taken over the affairs of the state.' It was not true: Chancellor Ebert was still in power, although sorely tried. He issued a cleverly worded statement, calling on the 'majority of loyal Germans' to support the elected government: 'Citizens, the leaders of Spartakus have proclaimed the end of the legal government; murder and a bloody civil war will be their means to establish a red dictatorship; anarchy and hunger will be the result.' The 'loyal Germans' listened and the tide turned. The first crack in revolutionary unity occurred when the Volksmarine Division chose to remain in their barracks. With that, the military position of the government improved rapidly. The revolutionaries had overlooked the importance of taking over the one building that symbolised power in Germany, the Reichstag. Forty unarmed loyalists scrounged some weapons, shut the doors of the Reichstag, and also manned the Brandenburg Gate, blocking the main axis through the capital (as did an infamous wall years later). Action erupted: a machine-gun fired from behind the pillars while bullets thudded into the sculptures on top of the giant Victory Gate. More fighting broke out around the Anhalter Bahnhof. In these opening skirmishes both sides suffered heavy casualties.

By 8 January, it became clear that Ebert was willing to use aggressive military tactics to bring the situation under control. He issued the order of the day: 'Fellow citizens, Spartakus fights to gain absolute power! The government has taken all necessary measures to destroy the threat of a terror regime. The hour of revenge is near'. Pushed beyond its capacity, the Revolutionary Council folded on 9 January. Now, Ebert took the decision to commit loyal units to storm the buildings still in rebel hands. During the night of 10–11 January, the Maikäfer Regiment went into action in the press district. Heavy fighting broke out for possession of the *Vorwärts* building. Its editorial offices were located in a factory that the rebels had turned into a formidable fortress. Colonel Reinhardt and Major Stephani led the assault. The building was surrounded by troops; three 105-mm howitzers and half a dozen Spandau machine-guns were put in position. The Spandaus fired the opening shots, followed by the heavy guns. Big holes were ripped into the side of the building as machine gun fire poured in through its sandbagged windows. The rebels fired back, holding out for two hours. Finally, they tried to negotiate a ceasefire. Major Stephani demanded their unconditional surrender: he had already received specific orders from the Freikorps commander to shoot all captured revolutionaries out of hand. The Spartakists did not accede to his demand. The Freikorps soldiers then attacked with flame-throwers and heavy mortars. No quarter was given.

Wherever a head popped up, it was shot off. Bodies tumbled into the courtyard. 'Whoever is found with a weapon will be shot.'

The Spartakists realised that their position was utterly hopeless. Seven rebels with their arms raised emerged from the shelled building to negotiate a surrender. Among them was the author Wolfgang Fernbach, an intellectual Spartakist. Only twenty-four hours before, he had published a call to arms: '*Auf zum Streik. Auf zu den Waffen!* Rise up to strike and take up your weapons!' This was not something that made him popular with the regular troops, who had suffered great casualties. The seven were stood up against a wall and shot. The Spartakists answered with a barrage of fire and the Freikorps gunners pumped more shells into the building. It was another hour before the door opened and the remaining Spartakists stumbled out, arms high, choking, coughing, some crying, all in a state of absolute panic. Some 300 were taken prisoner. All of them were beaten up and a good number were instantly shot in the courtyard. The rest were put in jail.[9]

Other battles broke out on the Alexanderplatz around the *Polizeipräsidium* (Police HQ), where Spartakists had armed themselves with pistols and guns taken from overpowered policemen. Two companies of the Maikäfer Regiment under a Lieutenant Schulze launched an attack on the building complex on the morning of 12 January. The first action took place around the Alexanderkaserne where the Spartakists held 600 policemen prisoner. Lieutenant Schulze stormed the compound, delivered the policemen, and armed them with the recaptured weapons. Several Spartakists were shot in the courtyard. As the first artillery piece took up its position on the Alexanderplatz, a burst from a machine-gun placed on top of the police HQ killed every gunner behind it. A Sergeant Westphal took his platoon of fifty men, loaded them on

[9] F. Runkel, *Die Deutsche Revolution*.

trucks, and drove them to the back of the police compound. As they turned the corner into the Prenzlauerstrasse, they were met by a hail of fire that killed the driver of the first truck. It crashed into a house and injured or killed most of the soldiers riding on it. While the survivors attempted to crawl back to safety, snipers picked them off. Another armoured car inched forward, followed by soldiers. Fire poured down from the rooftops and basement windows, rattling and thunking all around them. Bullets ricocheted into cars and bodies. Survivors grabbed their wounded comrades and dragged them out of the line of fire. A bullet sliced above Sergeant Westphal's head into a wall. Crouching behind a lamp-post, he saw a head pop up. He fired and the head disappeared. The soldiers lobbed grenades through the lower windows and momentarily broke the rebels' resistance. Another howitzer took up the action, and fired fifty rounds in rapid succession into the building. The result of this concentrated fire was devastating; bodies were blown from windows. A man, obviously wounded, stood clearly outlined in the frame of a third-floor window, clutching his midriff. Three soldiers fired and the body tumbled out into the street below.

Westphal advanced with two men. A shell hit the side of the building: brick and shrapnel bounced off their steel helmets. The firing was still heavy when the sergeant sprinted to the barricaded main door of the building. Suddenly the door was pushed open. Half a dozen Spartakists came out, unarmed and with their hands raised. Westphal asked if they were ready to surrender, and they said yes, but they had no leader who could negotiate. Westphal suggested that they immediately choose a leader from among themselves, and added: 'Unconditional surrender.' When they hesitated, Westphal told them it was either that or die inside the building. One of the Spartakists went back inside to speak to the others. After some minutes, the door opened wide and a group of 150 Spartakists emerged from the smoking ruin. Lieutenant Schulze and Sergeant Westphal entered the dark interior of the building; shots cracked from everywhere. Schulze screamed an order over the din to cease firing, and declared in an equally loud voice that anyone found with a weapon would be shot. That did it. The fight for the police building was over, [10] but this did not stop the killing. At least five hard-core Spartakists were executed in the courtyard.

In other parts of the city the fighting continued. Groups of Spartakists at strategic positions continued to fire on Freikorps units. Many more died: Spartakists, soldiers, and innocent bystanders. The Reichstag Regiment suffered over a hundred casualties. To end the killing, Friedrich Ebert needed a show of force. Garrisoned near Berlin was the Guard Cavalry Division of General von Hoffmann. The chancellor feared the consequences of ordering an aristocrat general to move against the proletarian masses. He therefore appointed one of his own men, the Gustav Noske of Kiel fame, as his military chieftain. When Noske received the order, he said: 'One of us has to be the bloodhound. I'm not afraid of the responsibility,' and he marched on the capital at the head of 3,000 loyal troops, renamed for the occasion the Freikorps Noske. They arrived around noon on Saturday, 11 January, too late to make any difference to the major action. Before Noske got there, the battle had been decided. However, his men put on a show as they paraded grim-faced down the Kurfürstendamm. It helped to reassure the Berliners.

On 13 January the workers' councils declared an end to the general strike, the workers went back to their factories, and 'Spartakus Week' was over. The subsequent cleaning-up campaign led by Noske and his units was as bad as anything that had taken place at the height of the White Terror of the tsars. Soldiers smashed down doors with their rifle butts, arrested people without court orders, and trucks went out

[10] As reported by Lieutenant Schulze during the subsequent inquiry.

every morning picking up hundreds of rebel sympathisers. The Spartakists were the most exposed group. Government soldiers ransacked the Central Committee offices of the KPD. The outcry against the revolutionary leaders was pushed to fever pitch in a series of editorials. The government press went into top gear, as was proved by a poem in *Vorwärts* by Arthur Zickler: *Many hundreds dead in a row – proletarians! Karl, Rosa, Radek, they are not among them . . .*

Freikorps leaders suggested rounding up all the Communist leaders and writing a quick finis to all this nonsense. Leaflets called for the death of Luxemburg, Liebknecht, and their clique. The tragedy took its destined course. A sum of 100,000 marks was put up as reward for the elimination, dead or alive, of 'the traitors Luxemburg and Liebknecht'.[11] They were hounded across town, fleeing from one hideout to the next; no place was safe. Even after the summary execution of some of her collaborators, Rosa still did not believe that she was in any real danger. They would not dare touch her! They spent the night of 12–13 January 1919 in a worker's flat in Neukölln. When soldiers came up the stairs, they climbed down the fire escape. The next night they moved into a bourgeois neighbourhood where Rosa wrote her last article under the cynical title: 'Order reigns in Berlin'. It was a devastating attack on the bourgeois idea of order with all its brutality and oppression: 'The revolution has no time to lose; it storms ahead full steam, over open graves, victory and defeat, unstoppable in achieving its final aim.' To prevent this from happening, it was time to seal her mouth for ever.

Rosa and Karl were betrayed. Their final hideout was a stately home in Wilmersdorf, at 53 Mannheimer Strasse, in the apartment of Rosa's friend, Mrs Markussohn. The presence of two strange characters in this bourgeois neighbourhood had not gone unnoticed, and someone denounced

---

[11] As the ultimate irony, this sum was offered by Scheidemann, a Socialist whose party affiliation for the past two years had been that of the hunted couple.

them to the right-wing Citizens' Committee. It was late at night on 15 January 1919. Wilhelm Pieck, a member of the KPD's Central Committee, had just arrived at the apartment to provide the couple with false papers, when soldiers under Lieutenant Lindner, together with Mehring, the chief of the Wilmersdorfer Citizens' Council, broke down the door. Rosa was lying on a sofa, suffering from migraine. First she tried to bluff her way out by showing their forged papers, but that did not work. Rosa knew that another stretch in jail was unavoidable, so she packed a small suitcase with a few belongings and some books. While she was in the bedroom, Liebknecht was led away to a waiting car. Luxemburg and Pieck followed under heavy guard in another car. All three were driven to the Hotel Eden, which served as headquarters of Noske's Gardeschützen (grenadiers of the guard) Division. As Liebknecht entered the hotel lobby, he received two blows from the butt of a gun to his head and collapsed to the ground. The soldiers refused to bandage his profusely bleeding wound. Soon afterwards Rosa was pushed into the lobby and was met by insults and catcalls. She saw the prostrate body of Liebknecht and tried to help him to his feet, but was prevented by soldiers who prodded her with fixed bayonets. Lieutenant Lindner led the prisoners to the first floor to the office of the divisional chief-of-staff, Captain Pabst, who was in charge of the 'arrest proceedings'. Pabst kept his prisoners standing while he talked on the phone. From time to time he looked up at them and just said to the person on the end of the line: '*Ja, ja. . . . Ich habe verstanden . . . jawohl.* Yes, yes . . . I understand . . . yes.' It has never been established who issued the order, or who knew of the plan to execute the two Communist leaders.

Pieck was placed under guard in the corridor while Captain Pabst interrogated Liebknecht and Luxemburg. Pieck could hear loud voices; he guessed that Rosa's biting remarks had provoked her interrogator to white-hot fury. The door

opened. Perhaps to give the illusion in the presence of witnesses that nothing out of the ordinary was about to happen,
Captain Pabst said loudly: 'Take them to the prison at
Moabit.' Pieck, still in the ante-room, clearly heard the
captain issue a subdued instruction that the two were not
to leave the cars alive.

The first to come down the stairs was Liebknecht. He was
still unsteady on his legs from the injuries he had received;
Otto Runge, a ruffian on guard at the door, struck him once
more over the head with his rifle butt. Liebknecht fell to the
ground and was dragged unconscious across the lobby by two
soldiers, to the snide remarks of drinkers at the hotel bar:
'Those man-eating Spartakists don't look so terrible after all.'
Liebknecht was pulled into a waiting car, which was driven
by Lieutenant Captain Horst von Pflugk-Harttung. The other
passengers were Captain Heinz von Pflugk-Harttung and
Lieutenants Liepmann, von Rittgen, Stiege, and Schultz, plus
the private soldier Friedrich. The car left the hotel but did
not head for Moabit prison. Instead it drove in the opposite
direction, towards the Berlin Tiergarten, which at this time of
night was completely dark and abandoned. There, the soldier
dragged the half-conscious Karl Liebknecht from the car and
ordered him to walk away. He stumbled off, illuminated by
the headlights of the car. The shot that killed him was fired by
Lieutenant Captian Horst von Pflugk-Harttung. Liebknecht's
body was discovered along a side path by strollers and taken
to the morgue as some unknown caught in the fighting. The
official version put out was that the car had broken down,
and when Liebknecht tried to jump into a thicket, an officer
had shot him.

Meanwhile, Rosa Luxemburg was brought down to the
Eden lobby where soldiers heckled her. A Lieutenant Kurt
Vogel spoke a few words to Runge, a demented soldier,
who stepped forward and smashed her over the head with
his steel-backed rifle butt. Without a sound Rosa Luxemburg

fell to the ground. They dragged her lifeless body outside and threw her into a car waiting outside the hotel entrance. The car took the same route to the Tiergarten, where they threw her body out of the car. As they were about to drive off, Lieutenant Vogel realised that she still showed signs of life. Marine Lieutenant Hermann Wilhelm Souchon fired a bullet into her head.[12] They wrapped her body in a blanket, weighed it down with stones, and dumped it into the Landwehrkanal from the Liechtensteinbruecke. Lieutenants Vogel and Souchon returned to the Eden Hotel to report the version of events that had been agreed on: they were on their way to Moabit prison, when a crowd forced their driver to stop the vehicle and pulled their female prisoner from it. What they then did to her was unknown. Her corpse drifted ashore in May 1919.

But even long before that, the truth came out. The first report to raise doubts about the official version appeared in *Vorwärts*. The cold-blooded killing was too much for Berlin's decent citizens. In an editorial the paper demanded the punishment of those 'guilty of murder'. It was the first time that such harsh words had been used. To stave off an outcry by the working class, the government found itself forced to issue a tame statement: 'The government has immediately ordered a full investigation concerning the violent death of Dr Rosa Luxemburg and Dr Karl Liebknecht. The two, though having sinned greatly towards the German nation, had the right like any other citizen to a fair trial.' In contrast, the republican *Taegliche Rundschau* stated in its lead article: 'Blood called for blood! The blood bath instigated by Karl Liebknecht and Rosa Luxemburg called for revenge. This was swift and, in the case of Rosa Luxemburg, cruel but just.' By April 1919, not only did the government know the truth about the murders, but so did the public. This was because the lunatic Otto

[12] For many years it was believed that Lieutenant Vogel fired the fatal bullet. Recent investigation has shown it was the other officer in the car, Lieutenant Souchon.

Runge felt that his role in the brutal executions had not been sufficiently praised; he boasted to the press of his fifteen minutes of glory. The government finally had to give in to pressure from the public, and a military tribunal conducted a trial. The only accusation levelled against Lieuntenant Vogel was that of 'hiding a corpse and falsifying a report to a superior'. He was sentenced to a minimal prison term, but friends delivered him from jail the same week and helped him across the Swiss border. Otto Runge, the crazed killer, was accused of 'using his service weapon to inflict harm,' and sentenced to two years in jail. Those who were truly guilty were never brought to trial.

Rosa Luxemburg dared to knock on the class barriers that had shaped Germany's dominant social system for generations. Her attempt ended in failure. Her works were publicly burned after Hitler took power. Her monument was destroyed. Many of her disciples paid for their loyalty in Hitler's concentration camps or in Stalin's gulags. Even worse, her own side misused her name by spreading ideas which were not hers and which she would have never sanctioned. Finally, they tried to destroy her memory. But the spirit of Rosa Luxemburg lives on, as no funeral pyre nor dictatorial decree can ever bury a thought once it is planted in the minds of people. Her most fitting epitaph could be the comment of Oscar Wilde:

'It is personalities, not principles, that move the age.'

And then . . .

It is one of the great tragedies of modern history that Germany's first encounter with a democratic government was associated with defeat and misery. The debacle can be blamed in full on the use of bullets to solve a political problem. The

Communists, listening to foolishly optimistic advice, built their plan on brute force, then committed a tragic error that led to the crisis. The Social Democrats, accepting the might of the military in order to maintain order, suppressed the Communist revolt by using equal brutality.[13] With the pitched street battles of January 1919, which the historian Rudolf Hilferding called 'Germany's Battle of the Marne', revolutionary activity reached its zenith. The final act of the German Revolution was to bury its fallen at the cemetery in Berlin-Friedrichsfelde on 25 January 1919.

The murder of their leaders, and the intolerance and hatred with which Spartakist–Communist accounts were settled, captured the centre-stage of Germany's political scene for years to come.[14] The savagery displayed by Noske's *soldateska* (unruly bunch) drove many into the camp of the opposition. The murders implied that the state was so fragile that its preservation depended upon the slaughter of its opponents. It followed a time of confusion; the hesitant took the side of the government and the less hesitant formed new parties. One of these was started in the cellars of a Munich brewery. In the beginning they were few, until they found a charismatic leader in an Austrian Corporal who would not hesitate to make terror his weapon.

The main political organisations were cobbled together to form the Weimar Republic. It proved a total failure, as was Hindenburg's presidency. The agony inside the Reichstag continued. Inflation destroyed the country's economy. From this confusion grew a new party under Hitler who united in him the three elements of tyranny. These were the popular version of the kaiser principle, demanding unquestioned obedience and loyalty to his person as the uncontested Führer; a lack

[13] Including the regime of Kurt Eisner in Bavaria.
[14] Georg Grosz, the famous humorist, drew a cartoon which shows an officer and a businessman at lunch while soldiers bayonet workers: the Communists fall while the money piles up.

of scruples; and the opportunism to change, or even abandon, any published political programme. His charismatic speeches, carrying racist overtones, were food for the masses. They assured him of the first; to create a climate for the second, he engineered disorder in the streets; as for the third, he promised anything the masses wanted to hear, while never intending to fulfil those promises. His pet saying was: '*Das deutsche Recht ist der Wille seines Führers.* – The German law is the will of its Führer.' With this, Hitler buried the budding German Republic.

Interlude

1920–1944

'Non-violence is the greatest force at the disposal of mankind. It is mightier than the mightiest weapon designed by the ingenuity of man,' preached Mohandâs Gandhi. With this phrase, he set out to prove that the power of arms could never prevail against the force of the spirit. In 1930 this half-naked fakir exhorted people to civil disobedience against an unjust British law governing the production of salt, then gathered his followers in 'a march to the sea to make their own salt'. People from every part of the country and every class of society joined his march. It shamed the English into negotiating with this man of peaceful persuasion. It was the beginning of a non-violent mass struggle for Indians to obtain freedom from their colonial overlords. He maintained a hunger fast until his people, both Hindu and Muslim, agreed to live together in harmony.[15] For this, one of them murdered him in 1948. Mohandâs Gandhi, the apostle of non-violence,

[15] The implacable hatred between Muslims and Hindus began with the Islamic conquest of Sultan Mahmud-al-Ghazna in 1000 AD.

was and is the exception. Two of his heirs, who took lessons from his non-violent approach, were Nelson Mandela and Martin Luther King.

Not all revolutionaries of that era acted with the restraint of Gandhi and his disciples. The thirties saw an individual rise to power who preached extreme nationalism, ethnic hatred, racism, and state-organised murder. For some time, the world failed to understand that Adolf Hitler was more of a threat to democracy and peace than Communism had ever been. His demands increased, his personality seemed irresistible. An appalling fate befell those who refused him. Hitler's rise was relentless, as was the way he subdued his next-door neighbours. He did not have to fight. He had only to convince the world powers that he intended to fight. Most countries simply gave way and submitted, despite the big noises made by their politicians. These poor little men with their creased suits and their funny hats, humiliated by the polished jackboots and stylish olive-green uniforms of Nazi generals, looked on as their countries were occupied and taken apart as one fillets a fish of its bones.

The German war machine rumbled unchallenged across Europe until at last the fortunes of war changed. By 1944, the situation for Germany was not only desperate, it was hopeless. In June of that year, with Allied pincers moving towards the Rhine and the Soviets ready to strike at the heart of Germany, Hitler had to be stopped, but not by the Allies; by someone from the inside. Some brave Germans conspired together. They knew that exposure meant barbaric torture or agonising death. And many were prepared to lose their lives in order to spare Germany the horror of defeat. What it took was a rebellion. It was a mad plan, a mission into hell.

6

20 July 1944

'Ein Volk, ein Reich, ein Führer'

Ein Volk, ein Reich, ein Führer.
One realm, one people, one leader.
Nazi party slogan, early 1930s

Wir haben das Letzte getan für Deutschland.
We have done our best for Germany.
General Friedrich Olbricht

'You are the man we need,' said General Friedrich Olbricht, deputy chief of Germany's home army, to the tall colonel with the eyepatch. The general was not speaking of gaining some illusory 'final victory', but of a more serious and immediate problem. He knew the colonel as a brilliant planner and a brave man. In the African desert he had been permanently disabled during a strafing run by American planes. Men of his calibre were rare, and, despite his physical handicaps, the German High Command had appointed him ADC to the commander of its reserve army, Generaloberst Fromm.

These were harsh days for the Third Reich. Around its borders Nazi and Allied forces were locked in a titanic struggle. The Germans were reeling under the relentless assault of the Red Army in the East and the combined forces of the

Americans, French, and British in the West. Germany was faced with destruction, and the German race with annihilation. Nothing, not even the fiction of some all-destructive *Wunderwaffen* (magic weapon) could hide the fact that the nation was headed for losses on a cataclysmic scale. For good German men it was the moment to act to prevent their country's headlong rush towards the precipice.

The general studied this man who had courageously brought back his regiment from the bloody Gethsemane of Kasserine Pass. He saw a face undisturbed by even the merest flicker of emotion. 'For years,' General Olbricht said, 'I have been walking on the very brink of hell, treading between truth and lies, good and evil. If I had ever spoken out against the tyrant, I would die as a martyr, and this would achieve nothing. God knows, there are already enough martyrs in the prison camps of our glorious Third Reich. But I cannot be silent any longer with my poor country moving into a world of infinite darkness. In that I am not alone.' Listening to the general, the colonel knew that he was about to become linked with a conspiracy at the highest military level. 'Our ultimate aim is to achieve a negotiated peace,' continued the general, before looking the young colonel straight in the eye. 'For this to happen we must eliminate Hitler. Are you with us?'

Colonel Claus Schenck Graf von Stauffenberg looked out the window. What had once been the glittering capital of Prussia, home of great men of literature and thought, was now a cratered moonscape. Yes, the general was right: four long years ago they had given up everything, family, home, even a future. And now the Fatherland was a cemetery. He did not hesitate. 'You can count on me, Herr General.'

'Herr *Oberst*, I can see we are going to understand each other. You are a man of unsuspected talents. The operation order is a secret known only to a few. To put our plan into operation, the code name is *Operation Walküre* (Operation Valkyrie).'

* * *

The serious setbacks experienced by the German forces prompted a number of high-ranking German officers to break Hitler's brutal grip on the nation. Counting on a widespread, popular uprising was out of the question under Germany's totalitarian regime. Ever since the beginning of the war Hitler had kept himself incommunicado, protected day and night by personal guards. Only a group of his yes-sayers had direct access, men like Himmler, Göring, Goebbels, or most sinister of them all, Martin Bormann, the one self-effacing man of mystery among the bemedalled Caesars of the Third Reich. The attempt on Hitler's life, if such an attempt were to succeed, had to be made by a small but well-organised unit of high-ranking officers who sometimes gained direct access to Hitler. There had been previous attempts which had ended in failure. The closest anyone came to killing the Führer was on 13 March 1943, when he was visiting the Central Army Group on the Russian front. A bomb was placed on his personal aircraft, jammed in between two bottles of schnapps. The pre-set timed fuse failed to work, and Hitler's plane landed safely without anyone on board being aware of their miraculous escape. One of the plotters, Count Fabian von Schlabrendorff, showed great courage when he dashed into Hitler's HQ to remove the device from the aircraft before it was discovered.

Opposition to Hitler within Germany became more widespread[1] as its military failures increased, but the key elements remained among the disenchanted officer class. Field Marshal von Witzleben; General Ludwig Beck, former chief-of-staff of the army; Generaloberst Fromm, head of the reserve army; and his second-in-command, General Friedrich Olbricht; Dr Karl Goerdeler, former lord mayor of Leipzig; Ambassador

---

[1] In February 1943, two Munich University students, Hans Scholl and his sister Sophie, founded the Weisse Rose anti-war group. Both were arrested and beheaded.

Ulrich von Hassel – and Admiral Canaris, head of the German Abwehr (counter-espionage). The rest read like a *Who's Who* of Prussian junkerdom: Count Helmuth von Moltke, Count Fabian von Schlabrendorff, and Count Claus Schenck Graf von Stauffenberg, ADC to General Fromm at *Oberkommando Heer* (army high command).

The conspiracy was elaborate in its organisation since it had to encompass the likelihood of defeat and the possible disintegration of the entire nation. By the end of 1943, General Olbricht had completed a draft outline: kill Hitler, take control of the Wehrmacht (the German armed forces), and eliminate the SS. Then go for a compromise peace treaty with the Allies. The key was the elimination of Hitler, a task that Graf reserved for himself. *Operation Walküre* was an apt name: struck by the fury of the Valkyries, Hitler and his cronies would meet their end on a fiery funeral pyre.

This plan was discussed by the conspiracy's inner circle: Count Ulrich Wilhelm von Schwerin-Schwanenfeld, Adam von Trott zu Stolz, Count Fritz Dietlof von der Schulenburg, Colonel Albrecht Mertz von Quirnheim, Colonel Georg Hansen, Lieutenant Caesar von Hofacker, and Count Peter Yorck von Wartenburg. All were the scions of old-fashioned German junkers and stiff-necked noblemen, no match for the gutter fighters of the Brownshirt days or the Nazi careerists at Hitler's elbow. But all were willing to die for their patriotic ideals, if they could only decide what they were. 'What we want is men who will pull the trigger for what they believe in,' stated General Olbricht. 'We need a quick result. The Allies will be landing somewhere along the coast of France this summer. Then the two-war front will become a reality for our army. Since all of you have earned a trusted role in our plans, the time has come to know about them.'

Claus Schenck, Count von Graf, was not a revolutionary but a German of great nobility who rebelled against the repressive dictatorship of Hitler and his henchmen. Stauffenberg's head-strong personality brought new impetus to the conspiracy and he became the driving force for the *coup d'état*. However, he was no assassin and he was certainly the wrong man to kill Hitler. His wounds had severely handicapped his movements: he had lost an eye, his right arm was paralysed, and on his left hand two fingers were missing. This prevented him from using a hand-gun, leaving the only alternative: a powerful bomb.

Just like the German High Command, the conspirators were taken by surprise when Allied forces landed in Normandy on 6 June 1944. Stauffenberg made his first assassination attempt on 11 July, and again on 15 July. On both occasions Hitler failed to make an appearance. On 17 July, part of the plot was discovered. The plotters did not underrate the efficiency of *Gestapo* interrogators. General Ludwig Beck, General Olbricht, and Colonel von Stauffenberg decided that the next opportunity to get close to Hitler had to be the right one. It happened sooner than expected.

On 18 July, General Olbricht called Stauffenberg into his office: 'Our Korporal [Hitler] has ordered a briefing about our state of readiness.' Olbricht handed Stauffenberg a message. 'You will proceed to *Wolfschanze Eins* [Wolf's Lair One][2] on the twentieth.' He shook the colonel's hand. 'Our time has come . . .' The third attempt on the Führer's life was at hand.

The military situation was desperate. Hitler knew it and his generals knew it. And yet, while washing down his daily dose of pills with tea to steady his nerves, he kept on saying: 'It is part of the German greatness that victory can be forged in the face of defeat.' The reality looked quite different. The Red Army had liberated Leningrad and taken Minsk, Vilna, Pinsk,

---

[2] *Wolfschanze* (Wolf's Lair) was the code for Hitler's HQ. There was also a *Wolfschanze Zwei* (Wolf's Lair Two) for the Western theatre of war near the village of Margival in eastern France.

and Grodno. A German force was on the brink of becoming encircled in the Baltic States as a Russian drive threatened East Prussia. On the home front, Allied bomber fleets visited German cities with monotonous regularity and buried them under a deluge of bombs. On 4 June, Allied forces had walked into Rome, and two days later, a vast armada had landed on the shores of Normandy. Hitler had begun to feel what a war on two fronts really meant. His health had deteriorated. He was pale and listless. During meetings with his staff he played nervously with his spectacles or chewed on a pencil. He had to sit while his generals pored over maps of a rapidly shrinking Nazi Europe. Hitler was a bitter man; he felt betrayed and blamed his generals for allowing the Allies to land in France. He was incapable of issuing coherent orders and would rave in monologues about fantasy weapons, his *Vergeltungswaffen*, with which he would smite the enemy. His paranoia knew no bounds and he lived in permanent fear for his life.[3] He never travelled without a bulletproof vest and even his cap was armour-plated. He had food tasters, and a quack physician prescribed him pills and medicines. He continued in his belief in his own destiny, which was read to him daily by his court astrologer. 'The German people don't deserve me,' he kept repeating to his entourage.

Hitler had spent the first two weeks of July with his mistress, Eva Braun, at his residence on the Obersalzberg. That is how he escaped the two previous planned attempts on his life. In the third week of the month he flew back to his field headquarters, the *Wolfschanze*, in a forest near Rastenburg in East Prussia, as he was expecting a visit by Benito Mussolini on 20 July. For that reason his staff had advanced the daily *Führer Lagebesprechung* (situation report) for 12.30 p.m. Because of the sweltering heat, the meeting was moved from the usual concrete bunker, whose solid walls would have

---

[3] As did another dictator, Joseph Stalin.

added greatly to the blast effect, to a ventilated log cabin in the woods. This move proved to have critical consequences.

On 20 July 1944, accompanied by a conspirator, Ober-leutnant (1st Lieutenant) Werner von Haeften, Count von Stauffenberg took a courier flight from Berlin to Rastenburg where he was expected to deliver a brief on the positioning of newly created front-line units, pulled from the reserve army. In his briefcase were not only his notes, but an explosive device using the most lethal substance then known: one kilogram of hexonite, connected to a chemical time fuse[4] which would go off within minutes, once the glass vial was broken. Stauffenberg's plane landed at Rastenburg at 10.15 a.m. From the airstrip he was driven to the HQ complex where he passed the numerous SS control posts without hindrance. General Keitel stepped from the wooden hut.

'So, Stauffenberg, did you bring us good news?'

'I hope so, Herr General . . .'

Keitel preceded the colonel into the briefing room, where Hitler was surrounded by his generals and personal staff.[5] They were bent over a map laid out before them on a heavy wooden table and took no notice of his arrival. Stauffenberg stationed himself beside Colonel Brandt who was standing next to Hitler. He had already broken the vial of the fuse, and the bomb was set to go off within minutes. He placed his briefcase on the floor and used his foot to slide it under the table, before turning to Keitel and whispering: 'General, will you excuse me for a minute, I must call Berlin.' The general nodded and Stauffenberg left the room. It was 12.50 p.m. He had hardly stepped from the log cabin (it was certainly no more than one minute later), when a violent explosion blew the map-room apart. The roof was lifted off and the

---

[4] He used a captured English chemical fuse as it proved more reliable.
[5] Keitel, Jodl, Warlimont, Heusinger, Buhle, Bodenschatz, Scherff, Korten, Voss, Puttkamer, Brandt, Below, Assman, Waizenegger, Buechs, Fegelein, Guensche, Sonnleithner, Berger.

wooden walls splintered into a thousand pieces. While he ordered his driver to make in all haste for the airport, he saw a black cloud rising above the treetops. Once again luck was with him; in the confusion no order had gone out to the perimeter posts to stop any traffic leaving the camp.

The cloud of dust and debris settled, the wounded moaned, guards yelled, sirens screamed – and Hitler stumbled from the ruin! *Alive!* His right trouser leg was missing, he was covered in dust and blood, his hair was singed and his right arm dangled lifeless by his side. There were severe burn marks on his legs and a deep gash on his back where a falling beam had struck him. His eardrums had been damaged and he was shaking his head in an attempt to clear his hearing. His eyes registered deep shock and complete disbelief. Everyone else at his end of the room was either dead or badly wounded. Hitler's life had been spared by the heavy table, which had protected his upper torso, and by the flimsy walls, which had given way under the blast effect. Hitler stumbled around, numb and dazed, mumbling: *'Es gibt eine Vorsehung . . . Es gibt eine Vorsehung!* There is providence!' He thought that he had escaped an aerial bombardment, and only much later did it dawn on him that it had actually been an attempt on his life – from the inside.

In the chaos following the explosion, Count Stauffenberg bluffed his way past the SS guarding the HQ compound and his He-111 bomber took off for Berlin. He had a front-row view of his work as the plane passed over a black patch in the forest and the last he saw of it was people running about like nervous ants.

The nucleus of the conspiracy had gathered in the office of General Olbricht at the headquarters of the OKH *Ersatzheer* (reserve army) in Berlin's Bendlerstrasse. Present were Field Marshal von Witzleben, General Beck, General Hoeppner, and Olbricht. Their first task called for an announcement by radio, warning the nation that a dissident group of ruthless SS leaders had tried to usurp power from the Wehrmacht. To foil this attempt, Generals Beck and Witzleben had found it necessary to assume power following the assassination of the Führer. On a military level, locally based Wehrmacht reserves were to disarm the SS in Berlin, occupy the radio stations, and seal off the government sector. The conspirators counted that, with Hitler dead, regular army officers would no longer feel bound by their Treueid, the oath sworn to the Nazi leader. Everything hinged on two factors: one, Hitler being dead; and two, a cut in communications between Hitler's field headquarters and the government offices in Berlin.

It took Stauffenberg's plane two hours to make it back to the capital. He landed at 15.45, and drove straight to the Bendlerstrasse, where he reported that nobody could have possibly survived the blast. His assessment was based on the conflagration cloud and his overflight observation. Unfortunately he was wrong. The plot could have still worked, had it not been for that second factor: the communications system had not been cut between Berlin and the *Wolfschanze*, which was to lead to the failure of the conspiracy. With Stauffenberg's 'kill report', General Olbricht rushed into General Fromm's office and insisted that the commander-in-chief of the reserve army immediately issue the signal for *Operation Walküre*. Fromm was hesitant, as no final confirmation (other than Stauffenberg's verbal report) had come through about Hitler's death. He refused to give the order and a scuffle took place in which the general was overpowered and locked up. In the meantime and without instructions from General Olbricht, Mertz von Quirnheim had already released the initial Walküre order. It went out at 16.05 to the army garrisons in and around Berlin. Although the orders were confusing, army units obeyed: from the tank training centre at Krampnitz and Gross Glienicke, from the infantry school at Doebernitz, with a battalion from the Ensign Training Corps from Potsdam, they moved on Berlin. Finally, one more unit was ordered into action. The Wachbataillion Grossdeutschland was given the task of occupying key ministries in the government district.

When the battalion's communications officer, Lieutenant Hagen, read the order, it struck him as odd that it had not been signed by the commander-in-chief of the home army, but by a staff officer. He talked the battalion commander, Major Otto Ernst Remer, into verifying the order with the Minister of Propaganda, Dr Josef Goebbels.

The result proved devastating for the leaders of the putsch as Goebbels arranged for a telephone link for Major Remer with headquarters at Rastenburg. A man came on the line: '*Do you recognise my voice?*'

Remer was thunderstruck; his knuckles went white around the receiver, before he replied: '*Jawohl, mein Führer.*'

Hitler told Goebbels to order Remer to break up the plot with the utmost vigour.

With one phone call, the situation for the conspirators became untenable. Dr Goebbels called the Deutschlandsender radio station and told them to broadcast a special bulletin that a group of army officers had attempted a putsch, but that the Führer was alive and well, and would soon address the nation. No sooner had the rumour spread that Hitler might still be alive than many of the officers awaiting the outcome of the assassination attempt switched sides. One of them was General Fromm, who spoke by phone to General Keitel in Rastenburg. Keitel confirmed 'the miraculous escape of the Führer'. Was Hitler really alive? Fromm was not about to take a chance. So the conspirators locked him in his office. While this confusion went on, Major Remer marched with his Wachbataillion on the Bendlerstrasse.

A tired Field Marshal von Witzleben had just temporarily left his office when a message was received by the communications officer in the Bendlerstrasse that Heinrich Himmler of the SS had been appointed as new head of the reserve army. This signal aroused the suspicions of an officer on the staff of General Fromm. Colonel Karl Pridun, ADC to General Olbricht, called his staff into his office and reminded them of their oath of loyalty to Hitler.[6] Curiously enough, none of those who had been ordered by Goebbels to put down the putsch had, until now, made an appearance at the Bendlerstrasse: neither SS Obergruppenführer Kaltenbrunner of the Gestapo, nor the head of Hitler's Special Forces, SS Colonel Otto Skorzeny. Also Remer's battalion was delayed by transportation problems. It was left to the Pridun group inside the Bendlerstrasse building to take action.

History might never have known what next took place had it not been for an eyewitness who was not only overlooked and forgotten, but who managed to survive the war. This was Major Georgi, working in the headquarters of the German air force. He was also married to General Olbricht's daughter. At 9 p.m. Olbricht called his son-in-law and told him to meet him right away at the Bendlerstrasse.[7]

> *Väterchen* [my father-in-law] sat in his office smoking a cigar, a glass of Cognac in front of him. 'At noon,' he said to me, 'Count von Stauffenberg dropped a bomb on Hitler. We were told that he had been killed; Field Marshal von Witzleben took power. But we found out that Hitler had survived, and most of our supporters have changed sides. We may be able to hold out for a short time. Perhaps one night, perhaps two, but we might also be done for in an hour. I shall die here like a soldier. I shall die for a good cause, of that I am convinced. *Wir haben das Letzte getan für Deutschland.* – We have done our best for Germany.' My father-in-law then told me to

---

[6] Karl Pridun, *20 Juli 1944, Stellungsnahme.*
[7] Georgi's typewritten account of the meeting was written at 01.00 hrs on 21 July 1944; in other words, barely ninety minutes after the event.

leave immediately and save my family. It was ten minutes to eleven, when six to eight staff officers entered the room with guns drawn and demanded to know what these conflicting orders were all about. My father-in-law tried to stall them but they insisted on speaking directly with General Fromm. At that moment the door opened and Stauffenberg entered the office; he told them that he would check whether Fromm was available. As he left the room, the count suddenly slammed the door shut and a shot rang out. It was followed by several more. My father used this opportunity to shake my hand, then took me by the elbow and shoved me from the room. His antechamber was now full of men with guns. In the confusion I put my hands above my head and marched out. Nobody stopped me. I was now certain that I had seen my *Väterchen* for the last time.

In fact, a group of officers loyal to Hitler led by Lieutenant-Colonel Franz Herber rushed into Olbricht's office to demand an explanation. That is when Colonel von Stauffenberg entered and his personal ADC, Captain Klausing, saw the guns drawn. It was Klausing who fired first, before the officers shot back. Stauffenberg was slightly wounded but managed to escape into another room by slamming the door.[8] At the point of the staff officers' guns, Olbricht was marched along the corridor to Fromm's room where General Fromm 'was set free'. Fromm's dubious role in the proceedings put him in grave peril and he felt a great need to demonstrate his allegiance to the Führer. He ordered the immediate arrest of Olbricht, Stauffenberg, Mertz von Quirnheim, and Lieutenant von Haeften.

Another conspirator at this time still inside the Bendlerstrasse complex was General Ludwig Beck, a man too senior in rank

---

[8] Von der Heyde, *Der 20, Juli 1944 im OKW-AHA.*

to touch without a direct order from Hitler. But he knew too much about Fromm's part in the affair and had to be eliminated. Fromm confronted him. Beck took his service pistol and fired two bullets into his own chest. He was still alive when Fromm ordered a sergeant to administer the *coup de grâce*. To forestall any attempt to connect him with the failed conspiracy, Fromm announced that an immediate trial had been conducted. He didn't say who the members of this kangaroo court were, but ordered the death penalty for '*den Oberst im Generalstab Merz, den General der Infantrie Olbricht, diesen Oberst dessen Namen ich nicht mehr kenne* – whose name I do not wish to know any longer [with this he pointed to Stauffenberg] *und diesen Oberleutnant* [Haeften].' The sentenced foursome were marched down the stairs and pushed into the courtyard. A pile of sand had been heaped in front of a basement window as added protection against air raids. Olbricht, Stauffenberg, Mertz, and Haeften were shoved towards the sand pile.[9] It was ten minutes past midnight. Two parked trucks switched on their headlights, catching the four condemned officers in their glare. A detachment of ten men from Remer's battalion took up their positions. It happened very quickly. '*Auf mein Kommando*' – on my command!' In the momentary silence that followed the sharp order, only the deep growl of the idling engines was heard. '*Auflegen* – take aim.' Claus Schenck von Stauffenberg suddenly took a step forward and, without the slightest tremble in his voice, shouted: '*Es lebe unser heiliges Deutschland!*'

'*Feuer!*' Ten guns spat out a hail of bullets and four bodies sank to the ground.

SS Colonel Otto Skorzeny, the hard man who had liberated Benito Mussolini after his arrest by the dissident Italian army, was aboard a train in Berlin's central station when the news

---

[9] The site today is marked by a plaque and visitors can see the impact of the bullets in the wall.

reached him. He rushed to the Bendlerstrasse where he found the four dead conspirators; Generaloberst Fromm had already gone home. This aroused the suspicions of Skorzeny; why would the head of Germany's home army, whose deputy and closest collaborator was the bomb carrier, leave his command post on a night such as this? For a time, the SS colonel kept his misgivings to himself and instead arrested Stauffenberg's brother Berthold, Yorck von Wartenburg, Ulrich von Schwerin-Schwanenfeld, and Eugen Gerstenmaier. In the courtyard he stripped them of their medals and locked them up for trial.

At the same time, Hitler went on the air in a nationwide broadcast: 'I speak to you today so that you may hear my voice and know that I am uninjured and well. You will also learn the details of a crime that has not its like in German history. A small clique of ambitious, wicked, and stupidly criminal officers forged a plot to eliminate me and along with me virtually the entire Wehrmacht leadership. The bomb, planted by Count von Stauffenberg, burst two metres to the right of me . . .' He ended his tirade with a prophetic phrase: '*We shall settle accounts the way we National Socialists are accustomed to settle them!*'

And then . . .

The traditional German officer corps had become entangled in something far more complex than their elementary task of fighting and dying for the *Vaterland* (Fatherland). Politics were no pastime for soldiers and they would all swing by the neck for it. Hitler knew that the conspiracy involved not just a small clique of class-minded officers but many of his closest collaborators and generals. Those spineless junkers (aristocratic officer class) who envied him his iron will and military genius, how dare they call him 'the little corporal'! It was mortifying that the instrument he must rely on to achieve his aims was fundamentally opposed to him. His personal hatred was now directed against the entire officer class and it sent him into an uncontrollable fury. He gave strict orders that anyone connected with the plot be executed in the most barbarous manner: '*aufgehaengt wie Schlachtvieh*' (butchered like cattle).

Many were dragged before the merciless and paranoid judge Dr Roland Freisler, Hitler's appointed henchman of the special People's Court.[10] 'By authority of the Führer!' The trials went on for weeks and the list of condemned read like a register of the German military hierarchy. Hitler's mania bore a likeness to Stalin's Tuchachevsky purges, when the Red tsar decapitated the entire Soviet High Command. It was a time for getting rid of cumbersome opponents and dissidents, intellectuals, aristocrats, industrialists, clerics, writers, and academicians. With no recourse to the principles of basic justice, all were found guilty, all were strung up with piano wire on meat hooks in the prison basement of Berlin-Ploetzensee, while film units recorded scene after grisly scene so that their final agony could be shown to the dictator. Hitler felt no pity because he knew no pity.

It was also the beginning of an unimaginable nightmare, the promulgation of the *Sippenhaft* decree (sibling arrest). Family members of suspected conspirators were rounded up and 'guilt by blood' was passed on to them. No one was spared, not even the greatest of German heroes, Field Marshal Erwin Rommel. The Desert Fox had not been directly involved in the conspiracy; however, his biting criticism had offended dangerous characters such as Himmler, Goebbels, and especially Hitler's *éminence grise*, Martin Bormann. He dispatched Generals Wilhelm Burgdorf and Ernst Maisel

---

[10] Freisler was crushed to death by a falling beam in his court chambers during a Berlin air raid.

to Rommel's home in Herrlingen (Suabia) where he was recovering from wounds. For once, Goebbels was unable to distort the truth or twist it into the lies that condemned others before the People's Court. Rommel was offered a Socratic finale. The field marshal accepted a vial of cyanide as a noble way out. His death was tearfully announced in the *Voelkischer Beobachter* as the result of a war injury and he was laid to rest with military honours.

Generaloberst Fromm, who had ordered the immediate execution of Stauffenberg and Olbricht to cover his own part in the affair, was arrested, accused of 'cowardice in the face of the enemy', and executed.

The putsch of 20 July 1944 found a fitting epitaph in the pages of the *New York Herald Tribune*: 'The moment that Hitlerism takes its final stand by destroying Germany's military tradition, it lifts a great weight from the workload of our Allied forces.'

There is a personal postscript to this episode. On a warm summer evening of 1960, I met the man that the Allies had dubbed 'Commando Extraordinary', Colonel Otto Skorzeny of the Third Reich. His veins held enough ice to sink another *Titanic* and his eyes were those of a man who knew little pity. Sitting on his terrace in Madrid, we talked about his role as commander of Hitler's special intervention unit. He had only done his job, he said, which was to eliminate the enemy by whatever means. 'I hated nobody,' he told me,' not even the enemy.' Our conversation drifted to the events of 20 July, and the part he had played in it, I was curious to know what he thought of the conspirators, and why their attempt to kill Hitler had miscarried. '*Stümpers* – bunglers,' he said. If his eyes communicated any emotion at all, it was wholly that of contempt for those who had tried and failed. 'If you have to eliminate a specific target, you don't shove a bomb under a table and walk out.'

'How would *you* go about it?'

'Walk into the room, pull a gun, shoot the target – twice, to make sure. Before the bystanders recover from their shock and crawl from underneath the table, you're already halfway to London or Moscow.'

'And if you can't use a gun?'

'Wrap a man in dynamite, have him blow up the target and himself.'

He was right, of course – there is no defence against a human torpedo. Fortunately, in every one of us there is a highly developed sense of guilt. That is what stops most men from going beyond the edge. Most men. Except a humanoid machine wound up like clockwork. A man with a stick of dynamite in his pocket and his thumb on the trigger. A suicidal robot pre-programmed to kill.

Stauffenberg's attempt, as noble as it may have been, was doomed because he thought and acted like a human being.

Interlude

April–August 1945

'Whom the Gods wish to destroy they first make mad.' In the accounts of human lunacy, one man stands out: Adolf Hitler. He had a race exterminated just for existing and thereby set a new example of madness; 'man is defined by what makes him inhuman.' His megalomania ended on a Viking pyre. At 3.30 p.m. on 30 April 1945, as Russian troops were about to enter his last redoubt, he stuck a pistol in his mouth and pulled the trigger. His body was doused with gasoline and incinerated.[11] His bones were never found.

---

[11] Together with that of his newly wedded wife, Eva Braun.

The war in Europe had come to an end, but the war itself was not over. The focus shifted to the Pacific theatre, where a Japanese emperor, whose generals would admit neither defeat nor surrender, was faced with a seemingly insurmountable problem; how to bring the war to a close. The Japanese army's last battle was not directed against a vastly superior enemy – but against the heart of Japan itself, its divine emperor.

7

15 August 1945

'Tenno Heika Banzai!'

Tenno Heika Banzai!
Long live the emperor!

The time has come when we must bear the unbearable.
We swallow our tears . . .
Emperor Hirohito, 15 August 1945

The celestial monarch of the Empire of the Rising Sun spoke: 'Why could they not understand what was on Our mind?' Black despair overwhelmed everyone in the room; nobody dared to raise his eyes to the divine presence. They were unsure of themselves, still worried that some fanatical officer was lurking in the shadows. Only the calm bravery with which the emperor had faced the crisis gave them hope for the future. Through the windows they saw a cloud of smoke from burning documents.

In a house that had survived the onslaught of the US Air Force firebombing Tokyo, an officer bowed his head and stared at the body on the rice mat. He picked up the paper, a suicide poem. A few drops of blood had splashed on the thick, firm ink strokes.

An old man spoke: 'Your husband will return home in an hour. My daughter, are you prepared for the news?'

'I am, my father.'

'He has killed himself.'

The girl had been trained to show no emotion. 'I have been prepared for it.'

Japan was living through its longest day.

The *tenno* was the Chosen One by the grace of God. The notion of the sacred emperor, linked only to God, was the source of the *tenno's* omnipotence. It conferred on him special earthly responsibilities and was at the heart of Japanese monarchical doctrine. A fanatical belief in the divine power of their *tenno* forged Japan's soldiers into the most formidable army in Asia, willing to sacrifice their lives for their emperor, a divinity who embodied the spirit of the entire nation. They had fought hard and would die well to protect their monarch, because to die for Him was the ultimate honour for any man. To submit to an enemy, however, was dishonourable; it was better to commit *seppuku*[1] than live in shame.

'A Japanese soldier will never surrender! His life belongs to His Divine Emperor!' The Japanese army had given proof of their steadfastness on Tarawa, a slip of sand in the Pacific Ocean. Of its 4,836 defenders, only seventeen Japanese soldiers were taken prisoner. The rest died heroically – either from bombs, bullets, or by their own hand.

August 1945. There were still 6 million Japanese men under arms who would willingly obey their emperor's command that they make the supreme sacrifice, like the defenders of Okinawa and Iwo Jima, glorious names with glorious martyrs. They had been doing battle with a cunning enemy and had no illusions about what lay ahead: more desperate battles on the beaches and more massive bombs falling on their homes. Beneath the rubble their families lay buried, but the Japanese army was still very much alive. Those long-nosed

---

[1] Also known as hara-kiri.

white devils had overlooked one thing: their bombs had turned Japanese cities into the perfect killing ground on which to fight the aggressor. They would defend every field, every brook, every village, and every house and they would extract a terrible toll to avenge their loved ones. Most important of all, nothing would divert the Japanese soldier from his sacred duty to protect his *tenno*. In those hot summer days of 1945, the will of the Japanese soldier remained unbroken, his faith in his celestial emperor intact. Seven hundred years before, a kamikaze (or 'divine wind') had stopped a mighty Mongol invasion fleet from violating Japan's shores. Now they would also wreak terrible destruction on the foe; the bodies of his drowned and slain would litter the beaches and mountains of their home islands. The Japanese soldier would stand, fight, and die. With his ultimate sacrifice he would ensure for himself a place in the afterlife.

And now they heard of this shameful betrayal by their traitorous politicians who had dared to force *their emperor* to read an announcement which would be broadcast to the nation.

From early in the morning, a message had repeatedly interrupted the martial music sent out over the national radio network: 'A broadcast of the highest importance is to be made at noon today. Will all listeners rise . . .' At midday people across the land would hear for the first time in the 2,000-year history of this proud country the Voice of the Crane, their celestial *Showa-tenno*, known to the rest of the world as Hirohito, Emperor of Japan. It could not be, it must not be – no, they would not allow the Voice of the Crane to be defiled. A cry of fury went up from the young officers who had sworn to carry on the sacred traditions of bushido; the knights of an honourable society, the samurai. As an initial step, Japan must be cruelly purged of its internal enemies – and thus there dawned for Japan a day that was to change fundamentally the future of the nation, and its emperor.

Noon. All of Japan huddled around their radio sets, in villages, in trenches, in shelters, in schools and next to the smouldering ruins of their cities. At noon precisely, a people rose to their feet. The only one who did not was the emperor himself. With his head bowed, he sat frozen in a bomb shelter, surrounded by his closest advisers. Across the global ether, from Tokyo to Osaka, from Chungking to Moscow, London and Washington, the whole world tuned in to the wavelength of the Nippon Broadcasting Company. After some crackling static the voice of an announcer came on the air: 'This is Radio Japan. We bring you an important message.'

It was followed by a recorded, rather high-pitched voice:

'To our good and loyal subjects. After pondering the general trends of the world and the actual conditions obtaining in our empire today, we have decided to effect a settlement of the present situation by resorting to an extraordinary measure . . .'

It had been Japan's longest day, 15 August 1945.

In the seventh century BC a demi-god descended from heaven, the offspring of Ameterasu, goddess of the sun. His name was Jimmu Tenno and he laid the foundation for the Empire of the Rising Sun. His dynasty was to last 2,600 years. Every subsequent god-emperor was considered above any living being on earth. No mortal would ever dare to raise his eyes and look into his celestial face; since his eyes would be burned out, if not by the sun, then by the emperor's bodyguards.

Going back a long time, and Japanese emperors do go back a long time, there is no record of any of these divine beings, no painting, no monument carved of stone. When a monk, Kobo Daishi, introduced a revolutionary concept, the religion of Shintoism, a caste of soldier monks came into existence, men who lived by the inflexible honour code of bushido, 'ready to die on the scorched earth or on the stormy sea'. They called themselves samurai. With their increasing predominance in matters of conquest and defence, the power of the emperor diminished to a ceremonial role. While a series of ineffective and weak emperors held court in Heian-ko (Kyoto), soldier–lords began to rule over the *shoen* (provinces). For the emperors of Kyoto and for the country, this was the beginning of a troubled time. From 823 to 1338 forty-three emperors sat on the imperial throne, of whom twenty-three abdicated or were murdered, mainly by family members, and three were deposed. A soldier clan, the Fujiwara, had carved out a power base at Kamakura. This created a dual leadership: that of the divine emperor, and that of his 'faithful' military commander, or shogun,[2] the real power.

In the 'black year of 1281', Japan faced its greatest threat. The Mongol Emperor Kublai Khan dispatched a mighty invasion fleet to conquer the island chain off the coast of China. As the ships were on their final approach to Japan's shores and Kublai Khan's forces made ready to disembark, a *taifun* (typhoon) struck the armada and the Mongol hordes drowned. The Japanese gave thanks to the gods for their deliverance and called the storm kamikaze, the 'divine wind'. No further foreign invasion had been attempted until the Allied armies were poised to storm ashore in the summer of 1945.

In the mid-eighteenth century, a new foreign power entered the Pacific theatre: the United States of America showed its flag off Japan's shores under the pretext of whaling. To support their maritime interests in the face of mighty Britannia, the United States needed a strong navy and a foreign anchorage. Thus a certain Lieutenant Pinkerton came to call on Madame Butterfly – although actually it was Commodore Matthew C. Perry with his 'black ships'. In February 1854, three US navy steam frigates and five ships of the line entered Tokyo Bay and trained their guns on the city while the US

---

[2] *Shogun*, or *sei-i-tai shogun*, meaning 'great barbarian-subduing general'.

consul, Townsend Harris, 'convinced' the shogun to sign the Treaty of Kanagawa, which opened three seaports to American traders. A conspiracy of 'young officers'[3] brought down the 'traitorous shogun' over this humiliating treaty. It was the end of the shogunate. The young Emperor Meiji led a country with a three-millennium Asian past into a European-style future. Foreign trade missions were set up which introduced the Japanese to a wide spectrum of Western knowledge. Japan not only survived the assault on its ancient culture but actually turned it to its advantage. Meiji proved himself an astute politician who grasped any opportunity offered to him. In 1900, the Chinese dowager empress was beset by internal strife in the anti-foreign uprising known as the Boxer Rebellion,[4] and Japan used the pretext to invade China. Four years later, Russia and Japan were at war, when Russia tried to break out of its maritime bottleneck: it had no ice-free port in winter. In 1905 Admiral Togo ambushed Russia's imperial fleet in the Tsushima Straits and sank it. In a suicidal frontal attack the same year Japanese soldiers captured Port Arthur and then overran Korea. US President Teddy Roosevelt initiated peace negotiations between tsarist Russia and imperial Japan; this won him the Nobel Peace Prize. Japan became the Far East's leading naval and terrestrial force. During the First World War, the emperor joined the Allies and annexed Germany's trade possessions in China.

Meiji created in Japan's modernised army a formidable tool of imperial power. This move gave rise to a new ruling caste, the military professionals. Although this scenario worked well for a strong ruler such as Meiji, it proved a serious handicap for a weak one, like his son Yoshihito, known as Taisho. While Japan witnessed a rapid industrial expansion and an economic explosion, on the political

---

[3] The term 'young officers' is used to include ranks up to that of lieutenant colonel.
[4] The term 'Boxer' means 'The society of the harmonious fists'.

scene things were not going well. Emperor Taisho lacked the moral fibre of his father. The new military caste used this as an excuse for seizing power, which wrecked Meiji's democratic culture, pitched the country into a series of conflicts, and marked the Taisho era with political repression. Prime Minister Hara, who dared to stand up to the army, was assassinated, and General Terauchi led his forces on a politically foolish adventure, an unsuccessful invasion of Red Siberia. In 1921, Taisho's son Hirohito took effective control of affairs of state and ascended to the throne in 1926 with the name of Showa, or 'enlightened peace'. To explain his choice of name, Hirohito declared in his coronation message, which was read to the people and the army: 'I have visited the battlefields of the Great War in France. In the presence of such devastation I understand the blessing of peace and the necessity of concord among nations.'

His reign began with a global economic disaster, the Crash of 1929, which did not bypass Japan. Without natural resources and little arable land to feed its rapidly increasing population, it became one of the worst-hit nations. This brought the masses into the streets demanding a 'policy of national prestige'. Japan's military saw 'Red as in Communism' everywhere and looked for a way to divert the country's attention. It discovered one in Manchuria. Japan's imperialism began its long march, which did not end until August 1945.

Hirohito, revered by his nation as a warrior–god–emperor, was none of these things. A quiet man who shied away from the glare of public life, he neither drank nor smoked, and ate a simple diet of black bread, vegetables, or dumpling soup. Following a morning's prayer at the Kashiko dokoro (temple), he took his walks in the inner garden of the palace before reading the daily newspapers. He seldom left the sanctity of his imperial palace. He spoke in a soft voice; his military hierarchy considered this weakness and acted accordingly. In theory, every general was responsible to his emperor, yet every general did precisely what he wanted. So it was the large and powerful Japanese army, and not the emperor, that decided foreign policy.

On 18 September 1931, Japan's giant Kwantung Army, stationed in Korea, decided to commence hostilities 'to stop the spread of Communism'. To justify their aggression they created the 'Mukden Incident', in which they faked an act of sabotage on their own supply railway.[5] Their artillery poured fire upon some hapless defenders and then quickly overran the city of Mukden spilling out into Manchuria. The news of this blatant assault shattered the emperor. He summoned Prime Minister Inukai: 'We believe that international justice and good faith are important for our country. We are striving for world peace – but Our forces overseas do not heed Our command and are recklessly expanding the incident.' He ordered the army commander, General Kanaya Hanzo, to restrain the Kwantung Army from further aggression. The army, however, continued to advance. It showed the power of the generals that, while professing loyalty towards their divine emperor, they in fact ignored his directives.

In May 1932, the cabinet of Prime Minister Inukai tried to put the brakes on the army's power. Junior officers gunned him down. The army's chief-of-staff, Lieutenant General Sadao Haraki, flatly stated: 'As far as I can see, this event was designed to pacify politics.' Nor did it end with one murder. At dawn on 26 February 1936, a group of 'young officers', supported by 2,000 soldiers, stormed Tokyo's government buildings. Fortunately for Japan and its emperor, once they had occupied the radio station and the government buildings, and had shot a few assorted ministers, they had no idea what to do next as they had made no further plans. So they quietly gave up. Everyone was baffled by the army coup,

[5] Hitler copied this tactic when he created a similar incident at the Polish border to start the Second World War.

and its intentions. That included the German ambassador who called on a certain Dr Richard Sorge to explain to him the putsch's significance, the same Dr Sorge who was to play such a decisive role in the outcome of the war in Europe. As Stalin's super-spy he advised the Kremlin in 1941 that Japan would not attack Siberia.

On 7 July 1937, matters finally came to a head in the clash that the emperor had so feared. It was to draw the great powers into Asia. The 1st Japanese Infantry Division, camping outside the Chinese city of Wanping, ordered the Chinese commander to open the town gate 'to allow a search for a Japanese deserter'. The Chinese refused. Japanese artillery turned Wanping into rubble and the undeclared war with China began. Emperor Hirohito immediately called his generals to heel. 'You will not move a single soldier without my specific orders.' As before, his generals ignored the imperial command, much as his new government, this time made up of bellicose generals and warlords, ignored Western protests. In early December, world opinion received a further shock when Japanese troops stormed into Nanking and butchered thousands of its hapless citizens in the notorious Rape of Nanking. That same day, a squadron of Japanese bombers, with red suns blazing on their wings, dived on the US gunboat *Panay*, which was lying at anchor in the Yangtse River. Their bombs sank it. Its executive officer, shot through the throat, scribbled the command to abandon ship. While the crew was making for shore on life-rafts, planes strafed them with machine-guns. Three Americans were killed. It had all the appearance of the Japanese generals really wishing to embroil America in a war in Asia. The *Panay* Incident led to increased pressure from the West and soon all the signs pointed to a major conflict ahead, although everyone ignored them.

The Japanese trampled across China. The major centres of Shanghai, Wuhan, Canton, and Peking fell. During the battle for Shanghai, 250,000 poorly fed, poorly armed Chinese conscripts died. Yet the Chinese showed an incredible ability to recover, even after Nationalist and Communist forces combined to form a single front against their common foe. This alliance did not fit at all into the global scenario imagined by the democratic nations of the West, and the League of Nations issued a toothless warning to Japan. By now the West's attention was focused on Europe, where fascism was reaching new heights and a civil war was tearing Spain apart. With their hands untied, in 1938 Japanese forces cut the British-controlled railway link from Canton to the middle of China. To break the blockade, the British started to build one of the most ambitious road projects ever attempted, the famous Burma Road. By 1939, China had become of secondary importance for the Western powers as events shifted to a new stage.

The initial bombshell fell with Hitler's ten-year non-aggression pact with Stalin, signed in August 1939. A week later, Hitler invaded Poland and started a world war. In September 1940, Japan signed the Tripartite Act with Germany and Italy, then amazed the Allies by signing a non-aggression pact with the Soviet Union. Japan needed assurances of a pacified northern frontier (Siberia–Manchuria), before it could turn south to conquer the rest of China. On 12 July 1941, 50,000 Japanese troops landed in French Indochina (now Vietnam) and proclaimed a Japanese 'protectorate'. The United States stood by and observed, merely dispatching a protest note, which Japan ignored. On 25 July 1941, US President Franklin D. Roosevelt finally imposed an embargo on high-octane fuel, which was indispensable for Japan's air fleets. The sanction soon proved crippling to its war machine. But Japan would not allow itself to be strangled! Should America refuse to deliver the fuel vital for Japan's continued expansion effort in Asia, then the Dutch oil wells in Indonesia would be seized. But getting at the Dutch wells meant taking Hong Kong and Singapore, both English crown colonies; that again would assuredly lead to a flashpoint with the huge industrial power on the other side of the Pacific. In late summer, Japan tried a final diplomatic solution, offering the United States a sharing of power in a 'peaceful co-existence sphere in Greater East Asia'. America flatly rejected the Japanese proposal.

In September 1941, the chief of the Imperial Navy, Admiral Nagamo Osami, advised his emperor: 'We must go to war, our oil reserves are dwindling.' He then promised his divine sovereign that the might of the Imperial Navy and army would control the entire southern Pacific within three months. The admiral's predictions, far from being exaggerated, turned out to be true. Where he erred was in the ultimate reaction of the United States. The emperor had a private discussion with Japan's most brilliant strategist, Admiral Yamamoto. 'Your Imperial Majesty, should You order me to enter into a conflict without considering the consequences, I shall obey Your command and fire from all tubes for six months. But thereafter I cannot promise success. My advice is: avoid a war with the United States.'

General Hideki Tojo, the new prime minister, was a bellicose militarist, although many believed him to be capable of restraining the army from open hostilities with the United States. On 10 November 1941, the American president told his nation: 'The war is coming very close to home.' Despite that, nothing was done to put America's armed forces on the alert. A last-minute attempt by a cabinet 'peace faction' to have Emperor Hirohito meet directly with the American president failed when Washington committed a diplomatic gaffe, which was considered an 'insult to the Divine Majesty'. It led to an acrimonious exchange of ultimatums, while General Tojo and the Japanese general staff decided that it must be war. But for such a step he needed the emperor's acquiescence, and the emperor was reluctant to see Japan at war with America.

A practice run, so secret that it was kept even from Emperor Hirohito, had been carried out in November. The *Taiyo Maru*, with two high-ranking naval officers aboard, Captains Suzuki and Maejima, sailed the planned attack route and landed in Honolulu. For days they observed ship movements at Pearl Harbor and made a sketch of the anchorage of the US Pacific battle fleet.

On 1 December 1941, Tojo and his cabinet, which was made up entirely of the military, informed the emperor that he could no longer delay his approval for the attack without seriously endangering Japanese security. By this, Tojo was referring to the dwindling oil reserves for the navy and air force. In any case, it was too late to change their plans because, without the emperor's knowledge, war was already on the horizon. A week before the imperial council met to decide the issue, the Imperial Navy had already slipped undetected from the Kuriles Islands on their long journey towards world conflict. Under Vice-Admiral Nagumo, a vast armada of aircraft carriers, battleships, cruisers, and tankers accomplished the 5,600-kilometre voyage without being sighted. Its code name was *Kurai Tanima* – the dark valley; its target, the US Pacific Fleet at Pearl Harbor.

Prime Minister Tojo gave the hesitant emperor the harsh facts: 'Your Imperial Majesty, Your navy is already on its way.'

The outspoken opponent to war with the United States, Admiral Yamamoto, for once supported Tojo: 'If I am to continue in command of the Imperial Navy, this strike is unavoidable.' Forced into a resolve taken by others on his behalf, the *Showa-tenno* finally ratified the decision to go to war and the world headed for a global holocaust of dimensions never before witnessed by mankind. The strike date was set for a Sunday, 7 December 1941.

Across the Pacific, the United States were well aware of Japan's desperate need for oil and that is why their strategic analysts pinpointed likely targets for a Japanese attack outside America's dominions. They correctly identified British Malaya and Dutch East India – but they overlooked Hawaii and the Philippines. In addition to this there was an astounding factor that has never been properly explained. With his code-breaking machine dubbed 'Magic', the US cryptanalyst Colonel William Friedman had broken the Japanese imperial diplomatic code. In Honolulu, on Saturday, 6 December 1941, twenty-four hours before the attack, a cipher clerk in US Naval Intelligence, Dorothy Edgers, rushed into the office of her superior – she had just intercepted a Japanese message that an attack on Honolulu was imminent! Her chief told her this could wait until Monday. Several hours later, the US army chief-of-staff, General George Marshall, was handed another intercepted message. He took immediate action and warned US bases around the world; but the devil played his hand, and adverse atmospheric conditions made radio contact with the US Pacific naval base of Pearl Harbor impossible.

Aboard his flagship *Akagi*, Admiral of the Imperial Fleet Yamamoto sat down behind his desk and composed a poem: *It is my sole wish to serve the Emperor as His shield – I will not spare my life or honour.* The Japanese fleet plunged through heavy seas only 230 miles north of the island of Oahu (Hawaii). The attack planes were lined up on the deck of Japan's six mighty aircraft carriers; the pilots were in their cockpits with their bombs and torpedoes slung beneath their aluminium wings. The engines sprang into life with a roar. At 7.55 a.m. on Sunday, 7 December 1941, Commander Misuo Fuchida, leader of the first wave of 183 Japanese carrier planes, issued his famous order for attack: '*Tora! Tora! Tora!*'[6] and the war in the Pacific had begun. The battleship USS *West Virginia* was struck by six torpedoes, the *Oklahoma* by five, the *California* by two, as was the

---

[6] An abbreviation of *Totsugeki* – 'Charge!'

Utah. Also hit were the *Tennessee, Maryland, Pennsylvania* and *Nevada*. The *Arizona* blew up. A message went out from Ford Island: AIR RAID PEARL HARBOR – THIS IS NOT A DRILL, REPEAT, THIS IS NOT A DRILL!

Thousands of miles away, confusion reigned inside Japan's embassy in Washington. The ambassador had received the order to hand over personally a declaration of war to the US secretary of state, timed to be presented *one hour before* the attack. A secretary who had never before used a Western-style typewriter typed the translation; this caused a delay and led to the declaration being delivered *one hour after* Japanese planes struck Pearl Harbor. The 'day of infamy' speech made by the US president to the US Congress was the preamble to the dropping of the atomic bomb.

In the Philippines MacArthur's air force was annihilated. Two days later, the era of the battleship became a thing of the past when two British capital ships, *the Prince of Wales*[7] and *Repulse*, were sunk by land-based aircraft. Hong Kong fell, then Singapore and the Philippines. In a typhoon of conquest nothing stopped the robot-like armies from rolling across the Pacific. In Japan each victory was celebrated by masses of flag-waving schoolchildren. The country was swept by euphoria, while an air of defeat settled over Washington. When the gloom was at its height, the US president signed Executive Order 9066, which gave the military the right to round up 127,000 Japanese-Americans and intern them in ten concentration camps.

But all was not well in Japan. The general staff faced some fundamental problems. Most of all, how to secure the defence of their vastly dispersed empire and, at the same time, bring about a speedy peace settlement with the United States, before US production machinery went into high gear. Japan's supply line became overstretched, its victorious army was blunted at

---

[7] Of *Bismarck* fame.

Kohima, and the navy's pride, its four main aircraft carriers, were sunk by US carrier planes off Midway. Eighteen months after Pearl Harbor, Japan began to lose the war. America's heavy industry performed miracles, while its scientists worked on an ultra-secret undertaking, the Manhattan Project.

North of Santa Fe in New Mexico lie the Jemez Mountains, a chain of arid hills ringing a high plateau of the *mesa*, as the Spanish conquistadores had called Los Alamos. It became the site of the world's first plutonium separation plant and it was run by physicists, chemists, and mathematicians from all over the globe. Nuclear science was to become their religion, although some, notably Jacob Robert Oppenheimer, could not shake off a certain apprehension about the possible consequences of their work.[8] They had been warned by a close call. Louis Slatin, a Canadian scientist, prevented an accidental chain reaction when he tore apart two critical masses. He became the first known victim of a new and deadly illness, radiation sickness.

By 1944 General MacArthur's units began island-hopping around the south-west Pacific, followed by Japan's naval disaster at Leyte Gulf in which she lost four battleships, five carriers, and sixty other vessels, plus 7,000 irreplaceable aircraft and their pilots. A naval admiral, Baron Kantaro Suzuki, replaced Prime Minister Tojo. On Iwo Jima the remnants of the defenders gathered around their commander, General Kuribayashi, and blew themselves up inside their bunker. Their sacred oath of 'fidelity to the death' included practical rules for dying. Japan entrusted its defence to some heroic but untrained youngsters, the 'pilots of the divine wind', the kamikaze. 'Safe hit, safe death,' was their motto. They were formed into an elite corps by Admiral Takijiro Onishi, commander of the 1st Air Fleet, and their initial strike hit the aircraft carriers *Saratoga* and *Bismarck Sea*, killing 500

---

[8] One of them was a German scientist, Klaus Fuchs, who turned Soviet agent and gave away to the Russians the entire bomb's design.

American servicemen. Altogether, kamikaze attacks sank or severely damaged 300 American vessels. But just like Japan's ground forces, the 'divine wind' was unable to stem the Allied tide rushing for its shores.

During the night of 9–10 March 1945, US air force General Curtis LeMay ordered 279 giant B-29 bombers to attack Tokyo with a new weapon, the M-69 napalm bomb, a jellified mixture of rubber and gasoline. The citizens of Tokyo chose to ignore the sirens and remained in their wooden houses. Two pathfinder aircraft marked with a flaming X the centre of the city and waves of bombers unloaded 1,900 tonnes of napalm. It created a firestorm, which reached temperatures of 1,800°C and lasted for four days. The bombs killed at least 80,000, left over a million homeless, and turned a quarter of the city into smouldering cinders. The super-battleship *Yamata* sailed on a suicide mission and was destroyed. American submarines put a noose around the islands; in sunken tonnage they far outdid the German U-boats.

On 21 June 1945, Okinawa was in American hands. Of the 120,000 Japanese defenders, only 7,000 survived. Their commander, General Misturi Ushijima, and his entire staff committed *seppuku*. The following day, Emperor Hirohito called his Supreme War Council and suggested an immediate ceasefire, followed by negotiations with the enemy. The military faction, led by War Minister General Korechika Anami, insisted on a continuation of the hopeless struggle. With the fall of the last island fortress protecting the main Japanese islands of Hokkaido, Kyushu, Sikoku and Honshu, the Americans assembled a gigantic invasion fleet of forty-two aircraft carriers, twenty-four battleships, and 750,000 men. At the same time, a highly secret operation was set in motion and the 509th Composite Group of the 20th US Air Fleet, was posted to the Pacific atoll, Tinian. At 5.25 a.m. on 16 July 1945, the team of J. Robert Oppenheimer exploded the first nuclear device at a test site. The great scientist said: 'I am become death, the destroyer of worlds.'[9] On 26 July 1945, the Allied Potsdam Conference decided to accept nothing less than Japan's unconditional surrender, or Japan would face 'complete and utter destruction'. They did not say what means would be used to achieve it. The world soon found out.

The prospect of what lay ahead weighed heavily on the mind of His Imperial Majesty. A terrible fate awaited the country, trapped in a nightmare of more monstrous bombs incinerating its cities. The military outcome became a foregone conclusion. The only question was: how could Japan preserve its integrity and honour in the face of certain defeat? Only the person of the emperor could strengthen the nation in the face of a catastrophe that was inevitable and, at the same time, save the country from the carnage of total anarchy. The emperor stepped to the window and watched the sky glow red beyond the moat which separated the imperial palace from the horrors of a burning Tokyo. How to convince his own military that a ceasefire, on whatever conditions the enemy dictated, was the only way to save Japan from total destruction?

On 27 July 1945, the Supreme Council for the Direction of War met to discuss the Potsdam Declaration of the previous day. Foreign Minister Shigenori Togo flatly stated: 'The army will never accept the Proclamation the way it stands.'

Everyone in the room waited for the reaction of War Minister General Korechika Anami. If Anami's eyes communicated any emotion it was entirely one of contempt. 'Dispatch a strong note of protest to the Allies.'

'No,' argued Prime Minister Suzuki and then added a word

---

[9] Lord Vishnu from the *Bhagavad Gita*. For his opposition to the nuclear bomb programme, Oppenheimer was dismissed in 1952 and charged with treason during the 'Red Scare' period of McCarthy. He was cleared of these charges, but was never again given access to nuclear data.

that was to become famous; 'we will simply *mokusatu* [kill with silence] their Proclamation.'

It was a fatal error, as Washington concluded that their demand had not been taken seriously. US Secretary of State Henry Stimson declared: 'We had to demonstrate that the ultimatum meant exactly what it said, the inevitable and complete destruction of Japanese armed forces and the utter devastation of the Japanese homeland.'

At 2.45 a.m. on 6 August 1945, the American B-29 Superfortress *Enola Gay* rumbled off the runway of Tinian Atoll. Its pilot was US air force Colonel Paul W. Tibbets. His orders from US air force General Thomas T. Handy were quite specific: ' . . . to deliver the special bomb to the target *depending on good weather conditions* and to drop it on one of the following targets: Kokura, Niigata, Hiroshima, Nagasaki . . .' It was at 8.15 a.m. and 17 seconds on 6 August 1945 that the world entered the nuclear age. The co-pilot of the *Enola Gay*, Captain Robert Lewis, yelled: 'My God, what have we done!' There was something awesome and terrible about the sheer power released to create such wanton, total destruction. A blinding flash had become Japan's unthinkable future and changed the rules of warfare. The scientific mind had created a Promethean monster and put into the hands of man the fire of the sun itself.

The following day, Lieutenant General Torashiro Kawabe, vice chief-of-staff, had the unpleasant duty of informing his emperor that a single bomb of unknown power had wiped out the entire city of Hiroshima. Upon receiving the news, the emperor told his prime minister: 'In view of this new type of weapon, Japan is powerless to continue the war.' And he added that the tragedy of Hiroshima must not be repeated. The Suzuki government, which until then had hoped to use the good offices of the Soviet Union to bring the Pacific conflict to an acceptable end, were sorely disappointed when, on 8 August 1945, the Soviet Union declared war on Japan and its armies overran Manchuria within three days. The shock was devastating, especially since on the same morning another Japanese city, Nagasaki, was obliterated by a second atomic explosion. The Japanese empire was left with no choice but to accept the shameful, unconditional surrender. Still the army refused to give in: 'They shall not have my sword,' said General Umazu,[10] and he contended that Japan had not lost the war. With statements such as this it became clear that the army preferred to be totally annihilated rather than give up in dishonour.

On Thursday, 9 August, the cabinet met to decide Japan's fate. Navy Minister Admiral Yonai opened the proceedings when he stated flatly: 'We will win the first battle but not the second. The war is lost to us and we must forget about saving face and surrender as quickly as we can.'

War Minister General Anami disagreed vehemently. 'It's far too soon to say the war is lost. Our army will not lay down their arms, they know they are not permitted to surrender. *For us there is no alternative but to continue the war.*'

'But that mammoth bomb . . .'

'It was just an ordinary bomb, perhaps somewhat bigger, but still only an ordinary bomb,' cut in General Umazu. 'Remember the tale of the warrior who ran away because he mistook the beating of birds' wings for the trampling of his enemy's boots?'

To break the deadlock within the ruling clique, the prime minister took a step that no one had ever dared before: he humbly asked for a special conference with the Imperial Presence. Under ordinary circumstances, the responsibility for political decisions had never been that of the divine emperor, but had been left to his closest advisers. This time it was different; only a *deus ex machina* could resolve the problem and save the country. Until now the emperor had not

---

[10] It was the same General Umazu who would eventually be forced to sign the surrender protocol for Japan aboard the USS *Missouri*.

taken sides, only approved (or in some cases, disapproved) the government's decision. His cloistered existence was suddenly interrupted by the dire need for a Salomonian judgment.

9 August, midnight. His Imperial Majesty walked along a dark and narrow passage that sweated moisture in the dim light. The council chamber was located in a concrete bomb shelter with a steel-beamed ceiling and dark wood wall-panelling. It was badly lit and poorly ventilated in the stifling August heat. At two rows of tables, eleven Supreme Councillors in formal morning clothes or freshly starched uniforms bowed with their eyes fixed on the floor. Baron Suzuki asked the Cabinet Secretary to read aloud the Potsdam Declaration: 'Japanese militaristic advisers have brought the Empire of Japan to the threshold of annihilation . . .' It ended with: 'We call upon the government of Japan to proclaim now the unconditional surrender of all Japanese armed forces, and to provide proper and adequate assurances of their good faith in such action. The alternative for Japan is prompt and utter destruction.'

After a moment of silence, the emperor nodded and the Premier called upon his foreign minister, Shigenori Togo, to recommend the immediate acceptance of the Potsdam Declaration. The War Minister, General Anami, drew himself stiffly to attention as if this was some play in which they all shared, and he was eager to act his part. 'The outcome of the Battle for Japan is not known until it is fought. A situation without parallel will be created if the cabinet authorises the surrender.'

The Premier bowed towards the emperor. 'Your Imperial Majesty's decision is requested . . .'

For the emperor, this then was the ultimate moment of decision. The next step would be irrevocable and would spell the end of 2,600 continuous years of divine Tennoism. His ancestors had always regarded themselves as the incarnate representatives of absolute power, both temporal and eternal.

To give in to the demands of his armed forces was beyond both their capabilities and his wishes. The decision was a moral one, but for the emperor, it was also philosophical. That slight, almost frail man was imbued with great reserves and courage, and in adversity he had not lost his strength of will. He had given his whole life to this effort of will. Yes, there was another way. The old system of governing the empire, moribund though it might be, was not yet dead. Japan had to be recreated. Only then could it resume the place that rightly belonged to it; only then could it once more seize the opportunity its generals had thrown away and become the leader in Asia. A rejuvenated Japan, under a government that would carry out the will of its people, and not the will of a divine emperor or some warmongering general. Therefore he must act quickly, to checkmate the 'war faction'. His divine will was all that counted. For a few minutes, only the laboured breathing of twelve men could be heard. Into the stillness fell the quiet Voice of the Crane: 'That it is unbearable for me to see my loyal troops disarmed goes without saying. *But the time has come to bear the unbearable.*' Without another word he walked past the bowed heads. The emperor had spoken and his will was that of God.

Emperor Hirohito assured Marquis Kido that his own safety was of little concern when it came to saving the nation, and that he was willing to undertake any step to ensure an immediate surrender. The marquis advised an unheard-of step: a radio broadcast by the emperor to his people. Hirohito agreed and at the same time asked Foreign Minister Togo to dispatch a note accepting the Allied demand. It took another four hours before a communiqué was ready to be released through their ambassadors in Sweden and Switzerland. It stated: 'The Japanese Government is ready to accept the terms enumerated in the joint declaration issued in Potsdam ... with the understanding that the said declaration does not comprise any demand which prejudices the prerogatives of His Majesty as Sovereign Ruler.'

In Japan, apprehension mounted as they awaited the enemy's reply. In Washington, Secretary of State Henry Stimson strongly advised President Truman that the dignity of the Imperial Presence be preserved to facilitate the surrender. Probably in the euphoria of certain victory, the State Department added an unfortunate phrase to the official communique. When the cable arrived in Tokyo, its demand created a shock: 'THE EMPEROR AND THE JAPANESE HIGH COMMAND WILL BE REQUIRED TO SIGN THE SURRENDER TERMS.'

A historian has commented:

'Unfortunately for the aftermath of the war, Japan's political centre of gravity eluded the vision of the American President and his advisers. It lay in the person of the *tenno*, the Heavenly God, and because he was the godhead of the armed forces, and in the eyes of his people a divinity, he was the supreme symbol of Japanese life and thought. Yet there was one thing he could not do, and that was to order his people to *surrender unconditionally* and thereby acquiesce in his becoming a war criminal, to be placed on trial or shot at sight.[11]

This diplomatic blunder was bound to cost the Americans dearly. In effect, their demand spelled an end to the emperor's rule and incited the Japanese army, honour-bound to die for their celestial lord, to continue in a senseless struggle, from town to town, street to street, house to house. That same evening, Tokyo broadcast a message by General Anami: 'We have but one choice: we must fight on, for in our death there is a chance of our country's survival.'

[11] J.F.C. Fuller, *The Decisive Battles of the Western World.*

At the same time that Radio Tokyo put out the call, 'No Surrender,' another, even more significant event took place. In the basement of Japan's War Office on Ichigaya Heights, fifteen *young officers*[12] met to decide what steps to take to 'protect' their emperor's integrity and the sacred honour of the imperial forces. The leader of this conspiracy was a delicately pale, fanatical young officer, Major Kenji Hatanaka. The ignominy of what the Americans demanded of his divine emperor burned his heart. Worse still, he could not allow his divine lord to suffer infamy at the hands of his own ministers, who were now forcing him to sign such a surrender. There was fire in his eyes when he declared: 'The traitors have to go.' With this, Hatanaka singled out the 'peace faction' inside the government. Premier Suzuki, Foreign Minister Togo, and the Lord Privy Council, Marquis Kido, who had direct access to His Divine Majesty: these three were marked down for immediate assassination. The key to the conspiracy would be the reaction of Lieutenant General Takeshi Mori, who commanded the hand-picked Imperial Guard and without whose consent they could not get past the honour battalion and enter the imperial palace grounds. If Mori refused to join the plot, then he too would have to be eliminated. The conspiracy was joined by a valuable newcomer, the equally fanatical, Major Hidemase Koga, a dashing daredevil who had been seconded as a staff officer from the Imperial Guards Division. Furthermore, he was the son-in-law of a former prime minister, the deposed General Hideki Tojo who could still exert great influence in army circles. Koga, like Hatanaka and so many millions across the nation, had been informed of 'the immense betrayal by the clique of politicians' via leaflets dropped by American aircraft, which supplied the precise text of the Japanese surrender note.

The Americans dropped these leaflets in good faith to

[12] This is a Japanese expression from the Meiji revolution rather than a term denoting junior rank.

stop further bloodshed; but to the average Japanese it was unacceptable that their divine emperor be forced to bow before a foe. Marquis Kido showed one of the leaflets to the emperor, warning him: 'We must act quickly or the army will rise.' The emperor agreed. He ordered the radio broadcast to be prepared for recording, and told Premier Suzuki to call another imperial council meeting. What he had to tell his assembled ministers and army commanders, all of whom had tears in their eyes, was that His August Mind had decided to address the nation. 'I am not concerned with what may happen to me,' he said in a quiet tone. 'I desire the cabinet to prepare an Imperial Rescript to announce the termination of the war.'

General Anami summoned Lieutenant General Mori to the palace and told him of the emperor's decision. The commander of the Imperial Guards replied: 'Then we must abide by it.' With this phrase he signed his death warrant. He then sent the following message to all army units:

'THE MINISTRY OF WAR, 14 AUGUST, 02.30 P.M. THE IMPERIAL FORCES WILL ACT STRICTLY IN ACCORDANCE WITH THE DECISION OF HIS IMPERIAL MAJESTY THE EMPEROR. (SIGNED) GENERAL ANAMI.'

The war minister had taken sides. The commander of the Eastern Army, General Shizuichi Tanaka, immediately followed up with a similar order:

'14 AUGUST. THE IMPERIAL FORCES WILL ACT IN ACCORD-ANCE WITH THE EMPEROR'S JUDGMENT. (SIGNED) GENERAL TANAKA.'

Major Hatanaka decided that there was no time to lose and he must act. He contacted his fiercest supporter, Lieutenant Colonel Masataka Ida of the Military Affairs Section.

Ida was hesitant: 'No, Hatanaka, a fire on which water has been poured will not burn again.' Hatanaka refused to be discouraged. Accompanied by Lieutenant Colonel Shiizaki, he bicycled across Tokyo to the headquarters of the Imperial

Guard Division. He feared that once the emperor had read out his Imperial Rescript it would be too late.

When he reached Colonel Toyojiro Haga, commander of the 2nd Battalion, Imperial Guards Division, Major Hatanaka immediately burst out with a lie: 'The minister of war [Anami], the commander of the Eastern Army [Tanaka], and the imperial divisional commander [Mori] support the *coup d'état.*' The battalion commander hesitated, but not for long.

On the way back to army HQ, Lieutenant Colonel Shiizaki asked: 'What if Mori calls your bluff and doesn't give us the green light?'

Hatanaka replied: 'He will.'

'And if he doesn't?'

There was fire in his dark eyes and furious energy in his reply: 'Then as a final resort we will have to kill him.'

At midnight, Emperor Hirohito, dressed in a generalissimo's uniform, arrived at the Imperial Household Ministry where the radio team waited to record his address to the nation.

'To our good and loyal subjects,' he began, 'after pondering deeply the general trends of the world and the actual conditions in Our Empire today, We have decided to effect a settlement of the present situation by resorting to an extraordinary measure . . .' He signed off with a phrase that would establish the future course of Japan: 'Unite your total strength, to be devoted to the construction of the future. Cultivate the ways of rectitude, foster nobility of spirit and work with resolution, so that you may enhance the innate glory of the Imperial State and keep pace with the progress of the world.' These proved to be prophetic words.

The recording was then handed to two imperial chamberlains, Tokugawa and Toda, who vouched for the safe keeping of the waxed disc. Tokugawa locked it in a small private safe, then piled loose papers in front of it to hide the metal box from view. Little did he realise that his move would protect the recording from destruction.

At the recording studio, Press Minister Shimomura gave a sigh of relief: 'The emperor has made the recording. We're in the clear.'

To which his assistant replied: 'The night isn't over yet.'

Major Hatanaka heard about the recording from a conspirator inside the radio station. He turned to Takeshita. 'Mori is still not with us.'

'And Anami,' Lieutenant Colonel Takeshita added. 'Whatever happens, he'll stick by his word.'

'Then you must go and convince the war minister,' said Hatanaka.

Lieutenant Colonel Takeshita now stormed into the office of his brother-in-law, War Minister Anami, in a highly agitated state of mind. He accused the general of betrayal should he fail to call out the army to stop the emperor from signing the armistice.

Anami shook his head. 'The emperor has made his decision and I must obey my emperor.'

Takeshita shouted so loud that he could be heard along the corridors: 'The surrender must not take place or you will have to take your life with your sword.'

The war minister kept silent. For him a decision either way created an insoluble dilemma. While his duty lay with the army, his loyalty was to the emperor. And the emperor had spoken. From that moment on, Anami knew there was only way out he could possibly take.

Hatanaka meanwhile had gone off to confront General Mori at Imperial Guards HQ. Mori was in conference with his deputy, Lieutenant Colonel Shiraishi, when Major Hatanaka and Captain Uehara burst into the room without asking permission. What happened next will never be fully explained, as there were no direct witnesses. The two conspirators had been in the general's office for only a minute when the sound of a shot was heard, followed by several screams. Then Hatanaka appeared in the doorway, pistol in hand. 'There was no time to argue so I killed him,' he yelled. Captain Uehara rushed out of the open door, wiping blood from his sword.

The murders of Mori and Shiraishi eliminated any chance Hatanaka might have had of obtaining help from the army. He therefore had to act quickly. With Major Koga, he issued Imperial Guards Division Strategic Order No. 548. The coup now went into full swing. The order stated:

1. THE DIVISION WILL DEFEAT THE ENEMY'S SCHEME. IT WILL PROTECT THE EMPEROR AND PRESERVE NATIONAL POLICY.

2. THE COMMANDER OF THE FIRST INFANTRY REGIMENT WILL OCCUPY THE PALACE TO GUARD THE IMPERIAL FAMILY. THE COMMANDER WILL ALSO ORDER A COMPANY TO OCCUPY TOKYO BROADCASTING STATION AND PROHIBIT ALL BROADCASTS.

This was followed by a series of specific targets for the rest of the division. Major Hatanaka had stolen General Mori's private seal from his blood-smeared desk and had affixed it to the bottom of the document to legalise the order. It was, however, a complete forgery. Major Hatanaka next rushed to Colonel Haga's HQ and told the battalion commander that he was the special envoy of General Mori; also that the 2nd Battalion of the Imperial Guards had been ordered to occupy the palace 'to protect His Divine Majesty', to round up the ministers found in the palace grounds, and, most important, to locate the recording with the proclamation that the emperor had been forced to record 'by the traitors'.

Inside the palace, Prince Konoye, brother of the emperor, asked Marquis Kido to see him immediately: 'I've heard some disturbing rumours about the Imperial Guard Division. Have you heard anything?'

'We have done our best for Germany.'
20th July 1944. The leader of the anti-Hitler conspiracy, General Friedrich Olbricht.

'Long live our holy fatherland.' 20th July 1944. Claus Schenck Graf von Stauffenberg, the man who placed the bomb in Hitler's bunker, shortly before his execution.

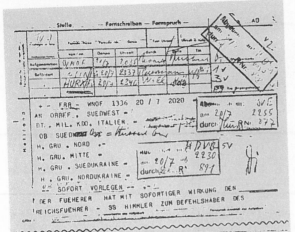

20th July 1944. The telegram dictated by Hitler to his chief-of-staff, Keitel, in which he appoints SS Chief Himmler as head of the Reserve Army. The date and time of dispatch are important: 20th July, 20.20 hrs. While the conspirators in Berlin were still hoping for a miracle, Hitler already knew the names of all the principal putschists, Fromme, von Witzleben and Hoeppner.

'We shall settle accounts the way we National Socialists are accustomed to settle them!'
20th July 1944. Hitler to Mussolini, inspecting bomb damage, hours after the attempt on his life.

'When they were friends.'
January 1959. Castro and Guevara on the day they entered Havana as victors.

'He was killed in an ambush.'
9th October 1967. Che Guevara's body in Bolivia. The official version
held for only twelve hours before the truth came out.

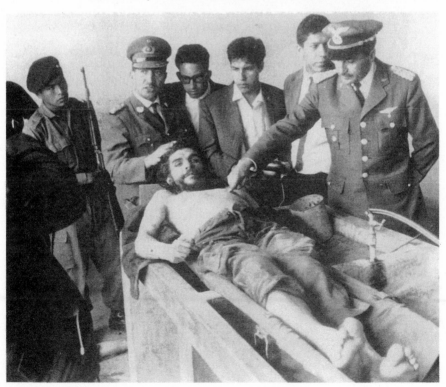

Above: 'I feel that perhaps there is a Supreme Being who is guiding me.'
His Imperial Majesty, the Shah-in-Shah, Reza Pahlevi.

Left: 'Allah is great, Khomeini is our leader.'
Ayatollah Ruhollah Khomeini.

'*In the face of adversity, it is wise to keep one's distance.*' 16th January 1979. The Shah leaves Iran from Tehran airport. General Abdollah Badrai, who kissed the ruler's hand was executed by the revolutionaries the following day.

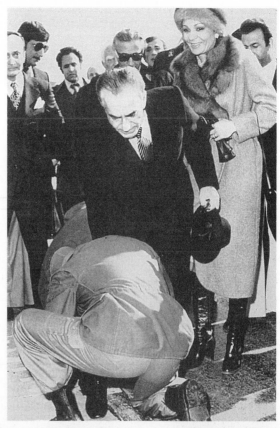

'*A victory of the faithful.*' 1st February 1979. Ayatollah Khomeini, enters Tehran in triumph.

'Death in the marshes.'
28th February 1983. Iraq–Iran war, Howeiza Marshes.

'When I join a funeral procession, I march all the way to the cemetery.'
November 1958. Fidel Castro to the author in the Sierra Maestra.

'I apologise to His Imperial Majesty for my supreme crime.' General Korechika Anami, Minister of War, committed suicide by seppuku.

'I would rather take the course of remaining a loyal Japanese, even if it means that in the end I must be called a traitor.' Major Kenji Hatanaka, chief conspirator, shot himself.

Above: 'The time has come when we must bear the unbearable.'
9th August 1945. Emporer Hirohito relayed his decision to
surrender to the Imperial War Council.

Left: The cover of a pamphlet,
distributed to the Imperial troops,
which incited the Japanese soldier
to kill his enemy and fight to the
bitter end.

Kido shook his head, and was about to bow his way out when out of the window he saw a group of heavily armed soldiers march into the courtyard. They were from the Imperial Guards 2nd Battalion, commanded by Colonel Toyojiro Haga. Within minutes the entire imperial compound was in the hands of the insurgents. Whoever was found there, regardless of status or age, was locked up in a dungeon. They failed to get their hands on Tokugawa and Toda, who knew where the recording was hidden. When the two imperial chamberlains heard the trampling of boots outside their door, they escaped through an underground passage into an unmarked storeroom. Soldiers ransacked parts of the palace trying to find the precious recording, while the one person who could have changed the situation by his mere presence was unaware of the ongoing *coup d'état*. Even in a critical situation such as this, nobody dared to disturb the sleep of His Divine Majesty.

General Tanaka, commander of the Eastern Army, was finally apprised of General Mori's murder. He issued an order to all his units: 'ALL TROOPS SURROUNDING THE IMPERIAL PALACE ARE ORDERED TO DISPERSE IMMEDIATELY.'

Lientenant Colonel Ida handed Hatanaka a copy of this order: 'It's all over. The Eastern Army isn't with us.' But Hatanaka was a volatile, impulsive man. His will to serve his emperor, who, he felt, was shamefully betrayed by his court lackeys, had become so single-minded that nothing – except death – could deflect him from his purpose.

Lientenant Colonel Takeshita raced across town to see his father-in-law, General Anami. He found him writing a farewell note: 'For my supreme crime, I beg forgiveness through the act of death. Korechika Anami, the night of 14 August 1945.' Perhaps he was thinking of the fate of one of his illustrious predecessors, the chief of the Imperial Japanese Army under Emperor Meiji, General Nogi, who had taken his life over a failure in command, to arrive now at this desperate and final step. To Takeshita he said: 'The emperor's broadcast will be made at noon tomorrow and I could not bear to listen to it.' A chill wind had entered the room; death itself had come to join them. General Anami was preparing himself for a long sleep.

General Tanaka called Colonel Haga from his Eastern Army HQ. He informed the 2nd Battalion commander that Mori had been assassinated, that order No. 548 was a blatant forgery, and that Haga was to remove his unit instantly from the palace grounds. With anger in his eyes, Haga turned on Hatanaka, who happened to be standing next to him: 'Now I understand, this whole thing has been nothing but a lie. It is not to save the life of the emperor. This is outright rebellion and I want no part of it.'

Hatanaka's face lost all colour. Without a word, and before the colonel could stop him, he turned and left the room. He managed to get out of the palace minutes before General Tanaka arrived to take overall command and set matters right.

Meanwhile Anami was kneeling on a tatami (rice mat), with a blood-covered dagger in his hand. His upper body moved back and forth, like a pendulum while more blood soaked his white ceremonial shirt. He had committed *seppuku*. His soul had already left him, but his body would not die. Lieutenant Colonel Takeshita stood behind him and watched his beloved general's agony, until he could not bear it any longer. He removed the dagger from the dying man's hand, and plunged it into his neck. Slowly the body of General Anami, War Minister of His Imperial Majesty, toppled forward.

With calm restored, Imperial Chamberlain Toda emerged from his hiding place and inspected the damage that the soldiers had wreaked in their search for the imperial recording. 'I never thought I would live to see it – Japanese soldiers attacking their emperor!' He sighed with relief when he found the safe intact, and in it, the invaluable recording.

Dawn, 15 August. Major Hatanaka had escaped the drag-net laid for him and was bicycling to the radio broadcast building, which he found unguarded and in a state of utter confusion. There were unconfirmed reports of a *coup d'état*, and harried journalists were trying to obtain confirmation, but telephone lines to the palace had been cut and its entrances were blocked by armed units with orders to shoot anyone trying to get in. Hatanaka stormed unchallenged into the announcer's studio and demanded to be given access to go on the air. The baffled technical staff said it could not be done because of a power cut and because no line was open for a transmission. Hatanaka waved his pistol, but was unable to overcome technical problems he did not understand. Now he too knew that it was over. The paper containing his prepared statement slipped from his fingers and he staggered from the building.

At 7.21 a.m. Tokyo time, the radio announcer came on the air: 'His Imperial Majesty has issued an Imperial Rescript. It will be broadcast at noon today . . .'

At 8 a.m. the 2nd Battalion of the Imperial Guards, with colours flying, returned the imperial palace into the hands of the government.

At 8.10 a.m. the Grand Chamberlain Fujita was received by the emperor who merely said: 'Why could they not understand what was on Our mind?'

At a temporary HQ inside the palace, General Tanaka issued an order for the arrest of Major Hatanaka and his conspirators. Captain Shigetaro Uehara, the killer of Lientenant Colonel Shiraishi, was arrested by the Kempeitai (the Japanese military secret service), but was released on a promise that he would commit suicide. Others were arrested, but not the ringleader, Kenji Hatanaka. He was where he was least expected to be, kneeling on the gravel in front of the imperial palace. He used the same pistol with which he had killed General Mori to blow out his brains. His co-conspirator Lieutenant Colonel Jiro Shiizaki watched his friend die, then drew his ceremonial sword and ran it through his own belly.

Admiral Takijiro Onishi, father of the 'divine wind', and the officers of his staff assembled in front of the imperial palace where they knelt down and committed ceremonial suicide, for they were now to serve their emperor in another world. The last of their kamikaze pilots took off and crashed their planes into the sea.

The broadcast by His Imperial Majesty to his nation went on the air as scheduled. It was precisely twelve noon, 15 August 1945.

And then . . .

'The human tragedy reaches its climax in the fact that after all the exertions and sacrifices of hundreds of millions of people and the victories of the Righteous Cause, we have still not found Peace and Security, and that we lie in the grip of even worse perils than those we have surmounted,' wrote Winston Churchill in his epic work, *History of the Second World War*.

After six terrible years, the Second World War finally ended aboard an American battleship in the Pacific. But what had the war achieved? And who were the real victors?

In 1941, America went into the war totally unprepared. It lost its fleet at Pearl Harbor and its air force in the Philippines in just twenty-four hours. Within months, the Pacific had become a Japanese lake. Then came the aircraft-carrier battle at Midway and the tide began to turn. In eighteen months, the might of American industry had managed to produce the biggest war machine ever to sail the sea. While the main theatre of war was still Europe, where armies were locked in fierce and desperate battles, while the German panzers were driven from Russia, while Normandy was invaded and France liberated, the war in the Pacific continued almost unnoticed. After its irreplaceable losses at the battle of Leyte Gulf in October 1944, it was out of the question that Japan could win the war. It is the tragedy of both countries, Japan and the United States, that American leaders failed to recognise the larger, political significance of their victory in what has been described as the greatest naval battle in history. Having supplied the main effort to bring the island nation to its knees, it was in the utmost interests of the United States that it achieve an immediate 'victory in the Pacific, unshared with its allies' and achieve thereby the highest profit from the nation's tremendous war effort. This meant that America had to win single-handedly to avert later complications, especially with the Soviet Union whose expansionist policies were well known, and before their war ended in Europe. The Americans lost all political advantage in Asia when the Soviet Union declared a last-minute war on Japan and was given a free hand to expand its Communist influence over the whole of the Far East and South-East Asia. As a result, the American crusade for 'Peace in the Pacific' was soon turned into a confrontation between the two superpowers, which was to lead to trouble in China, Korea and Vietnam in the years to come.

What the emperor had predicted did happen. In December 1945, the Shinto state, for a thousand years the bulwark of an emperor cult, was abolished. This proved a genuine watershed in Japanese society and a major generator of change. It led to the now unavoidable next step. The divine emperor himself became the most powerful image of the nation's healing. On 1 January 1946, in a brief announcement that took his country by surprise and was received by his people with great sadness, Emperor Hirohito declared: 'The ties between the emperor and his people do not depend on myths and legends. They are not predicated on *the false conception that their emperor is divine*.' With a simple phrase, the celestial descendant of the sun relinquished his right, and that of his successors, to be considered a divinity. A new era, that of democracy, was on its way.

Emperor Hirohito passed away in his sleep in his eighty-seventh year.[13] With him died Japan's ancient history. Huge crowds knelt outside the imperial palace to pay their final respects no longer to a god, but to a man, greatly beloved by his people. This was a ruler who had always wished to be close to his people, a closeness that his celestial stature would not allow.

Interlude

1945–1959

Hitler was dead, Mussolini had been executed, and Japan had surrendered. The map of the world was changed, and nations on every continent had to choose between two camps, progressive and conservative, East and West. Any thought of neutrality was just self-delusion. For a while, an armed conflict in Korea ruffled the complacency of an aloof stand-off, but it never went over the brink. The threat of a nuclear holocaust was too horrible to contemplate. Between the two atomic superpowers, a status quo was being established. 'We won't touch your cake if you don't eat ours.' This worked fine for years, thank you, until trouble occurred in a part of the world where none had been expected and it almost sent the rockets into orbit.

The scene moved from Washington and Moscow to a

[13] On 7 January 1989

Caribbean island, Cuba, where the Mafia had installed a string of luxury hotels and casinos, where daiquiris flowed freely, where a president smiled on the black economy and collected his slice of the profits, while the ordinary *campesino* (peasant farmer) suffered from abject poverty. This was fertile earth in which to plant the seed of egalitarian socialism. On 26 July 1953, the day that United Nations and North Korean negotiators signed an armistice in faraway Panmunjon, the son of a sugar plantation owner picked up his hunting rifle and stormed the military barracks of Santiago de Cuba. That was the start of the trouble. The uprising failed; the young firebrand was captured and sentenced. Then he was released courtesy of a bishop and exiled to Mexico. Two years later, Fidel Castro tried again. He packed his band of rebels onto an eighteen-metre motor yacht and landed in a remote part of Cuba. But his plans had been betrayed and most of his band were killed or captured. Only Castro and twelve of his closest *compañeros* (colleagues) escaped. For two years, Castro's *barbudos* (bearded ones) hid out in the mountainous region of the Sierra Maestre while their following increased steadily. A revolutionary council was formed under the leadership of Fidel. The rest were all Cuban veterans; his brother Raul, Camilo Cienfuegos, Juan Almeida, Hubert Matos, Efigenio Almejeiras, Christino Naranjo, Faustino Perez. All Cubans. And one Argentinean who had joined the rebellion, Dr Ernesto Guevara.

The world's press reported that their political *Weltanschauung* (world view) was a mixture: in part the philosophy of gung-ho Robin Hoods with big revolvers, and in part the egalitarian philosophy of Karl Marx. With few exceptions, they were neither.[14] Castro's disciples were neither left nor

[14] The author spent several months with Castro in the Sierra Maestre. Fidel's favourite bedside reading was *Commando Extraordinary*, the story of Colonel Otto Skorzeny. There was no Communist literature on his bookshelf. The author, who during this period spent much time in the company of Fidel, does not wish to speculate on what made Castro change his mind.

right; they were simple Latinos. Their sole credo was the need to overthrow a corrupt president and his clique of officials. Then they would replace the feudal system that Cuba had inherited from the Spaniards with true democracy: a step unheard of in Latin politics and one that was bound to put them on a collision course with established financial interests. Fidel Castro was relatively 'clean'; his opinions were, as could be expected, those of a revolutionary socialist. Brother Raul was a hardline Communist. Camilo Cienfuegos was a concerned Cuban. The Argentinean, *El Che*, was different: an intellectual and pure Latino Trotskyist, who believed that violence was the only means of achieving victory. In a feat of arms at Christmas 1958, Ernesto 'Che' Guevara captured the vital city of Santa Clara and finally opened the road to Havana.

8

8 October 1967

Hasta la victoria siempre!

Hasta la victoria siempre!
Until eternal victory!
Ernesto 'Che' Guevara, Bolivia, 1967

It doesn't matter where death overtakes us,
it will be welcome as long as our war cry will be heard . . .
Ernesto 'Che' Guevara, Bolivia, 1966

Tierra Muerta, the Dead Earth, the *indios* call the place. The skeleton of a rusty jeep, stripped to its carcass, lies forlorn near the entrance of the village. It bears the faded insignia of the Bolivian army. A collection of rough, mud-walled buildings with flaking plaster cling to the hillside, baking in the equatorial sun. No church, only a wooden cross on top of a bolder, which serves as a place for communal prayer. *Indio* women in drab blue skirts, their olive skins shaded by the slouched hats of the Andes, work outside their huts. A stray dog slinks around, searching for a tasty morsel of wild rabbit. A child chases a reed hoop along the rust-coloured sand track, which leads through the middle of the hamlet. A place that smells of poverty, so poor that even the pigs are skinny.

The village of La Higuera in the Rio Grande province of Bolivia is the most unlikely place on earth to attract attention. And yet it became the world's focus for one day. On 9 October 1967, an electrifying message flashed around the globe: THE BOLIVIAN ARMY HAS KILLED THE MYTHICAL REVOLUTIONARY . . .

La Higuera? Where was the nearest airstrip? How were they going to get there, to beat their competition to the story of the decade? News editors studied maps of Latin America, secretaries booked plane tickets for their ace reporters, television networks chartered jets. People in a more clandestine business, posing as photographers, made their own arrangements. All to see a corpse! Not just any corpse, but that of the Argentinean, or, as he was to go down in history, *El Che*.

Havana, Cuba. The president's New Year's ball of 1958 had been in full swing since nine that evening, a big affair with all the glitterati in attendance. At fifteen minutes before midnight President Fulgencio Batista, dressed in his customary white suit, got up from his table and waved to General Cantilla. The crowd opened a path for him and applauded their smiling president as he passed through the dancing couples towards the exit. Senator Rolando Masferrer, leader of a private army reputed for its brutality, found it strange that the president should take his leave before celebrating the New Year. Discreetly he followed and watched Batista step into a car. It was odd, as were most of the events that had shaken the capital in the last seventy-two hours, ever since the devastating news of Che Guevara's crushing victory at Santa Clara. Masferrer called for his own driver and ordered him to follow the president's limousine discreetly. When the president's car turned into Airport Boulevard, Masferrer realised that the balloon was up. Fulgencio Batista was abandoning his cronies to their fate. Whilst Havana was ringing in the New Year, and champagne corks popped in casinos and ballrooms, a plane would be flying across the Atlantic, carrying a disillusioned dictator into exile. The worst that can be said about Batista, a sergeant who promoted himself to general and from there to president, is that he was corrupt and under the influence of American mobsters. In a way, his regime was nothing like as dictatorial and as oppressive as the one that was to follow it.

The era of Castroism began precisely on the date that Fidel Castro was discovered by the world press: A NEW FIGURE IN HISTORY. He fired on the masses with empty rhetoric and understood that popular support could carry more weight than a police force backed up by guns. He took a lesson from the great orators that, in any message to 'the people', style mattered more than substance. Through the smoke of a cigar he declared to a cheering crowd that 'the feudal system has given way to true democracy'. He pledged free elections but did not say when they would that place. He spoke about rebuilding the nation's constitution on law and justice but gave no such orders. He promised leniency and forgiveness to his enemies but had all of them shot. The victors savoured their victory, while the ordinary citizen prayed that Fidel Castro would not turn into the kind of ruler he had struggled to overthrow.

Fidel Castro entered Havana with all the clout of a victorious revolutionary. That day the world held its breath, watching in fascination the prospect of a democratic millennium in Latin America. There was little violence. That would come later. It was the dawn of a new promise for Cuba, a dawn of great hope and expectation that was to turn to frustration and despair. One in which *libertad* became the key phrase for suppression, and *democracia* was replaced by dictatorial terror, not only for the ordinary citizen, but for the revolutionary leaders as well, most of whom were to end up in prison or in an early grave.

Laying their hands on the panoply that went with power posed no embarrassing problem for the new conquistadores. They simply took. It was a time for distributing the spoils. Revolutionary justice was a farce; it needed no ideological pretext to kick a *rico* family from their home. Revolutionaries took their houses, their cars, their chickens, and their rum to celebrate long into the tropical nights. The *barbudo* had become an honoured citizen beyond suspicion or reproach. Privilege was fun. But that was not all. In the confusion of hysteria, enthusiasm, and sudden waves of terror, the former underprivileged hunted down the usurers and bosses of the former ruling clique who had been unable to get away in time. They were rounded up and driven along with staves and rifle-butts, or left lying beside the road in pools of blood. It was also a time for reckoning. Then came the first distressing signals from the island, of show trials and blatant persecution. Castro had given the signal when he said: '*La Historia me absolverá!* History will absolve me!'

What concerned Cuba's foreign neighbours were the revolutionary commanders who rode on the same tank into Havana. Most were political enigmas. Especially one, Ernesto 'Che' Guevara, the architect of Castro's victory.[1] 'To defeat a dictatorship was easy; what is not easy is to build a new society. Socialism has to create a new type of man,' pronounced this theologian of *socialismo tropical*.

Ernesto Guevara de la Serna was born in 1928 in Rosario de Santa Fe, a steamy wheat port on the Rio Parana in the Argentine. He was a sickly child, suffering from bouts of asthma. While studying medicine in Buenos Aires, he began to show an obsessive concern with the suffering of the ordinary *peóns*, and took against the violently anti-revolutionary Catholic *pobresitos* (the class of the poor) who refused to participate

---

1 During the only battle of Castro's revolution, which took place at Santa Clara in December 1958, Che destroyed Batista's famous armoured train and took the town. This split Cuba in two and forced Batista to flee.

in a class struggle. He was never tied to institutional rigidities; his concept of socialism was a combination of Marcuse's analysis of capitalism, Trotsky's criticism of bureaucracy, and Mao's 'Cultural Revolution'. The fusion of these ingredients proved highly explosive, as he foresaw that the 'power of the peasant', allied to Chairman Mao's vision of millions of human atoms making an explosion of their own, would shake the world as much as any nuclear bomb. In Cuba, the Argentinean was looked upon as the outsider and he suffered from its xenophobic island mentality. He could not accept Cuban laxity in the drive to become truly independent. He openly voiced disappointment about the national mentality: 'We've seen that Cubans are willing to die for the revolution, but we haven't seen that they're willing to work for the revolution.' Castro handed him the Ministry of Industry – Cuba had no industry, only some run-down sugar mills. Then he gave him the National Bank in a country without an economy. Guevara always got the jobs that others did not want or in which they knew they would end up as failures. Che took both jobs and was a failure in each of them.

The old order based on patronising American imperialism was swept away by the scalding torrents of Fidel Castro's newly proclaimed Latin nationalism. A third world country dared to flaunt its sovereignty before the world! The ultimate break with the United States came over a speech by the newly inaugurated American President John F. Kennedy, who called on the 'captive people of Cuba to overthrow their government'. The Cubans dug in their heels and responded with defiance.

Hundreds of foreign journalists flocked to a movie theatre in central Havana to hear what Comandante Che had to say. Following a long speech which revealed little new, a reporter raised his hand to ask: 'Comandante Guevara, what will become of American holdings on the island?'

Guevara answered in a tone that clearly showed he was

bored by the question. 'Señor, as our leader has already stated, nothing will be touched of foreign properties. Of course, foreign owners must comply with the new situation.'

'Could you be more specific?'

'I really don't see the need to be specific. Our revolution was fought to bring equality and justice to all.'

At the word 'justice', the reporter cringed. Another journalist stood up.

'Comandante, what will become of your political prisoners?'

'Their crimes cannot be forgotten. We cannot have pity on those who helped the cause of a ruthless dictator. We must show inflexible rigour towards the criminals who have betrayed the Cuban people.'

'How many are there, I mean those you now call traitors?'

'I cannot give you an exact figure. But I can tell you this: we cannot hope for prosperity as long as the last traitor still breathes. We mustn't only punish those who have betrayed, but those who have done nothing to stop the scoundrels, who just sat by and watched.'

'That sounds like political terror, Comandante.'

'We call it justice.'

More hands came up. Guevara pointed to an old news hack who thought he had seen it all and heard it all. He asked in a condescending manner: 'OK, Mister Guevara, let's stop playing with words. Listening to you, I get this feeling that you find terror justifiable.'

A thin smile curled the Argentinean's lip. The capitalists were getting anxious about their investments and their corrupt friends. In that order. Good, 'I've already stated that we practise revolutionary justice. But to satisfy your question: if this country had not been troubled by conspiracy, if *nuestra patria* had not been the victim of a dictator's terror let me add, abetted by the United States government – of course, nothing would be simpler than to govern with peace.'

'Is your solution to lead the Cubans onto a path of virtue by denouncing their neighbours?'

'It is the duty of all good Cubans to unmask those who benefited from the tyranny. A nation that doesn't defend itself defends nothing and it is our duty to teach them this virtue.' He began to sound like another Robespierre: *'The cemeteries will overflow – not the prisons.'*

The room fell into stunned silence. With a single phrase, Ernesto 'Che' Guevara, after Fidel Castro the most influential man in the country, had condemned hundreds of political opponents to the firing squad. Even more prophetically, he had opened the door for legalised terror, which was to push Cuba into the abyss.

Both sides of the Florida Straits showed great apprehension about future relations between their countries. Much of the worry of its giant neighbour only ninety miles away was that Castro's example would trigger a whole series of national liberation movements throughout the Latin hemisphere. Instead of providing an example to Latin-American nations of a free-standing independence, Castro had turned the island into a prison, its people into refugees, and himself into the leader of an oppressive Moscow-guided regime. A 'cane curtain' descended and Cuba found itself in total isolation. Castro boasted of his mercilessness towards the enemies of his regime: 'My revolution has not shrunk, and will not shrink from serious decisive measures if dictated by necessity. The proof of this is the shooting of military and political criminals.' Such remarks gave pause to those who still viewed Fidel Castro as a romantic, misunderstood figure.

By 1962, the Russians were engaged in a dangerous game of internal power politics. A small Caribbean island, half a world away, became the pawn in a contest that had little to do with Marxist ideology, but which was primarily

concerned with a struggle for power in the upper eche-
lons of the Soviet hierarchy. It resulted in First Secretary
Khrushchev's suicidal gamble in placing atomic missiles on
Cuba. In so doing, he created a strategic liability that the
Soviet Union could not possibly defend against a determined American attack. During some frantic days in October
1962, when the world held its breath, President Kennedy
forced Khrushchev to remove the Russian missiles from the
island. This done, the Soviets dumped Castro, caring little
about their socialist brothers. Many saw this coming, but
only one man reacted. A committed Latin revolutionary,
whose Trotskyite views would not bend to Moscow's dictates.
The moment that he dared to predict the future and speak
out against the idea of Soviet world hegemony, he became
an outcast. This man was Ernesto Guevara. *El Che* was
different. He opposed the cold-war politics of a stand-off
co-existence between the Americans and the Russians, which,
as he foretold, could only lead to each superpower's creating
its own sphere of influence and parcelling out of world
between themselves.

A blow-up between two equally ambitious men – Castro,
the Cuban who had traded in his revolutionary fervour for
advantages derived from Communism, and Guevara, the
Argentinean who remained a Latino purist was inevitable.
The break came in February 1965; Guevara addressed the
Third World Conference in Algiers and castigated the 'new
socialist imperialism' of the Soviet Union. He stressed that
help from friendly socialist powers should be given without
strings attached, but in the case of the Soviet Union such
bonds were often more politically restrictive than those of
Satan himself: the bankers of New York. The reaction to his
speech varied from stunned shock to thunderous applause.
Needless to say, it infuriated the Soviet leadership; they had
been stabbed where it hurt the most, in an arena where, given
the political vacuum created by the recent move from colonial

dependency to free nationhood, no real political line had as yet been drawn and no allegiances formed. Furthermore, 1965 was the year when the Negro communities in the United States broke out in open riots. The black ghettoes of Watts and Detroit went up in flames, and the black revolutionary Malcolm X was assassinated. The Soviets had counted on these events as a shock effect to draw black African nations into their sphere of influence – and now there was this devastating accusation from someone who was part of their global strategy! The impact of his speech on the African nations cannot be measured in real terms, yet there is no doubt that it greatly affected Latin America. It therefore not only angered the Soviets but also the man who tried to portray himself as the new liberator, Fidel Castro. To Moscow and Havana, one thing became clear: Che Guevara had to disappear from the political stage.

Following his address, Che returned to Havana aboard a Cubana plane. This time, there was no military band on the tarmac and there were no photographers[2] to record the arrival of a returning hero. Fidel met Che in the arrivals hall, screened off from the usual, flag-waving reception crowd. Events moved rapidly towards a climax. Che and Fidel spent two whole days secluded behind closed doors. There were no witnesses to what was said. 'Donde está el Che? Where is Che?' The simple fact that his picture never again appeared in a Cuban newspaper, nor was his name ever mentioned in articles, speaks for itself. Che had become a non-person. In March 1965, only a few weeks after the secret meeting, Che said farewell to his daughter Hildita, and vanished from Havana. Some newspapers reported him in Hungary, in Chile, even in Palestine. But nobody actually saw him. Finally, someone did, and it was in the Congo. He led 200 Cubans to the former Belgian colony to try to assist

---

2 One photograph was taken, which appeared in *Granma*, the official newspaper, but it gave no indication where it was taken.

the local liberation movement of Pierre Mulele against the American-supported dictator Mobutu.[3]

Che could not understand African politics and the African mentality. He took a fateful decision: he chose Bolivia – a country holding the world record of military putsches and the poorest of all the Latino nations, under the fist of General Barrientos. Guevara picked Bolivia because he thought that the climate there was ripe for a movement of liberation to overthrow the general's dictatorial powers. But Bolivia was (and still is) a medieval place, whose politics were characterised by barbaric brutality, personal bias, and deep religious involvement. This was a country where people were superstitious, praying to Christ in their front rooms and worshipping some heathen deity in their backyards. Its *indios* stood transfixed by the spirit of darkness, considered modern medicine a gift of the devil, and believed in their local healers who divined the future and diagnosed ailments by reading coca leaves. They looked up to their Catholic priests as one would to some extraterrestrial divinity. Such people did not have the slightest notion of the word *revolución*. However, Che Guevara was imbued with the driving spirit of a Simón Bolívar: 'Let's have a go at it and see where it will lead us.'

Another handicap was the people who went with Che to Bolivia. He could not count on specialists, as they had not been chosen for their military qualifications. His hard-core of Cubans belonged in one of three categories: political failures at home, those who did not agree with Fidel's policies, and those who were liable to create a future problem for Fidel. Even Nunez Acosta, appointed by Che to lead his second front, was a loser in Havana. These men had no experience in guerrilla activity, had never been to Bolivia, and stuck out because they spoke with a 'funny accent'. On top of all this,

3 One of Che's lieutenants was Laurent Kabila, who overthrew Mobuto in 1997, and is today's strongman president of the Congo.

Che was beset by debilitating asthma[4] and every bout brought with it sudden panic attacks.

In November 1966, Che returned secretly to Cuba to collect his sixteen followers. They embarked separately for La Paz, Bolivia.[5] Guevara, alias Rámon Benitez, travelled via Moscow, Prague, Zurich, and Frankfurt. Wearing glasses, clean-shaven and bald, he arrived in La Paz on 3 November 1966 and took a room in the modest Hotel Copacabana. His local contact was a German girl and sometime bed partner, Tania, who put him in touch with the local Communist union of mine workers. Negotiations with the labour organisers, and the Bolivian Communist Party boss, Mario Monje, came to nothing. The Bolivians insisted on taking control and deciding any action, and Che found himself isolated, his dream of a general rising by the masses quashed. They were fifty and would never become more. Che put up a jungle base on the River Nancahuazu in Santa Cruz province and his code name became Rámon.[6]

His colleague Antonio Pacho dared to say it out loud: 'You might as well forget about help from Cuba. All they ever wanted was to get rid of us.'[7]

To which Che, slowly putting down his pipe, replied: 'You really like stirring up shit.'

It went to show that Che still believed in Castro and his help in extricating them should the need ever arise.

4 Asthma does not prevent the affected person from breathing, only from exhaling.

5 During a press conference given in late October 1967, the Bolivian authorities presented the journal which Che Guevara wrote during his guerrilla activities. It was discovered in a rucksack near the ambush site. Che had noted down everything in a diary he had purchased during his transfer stop in Frankfurt airport. His notes are eloquent and give a fair picture of the group's suffering, his own fading hopes, and his end.

6 His closest companions were Marcos, Benigno, Rolando, Coco, Joaquin, Alejandro, Luis, Moro, Medico, Urbano, Pombo, Pacho, Tuma, Loro, Inti, and Jorge: all Cubans.

7 This theory is also supported in a book by Paco Ignacio Taibo, a survivor of Bolivia.

He never even gave betrayal a thought. That night, two guerrillas deserted the base and denounced Che's presence to the Bolivian authorities. The secret was out. Bolivian army units threw a cordon around the area, creating a *zona roja* (red zone) and blew Che's underground network in La Paz. Che could no longer count on outside support. Only Tania slipped the dragnet to join Che; she brought along a French philosopher, Regis Debray.

It did not take long before blood began to flow. The guerrillas ambushed an army patrol in a river gorge and killed seven soldiers. National radio blared: 'Our country has been invaded by foreign mercenaries. It is the duty of every Bolivian to fight the intruders.' The message set off hysteria in the cities; in the villages, priests told *campesinos* that these bandits would come to take away their animals. This was the start of a gigantic manhunt involving 2,000 soldiers, aided by an air force that dropped napalm on the jungles and burned black patches in the foliage. Along a tree-covered creek an army patrol came across the rebels. Rubio was killed; the rest vanished into the protective jungle. They ran into another patrol and although the soldiers suffered more casualties than Che's men, they could replace their losses whilst the rebels could not. Che had no choice; to escape pursuit he split his forces. While crossing a river, the group with Joaquin and Tania collided with the Bolivian army. In a brief, murderous gunfight, all were killed. Che's group made for the high mountains.

A series of clashes, reported in five-column headlines, led to increased panic. Peace Corps workers relocated their families and *hacendados* armed their *peóns*. Bolivia asked for help and the Americans stepped in.[8] A team of instructors from the battle–hardened US 1st Airborne under Captain 'Pappy' Shelton were transferred from Vietnam and began to train

8 This has led to the suggestion, albeit false, that Americans captured Che.

Bolivian units. The astute Barrientos used the situation to declare a state of emergency and rid himself of all opposition. Hundreds of union bosses and leftist sympathisers were put in jail. Troops converged on the *zona roja*, thousands of well-armed soldiers pitted against a handful of exhausted guerrillas whose armed actions had led them to a situation of 'no return'.

In April 1967, Jan Stage,[9] a Danish journalist on a posting to Cuba for a major Scandinavian news group, was called into the office of Ismael Fundora, the head of Cuba's propaganda department.

'Señor Stage, you like travelling, don't you?'

'Only if there is a good story behind it.'

'In that case, I've got a good story for you, an extremely good one.'

Fundora provided Stage with a ticket to Bolivia. Che Guevara! It became clear to Jan that nobody in Havana had the slightest notion of Che's moves or plans. In La Paz, Jan made contact with 'local sources close to the revolution' and found a way to enter the off-limit *zona roja*. American engineers were relocating their families back to the States. This meant moving their belongings from Santa Cruz and Cochabamba to La Paz, and a Danish removal man was picked for the job. Stage went along as his handiman. It gave him a good appreciation of what was going on in Santa Cruz. When he returned to Cuba, he was met at Havana airport by Manuel Pineros, head of security in Cuba's Latin American section. 'Your reports are excellent. Please return immediately to Bolivia.' This time it was not a polite request, but more of an order. He agreed only after Che's wife, Hilda Gadea, begged him to get news of her husband. In La Paz he

9 Jan Stage is the best source for information about Castro's part in Che's Bolivian venture. He lived in Cuba during most of the early revolutionary period and was then married to a close friend of Hilda Gadea, Che's wife. Stage's personal account was substantial in putting together events as they happened, and the author gratefully acknowledges his invaluable help.

found that he could no longer count on his previous contacts; information was vague, unclear, even deliberately misleading. That's when it dawned on him: *Che had been cut loose.*

Eight months passed and a mood of despondency began to take hold of the guerrilla group. They had to stay on the move; the countryside was crawling with troops. Planes dropped flyers: '*Recompensa! Se ofreca la suma de 50.000 Pesos a auién entreque vivo o muerto al guerrillero Ernesto "Che" Guevara.* Reward! The sum of 50,000 pesos is offered to anyone for the guerrilla Ernesto "Che" Guevara, dead or alive.' Day after day they stumbled along stony paths, uphill, downhill, and uphill again, most of the time out of food and with little water. Che's health had seriously deteriorated; his asthma stopped him sleeping. He was a man on the run, surrounded by superior forces, in an environment that was foreign to him, with a population that wanted neither him nor his revolution.

On 22 September 1967 they reached the village of Alto Seco or, as the name so vividly describes it, the High Dry. They were received with a mixture of fear and curiosity. A *campesino* informed Che that the villagers had watched his column move uphill, and that the *alcade* (mayor) had gone to ask the army for assistance. There was nothing much they could do about it. Che's *guerrilleros* went from house to house and asked the people to congregate at the school for a meeting. The peasants listened to Che without showing the slightest reaction. For him, this was the final indication of failure. If these *campesinos*, subsisting on the minimum of what was humanly bearable, failed to understand his dream, then no one could. Dejected, the guerrillas left Alto Seco. A narrow path climbed steeply uphill. Before nightfall they stumbled exhausted into Picacho,[10] where the air was thin and cold. A few *indio* families in tattered rags shared whatever

---

10 At an altitude of 2,280 metres, this was the highest point in Che's march.

food they had, and danced and sang with their unexpected visitors. Che recovered his faith; these people were not hostile to him. It was only when he discovered that the four mud huts did not own a radio between them that he realised they did not know who he was.

Ten miles off – as the crow flies, a ranger captain studied his map. The rebels depended on water. He took a quick decision and stabbed with his finger at a point marking a tiny village. La Higuera.

From Picacho, a steep path led down to La Higuera. Che's men walked into a village devoid of life except for three women who stared suspiciously at the guerrillas. This was a bad sign, and Che decided to move on immediately. They would have to cross a 2,600-metre pass towards Yagüey. To scout the path, he dispatched an advance party of seven men. Shortly afterwards shots rang out. Benigno came limping back with blood pouring down his leg. Four of his men had been killed in the ambush. Che's men rushed down the bramble-covered slope to escape the noose, that was rapidly closing around them. For several days, Che's last seventeen men wandered the area, running out of water. Once a platoon of soldiers passed by, only a few yards away from them. They must get to water. To conserve energy, they moved only by night through a landscape devoid of all life until they heard a dog bark. Before them stretched a flat valley, covered with gnarled trees and bramble, and encircled by mountains. They camped under a cluster of trees while the Bolivian Willy scouted for a well. He came on a hut with a scrawny pig and some chickens but no people. Willy fetched the rest of the group who finally quenched their thirst from an earthen jar, before they stretched out under the broad shade of a tree. When Che opened his eyes, an old woman with three goats stood before him. He gave her fifty pesos and told her to keep quiet; she became friendly and gave them directions towards a canyon where they would find water and a trail that would take them across the mountains. The canyon was the Quebrada del Yuro. They set out before sunset. That is when a goatherd saw them and alerted Ranger Captain Gary Prado. Che and his small band reached the Quebrada del Yuro after dark and did not realise that they had entered a canyon ringed by cliffs. Under an overhang covered by low trees, they sank to the ground and removed their shoes to give their blistered feet a rest before covering themselves with their rough blankets. Che suffered another attack of asthma; so as not to disturb the others, he moved away. He stared up at the night sky . . . it had only been eleven months, but it seemed more like a hundred years. He felt that his odyssey was moving towards its climax. He closed his eyes . . . and woke up with a start. All was quiet, too quiet. He ran a practised eye over the gorge, which began to emerge from obscurity in the first light of a new day – and stared at hundreds of soldiers outlined on the rim of the canyon!

It was 8 October 1967. A Sunday. The inevitable had to happen. Che's men were strangers, marooned in a lifeless desert. The peasants they met could not, or would not, understand their revolutionary language. On the other hand, the Bolivian army asked questions and got answers. For days the noose had been tightening around them. Now there was no escape. They sat in a trap, in a walled-in canyon with its exit blocked. They had to dig in and bluff it through, in the vain hope that the troops were not quite sure of their presence. Che's men were invisible, hiding in the bushes, and all was silent except for the sounds of the wild and the buzzing noise of insects. At mid-morning, the silence was shattered. With a terrifying roar the ground around Che exploded, the canyon erupting in spurts of flame. Tracers from machine-guns stitched an intricate pattern across the valley floor. Bombs hurtled from mortar tubes. Many guerrillas were cut down in the first furious hail of bullets. Orlando Pontoja and Rene Martinez had their faces shredded by shrapnel from a mortar grenade. By a sheer miracle, Che had escaped the initial assault of bullets and bombs, and he fired burst after burst from his carbine. By 2 p.m. the noise of gunfire from his side faded; his men were dead, dying, or out of ammunition. Willy flung himself into the hole next to Che; he pointed excitedly at a path in the side of the cliff. The two moved quickly towards it, having learned that a single, unbroken movement is less conspicuous than a series of stops and starts, when a burst from a machine-gun raked the leaves. Che fell to the ground, struck in his right leg. His M-2 carbine was flung from his hand, its stock smashed by another bullet. Willy grabbed him by the jacket and dragged him deeper into the bushes. Despite his considerable pain, Che began to limp uphill. They had reached the canyon's rim – and came face to face with two Bolivian rangers with pointed guns, Corporal Balboa and Soldier Choque. '*Alto! Alto!* Hands up!' screamed the astonished Choque.

Quickly Che raised his hands: 'Don't shoot! *Io soi Comandante Guevara. Llame un jefe de prisa.* – I'm Comandante Guevara. Call an officer quickly.'

An officer came bounding down the path, Captain Gary Prado Salomon. The man he saw before him was nothing like the photo of the smiling revolutionary wearing a black beret. This was a dusty, grimy face, worn by fatigue and thirst. 'So you are Che Guevara?' Che nodded. Prado's eyes lit up; this prize catch would assure his future career.

Two soldiers helped Che to his feet. The slow procession had a biblical quality. They reached La Higuera. The only place that had a door with a lock was the schoolhouse, which was divided into two rooms: a windowless storage room and the classroom. 'This one in there. Che into the classroom.'

Prado turned to Sergeant Spinoza. 'You will vouch with your life for the two prisoners.'

The man grinned. '*Si, capitán.*'

The soldiers dumped their tied-up prisoners on the floor

and then began to hunt for souvenirs. When the sergeant tried to grab Che's pipe, his prisoner struck out with his good leg. 'Remember, you cannot treat Che Guevara this way,' he growled.

Captain Prado called division headquarters by field telephone: '*Cinco cento cansado*' (*cinco cento* was the code for Che, *cansado* for capture). When this electrifying news reached La Paz, the generals of Bolivia's junta were stunned. Although they had been pursuing him for a year, no contingency plans had been formed in the event of Che's capture! They had always taken for granted that he would fight it out to the end. Now *other arrangements* had to be made. General Barrientos, the smart politician, did not wish to get involved. He ordered Colonel Joaquin Zenteno Anaya to conduct an on-the-spot assessment. Zenteno radioed: 'Keep *cinco cento* alive for my arrival tomorrow.' That night, while soldiers in La Higuera celebrated their victory and the general staff debated the fate of their high-profile prisoner, Barrientos drove to the residence of the US ambassador for consultations.

Monday, 9 October 1967. In Higuera, no new orders had been received and matters were in a state of confusion. Somehow – perhaps because she was a handsome woman – the local schoolmarm, Julia Cortez Balderal, was allowed to enter the classroom. Che sat propped up against the wall, hands tied behind his back and his ankles fastened by rope. He seemed to be in considerable pain and blood seeped from his leg wound. His espadrilles were in tatters; his bleeding feet were covered in sores; his clothes were torn and stained.

I had expected to find a fanatic, instead I saw in front of me a man with kind eyes. We talked for a while. He asked me if I was the teacher, and then he began to discuss the drawings that my pupils had pinned to the wall. He said that my texts were wrong, and then he began to tell me about the schools in Cuba, where pupils were well fed and not dressed in rags. He asked what the village needed most, and I told him, a tractor. He promised to have one sent after he was set free. [This goes to show that Che still thought that he would be used in some bargain between Castro and the Americans.] He spoke to me in a low, stern voice and always looked me straight in the eyes. It left me in no doubt that I was in the presence of a very decent human being. I said: 'With your intelligence, how could you have ever put yourself into such a situation?' Che replied: 'It was for my ideals.'

Another prisoner was brought into the village, Chino Chang, a middle-aged, overweight Peruvian. A helicopter came in to make a dusty landing, bringing Colonel Joaquin Zenteno, Contra-Admiral Ugarteche, and the local CIA resident, Felix Rodriguez. They filed into the schoolhouse to view the captive whose reputation was enough to spread panic throughout the country. 'If any deals are to be made,' said a defiant Guevara, 'then I insist these are made through the local schoolteacher, Señorita Cortez.' Zenteno gave up, knowing it was hopeless. Captain Prado waited for specific orders.

The fatal decision was probably arrived at in La Paz around 10 a.m. on that Monday. The coded message was passed to Captain Prado, who handed it to Colonel Zenteno. It was clear and to the point: '*No prisoners.*' While Zenteno was on the radio to La Paz, the CIA agent Rodriguez dragged Che outside to have their photograph taken together. Che's eyes were downcast, his face drawn, and his hair lank.[11]

High noon. Schoolteacher Julia Cortez walked to the schoolhouse to take the prisoner a bowl of soup. Che

11 It shows the CIA agent Ramos to the right of Che Guevara. His presence in the picture became the prime source of the rumour that the CIA had ordered Che's execution.

looked at her in gratitude. 'It has been a long time since I've eaten so well. I think they will come now, but I shall never forget you.' Then he added in a quiet voice: '*Hasta la victoria sempre!*'

Zenteno entered the schoolhouse for the last time. When he stepped out again he nodded to Captain Prado. There was a brief delay when the CIA agent intervened: the CIA wanted to interrogate Che and was ready to fly him to Panama. But Zenteno's order stood, and Captain Prado called up his NCOs. Of the seven in his company, three volunteered, and two were chosen: Sergeant Bernardino Huanca and Sergeant Mario Terán. Their orders were to liquidate the prisoners and make it look as if they had been killed in battle.

At one in the afternoon on this hot Monday, Sergeant Huanca entered the room where Willy was kept. He ordered the prisoner to face the wall. Willy answered: 'Shoot me while I look at you.' A few short bursts from the automatic weapon cut him down.

For a few minutes, only the babble of hotly arguing voices came from the schoolhouse. Later reports state that Terán became reluctant and did not want to do it. Colonel Zenteno barked: 'Check your weapon, soldier.' The classroom door burst open and Sergeant Mario Terán walked in, his carbine at the ready. Without a word he pulled the trigger. Che was struck by nine bullets, which traced a line from the left side of his stomach to the right side of his throat. Incredibly, Che still moved, his fingers clutching the air. Terán fired one more shot, straight into Che's heart.

Julia Cortez was sitting at her kitchen table when she heard the shots. Somehow she knew that it was Che. Later she could not recall how long it took before her nerves were calm enough for her to run towards the schoolhouse. Through the open door she saw a body whose open eyes stared back at her. Ernesto 'Che' Guevara was thirty-nine.

*   *   *

The execution was timed to perfection. While Che was being liquidated, a press conference was being called in La Paz. 'Ernesto Che Guevara was killed yesterday, Sunday, in a battle which has resulted in the death of ten soldiers as well as the entire band of outlaws.' A special aircraft was laid on to fly the local and international press to Vallegrande to inspect the body. As their plane touched down, a helicopter came in to land, with a canvas-wrapped body strapped to its skids. The body was transferred to an ambulance and whisked away. The press corps was taken to an isolated laundry shed in Vallegrande's Maltese Hospital, where the body of the slain guerrilla leader had been put on display on a concrete slab. Colonel Zenteno made sure that he was in the picture as flash bulbs went off like firecrackers.

From the very beginning, something did not add up. Some members of the international press began to wander around the hospital until they came face to face with the two duty physicians, Dr Jose Martinez Casas and Dr Moises Abraham. That is when the killed-in-action story began to fall apart. It began with a chance remark by Dr Martinez, who told them that the body had still been warm when he received it, and that the blood in the wounds was not congealed. An Argentinean journalist asked Dr Martinez: 'How long has this man been dead?'

'Five, six hours at the most.' Following a moment of stunned silence, where the only sound was that of furiously scribbling pencils, another question was thrown at the doctor: 'What was the fatal wound, doctor?'

'A bullet into the heart.'

'Could anyone survive, let's say, twenty-four hours with such a wound?'

'Definitely not; death must have been instantaneous.'

The journalists checked their watches. It was now 6 p.m. on Monday, 9 October. In other words, *Che Guevara had died at noon that day, and not, as they had been made to believe, during a gunfight on Sunday!* The junta's well-laid plans had been shot apart by an off-the-cuff statement of the examining physician and some enterprising journalists' investigative footwork.

Back in La Paz, General Alfredo Ovando Candia stormed out of a press briefing, relieved Captain Prado of his command, and ordered that soldiers pull down the schoolhouse to eliminate all traces. Before this happened, one person was allowed into the building: a Dominican father, who had come to La Higuera on his regular visit to the village. The guards did not dare to prevent the priest from entering.

When I arrived early Tuesday morning and went inside the school, the rooms hadn't been cleaned up. None of the soldiers felt like going in, because of the flies, they said. In the room where Willy had been killed, the floor was covered with blood. It was hard to breathe, there was a stuffy stench of death and flies buzzed in the oppressive heat. On the wall opposite the door I noticed a number of bullet holes at head and chest height. In the classroom, there was also a great amount of blood. Here the bullet holes were about two feet off the ground. I extracted three bullets and some hair. The village was relatively quiet; people had been ordered to stay in their houses and the captain seemed quite busy preventing his soldiers from finding out more than they already knew. I visited some villagers; they were afraid. 'What is going to happen to us, Father?' They feared that friends of the dead guerrilla would come and take revenge.

Throughout Tuesday, Che's body was on display on its slab. The population of Vallegrande filed past; more photographs were taken of soldiers pointing their rifles at a corpse who stared with open, life like eyes at the ceiling. The bodies of the Cubans Antonio and Arturo, whose faces had been ripped off, had been placed dramatically against the legs of the table to enhance the horror. Before sunset, women began to arrive with candles, moved more by their deep religious respect for the dead than admiration for a revolutionary whose cause they never understood.

In La Paz, General Ovando got himself back into the news when he issued a series of contradictory statements. First he claimed that Che's body had been buried in an unmarked grave and the corpse covered with quicklime. Later he changed his story; now the body had been incinerated and the ashes scattered to the winds so that nobody would ever again worship the *asesino* (murderer). While wire services around the world buzzed with few facts and many rumours, something strange began to take place in Vallegrande. Che's picture, reproduced from a magazine article by a local photographer, appeared in windows and shop fronts. It was not the photo of the corpse staring with dead eyes at the ceiling, but the portrait of a smiling Che with a black beret. A picture that would soon spread across the world.

And then . . .

A battle cry was born. 'Comandante Che Guevara!'

'*Presente!* Here!' screamed children and adults from Havana to Hanoi. Che's smiling face stared from billboards around the world. His image outperformed the legendary Fidel himself. The Cuban leader exhibited his outrage by staging a mass rally in Havana's Plaza de la Revolución. It was a rally of a size Havana had never before witnessed. 'Comandante Che Guevara!' yelled the bearded leader of *socialismo tropical*. From a million throats came the reply: '*Presente!*'

Similar rallies were held from Mexico to Santiago, Algiers to Angola, Cairo to Calcutta. The population of Budapest and Prague lit candles; the picture of a smiling Che appeared in London and Paris. The very thing that the generals and politicians had tried so desperately to prevent was taking place: the world had found a martyr. And when a few months later, riots broke out in Berlin, Paris, and Chicago, and from there the unrest spread to the American campuses, young men and women wore Che Guevara T-shirts and carried his pictures during their protest marches. No, in those heady months of revolutionary 1968, Che Guevara was not dead. He was very much alive.

Ernesto Che Guevara was the last of the great romantic revolutionaries, a Don Quixote in search of an impossible dream. His motives were best expressed in a letter to his parents, sent from Bolivia. 'I believe that armed struggle is the only solution for the people who wish to liberate themselves. Many call me an adventurer – and I am – but of the kind who is willing to risk his own life in a test of the only truth he believes in.'

Bolivia was Che's idea, not Fidel's. Bolivia lay on the road to his ultimate goal: the liberation of Argentina. As a first step, Che tried to incite the Bolivian rural population to wage a class struggle against capitalist oppression – except that there were no visible capitalists in the country. President Barrientos had parcelled out tracts of land to the rural population, turning serfs into minor landowners. Wherever Che preached his social revolution, the deeply Catholic peasants did not understand him. To the urban intelligentsia, Ernesto Guevara was an imported troublemaker and an envoy of Fidel Castro's Latino brand of Communism. Fear of falling into a Cuban-led Soviet trap had stopped Bolivia's Communist party from supporting him and Che failed to recruit a single Bolivian to join in his cause.[12] For Che, Bolivia was a no-win proposition from the outset.

12 The three Bolivians in his group had come with Che from Cuba.

One may well argue that the disaster arose from his own miscalculation. Yet one unanswered but vital question remains: why did Castro not even try to disengage Che from an impossible situation? Che was a big name, and he was leading the most important operation that Cuba had at the time. Havana was aware that Guevara had no alternatives, no options, and no way to survive. Why then? *Because the Cubans did not really care what Che was doing!* They could have sent a rescue team, but they did not. They took a cynical view: 'Let's see what happens. If he wins we have a victory. If he dies we have a martyr.' Che's death was a monumental propaganda victory and so it continues to be.[13]

His enigma still haunts the world. *El Che* died alone. Those who might be able to tell the full story are also dead. President General Barrientos died in a helicopter crash. General Ovando died of cancer. Sergeant Mario Terán vanished into an army camp.

The mythical Che and the real Che have received blow after blow. Not much is left of his dream of a 'certain tomorrow', an all-encompassing socialism. Latin America today is what it has always been, a corrupt, reactionary continent. The only experiment in Latino socialism, Allende's Chile, failed. It is surprising that someone as lucid as Che should have overlooked the social and economic disasters in the Communist world, or the oppressive totalitarian politics practised by its masters. In a way, *El Che* became a prisoner of his unshakeable belief in old-style Marxism 'for the good of *all* the people', a political system that, even then, no longer existed. He failed because the God-fearing people of a God-fearing country refused to adhere to his atheist gospel. Instead they listened to the words of a prophet whose

13 Castro launched a well-publicised operation to search for Che's remains. In 1997, a team of geologists was sent from Cuba and found some human remains near Vallegrande. These were repatriated to Havana and received by Castro with great military pomp and honours.

teachings have survived two millennia, and will continue to do so long after all the revolutionaries of tomorrow have been forgotten. The greatest revolutionary of them all, Jesus of Nazareth.

There is a monument in the village of La Higuera, the crude bust of a man wearing a beret. It was done by local *indios* and it is painted in vivid colours, which is how the peasants remember the face of 'the man who came down from the mountain', Che Guevara. And on the wall in the schoolroom is a plaque with his name. Today's children look at it and wonder: who was he? It is like his own life, a long goodbye . . .

Interlude
1968–1979

In the West, stock markets boomed and the economy flourished. To feed the voracious furnace of modern industry, one ingredient was required: oil. That was to be found cheap and aplenty in an area of the globe made highly unstable by political squabbling and inter-religious strife. Saudi Arabia, Israel, Syria, Jordan, Egypt, Iraq: countries wrecked by territorial wars and political insurrection, by heedless terrorism and racial bloodshed. It was a time when America began to extricate itself from Vietnam and Russia was about to enter its own Vietnam in Afghanistan; a time when the Arab oil-producing countries united in an 'oil shock'. The industrial world began to worry and to search for secure supplies of the precious black gold. Out of the turmoil one nation rose to predominance. It seemed solid and could count on the best-equipped army in the region. It controlled a flow of oil that could pledge regular delivery. And it proved to be a steadfast ally of capitalism. The Shahdom of Iran. All went well until a troublesome monk entered the scene.

9

16 January 1979

'Allahu maa es sabrin!'

Allahu maa es sabrin!
Allah is with the steadfast!

Oh Prophet, urge on thy believers to battle.
If there be of you twenty steadfast, they shall
  conquer two hundred.

The Holy Koran

The wind was icy, as it always is in winter on the high plateau. The more affluent sections of the capital were deserted; the majority of its wealthy citizens had fled or had barricaded themselves behind iron railings and closed shutters. The country was paralysed by strikes. A helicopter skimmed over the rooftops, gaining height to allow its passengers a final glimpse of the city that sprawled over valleys and hilltops, before depositing its passengers in front of the royal pavilion at Mehrabad airport. The officer of the guard of honour, with tears in his eyes, stepped up to the slight, fine-boned, bareheaded figure in a charcoal-grey suit, who stared at the sky as if checking the weather. The officer bent down and kissed his hand.

'Do what you judge is necessary. I just hope there will be no more dead.'

The officer gave his monarch a final salute before the royal couple walked slowly along the red carpet and stepped into the Boeing 707 which bore the name *Shahin*, the Royal Falcon. It was eight minutes past one, on 16 January 1979. While a four-engine blue and white aircraft raced for the skies, with the sovereign at the controls, from the canyons of the streets echoed the roar of millions: *'Allahu maa es sabrin! Allah is with the steadfast!'*[1]

Radio and television interrupted their programmes with a terse announcement:

'The Shah has left the country!'

In 1878, the year that a boy was born to a poor subaltern in a remote mountain province, Persia was the most backward country in the Middle East. As were its people, a racial amalgam produced by invasions of Sumerians, Babylonians, Assyrians, Greeks, Romans, Arabs, Mongols, Kurds and Turks, bringing troubled times and varying fortunes for Persia's many rulers. These invaders imported their language and their laws, their customs and their religion. To keep them united became the overriding concern of every shah. Roads were non-existent and travelling was hazardous; brigands roamed the countryside. Education and justice remained firmly in the hands of the mullahs. They interpreted their power as giving them the right to decide for others, to impose their institutions and promote their own way of life. That kind of leadership could never lead to peace and stability, since religious strife had been the country's major problem throughout history. The religious majority was split in two, the twin enemies of Islam, the Sunnis and Shi'ites. In the north were the rebellious Kurds and in the mountains near Yazd lived the remains of Persia's original cult, the *Zoroastrians*, followers of Zarathustra, who left the

---

[1] The Koran, 2: 153.

bodies of their departed on the flat roofs of towers exposed to the vultures.[2]

The real rulers were the Russians and the British, whose predominant motive was the expansion of their trading interests, which called for protection of the passage from Europe through Persia to Afghanistan and from there across the Khyber Pass, to India. This route led to the establishment of trading posts surrounded by areas of colonisation. In 1872, the British railway tycoon, Julius de Reuter, beat the Russian tsar by a nose for the right to build a Persian railroad. But roads and railways alone did not lead to the creation of the vast agrarian settlements that had been developed in the West; the country that would have to be pacified was too vast, and the stony soil was too poor to till. Lawlessness ruled, and when it threatened the capital, the Kadjar Shah decided to create a force of Cossacks, trained by and under the command of tsarist officers. A fifteen-year-old boy, Reza Pahlevi, enlisted as a private in this Cossack force. His unique talent made him rise quickly through the ranks.

At the outbreak of the First World War, the Kadjar Shah sided with the Germans. This could not be allowed, since British naval vessels had now changed over from coal-fired to oil, and the Persian wells had to be safeguarded. With an 'agreement of mutual understanding', forced on the Shah in 1919, Persia became for all practical purposes, a British protectorate. But the Kadjar Shah, Ahmad Mirza, could not be trusted. The British, and in particular the Anglo-Persian Oil Company, decided to put a dependable ally on the Peacock Throne. Reza Pahlevi was made to understand that 'Persia's protectors' would not oppose his taking power – immediately! At the head of his Cossack brigade, General Reza Pahlevi

---

[2] As described in Nietzche's *Also Sprach Zarathustra*. The prophet Zarathustra, or Zoroaster, lived in the seventh century BC. His sermons were based on the adoration of the sun and its energy. The Parsi population of Bombay are refugees from Persia's Zarathustra cult.

Khan rode into Tehran and usurped power. In April 1926, the former peasant boy was crowned Reza I Pahlevi, Shahinshah of Persia. He changed his country's name from Persia to Iran in 1935. His next step was to muzzle the clergy, whom he considered an obstacle to his plans for a modernisation process.

His heir, Mohammad Reza Pahlevi (and his twin sister Ashraf), was born on 26 October 1919 in Tehran. In his youth his contracted diphtheria, typhoid fever, and malaria. While Reza Jun. was always feeble, his twin sister soon became known as 'the boy in the shah's family', a reputation that she was to maintain throughout her brother's rule, aiding him on many difficult occasions with her strength and advice. One day, when the boy was horseback riding, his horse reared and the fall nearly killed the boy. This accident was followed by yet another long period of convalescence. Reza Jun. spent his formative years at the Le Rosey School in Switzerland, which was reserved for scions of the very rich. With his dashing good looks he earned the dubious reputation of a *tombeur des filles* (ladykiller) and had to be speedily sent home when his relationship with a chambermaid shocked the school. Reza I scoured the Middle East for a suitable spouse for his heir. The best political choice promised a liaison with the royal house of Egypt. In 1939, at the age of nineteen, young Reza was married to the daughter of King Fuad I of Egypt and the sister of Farouk. Princess Fawzia gave birth to a girl and returned to her royal father. Next was Soraya Esfandiary who also failed to produce a boy. A student of architecture, Farah Diba, was sent to Paris to get herself a decent hairdo and a presentable wardrobe. With a flourish worthy of Pygmalion, she was transformed into the princess from *The Thousand and One Nights*. Within a year she presented the shah with a little Reza.

The history of modern Iran is the history of oil. In 1901, a

British adventurer, William Knox d'Arcy, obtained from the Kadjar Shah the right 'to explore and exploit, to transport and sell all the Persian oil'. Oil was (and still is) dominated by the Seven Sisters.[3] In the Agreement of Achnacarry of 1928, the major oil companies divided up the oil-producing world among themselves, going about it as one divides up a Camembert. Without bothering to check with the rulers of these nations, they allotted each slice of territory, and agreed on a price structure of 'what the market will carry'. Their profits rocketed from huge to gigantic, helped along by a Second World War that ran on oil. Just as the nineteenth century depended on coal for its steam engines, the twentieth century was the age of the internal-combustion engine. Without oil, the industrialised world would grind to a halt.

The shah recognised the stranglehold he had on international industry and transport, not to mention the international mechanised war machine. Oil, or rather the lack of oil, had driven Japan to war. His blow to the Seven Sisters' hitherto unchallenged monopoly came without warning. In 1957 the shah signed a deal with Italy's national oil company; the Italians invested 50 per cent in exploration for oil, in exchange for 25 per cent of the profits from its exploitation. This concession set a dangerous precedent and had the oil cartel trembling, more from fury than shock. The shah's initial deal was followed by similar concessions signed with the Japanese and the French.

Tampering with oil was a daring step, as Reza I had discovered to his loss. Under the 'Pahlevi doctrine', foreign diplomacy had become more prickly and uncooperative, even reckless. In 1932, Reza I committed the serious error of cancelling the Anglo-Iranian Oil concessions. He was forced to rescind and sign a sixty-year extension. He compounded

[3] The Seven Sisters are: Standard Oil of New Jersey (Exxon), Mobil Oil, Standard Oil of California (Socal), Royal Dutch Shell, Texaco, Gulf Oil, and British Petroleum (BP, formerly Anglo-Persian, afterwards changed to Anglo-Iranian).

his mistake by supporting Germany in the Second World War. In 1941, the Soviet Union and Britain invaded Iran and deposed the shah.[4] At the dictate of two foreign powers, his twenty-one-year-old son Mohammad Reza II was installed on the throne. Young and inexperienced, he was putty in the hands of the British and a puppet for the Russians. Winston Churchill defended this *coup d'état*: 'We have chased a dictator into exile and installed a constitutional sovereign pledged to a whole catalogue of long-delayed, seriously minded reforms and reparations.'

By 1944 another world power had begun to interfere in Iran's internal politics – the United States of America. In a memorandum to his secretary of state Cordell Hull, US President Roosevelt said: 'I'm excited by the idea of taking Iran as an example of what disinterested American politics can do.' America's suddenly taking notice of the oil-rich region ran contrary to British oil interests, and it did nothing to further the Russians' plans to extend their red empire to include a warm-water port, in fact, it interfered with their carefully laid plans. A Soviet-backed independence movement declared an autonomous republic in Iran's north-east, while the Tudeh Party, which espoused Soviet-style Communism, began to raise its head. For Britain and the United States, this mounting pressure represented a danger to the oil reserves. The shah declared martial law and his secret police did the rest. Arrests have never deterred a revolutionary movement and the troubles continued. With Muhammad Mussadegh, there arrived on the scene a shrewd manipulator who demanded nothing less than the nationalisation of Iran's oil. Prime Minister Ramzmara objected that Iran was in no position to repudiate its signed concessions. Four days later Ramzmara was dead, shot on his way to Friday prayers. More arrests followed and Iran's economy was jolted by a series of

[4] He died in exile in South Africa in 1944.

crippling strikes. To lead the country out of the impasse, the shah appointed Mussadegh as his prime minister.

For fifty years, Anglo-Persian (later Anglo-Iranian Oil) had been the instrument of British domination of Iran. In 1952, the seventy-three-year-old Mussadegh insisted on his country's fair share of the profits. With unaccountable foolishness, the British government refused to negotiate and withdrew its specialists from the refining facilities of Abadan. 'They cannot do it without our engineers,' claimed the English energy minister. He was wrong. Iran continued to extract oil and Anglo-Iranian reacted by inducing oil markets to boycott Iranian crude. Mussadegh reached a deal with the Soviet Union to buy up Iranian oil. At the height of the Cold War, with the paranoia of McCarthyism in America, the British Conservative government found it easy to brand Mussadegh as a Communist agitator. US President Eisenhower saw red and the CIA was ordered to prepare a contingency plan. The CIA resident for the Middle East, Kermit 'Kim' Roosevelt, grandson of President Teddy Roosevelt, was put in charge of Operation Mussadegh. While plans for an overthrow were in progress, the Shah sat cooped up in his palace, wondering what was going on. He even suspected that the British were co-operating with Mussadegh, until the CIA's Kim Roosevelt hid under a blanket, had himself driven into the Niavaran Palace, and outlined the counter-stroke for the shah.

In August 1953, Mussadegh dissolved parliament and assumed dictatorial powers. The shah tried to sack him and put in his place an ultra-right winger, General Fazollah Zahedi. But Mussadegh could rely on popular support and refused to step down. The street exploded with shouts of 'Yankee, go home!' Youths with red flags roamed the streets. Cars burned and people died. Violent demonstrations broke out in Tehran with flag-burnings and attacks on the offices of oil companies and foreign airlines. In a preview of things to come, the shah lost his nerve, climbed into a private plane, and fled to Rome. He arrived there like a penniless refugee and had to share a flat with a Persian businessman in the Hotel Excelsior.[5] This explosive situation held all the potential to inflame the entire Middle East. It was essential to bring it speedily to an end. CIA money went into action. Soon the shouts of 'Yankee, go home!' were replaced with 'Long live America!' and pictures of the shah reappeared in shop windows. On 19 August 1953, while having lunch in Rome, the shah was handed a cable:

MUSSADEGH OVERTHROWN. IMPERIAL TROOPS CONTROL TEHRAN.

In one of the most openly blatant CIA operations, and with the help of some key army generals in their pay, the US ousted Mussadegh. He was tried and condemned to death, but his sentence was commuted to a prison term by the shah. A beaming Pahlevi flew back to his nation's capital; champagne flowed and he was toasted by foreign journalists. He freely gave interviews that were essential to restore his tarnished image as the sovereign who had run away, abandoning his country to a civil war. What awaited him on his return were a ruthless, heavily armed police force, hidebound statesmen, glory-seeking politicians, and 'business partners' – native and foreign – intriguing for their personal ends. These shadowy manipulators fell on their knees and kissed the shah's hand. He murmured: 'I know that they love me.' With Mussadegh's 'popular overthrow', he clung to the false belief that he was immortal and beloved by all; this was one of the seeds of his tragedy. His megalomania knew no bounds; within months, signs of his deification were omnipresent. With the implementation of a savage press law, all critical discussion of the issues facing the country was in effect outlawed. Every daily newspaper had to lead with a front page story about Reza II, shahinshah of Iran, lauding his achievements, regardless of

---

[5] Everyone who helped the shah in this period was greatly rewarded.

what else went on in the world. His aim was to become the Napoleon of the Middle East. Oil revenues and US aid helped him create a huge military machine. Generals whose loyalty was beyond question were pampered and presented with splendid villas. Retired CIA chiefs and French generals, in the role of arms merchants, made the pilgrimage to Tehran to demonstrate the effectiveness of guided missiles and modern fighter aircraft. Petrodollars cascaded into the pockets of gun dealers. Between 1972 and 1977, Iran purchased 240 state-of-the-art fighter aircraft, 500 helicopters, 4 frigates, 3 submarines, and several Hawk missile batteries. The monarch justified his profligacy with a single phrase: 'We cannot achieve economic superiority without a powerful military force.'

If the shah was the anointed monarch, there was another personality as strong and influential as the divine shah himself. She was known as SAIPA, Son Altesse Impériale Princesse Ashraf. She was either much hated or much loved and she left nobody indifferent. Princess Ashraf contributed more to the image of the throne than any of Reza's three queens. Perhaps an Ulterior Being had mixed up their genes at birth and provided the girl with those intended for the boy. As the shah's ambassador extraordinary, she learned that diplomacy was the art of the feasible, and proved her value as a master of intrigue and compromise. When the Russians refused to evacuate Azerbaijan she went to see Stalin; he not only agreed to her request, but presented her with a magnificent sable coat. With the Americans she was instrumental in the ousting of Mussadegh; she opened diplomatic relations between Iran and Mao's China. Her many love affairs were the deafening whisper of the jetsetters bronzing themselves along France's Cote d'Azur. Her acute sense of business made her a vast fortune, but nothing untoward could ever be proved. Small wonder that in the 1970s all such affairs were conducted with Samsonite suitcases stacked with $100 bills, transferred by private aircraft to banks in Liechtenstein or the Cayman

Islands. A pay-off was the only basis for doing business with Iran. Corruption became a severe social disease, and the argument that 'everybody does it' was roundly approved. It was just that it was hard to fight when interests and habits were so deeply entrenched.

In 1963, Reza instigated a 'White Revolution' which called for a wide range of changes. What was intended as land reform became in reality nothing more than populist rhetoric. Land was bought from wealthy family holdings and sold back to rich landowners. Increasing numbers of poor peasants flocked into the cities where they tried to recreate their village life. Some newcomers found employment as menial labourers, but for most of them there was no work. Instead of bettering their existence, they became slum-dwellers in hastily thrown up dismal quarters on the outskirts of town. Their desolate existence added to the general discontent and they began to seek guidance from their mullahs. The shah erred also in his misconceived attempt at women's suffrage, a Western principle unheard of in Islamic countries. It was immediately denounced by 80,000 mullahs in mosques across the country. Princess Ashraf openly expressed her displeasure to the women who continued to wear 'that horrid black cloth of their grandmothers'. It made no difference; women continued to wear the chador.

The proposed female emancipation exacerbated the fierce struggle between temporal and spiritual power. It was here that Americans became the catalyst for the fall of the shah. Thousands of US military advisers and technicians now arrived to help make his war machine operational. They arrived by huge planes and seagoing transport. Booms swung out, winches creaked, and out of the holds of ships came the material of war. Artillery, ammunition, helicopters, crated missiles – and hundreds of cases of alcohol. The advisers brought with them their culture and their hamburgers; bucket brigades of Iranian labourers lugged canned bacon 'n' beans, hair curlers, and the thousand different items needed to stock a 'back-in-the-good-ol' US of A' supermarket. Their wives drove oversized cars to the 'you should see it, it's soooo cute' local market, dressed as if they were teenagers in sunny California, in short shorts and skin-tight T-shirts. They went to the beach, where their husbands lit barbecues to grill deep-frozen pork chops; 'the girls' meanwhile took a dip in skimpy bikinis. They overlooked the fact that they were in an Islamic country, with female modesty and prudish Islamic codes. These young American technicians had no experience of life abroad and the complexity of the strict religious Shi'ite laws escaped them. But this fact did not pass unnoticed by the local population who considered the influx of these invaders a new type of hostile occupation. It was bound to lead to trouble. By 1964, the issue of who had the right to judge the religious transgressions committed by American advisers led to the break between the shah and the man who was to become his nemesis, the Ayatollah Khomeini.

At the time, such questions were settled in a permanent fashion. There is no question that judicial murder had worked well for millennia as the symbol of the ruler's power, and in this, Iran became one of the most repressive and paranoiac regimes. Criticism of the imperial ruler was not tolerated. If there were policy disagreements within his government, then the most egregious opponents to the shah would pay for it with long jail terms – or their lives. Killing his adversaries only invited more secrecy and more opposition. In a move that fooled no one, the shah instigated a two-party system, then made certain of his 'opposition' when he hand-picked the candidates. 'We wish to avoid at all costs the recurrent experience in some democratic countries where the people give the government the opposition they deserve,' he declared. With the help of his internal security apparatus he held the country in a vice-like grip. The keeper of the shah's faith was the notorious SAVAK (National Security and Intelligence

Organisation), whose 80,000 agents (one for every mullah, it was said) did not need to account for their activities. Every part of Persian society was infiltrated, from minister to mine worker, from army officer to village headman, and a detailed report arrived daily on the ruler's desk. Sometimes he conducted show trials; at other times people simply vanished. In foreign countries, SAVAK agents harassed exiled opposition leaders and student groups. In the army, meetings of more than two officers were prohibited. Fear became the psychic template for revolt. This launched a process akin to contagion – throughout history, terror always begets more terror. The struggle changed its face. Soldiers who were still willing to die for their shah would one day be replaced by kids with looted rifles, willing to die for an ayatollah.

Reza Pahlevi behaved more and more as if his motto were Louis XIV's immortal phrase: '*L'état, c'est moi.*' But whilst the French sun-king had surrounded himself with men of genius like Colbert or Turenne, the shah thought he could do everything by himself. For this he had neither the talent nor the world status. Nevertheless, he held an unwavering belief in his divine mission. 'From the time I was six, I have felt that perhaps there is a Supreme Being who is guiding me.' Although the country suffered from a shocking level of illiteracy and a mortality rate worse than anywhere in the Middle East, all caused by the lack of schools and hospitals, in October 1971 the shah ordered an extravaganza of such proportions that it was sure to outshine anything ever seen before. The cream of Parisian fashion designers and chefs sewed and cooked for the occasion. Planeloads of royals were flown to a specially built airstrip. A huge tented city was erected in the middle of the desert, each tent equipped with a marble bathroom. Special perfumes were created; gala uniforms were embroidered with thread of solid gold; the three-star chef of Maxim's created a meal of poached partridge eggs and caviar. Since the Master of Protocol forgot to inform the expensive culinary expert that His Imperial Majesty never touched caviar, nobody else ate at the banquet – that is, not until the three-star *cuisinier* served the monarch some boiled leeks.

For the first time since the Congress of Vienna, when kings and statesmen divided up post-Napoleonic Europe, the ruling heads of the world were invited to discuss the future of the globe. Nothing less. One emperor, nine kings, three reigning princes, thirteen presidents, ten sheikhs, and one sultan. Reza Pahlevi considered himself the direct descendant of Cyrus the Great, who had conquered Lydia (modern Turkey) in 546 BC and then extended his empire from the Mediterranean to Syria and Egypt. His other great ancestor was Darius whose conquests reached the Indus Valley. The present shah there-fore combined the celebrations for the thirtieth anniversary of his own coronation with Iran's 2,500th anniversary as an empire. His choice for the site fell on the prestigious ruined city of Persepolis, still displaying much of the magnificence of ancient Persia. Persepolis bore witness to a colourful history. After Alexander the Great's crushing victory over the Persians at Gaugamela (or Gomel Su) in 331 BC, it was prophesied by Thaïs that Alexander would destroy the Persian past so that Greek culture could conquer the world. So Alexander had Persepolis burned to the ground. Such was the myth; the truth was probably that his troops were getting used to luxury and refused to move on. By destroying their quarters he solved the problem.

Mohammad Reza II Pahlevi, who had the history of Persia remodelled to his specifications, opened the festivities in his flat, monotonous voice: 'Cyrus, great king and king of kings, I, the Shahinshah of Iran, and his people, salute you!' This was followed by a costume spectacular which lasted for hours, beginning with the bearded warriors of the Persians and the Medes, the Sfedides and Kadjars. The power of Iran, once achieved by the cavalry of Xerxes and the war chariots of

Cyrus, was brought up to date by a display of the military might of the shah. Diplomatically speaking, Persepolis was a flop. The shah had given instructions to rank his invited guests in accordance with some medieval scale of royal precedence, which led to hysterical mix-ups. Kings without kingdoms were placed ahead of leaders of major world powers. The French President Pompidou refused to be relegated behind some minor princeling and sent his prime minister instead, an affront that the shah never forgave. The queen of England sent her daughter, Princess Anne; the queen of Holland dispatched her husband. But it was the absence of US President Richard Nixon that caused the greatest embarrassment. Vice-President Spiro Agnew, who according to aristocratic protocol was placed just one row ahead of the Chinese ambassador, represented America. Even worse, the expenditure of $300 million on this one-day extravaganza, in a land with an average annual income of $50 per head, provided ammunition to his enemies. The shah, however, considered Persepolis a success. He had passed on his message. Within a month he flexed his muscles and broke off diplomatic relations with Iraq. In a surprise move which upset the balance of the entire region, he took possession of three islands, Abu Moussa, Little and Big Tomb, small uninhabited rocks that straddled the Straits of Hormuz and thus controlled the entrance into the Gulf. With their seizure, he had achieved a stranglehold on all shipping entering and leaving the oil-rich region. This move was to have wide consequences.

The day of 22 December 1973 was significant in the economic life of the world. The six Persian Gulf oil ministers met in closed session in Tehran. Facing each other across the baize table were Sheikh Zaki Yamani, the Saudi oil minister, who pleaded for a drop in the price of Arabian crude, and the shah, who argued that the West should pay more. The initial session ended in a stalemate. The shah pulled his master stroke by calling a press conference. The grand hall at

Tehran's Intercontinental was jammed with the world's press and microphones sprouted like asparagus. The shah made his usual regal entrance and sat down behind the microphones. Before anyone could ask a question he raised his hands and brought the room to silence. He announced the shattering news: '$11.65 a barrel!' More than double the going rate of the previous day! He explained that his offer was 'on a basis of generosity and kindness'. In 1974, Iran's oil revenues jumped from $5 billion to $24 billion per year.

Oil was the issue. The West was not greatly preoccupied by internal Islamic problems; it was still reeling under the 'oil shock'. The Arabs (as they were generally called) caused market upheavals with their oil prices – and that was major news. As for their internal politics, apart from some Palestinian terrorists (also lumped together as Arabs) who had put bombs on Tel Aviv buses, the media did not have much to report. That was shortly to change.

For the Shi'ites (disciples of Mohammed's son-in-law Ali), and their mortal enemies the Sunnis (disciples of the Prophet Mohammed), their imams (Muslim leaders) represented more than just religion; they provided the spiritual guidance of laws laid down by the Holy Koran. With the reforms instituted by Reza I Khan in the 1930s, the imams had lost much of their influence in running the country. In despair, the Islamic fundamentalists regarded the shah as omnipotent and inflexible, protected by his formidable security and information apparatus. Mullahs had been involved in the assassination attempt on the shah in 1949 and had certainly supported Mussadegh, true to the local dictum: 'Any enemy of my enemy is my friend.' Their next great offensive began in the 1960s against the shah's 'White Revolution' of land reforms and women's emancipation – and the autocratic shah collided with Islam. All that was now needed was someone who possessed the spirit and the imagination that could lead to change. Such a man was an ageing, white-bearded Shi'ite professor of Islamic law, whose most remarkable feature were his eyes, burning with holy fire.

Ayatollah Sayyed Ruhollah Mousavi Khomeini was born in 1902 into a family of minor mullahs in the holy city of Qum. He was educated in strict obeisance to the Islamic faith. He wrote a pamphlet describing the shah as having forsaken the dictates of Islam. As his attacks grew in intensity, his audience increased in leaps and bounds. 'Today, the Holy Koran and Islam are in danger': this became his declaration of war on temporal power. By 1963, he was openly accusing the shah of being an agent of Israel. Khomeini's arrest caused bloody riots throughout the country in which several thousand were killed.[6] Prime Minister Assadollah Alam wanted to get rid of the bothersome ayatollah, but the shah prevented his execution. He grossly misjudged the priest's staying power. As far as he was concerned, there was nothing more tedious than a professional preacher of principle; no, the real danger lay with the underground agitators. In 1964, he sent Khomeini into internal exile but the imam refused to remain silent and his speeches stirred up more trouble. Once again he was arrested, and again the shah prevented his execution. He tried to persuade the ayatollah to leave politics to experienced politicians. Khomeini's reply was curt and to the point: 'Since the time of the Prophet, Islam has represented a political power and has not limited itself to religious practice.' The final break was inevitable and came in the autumn of 1964 over the issue of the American military advisers and their right to have their transgressions judged by American tribunals rather than by Iranian justice under Islamic law. In 1965, Khomeini fled into exile to Najaf in Iraq. The moment that the ayatollah crossed the Shatt-el-Arab, the river that separates Iran from Iraq, he moved from the dusty steppes of Asia into the history of Islam.

[6] It was the author's first contact with the Islamic Revolution.

*   *   *

In the seventh century, news spread about a strange event in Mecca, a windswept place in the wilderness of Arabia. Mohammed-ibn-Abdullah, who was born there in AD 570, had claimed himself to be the Apostle of God. People flocked to his house to listen to *his* message. Following the prophet's death in AD 632 Khalid-bin-Walid (known as 'The Sword of Islam') and a warrior host set out to conquer the Arabian peninsula, guided by nothing but an uncontrollable religious fanaticism. The decisive encounter came in AD 637, at Qadissiya near Najaf. In 'The Mother of all Battles', Saad-ibn-Waqqas defeated a huge Persian army. After Qadissiya, nothing could stop the spread of Islam, and the prophet's message was carried from the Fertile Crescent into North Africa, and from there across to Spain where it remained until the fall of Granada in 1492. Islam brought new impulses and effected a fundamental political transformation in all the countries it subjugated. In AD 656, the Prophet Mohammed's son-in-law Ali connived at the overthrow of Caliph Othman; his supporters stabbed Othman, who became the first caliph to be slain by another Muslim. Arabia trembled. A blood feud erupted and Ali was murdered. With these assassinations, Islam was split in two. It is Ali's son, Hussein ibn Ali, who is venerated as the founding saint of the Shi'ite'at Ali – the Party of Ali. In AD 680 Hussein received the divine summons to continue his father's caliphate in Kufa. With seventy-two retainers, driven by a fanatical determination to exterminate idolatry and indulgence, he set off from Medina. The Omayyad Caliph Yezid ordered the caravan to be intercepted and Hussein's followers put to death.[7] The 'massacre of the seventy-two' led to the Great Schism of Islam, into Sunnis and Shi'ites. The history of this division is one of incursions

---

[7] Hussein was buried in Kerbala, which, together with Ali's shrine in Najaf, is more sacred to the Shi'ites than the Kaaba at Mecca or the prophet Mohammed's tomb at Medina.

and expulsions, assassinations, wars, and devastation, and this lust for revenge continues into the present.[8]

In the beginning, Shi'ite was the doctrine of a minority, a rallying cry for all those with grievances against their Arab overlords. This gave birth to politically active extremists, such as the Assassins (from *hashashin* meaning 'hashish'), a sect founded by a Persian monk whose name became synonymous with murder. Shi'ite theology reveals considerable undercurrents of a pre-Islamic past; their martyrs were surrounded by divine light, just as were the ancient kings of Persia. Hussein's successors, designated imams, attributed to themselves the same qualities as those of the divine figures from the past.

Ayatollah Khomeini was a Shi'ite. The town of Najaf was a shrewd choice for an exiled ayatollah, since it was not only the most holy place for Shi'ites, but also the centre of Iran's state religion. From this bleak place of mud-walled houses, in the shade of the Ali Mosque, this fanatical twentieth-century disciple of 'the Apostle of God' launched his theological thunderbolts against the 'evil servant of dollars'. He denounced the cruelties committed by the SAVAK, praised the martyrs in the struggle against oppression, and urged the Iranian mullahs to take up active resistance. Tehran was wrong to consider these the ravings of a spiteful old man. In 1978, the laic Saddam Hussein, faced with a rebellious Shi'ite minority, threw them out of Iraq.

If the ayatollah was the engine of insurrection, it was always oil that led to the shah's demise. The Arabs did not trust a man who would sell oil to any buyer, including Israel. For once, the shah reacted; under his guidance the major oil-producing countries united into a club and achieved their first victories. OPEC, a loose federation, signalled the end of the old regime of concessions. Countries from Indonesia to Venezuela, and from Saudi Arabia to Mexico, managed to demand significant

[8] In the summer of 1998, Sunni Taliban forces overran several major cities in Afghanistan. They rounded up all Shi'ites and butchered them.

changes from the oil majors. With the creation of OPEC, the shah's reputation was riding the crest. But his fatal error was in attempting to usurp the oil crown, while simultaneously fighting the Seven Sisters. It became a war on two fronts, never a promising scenario. In 1973, while OPEC ministers were still haggling over the size of price adjustments, Egypt and Syria invaded Israeli-occupied territory. The shah supplied Israel with oil throughout the Yom Kippur War. The Arabs, led by Saudi King Feisal, declared an embargo on oil exports; queues formed at petrol pumps around the world. The Iranian oil minister, Amouzegar, acting under the orders of the shah, broke the ban when he conducted the first of a series of 'oil auctions' which raised the price from $6 to $17 a barrel. The Arabs were furious. US Treasury Secretary William Simon refused to visit Tehran, saying: 'The shah is a nut.'

Reza's flawed regime could only do the whole region more harm than good. It was time to dump him. There was no shortage of reasons and excuses. Religion was high on the agenda. The shah's symbolic decree banishing Islamic fundamentalism could discredit the very ideal that it aimed to embrace. The risks were too great and the possible gains too small. OPEC decided that the shah had to go. Strangely, up to that point, Iran's greatest support had come from the oil-producing Arab sheikhdoms, especially the kingdom of Saudi Arabia. They argued that as long as the shah was kept in power, oil prices would remain high. There was another nation that had always watched the friendly relations between the United States and the shah of Iran with an unfavourable eye. That nation was Israel. Not because Iran was Arab-friendly, which it was not, but because Iran was America's southern cornerstone in the containment of the Soviet Union. It did not please Israel that America supported two allies in the region. Another event of consequence took place in the summer of 1975, when Iraq's strongman, Saddam Hussein, and the shah put their countries' age-old quarrel to rest and concluded a typical oriental horse-deal. Iran agreed to stop supplying arms to the Kurds in their fight against Iraq, and Saddam Hussein opened the Shatt-el-Arab to Iranian shipping. This rapprochement turned Iran into an unstable liability.

For a while the shah survived on inertia. The West had invested too much in him to imagine abandoning him now. Western industrial powers argued that with the shah still the driving force behind OPEC, an easier oil policy with the Arabs would be feasible. This assessment was erroneous as the shah was now considered a traitor to Islam. The Gulf Arabs began to financially underwrite his opposition. It was the worst thing that they could possibly do. They did not appreciate how much worse things would become if the shah failed – at best he would be swept aside by nationalism, at worst by a new-born religious fundamentalism that could and would contaminate the entire Islamic Crescent.[9]

It did not need the help of his Arab neighbours; the shahinshah was digging his own grave. 'Freedom of thought, what is freedom of thought, what is democracy?' he threw at a journalist. 'With five-year-old children going on strike and parading through the streets? That's democracy? That's freedom?' In the days leading up to the crisis of 1978, a better understanding of the inherent problem, a stronger political will, and a greater honesty could have marked a turn away from the abyss, rather than a lurch towards it. Hard choices were called for: a change of government, a clean-up campaign directed against the profiteers. To bring stability rather than chaos to Iran would have required the confidence of the people. It was precisely this confidence that had been squandered by the shah and his ministers. The shah thought that he could make vast economic changes without making political changes as well. Only a year before, crowds

---

[9] The Islamic Crescent is the term used to describe the geographical area from Indonesia to North Africa.

had celebrated their country's elevation to world-power status (following Iran's seizure of the Straits of Hormuz); now the same people poured into the streets to protest the government's incompetence and the political crisis it had created. The troubles played into the hands of the Islamists. It was at this moment, when it needed a strong hand, that the shah's slide from elation to despair became precipitous.

Added to his growing internal problems, the shah was a sick man. In 1975, Dr Georges Flandrin, a famous Parisian surgeon, had been secretly called to Tehran. He diagnosed cancer of the blood, and suggested an immediate treatment of chemotherapy, followed by intensive radiotherapy. This diagnosis came as a severe shock and it is understandable that the shah's mind became distracted from the affairs of state. He suffered from bouts of depression, walking always in the shadow of his overpowering father, that Cossack who employed the methods of a Renaissance *condottiere* to subjugate an entire nation and then used an iron fist to run the affairs of state. Things were different now.

For years, the SAVAK had been preoccupied in exterminating Communism; they never dreamed there might be an insurrection based on religion. The shah refused to believe that for the past twenty years he himself had supplied the impetus for the agitation by the mullahs. The leader of the shah's government, Amir Abbas Hoveyda, a subtle, faithful prime minister, striving to fulfil his role, yet not using his position as a trampoline for personal ambitions, tried to warn his sovereign. 'Majesty, a situation of insecurity develops in our townships. The young people constitute a new power group, they flock into religious centres for guidance. We must treat them seriously, or disorder will invade the suburbs.' The shah ignored the warning, looking on youngsters as nothing more than a nuisance.

Ehsan Naraghi, an adviser who met the ruler on a regular basis, described the mood in the imperial court in the early months of 1978.

'Your Majesty, the Islamic revolutionaries have installed a system of loans without interest.'

The shah shook his head in disbelief. 'Where does the money come from?'

'Majesty, over the last few years several hundred mosques have been built in Tehran alone; a hundred thousand students have subscribed to these religious centres, hundreds of publications have been printed – all without the state paying a cent, only through Muslim solidarity.'

'Who are these people who support it financially?'

'They can count on external sponsorship and *Bazaaris*[10] also contribute to the endeavour.'

At another meeting, the question was the trustworthiness of Iran's foreign allies.

'You know what the English did to my father.'

'But, Your Majesty, the Americans are helping us.'

'Yes, the Americans are a different kind, but they allow themselves to be influenced by the English. They fear our military strength to control the region. It would suit them better to have a weak king in this part of the world whom they could manipulate.'

Nineteen seventy-eight was the year of decision. It began with deceptive calm, lulling the shah into the illusion of eternal imperialism. Less than a week after the New Year, the explosions of the autumn were echoed in a rash of minor demonstrations, which set in motion a chain of events that resulted in the destruction, not only of the shah, but of the 2,500-year-old Persian empire.

In January, trouble erupted in the holy city of Qum. The SAVAK had placed an article in *Ettélaat*, which insulted the exiled and almost forgotten ayatollah. A demonstration led by mullahs in defence of Khomeini's honour ended with an attack on a police station. It left sixty dead. The contagion

[10] *Bazaaris* are those who run all commerce in the bazaar.

spread. A week later a hundred people were killed during a pro-Khomeini riot in Tabriz. On 15 May, students of the University of Tehran rioted and troops stormed the campus. A month later, 200 more died in Mashad when a crowd followed a call by Khomeini to overthrow the shah. The victims were wrapped in green flags inscribed with verses of the Holy Koran, while the mullahs intoned: '*Inna lahum el janna* . . . because the paradise belongs to those who follow the righteous path of Allah, who kill and are killed, then they will achieve redemption.' The burial of the martyrs of Mashad turned into a demonstration of faith, and pushed Khomeini overnight to sainthood.

The disturbances could have been contained but for a series of unconnected events that tilted the scales. The first happened in the southern town of Abadan, site of the largest oil refinery in the world. On the hot evening of 19 August 1978, fire broke out in the projection room of the Rex Cinema. Panic ensued when the spectators found that the exits had been blocked from the outside; 477 died in the flames. It was arson, and the police blamed the Islamic fundamentalists. The mullahs blamed agents provocateurs of the SAVAK. Their accusation carried more conviction and was readily accepted by the population, even to the point of calling the cinema *Kebabi-ye Aryamehr*, the shah's shishkebab house. The opposition began to spread more rumours; for example, that the shah had asked for 20,000 Israeli soldiers to quell the insurrection. The atmosphere became tense: no longer the continuous baying of the pack, but an ominous silence punctured by shrieks. For the first time the ruling class was made aware that the country was on the point of rebellion. The shah's statues were sprayed with red paint but were not yet toppled from their bases; there was still time to defuse an explosive situation. To do so, the shah had to act, and act fast in order to put the lid on the unrest. He had to accept the prospect of bloodshed. He hesitated and the insurrection invaded Tehran with thousands surging through the streets. They were chanting something new: 'Khomeini is our leader!' It was a noisy demonstration but there were no injuries or arrests. Weakness, or good sense? Either way, the revolutionaries judged the moment ripe to seize the initiative.

The fatal day must be considered the turning point from civil disobedience to open revolution from which the shah was never to recover. On that day, 8 September 1978, many more thronged the streets and the military governor, General Gholam-Ali Oveissi, without asking his monarch, decided to take a stand. The crowd converged on Tehran's Jahleh Square. The limousine of a rich merchant was trapped and a *mustazafin*, one of the 'disinherited', leaped on top: '*Margh bar Shah!* Death to the shah!' The ultimate blasphemy! A shot rang out, the agitator tumbled from the car, and a shocked moan was heard. His body was wrapped in a blood-splattered green flag, and the revolution now had its martyr. The crowd howled for revenge. General Oveissi ordered his troops to block off the square. Heavily armed soldiers advanced slowly, compressing the seething masses towards the centre of the square. Demonstrators were pushed back with rifle butts. Foreign journalists on the scene could never establish with certainty whether the excited soldiers were to blame, or whether they were acting under the orders of their commanding officer. The troops opened fire, killing 122 and wounding 4,000. The shah was shattered; more than anything, he hated bloodshed.

Oveissi was not the only one at fault. The uprising was a reaction to the way that power had always been exercised, when troop commanders had standing orders to quell riots with the utmost vigour. Suppression bred violence rather than stifled it. The immediate effect of the government's display of brute force was to unite the masses behind their mullahs. Any further incident would only help to turn more ordinary city folk into an army of revolutionaries.

Previous clashes paled in comparison with this traumatic event and it set a pattern that was to be tragically repeated in the months to come. The movement had acquired a terrible dynamic. Thousands more joined in. To many fiery spirits this was their chance to join the heroic revolution of the prophet. Religion was still their symbol. It was in this highly charged moment that a political agitator stepped in and manipulated the emotions of these excited youngsters. '*Margh bar Shah! Death to the Shah!*' And the shah had never been a religious symbol, only of totalitarian monarchy. In a sudden release of anger after long years of repression, tens of thousands were driven by a demented hatred of the shah's authority to pit their slogans against the best-armed military force in the Middle East. The mob threw stones and petrol bombs; the army retaliated with bullets.

Disasters never arrive singly. A few days after Jahleh Square, a devastating earthquake struck the town of Tabas, killing 3,000. The shah flew to a nearby airstrip where he was photographed in his starched uniform with bowing generals and officials, while in the stricken town students and mullahs pulled their dead from the rubble. As a public relations move, the shah's lightning visit to the earthquake region was a fiasco. His health began to fade noticeably, his arrogance gave way to despair. Michael Blumenthal, US Secretary of the Treausury, had to tell the US president following a visit to Tehran: 'We've got a zombie in place. Do we have alternative plans?'

Washington may not have had a revised strategy, but Admiral Kamilladin Olahi, head of Iran's navy, did. He demanded an audience with his monarch to outline it: 'Allow the army to take control of the situation; arrest 5,000 business profiteers and 5,000 mullahs. It'll stop this nonsense cold.'

For a long time the shah remained silent. He stared out the window, at some distant point in time and space, before he replied: 'But that's against the constitution.' The constitution

– by now everything was against the constitution and the country was on the brink of disaster.

'Majesty, there is no other option. The revolution has already reached such an advanced stage that only the army can save our country.'

The moment was now, and that moment was lost. The shah remained indecisive, and Olahi left dejected. A king without will is a king lost. Thus, like Louis XVI and Nicholas II and all other fallen potentates, another sovereign gave up his last chance to save his crown and his country.

The shah's efforts to modernise Iran had disturbed the pattern of everyday life. There is no denying that the revolutionary mullahs played a vital part in shaping popular opinion and discontent, not that they were undoubtedly an important element in stirring up the masses. However, the huge crowds voicing their rage were by no means just passive, cleverly directed instruments.

Left-wing Islam had been a source of progressive and radical thinking for over a generation. It had fertilised political and intellectual circles, yet often bypassed the mosque itself. Some mullahs even issued statements contesting the archaic structures of their religious institutions and attacked the clerical hierarchy as part of a self-perpetuating society. This struck a chord among the young, and they came out screaming for change. It swept these youngsters into political activism, with a great thirst to run things for themselves, where solidarity with their fellow students became the great mobiliser. Observed from a safe distance, this may have seemed nothing more than an accidental dislocation, just one more disturbance in a disorderly month. As with most decisive moments in history, its ultimate consequence would not be visible for months to come.

In September 1978, Khomeini flew to France where he applied for political asylum. The French at first did not know what to do with him. Although they threatened Khomeini with immediate expulsion, they did not reckon with the stubbornness of an old, highly mediatic man. By accepting the ayatollah on French soil, President Giscard d'Estaing had opened Pandora's Box. With typical Gallic cynicism, the Quai d'Orsay was preparing the successor to an already written-off shah. French police were not used to stop the exile's political activities but to untangle traffic jams. A sleepy French hamlet now became a place of pilgrimage. The ayatollah's disciples camped nearby and locals had a hard time doing their shopping, so crowded were the streets of Neauphle-le-Château. Open white shirts and a three-day beard was the holy uniform, while girls used to climbing into tight-fitting jeans now hid themselves under an ugly black cloth called the chador.

The shah's hopes that the world at large, and his country in particular, would soon forget the old mullah were dashed. Because now a new phenomenon entered the ayatollah's medieval crusade: the electronic media. Khomeini gave interviews freely, which rapidly had an effect. Ably supported by men such as Sadegh Ghotbzadeh (his interpreter), Dr Ibrahim Yazdi (a physician from the USA), and Bani Sadr (his first political leader), foreign journalists became his cutting sword. Soon his modest bungalow on the outskirts of Paris was beleaguered by hordes of television cameras and newsmen. Satellite dishes sprouted thicker than weeds, articles were produced like cars on an assembly line. Journalists waited in queues, then removed their shoes before being led in to see this man of biblical overtones with his white beard, black eyebrows, and subdued voice, who pontificated to the press. A journalist asked the ayatollah if he approved of card games. 'Only if the kings are taken out and the queens wear chadors.' Khomeini's outpourings, given in a monotonous litany, were beamed by international radio services to the rest of the world, including Iran. For Khomeini there existed no separation between religion and politics. He ruled out a compromise with the shah – he would not talk to the personification of Satan. Sitting cross-legged on a threadbare carpet in a tent put up in an apple orchard, mullahs taped their imam's sermons and smuggled the recordings into Iran. 'The world is possessed of evil' was one of his catchphrases.

In Iran's mosques, the *mustazafin*, the 'disinherited' slum dwellers, gathered around their mullahs and listened to the imam's recorded words, inciting them to revolt. There can be no doubt that the most successful support for his mission came from the Western media. While the black-turbaned ayatollah was making headlines from a rural outpost in the Ile de France, support for his revolt was being mobilised in Iran. The radical current had grown ever since the shah's indirect involvement in the Yom Kippur War; Islamic militants considered his tacit support for Israel nothing short of high treason. These militants formed a revolutionary hard core. Men of learning, politically experienced and mature, who represented a Muslim elite and who were unaffiliated with any party, joined them. They added moral and intellectual weight at a crucial moment in Iran's history, and helped to swing the masses behind the radicals. These were the forces that coalesced to form the leadership of the Islamic Revolution. It was held together by ideology, not by organisation.

From October 1978 onwards there were daily demonstrations in Tehran and other cities. In a significant step, the entire workforce at the giant Abadan Refinery shut off the flow of oil in the pipelines. Within a week the land with one of the biggest oil reserves was running out of oil.

Ehsan Naraghi was summonod to see the shah.

'How do you see the situation since our last meeting?' the shah asked him.

'The strike movement is spreading all over the country, Your Majesty.'

'Can you please explain to me what causes all these strikes?

We must ask ourselves if there isn't something else behind these strikes.'

'I don't doubt that there is a political will which guides it all.'

'You mean to tell me, beside the wage claims there is something else? What?'

This conversation demonstrates that even at such a late date the shah was still ignorant of the real peril. By his continued inaction he had shown weakness and disloyalty to his fervent supporters, both civilian and military. There can be no lonelier moments in a ruler's life than the moment he finds himself bereft of friends and allies, set adrift like a castaway on a sea of disappointment, anger, recrimination, and distrust. He became torn between loyalty to friends and loyalty to his mission. And now he was being deserted by all those he had helped to gain fame and fortune. It left him so isolated that that he began to doubt in his divine mission. Unlike the revolutionaries who were prepared to resort to brute force, Reza Pahlevi, shah of Iran, was neither ruthless enough nor strong enough to see it through to the bitter end.

On 2 November 1978 a serious problem facing the USA in the Middle East was brought to the attention of President Carter with a cable from his ambassador to Iran, William H. Sullivan. It carried a loaded message and was to lead to a first-degree crisis: 'THE SHAH OF IRAN IS CONSIDERING ABDICATING.' Sullivan, who only weeks before had cabled: 'OUR DESTINY IS TO WORK WITH THE SHAH,' had with one message changed the rationale behind US foreign policy. The question that America had to answer within the next twenty-four hours was: should they support the shah, or dump him? It was all a question of cash. The US industrial armaments complex had an outstanding order to supply Iran with state-of-the-art weaponry worth over $12 billion dollars, big money that had to be protected. With this in mind, the

US Department of Defense dispatched a senior representative, Eric Von Marbod, to restructure Iran's military procurement programme, which was to take the changing situation into account. The psychological profile of the shah, prepared by the CIA, described him as 'a dangerous megalomaniac who is likely to pursue his own aims in disregard of US interests'. The shah's major ally began to waver. In Washington, the situation was almost as confused as in Tehran. The US president's decisions were contradictory and were openly attacked by former Secretary of State Henry Kissinger: 'Carter's policy is losing Iran for the West.'

On 5 November 1978, in defiance of the government's ban on demonstrations, a huge crowd flooded the streets of Tehran. A considerable segment was composed of women in black cotton cloaks. With yells of *'Margh bar Shah!* Death to the Shah!' the mob stormed banks, government buildings, state-controlled company headquarters, and alcohol distribution centres. They broke the windows of shops displaying luxury goods, overturned cars, burned buses, and wrecked the homes of wealthy citizens. The unprotected British embassy was sacked. Teenage rioters following instructions systematically smashed furniture and communication equipment before setting fire to the building. Karim Khan Zand Avenue was littered with broken glass and burning cars; the Bank Melli Tower was a smoking ruin, as was a luxury car showroom. This time the shah was overtaken by events. History swept him aside when he failed to halt a further effusion of blood by taking a firm stand. 'A monarch cannot retain power at the price of killing his own people.' Where his father, the old Cossack-shah, was always prepared to take hard decisions and led his cavalry from the front, Reza was basically a shy man who flinched at the sight of blood and left the killing to others.

The situation was spiralling out of control. Strikes paralysed the country; the bazaars shut down; there were more riots where the violence increased immeasurably. Violence paid. Violence made headlines. In a massive demonstration, over a million pro-Khomeinites clashed with elite units of *djavilan*, the Immortals of the Emperor's Guards, and *homafars* (Special Air Corps) units. The units blocked off the approach to the Niavaran Palace. Several processions united into one huge, howling mob: 'Death to the shah!' Shots rang out, this time not into the air, and the crowd replied with a roar of revenge. It was the deep bellow of a wounded dragon, which echoed through the canyons of high-rises and luxury hotels. Then a storm gathered as if the whole land had risen; a thousand, ten thousand undulated and rolled towards the armed soldiers, their fear replaced by frantic fury. *'Margh bar Shah!* Death to the shah!' More shots; the first rank fell; those behind poured over them, running and stumbling, making for the roadblocks. There was no stopping them. *'Margh bar Shah!* Death to the shah!' The scream rose above rooftops and was carried up the hill to the imperial residence. From windows came other screams as fire swept up elevator shafts and along hallways. There were many dead or dying. Some jumped from burning buildings; some were women with shopping baskets or old men who could not get out of the path of the surging mob and were trampled under its whirling fury. That day left the centre of Tehran littered with bodies, with carcasses of burnt-out cars, and scorched buildings. A black pall of smoke rose like some bloated mountain range. At least 600 died and over 3,000 were wounded. The incident shocked the shah beyond description; anxiety and fear seized him and his thought processes became unravelled. His failure to take immediate action had wide-ranging consequences. The White House shifted its overall thinking and now worked on a plan to support a military coup that would safeguard the vital oil installations, a step not considered a *coup d'état*, but rather a protective takeover by the military under the political guidance of the American-friendly Shapour Bakhtiar.

Washington realised that the shah had gone to pieces and the outcome was no longer in doubt. The tide had changed; the country had become an emotional tinderbox.

The shah was abandoned. In the Hall of Audience, the Great Master of Ceremonies, Amir Aslan Afshar, was on his knees.

'Your Majesty, Tehran is on fire, You must do something,' he pleaded.

'But my soldiers are already in charge of the city.'

'You have forbidden them to defend themselves. Majesty, we beg You, put a strong man at the head of your government.'

'Whom do you have in mind?'

'General Oveissi, Your military governor.' The general was known to put down fire with blood, as he had done in Jahleh Square in September.

'I'll see what I can do.'

But he did nothing. Or, at least, nothing that would defuse the situation when he named General Gholamreza Azhari to head the government. While Oveissi would have finished off the revolution once and for all, the weak Azhari only helped to further destabilise the situation.

Alexandre de Marenches of the French secret service paid a private call on the monarch. Having driven through the streets of a city seething with slogan-shouting mobs, and thus able to witness for himself the extent of the dilemma, the count was received by the shah in a blacked-out room.

'I shall never allow my troops to fire on my people,' the shah told him.

'Then, Sire, you are lost.'

On his return to Paris, Marenches went straight to the Élysée Palace to debrief President Giscard d'Estaing.

'*Alors*, Marenches?'

'He's another Louis XVI,' replied Marenches.

It was now clear that there could be no peaceful way out. A

whole generation was rising against a certain type of society. Demonstration followed upon demonstration. The thuds of exploding gasoline tanks could be heard inside the luxury hotels housing the world press. The glare from burning cars projected shadows of the fierce fighting on nebulous clouds of acrid gas. Lungs burned, eyes watered, heads bled, flags were waved. Teenagers threw themselves into the battle with incredible dedication; it was their chance in a lifetime to join a revolution. And what a revolution it was! The shah had done his Samson act; he had brought the whole structure down and buried himself in the rubble.

On Ashura, the tenth day in the holy month of Muharram, a demonstration of over a million marched towards the Shayad monument, put there by the shah to the glorification of his dynasty. The march was led by rows of *mustazafin* in shabby clothes, with stubbly chins and shaven heads, followed by mullahs in their black and white turbans, reciting verses from the Koran. The *mustazafin*, who had come to Tehran to find only misery, began to shout: 'We are holy martyrs like our Imam Hussein!'[11] A noise rose like the ocean's waves crashing on the shore: '*Allahu akbar – Khomeini rachbar!* God is great and Khomeini is our leader!' The Islamic Revolution was a fait accompli.

Next the Americans moved in. On 30 December, a high US official in Iran, Gary Sick, wrote a secret memorandum for the president's security adviser, Zbigniew Brzezinski, warning the White House of the possibility of a civil war. In which case Iranian hate would fall squarely on the 10,000 American oil engineers and their dependants residing in Iran. He suggested their immediate evacuation. Brzezinski read the memorandum and scribbled 'Done' across the bottom. The American exodus began. On New Year's Day 1979, the US ambassador, William H. Sullivan, visited the shah. He had

11 The founder of the Shi'ites.

two questions for which the president of the United States wanted an answer before he left for the summit conference in Guadeloupe. Would the shah approve a new government under Shapour Bakhtiar, and what would it take to get the shah to leave the country? The shah finally realised that the Americans were letting him down. His new prime minister designate was Shapour Bakhtiar, a man of intellectual curiosity, democratic style, and political skill. But by now the situation was hopeless. To be rescued from its endemic corruption and its ethnic, religious, and regional violence, the country did not need an impressive intellectual but a strong captain to lead it back from the brink. With his penchant for secular nationalism and religious tolerance, Bakhtiar was the wrong man at the wrong time.

The American and British ambassadors were summoned for an audience at the Niavaran Palace. The tired-looking shah was no longer able to conceal his emotions. Sick man that he was, the last few weeks of incessant pressure had taken their toll of his powers of endurance. He told them that he could see only three possibilities: stay and accept humiliation; barricade himself inside a naval fortress and let the army take over; or leave the country. Both envoys agreed that the only way out of the present situation was for the shah to leave the country 'temporarily'. The US ambassador had obtained assurances from Washington that a 'temporary visit for health reasons' by the monarch would present no obstacles; only a regal reception by the US president was ruled out. (Sullivan was to write in his memoirs: 'They threw him out like a dead mouse.') To allow the shah to retain some dignity, Egyptian President Anwar Sadat invited the imperial couple to make a stopover in Aswan – on their way to the United States. What made the shah finally decide to leave may never be known. Perhaps he was trying to reproduce General de Gaulle's master stroke: at the height of the revolution of May 1968, he pretended to flee France in order to lull his enemies into overconfidence, whilst all the time preparing his triumphant return.

The Iran issue, which had become so tangled through the conflict of loyalties, was now simplified. On 6 January 1979 the Guadeloupe Conference opened that was to finalise the fate of the shah. Carter told Helmut Schmidt, James Callaghan, and Giscard d'Estaing that the shah was lost and had to go. 'We cannot expect anything further from his regime. The military will take charge. We know them well, my generals talk to them on a first-name basis.' Carter really thought that familiarity with some Iranian generals could resolve the crisis. The plan was to put a moderate in place: the leader of the small Liberation Movement of Iran, Mehdi Bazargan. What the United States never understood was that their negotiations were in vain. It was no longer Bakhtiar or Bazargan – Khomeini had become the man of the hour. (Theodore Eliot, the US envoy who tried to strike a bargain with the ayatollah in Paris, never did receive assurances that Khomeini's plans would be politically acceptable to the United States.)

He goes, he stays, he goes, he stays. The suspense was brought to an end, not by Tehran, as one might expect, but by Washington, with an announcement from the Secretary of State, Cyrus Vance. It was couched in language that fooled nobody: 'The shah has decided to take a temporary vacation for reason of health.' He added that the US government 'concurred' with the shah's decision to leave the country. 'The Voice of America' and the BBC World Service carried the news as their top item. The reaction was immediate. In Tehran there was confusion. The shah felt only bitterness that his closest ally had publicly dropped him. In 'Khomeini country' drivers switched their car headlights on and honked their horns, their passengers giving the V-sign. The key was the army, and the army was divided. While high-ranking officers were bewildered, the recruits and lower ranks engaged in scenes of open fraternisation with Khomeini supporters; tanks had posters of Khomeini stuck to their sides and soldiers paraded with carnations in the muzzles of their guns. In the wealthy areas of Tehran a feeling of impending doom pervaded; in scenes of panic, hundreds closed up their mansions and rushed to board flights bound for Europe. One overriding question was on everyone's minds: of the twin forces of revolution, which would emerge as the eventual winner? The determined Muslim radicals, or the insidious Marxists, riding to power on the pretext of defending Allah?

One of the last courtiers to be received in an audience with His Imperial Majesty was the shah's adviser, Ehsan Naraghi. This was just two days before the shah's departure.

'So tell me, what is new?' the shah asked in a desperately tired tone.

'The biggest news is the announcement of the departure of Your Majesty.'

'Yes, I have decided to leave for a few weeks to give Bakhtiar a chance to settle affairs. Tell me, why did you not come sooner to tell me the truth?'

'Your Majesty always preferred those who dissimulated the truth.'

The shah frowned. 'You know, every time this country has faced up to a crisis, I have always listened to advice from our great poet Hafez. What would he have said now?'

'*In the face of adversity, it is wise to keep one's distance,*' replied Naraghi without hesitation.

'That is consoling ... Well, I hope we shall see each other again.'

They never did.

Tuesday, 16 January 1979[12] was a cold and windy day. In downtown Tehran, excited crowds were shuffling around in the snow and slush, waving pictures of Khomeini. For the

---

[12] In the Koranic calendar, 26 Dei 1357.

superstitious, a natural phenomenon had given them a sign: the night before, they had seen the face of the ayatollah imprinted on the moon. The shahinshah and the shahbanu passed through the gates of the Niavaran Palace for the last time. All the remaining court officials and loyal officers lined up along the red carpet. General Abdollah Badrai rushed forward, took the shah's hand and kissed it. He would later pay for this gesture. Many held the Holy Koran over the head of their departing monarch to call down on him Allah's protection on his last journey. From the courtyard a helicopter ferried the royal couple to the airport. A number of journalists had been admitted into the heavily guarded compound. The shah stepped up to the battery of microphones and issued a brief declaration: 'A new government has been formed. As for myself, I feel tired and need some rest. My voyage begins today.'

'How long will you stay away?' shouted a foreign journalist.

'I don't know . . . I really don't know . . .'

At 1.08 p.m. on 16 January 1979, the Boeing *Shahin* took off. The 2,500-year reign of the shahs of Persia was history.

Inevitably, the shah's private flaws led to grave consequences. His closest supporters hoped against hope that he would heed his mantra of personal responsibility. But his resolution was exhausted, and he had forfeited respect to the point of political impotence. He was left with no credibility or moral leverage to demand an end to the uprisings. It was not some mullah who had brought the sovereign to this pass. The shah's own demons had put him there. For years he had surrounded himself with flatterers, who told him what he wanted to hear. Only when it was much too late was the shah willing to listen to those who were shunned at court because they were too frank. He found himself abandoned by those whom he had helped to build up, those who had gained fortunes beyond their dreams: the urban middle class. Once the troubles started, he received no loyalty, no backing. They joined the opposition – not the workers or the peasants, but the minor intelligentsia, who were furious and bitter in their contempt. This then was the agonising, uncomprehending end to the Pahlevi adventure. His fatal flaw lay in his own insecurity. His aloofness and arrogance fell victim to a well-orchestrated campaign of hatred.

In the end, the shah wept. And soon, the country was to weep with him. But not on 1 February 1979, when 3 million people jammed the streets from the airport and fought to touch the car that carried the Ayatollah Khomeini in triumph back to Tehran. A religious dictator had replaced an autocratic king.

By making the Ayatollah Khomeini a martyr, the shah had raised him to a pinnacle of power and prestige unheard of in recent Islamic history. Now, this imam was revered as nothing less than the personification of a New Iran. Schoolchildren carried his banner: 'By the force of Khomeini, the shah has fled.' A new sign had appeared over night on the walls of the capital. It depicted a guerrilla holding up the sacred weapon of terrorism, the Kalashnikov, and underneath was written: *Afzal ul-jihad* – The better for a holy war.

At one o'clock in the morning of 1 February 1979, Air France flight 4271 took off from Paris Charles-de-Gaulle Airport. There were 168 passengers aboard the chartered Boeing 747, almost all of them journalists. A battery of microphones were thrust in the faces of several badly shaved men in rumpled suits with open shirt collars: Mohammed Yazdi, the ayatollah's spokesman; Sadegh Ghotbzadeh, who was to become foreign minister for a short time; and the cold, silent Bani Sadr, future president of the Islamic Republic. And one VIP passenger, travelling separately from the rest in the upper compartment of the jumbo jet. Wearing his well-known brown coat and black turban was the *Agha* himself, Ayatollah Khomeini. His secretary and confidante, Sadegh Tabatabai, accompanied him. During the flight, Khomeini asked Tabatabai to draw up a programme for a new government. He asked that it be exhaustive and that it be ready in three weeks. This meant that Bakhtiar was out. As the first rays of the sun shone through the porthole and the plane crossed over the mountain peaks along the Turkish–Iranian border, the ayatollah spread an Air France blanket on the cabin floor and knelt down in the direction of Mecca. He was giving thanks to Allah that he was going home.

The situation in Iran was far from settled. Would the army shoot down the plane? A squadron of Iranian air force combat planes was stationed at Khazvin. Flak batteries had been placed along the runways of every airport. And what about the soldiers of the Imperial Guard, would they arrest the passengers? How could a regime detain a planeload of the world's leading journalists without creating a scandal of monumental proportions? Was it for protection that the journalists had been allowed to accompany the ayatollah? The Air France pilot was not about to take a chance. To test their reception at Mehrabad Airport, the jumbo made a low passage over the field before it came down for a landing. It was 9 a.m. The ayatollah appeared at the top of the steps and walked towards the arrivals hall, where many of his close supporters lined up to greet him. Islamic guards had blocked the huge crowd near the Shahyad Monument on the Airport Boulevard. The only incident occurred when Tehran television, broadcasting the ayatollah's arrival live, suddenly interrupted their transmission with a picture of the shah, before the screen went black. This, more than anything, showed how tense and unsettled the situation was. Shapour Bakhtiar failed to make an appearance at the airport, a serious misjudgment that was to cost him his life.

'*Allahu akbar, Khomeini rachbar* – Allah is great, Khomeini is our leader.' Pandemonium broke out around the Shahyad Monument as the light-blue van bearing the ayatollah was swallowed up in the throng of hysterical millions. A helicopter had to be brought in to extract Khomeini and take him to the Behest-e-Zahra cemetery for his first public pronouncement on home soil. For three days, it became a stand-off between the prime minister, the army, and the mullahs. The ayatollah denounced Bakhtiar and threatened to unleash a holy jihad. Their problem was that a holy war could only be declared against infidels and Bakhtiar was a Muslim. The imam, a stubborn old man out to settle a personal score, was as much out of touch as the shah before him. And yet, he prevailed and rode to power on an archaic, puritanical form of Islam of the most depressing kind, based on a medieval anti-East, anti-West outlook.

On 3 February 1979, Khomeini created the Council of the Islamic Revolution. In doing so he released the seven avenging furies. Naive Westerners believe that all places are basically the same and that people the whole world over behave in the same rational way. It was assumed that, with the fall of the despotic shah, Iran would evolve politically; it was further assumed that once its economy began to grow, all reasonable Iranians would dress like everyone else and that prosperity would lead to liberal democracy. But Iran was, and still is, a different place. The West, but most of all, Iran's Arab neighbours, were soon to discover that the emergence of a virulent Muslim fundamentalism was now the decisive force in Iranian politics. On 7 February, the Khomeinites took control of the administration, the police, and the courts. Only three days later, a mutiny broke out within the army and most units joined the Islamic Revolution.

Prime Minister Bakhtiar could not be found; General Gharabaghi was in conference with the leader of the Liberation Movement of Iran, Mehdi Bazargan; and the status of the Iranian armed forces was uncertain. The ayatollah announced the formation of a Provisional Government under Mehdi Bazargan. Bakhtiar called it a joke, but it was not. Popular support was with Khomeini. The Imperial Guards moved into the military base at Farahabad Airport to put down the revolt by the *homafars* (non-commissioned officers). It turned into a fierce clash and over a hundred were killed. The news of the Farahabad massacre spread across Tehran, and resulted in wild street fighting between Islamic Guards and units loyal to Bakhtiar.

The showdown came on Sunday, 11 February. At 10.20 a.m. Tehran time, General Gharabagi announced the decision by the Superior Council of the Army that the Iranian armed forces were to remain politically neutral. This caught everyone by surprise. Prime Minister Bakhtiar hurriedly left his office and disappeared from view, while the mob stormed the armouries. By nightfall, all military installations were in the hands of the Islamists. Admiral Olahi escaped by walking across the mountains into Turkey.[13] A number of officers were less fortunate; dragged from their cars or their homes, they were savagely butchered by the mob. That same night, Prime Minister Bakhtiar boarded one of the last planes out of Tehran; he reached France. Mehdi Bazargan, the long-time chairman of the Iranian Committee for the Defence of Human Rights, became prime minister. The revolutionaries took over the shah's Niavaran Palace. Armed gangs roamed the city, breaking into the homes of the rich and making arbitrary arrests. General Abdollah Badrai, who had wept at the shah's departure, was murdered. The shah's loyal prime minister Amir Abbas Hoveyda was dragged before Sadegh Khalkhali, who was soon to earn for himself the sobriquet 'The Hanging Judge'. This small, insignificant man, whose thick glasses gave him the impression of a bug-eyed

[13] It has been said that he was aided by the Israeli Mossad.

monster, bragged to a journalist how he had sent 400 to their deaths during the first weeks of the revolution. 'We will govern from now on. This Islamic Republic will last for ten thousand years. Marxists can have their Lenin, we have Khomeini.'

The bombshell hit Washington during the early hours. At 11 a.m. EST that morning, a message arrived on President Carter's desk, sent by the military attaché in Tehran, Colonel Tom Schaefer: ARMY SURRENDERS. KHOMEINI WINS. DESTROYING ALL CLASSIFIED. With this message, the United States realised that it had lost its influence over Iran. The situation there now became perilous for any US representatives. The US consulate in Tabriz was sacked. At the US embassy in Tehran, Iranian guards had withdrawn and a mere twenty-two US Marines defended the compound. On 14 February 1979, St Valentine's Day, revolutionaries confronted 'Satan USA'. For the first time the American embassy was ransacked. '*Margh bar Shah!* Death to the shah!' had been forgotten. Now it was '*Margh bar Amrika!* Death to America!' Still, the worst was averted when Iran's new foreign minister, Ibrahim Yazdi, presented his official apologies to the American ambassador only moments after the ambassador had groped his way along a hallway into the basement to order that all classified papers and code machines be destroyed. America was forewarned: should it accept the deposed shah on US territory, every American diplomat posted in Tehran would be sent back to his home country – in a pine box.

The following day saw the first summary executions of officers. A beaten and bloodied General Nematollah Nassiri was produced before TV cameras. After a mock trial presided over by the sadistic mullah Sadegh Khalkali, which included Generals Rabii, Khosrowdad, and Naji, all four men were dragged to the roof of the Alavi School and shot. To demonstrate their power to the remaining loyalists, the scene was filmed and the pictures shown on Iranian television.

On 1 April 1979, the Islamic Republic of Iran was proclaimed. Prime Minister Amir Abbas Hoveyda was dragged into the courtyard of Qasr prison, tied to a ladder, and shot. When he did not die at once, a mullah pulled his head up by the hair and put a bullet through his face. Most of the shah's generals and Savakists suffered a similar fate. The Ayatollah Taleghani withdrew from the new government in protest over atrocities committed in the name of Islam. One of the revolution's most humiliating aspects was the intrusion of Islamic vigilantes. Claiming to be guardians of the revolution, these vigilantes waged a violent campaign to eradicate all signs of the former shah as well as of 'decadent' Western culture. The shah's statues tumbled and the inscriptions on their marble bases were plastered over with pictures of the ayatollah. Western literature and American cars were turned into giant bonfires, hotel bars were smashed, and alcohol was poured into swimming pools. Sporadic gunshots signalled the summary execution of high-ranking officials and officers. The first months of the Islamic Revolution proved to be bloody in the extreme. Monarchists were ruthlessly exterminated. Anyone who failed to show openly his belief in Allah was branded as an atheist, dragged from his house, and shot for 'corruption on earth'. Landowners were butchered, oil experts executed. Throughout the country, a proliferation of neighbourhood *komitehs* (committees) sprang up under the authority of some local mullah. The core of a *komiteh* was the mosque and the Friday prayers. They turned Iran into a patchwork of power centres. Prime Minister Bazargan pleaded with Khomeini to disband the *komitehs*. Instead, the ayatollah replaced the old-line 'moderates' with young, zealous 'hardliners'. This step allowed teenagers to commit excesses on a scale never previously experienced.

The National Front, many of whom were lawyers who

declared a platform of civil liberties and human rights, was replaced by the Islamic Republican Party. In a new constitution, Khomeini's position was elevated to that of *velayat-e-faqih*, the representative of God. He set out to silence his opposition but needed a pretext to divert public attention. The Kurds were an ideal target. In exchange for their support against the shah's army, they had been promised local autonomy. What followed was an example of how matters would be conducted in the future. Khomeini branded the Kurds 'devils fighting the will of the One God'. Their uprising was put down in reprisal raids and summary executions. Khomeini moved to the holy city of Qum, from where he dealt with some rebellious mullahs who had objected to his dictatorial powers. One of them, who had been instrumental in mobilising the anti-shah demonstrations in the capital, was Tehran's leading religious figure, the Ayatollah Taleghani. He held more tolerant views than Khomeini. 'The religious leaders must not take power in the Islamic Republic. The fate of this country must be put into the hands of personalities that have the respect of the entire population.' His emphasis on 'religious leaders' left no doubt about his attitude. An important factor here was the intelligentsia and the students, who had more confidence in Taleghani's moderate views than in Khomeini's inflexible stand. Shortly thereafter Taleghani 'died of heart failure' and was replaced by Ayatollah Montazeri, an incompetent but pliable character.

The new *Majlis* (assembly) voted for the death penalty *in absentia* for the shah and the shahbanu. The mullahs gave a demonstration that their arm could reach beyond their borders. The son of Princess Ashraf was gunned down in Paris on the orders of the Ayatollah Khalkhali who justified the murder by saying: 'We have to liquidate all the dirty lackeys of a decadent system.' The odyssey of the ousted shah had only just begun. For the remaining eighteen months of his life, he continued to scour the global map in search of a suitable refuge. He analysed the possibilities and found fault with them all. No country wanted him. The Swiss said no; the Austrian chancellor thought that his presence could become 'disturbing'. England's Iron Lady, Mrs Thatcher, said no. US President Carter, who at the time was under great pressure to free the American hostages, made his position quite clear: 'While our people are being held hostage I don't want the picture of a deposed shah playing tennis in America.' A faithful friend remained in the former US Secretary of State Dr Henry Kissinger, who tried to change President Carter's mind. Abandoned by all, the shah wandered aimlessly around the world, while his health rapidly failed. Morocco, the Bahamas, Mexico, and Panama became temporary stopping points. His odyssey came to an end in Egypt where he died on 27 July 1980. Mohammad Reza II Pahlevi had been shahinshah for thirty-eight years. Ex-US President Richard Nixon said what many felt: 'I believe that the way our government behaved will forever remain one of the darker pages in the history of our nation.'

A reappraisal of Western policy on Iran was already under way. Ever since the fall of the shah, this had become essentially an ideological project. Islam would always be an important part of world policy. Thereby, co-operation with Iran, and acceptance that America would have to deal with a new, revolutionary type of Islam, was vital. But it was already too late. American statesmen finally awoke to the realisation that they had never known a culture so personalised as the radical Islam of the ayatollah. Khomeini had cleaned out his opposition; those who had survived banded together in an underground organisation, the *mojahedin-e-khalq*. Meanwhile, the ousted shah had arrived quietly in New York. 'We protest that the United States have taken in our enemy . . . we shall demand that they hand him over to us. Let this be a warning.' This attitude was amply demonstrated when 'Iran's valiant students, outraged by Satan America's behaviour' stormed the US embassy and took hostages.[14]

The day before the planned attack, a statement signed by Khomeini transformed a heated atmosphere into direct action: 'We ask all students and theologians to expand their attacks against the United States and Israel, so that they may force the United States to return the criminal shah.' Khomeini played for high stakes. He was about to take on the most powerful nation on earth.

Who actually pulled the strings in Tehran? It is one of the riddles of the Islamic Revolution: were there actually two revolutions? The first one, everybody knows about. But what took place during the days preceding the American hostage crisis? Who gave the order to overrun the American embassy? The most plausible explanation is that it was the Islamic Republican Party under the guidance of Mohammad Behesti. He had held secret talks with US officials which could be construed as treason, and wanted any proof of these meetings destroyed.[15] It may well be that the order did *not* originate with the Ayatollah Khomeini and that he was taken by surprise. This theory is strengthened by the fact that some Iranian Foreign Office officials tried to warn the American ambassador to take preventative action. In revolutionary Iran there existed several factions of hardliners, all fighting for control. One group was headed by Rafig Doust, the leader of the Revolutionary Guards and chief of the powerful Foundation for the Disinherited. Asgar Oladi,

---

[14] Mutual hostility continued until 21 June 1998 when the football squad of Iran met that of the United States during the football World Cup in France. Iran won.

[15] This theory was strengthened by a denial in *Mojahed* (2 December 1980). It was published together with a cable of a reported conversation between Bruce Leingen and Henry Precht from the State Department, and Behesti: 'IT IS TRULY SHAMEFUL THAT THE SAME PEOPLE WHO TOPPLED THE BAZARGAN REGIME BECAUSE IT MET WITH BRZEZHINSKI WOULD CONSIDER THE EMBASSY DOCUMENTS TO BE INFAMOUS. WE ARE NOT AWARE THAT MR BEHESTI MET WITH OFFICIALS OF THE US EMBASSY AND ASKED THE HELP OF THE AMERICANS.'

who represented the *bazaaris*, the bearded ones, led the other. This faction controlled commerce and oil. Opportunists like Rafsanjani, always hovering in the background, helped to confuse the situation. Lastly, there has the leader of the hardline mullahs: Mohammad Beheshti. A key figure in the Islamic Revolutionary Party and in the Revolutionary Council, he thought that Khomeini was getting soft. Granted, the ayatollah was *velayat-e-faqih*, the representative of God, but Realpolitik was never decided in heaven. Even in a religious republic, politics were earthy realities. Of course, it can be argued that it was Khomeini who gave the order, fearing that his grip was slipping. Perhaps he was looking for an attention-grabber to mobilise public opinion behind his radical plans and to silence the growing opposition.

The Iranian Hostage Crisis broke on 4 November 1979. Since early morning, a group of militant students had begun to gather outside the gates of the US embassy. At around 10.30 a.m., the Iranian guards posted to protect the building suddenly disappeared and a crowd of some 3,000 students surged into the compound. The twenty-two US Marines who were guarding the embassy were overpowered, disarmed, and blindfolded. The crowd stormed into the building and made the embassy staff of sixty-six Americans their prisoners. Their hands were tied behind their backs, and their eyes blindfolded with tape. Soon it became apparent that what at first seemed like a spontaneous anti-American demonstration was a thoroughly organised hostage taking. By the time foreign news crews arrived on the scene, the embassy had been occupied and the blindfolded US Marines were paraded before the television cameras. The pictures were transmitted via satellite around the world. The United States was shocked beyond belief; Americans were glued to their television sets. Washington feared reprisals on Iranian students living on American campuses and the National Guard was mobilised to protect the universities.

Throughout the crisis, President Carter's main concern was for the hostages. His limited actions, and they were few indeed, could hardly be viewed as a vehicle for self-promotion. His major fault was that he thought like a reasonable human being and not like a terrorist; he counted too much on diplomatic pressure to free the hostages but the mullahs did not blink an eye. Or perhaps they themselves had become hostages of the hostage takers. When a delegation of the PLO tried to negotiate a release, the students refused to have anything to do 'with Yasser Arafat, the PLO, or anyone else'. Sent by Khomeini, Foreign Minister Sadegh Ghotbzadeh tried to assure himself of the condition of the hostages but was unceremoniously manhandled and kicked out by the student leaders. Television crews besieged the embassy gates; the world was shown a daily diet of pictures of Iranian students standing on the wall, waving flags – but they never got a glimpse of an American hostage. The fate of the fifty-two Americans[16] was a riddle; it was as if they had ceased to exist. More terrorist events swept the Islamic world. In the beginning of the holy month of Moharram a group of Shi'ite fanatics invaded the Great Mosque of Mecca. Many died. In Kabul, the US ambassador to Afghanistan was gunned down, and a crowd stormed the US embassy in Pakistan, killing two. It led to the evacuation of all non-essential US service personnel from the region.

UN Secretary General Kurt Waldheim, attempted to resolve the hostage crisis. His mission became hopeless when a Tehran newspaper splashed a front-page picture of him talking to the shah. 'The Canadian caper' did not help either. At the time of the hostage taking, six Americans had slipped away into hiding. Canada's ambassador had supplied them with passports and they had left Iran on a regular flight. In a prime example of how the highly prized freedom of the press

[16] A number of black women employees had been released.

can backfire, an article about this, written by an American, put a halt to efforts to release the hostages. The US State Department delivered a threatening note to Iranian President Bani Sadr: 'In order to avoid misunderstanding, we want you to know that in the absence of a transfer by Monday, 31 March, we shall be taking additional non-belligerent measures that we have withheld until now . . .' Bani Sadr replied positively; the Revolutionary Council even voted 8 : 3 to resolve the hostage crisis. And then Khomeini vetoed it. He may have been forced to demonstrate to the hardliners that he was not softening.

It dawned on Washington that there was no further hope of solving this problem by any means other than direct intervention, which meant a military scenario. The first suggestion was the destruction of Iranian domestic oil facilities if but one hostage would be harmed. Brzezhinski turned this suggestion down, fearing that with a bombing campaign, America would enflame the entire Middle East and limit its future options, if it ever had any. Time was running out. On 7 April 1980, the United States officially severed diplomatic ties with Iran. It was a muddled affair. The Iranian chargé d'affaires was met at the door of the US State Department by Henry Precht. With a sly grin, the Iranian told the American official how happy the hostages were and that some of them wanted to remain in the Islamic Republic. Precht simply replied: 'Bullshit!' The Iranian felt insulted and stormed from the building. The note advising him of his expulsion from the United States was delivered to him as he sat in his car.

Operation Eagle Claw, as the military rescue plan was called, was the most ambitious undertaking ever put into the hands of a Delta Force commando. As the Israeli General Rafi Eytan (the man in charge of the famous Entebbe raid) pointed out, the main problem lay in the great distances across enemy territory. For this, eight C-130 transport and tanker planes would be needed. On 24 April, the planes flew to a flat area of desert and landed on the hard sand. Commandos installed a defensive perimeter around the zone. Next to the landing strip ran a rarely used country road. Suddenly lights appeared. It came from three civilian vehicles. The first was a rickety bus carrying forty-three passengers plus the driver. The commandos flagged down the bus and the passengers were taken prisoner. But the second vehicle would not stop. It was fired on and burst into flames. The driver made good his escape by running off to jump on board a small pick-up truck that was following close behind. It made off into the night. Someone suggested (which turned out to be correct) that it was a band of smugglers who thought they had run into a police roadblock. The mission was still go. The men of the Delta Force of Colonel Beckwith took off in eight helicopters from the USS *Nimitz* stationed in the Gulf. The projected path of the helicopter force lay across 500 miles of the Dacht-el-Kavir desert. The American planners had counted on every eventuality, but not on the *bad-e-semun*, 'the all-destroying wind'. All went well until they suddenly flew into a dense sandstorm. Soon a warning light flashed on the blade inspection method indicator of helicopter no. 6 and the pilot did what every American teenager is taught to do in school when a flashing light appears on the dashboard of his car. He stops. The pilot of no. 6 did precisely that: he landed his ship and the crew was picked up by another helicopter. Next, helicopter no. 5 developed guidance instrument failure. The pilot turned around and flew back to the *Nimitz*. With the loss of the second helicopter, the rescue mission began to unravel; they only just had enough capacity to carry all the hostages. But their troubles were not over. Helicopter no. 2 developed hydraulic problems and required major repairs. It too was out of the mission. Colonel Beckwith was stuck. The dawn was breaking and five helicopters were not enough to complete the lift-out. He sent a crash signal to the White House operations room. Brzezhinski called Secretary of Defense Brown to get Beckwith's on-the-spot assessment. It came at 4.57 p.m. Washington time. 'The request is for aborting the mission.'

President Carter thought for a moment before he answered: 'Let's go with his recommendation.'

The final curtain came down when one of the helicopters lifted off. As it whirled up in a dense cloud of loose sand, the pilot lost his bearings and flew into a tanker plane that was loaded with high-octane aviation fuel. The plane exploded, killing its seven crew members. At 6 p.m. the direct line to the president rang again in the White House. He picked it up and his face turned white. 'Are there any dead?' he asked, before turning to the operations group to tell them of the explosion.[17] The following morning, Iranian cameramen, led by mullahs, took pictures in the desert of their shining victory over 'Satan America'. Stations around the world picked up horrific pictures of incinerated corpses and mangled machines. The commentary changed but not the images.

The failure of 'Operation Eagle Claw' was due to mechanical reasons, but the reaction to them was purely human. In this ambitious operation, highly trained American specialists had relied on complex technology. When their machines let them down, they reacted according to the instruction manual – 'When your car goes on the blink, drive it into a garage and get it fixed.' The United States of America and its military might were covered in ridicule. Iran's propaganda triumph was complete. On 19 January 1981, US Secretary of State Cyrus Vance signed 'the Algiers Accord', which established the pre-November 1979 situation. Its main clause was the restitution of frozen Iranian holdings in the USA. The next day, the fifty-two American hostages were released. On the same day, Ronald Reagan replaced Jimmy Carter in the

[17] Chief of Naval Operations, Admiral J.L. Holloway III, *Rescue Mission Report*. August 1980.

presidency of the United States of America. All along Jimmy Carter had been the fifty-third hostage of Iran.

The terror continued. Regardless of the tightest censorship, stories came out.[18] One was of an Iranian English teacher who was considered an intellectual of the wrong kind.

> First they dragged me into a basement and beat me, to make me confess that I was in the pay of America. Just because I spoke English! Perhaps I was one of the lucky ones, because another prisoner stumbled into our cell, his hands and arms hanging, his face smeared with blood. He collapsed on the floor and never said a word until he died. We were left standing out in the freezing cold in the prison courtyard. If anyone died, his cause of death was given as pneumonia. I was put into a special cell and given documents to translate that were recovered during the raid on the US embassy. One day we were all herded into the courtyard to watch the execution of some prisoners accused of anti-revolutionary activity. They put the nooses over a construction crane, then raised it and strangled them.

Ehsan Naraghi, one of the last people to see the shah, was arrested and thrown in jail. His story from the notorious prison is telling.

> A guard put a blindfold over my eyes and I was led into the central building. As soon as I felt that the guard had left, I lifted my blindfold in one corner. What I saw was a hallucinatory spectacle – fifty boys and girls, all blindfolded and tied to one another, lined the long hallway. They had been left there for hours, in constant

---

[18] One tale concerned a prisoner (name withheld) who managed to slip away on transfer from Qasr prison to Evin prison. (He paid a Kurd to pass him across the mountains into Turkey and lives today in Denmark.)

anguish about their destiny. Were they given a reprieve and herded back into their cells, or did their way lead into the courtyard before daybreak?

These were teenagers who had been subjugated by ideologist Marxist ideas. They thought that their comrades, under the leadership of Massoud Rajavi (who was in Paris), would overthrow the Islamic regime. Even in their ineluctable march towards death they remained blind to realities. Prison life was an infernal spiral. Interrogation was followed by beatings and deprivations to be followed by more interrogations. One morning, a young boy was pushed into my cell. 'Today it was the first time that I was interrogated without a blindfold,' he said. To me it was clear that the interrogators were no longer worried about being recognised. And so it was; next morning the boy was shot.

In February 1981, Iran's attorney general, Ali Ghoddussi, released the figures of the number of trials by revolutionary courts. According to him, there had been 11,565 cases, resulting in 2,600 verdicts of guilty, of which 406 had been condemned to death. Ghoddussi went on to explain: 'We do not use torture, we apply only legitimate Islamic punishment.' Western journalists got a taste of this when armed Revolutionary Guards burst into the hotel reserved for the foreign press and ordered journalists to climb aboard a bus.[19] Their bus came to a halt in front of the notorious Evin prison. They were led upstairs into a vast hall. It was a scene from Dante's *Inferno*. A huge wall painting of a benevolently waving Ayatollah Khomeini floated over a huge crowd, of perhaps a thousand prisoners. All were dressed alike: the boys in grey prison garb, kneeling in a block on the left; the girls, equal in number, in dark blue chadors. 'Long

---

[19] The author was one of them.

live the glorious Islamic Revolution – Death to America.'
While the cameras rolled, a parade of wretched creatures
was produced. In halting English, they proclaimed their self-
condemnation. Phrases such as 'the beneficial influence of
the Islamic Revolution', and 'the teachings of our beloved
velayat-e-faqhih' alternated with 'Death to Satan America
who put us on the path of evil'. One of the female prisoners
admitted that she had not been wearing the chador, the
sacred veil of womanhood. Another's crime was that she
had been caught reading Western literature. The foreign
correspondents were allowed to put questions to the few
prisoners who had crossed their path; all were tame and
could be trusted. Then the press was led into the presence
of the man with the dubious sobriquet of 'The Butcher of
Tehran', Prosecutor Assadollah Ladjevardi, who put on a
show of great modesty. It was difficult to imagine that, only
hours before, the same man had sent eighty teenagers to their
deaths. That night, the world's press and their viewers got
a glimpse of hell. This time the revolutionary propaganda
backfired.

The war between Iran and Iraq erupted on 22 September
1980. After an initial setback, the people of Iran united
behind their imam against the Iraqi invader. On 24 May
1982 Iranian troops retook the strategic Iranian port of
Khorramshar. This feat of arms led to great outbursts of
joy, and was proclaimed as 'The victory by the true believers'.
The call for foreign journalists[20] came at 6 a.m. 'We shall
fly you to Khorramshar; be ready in fifteen minutes.' The
approaches to Khorramshar were littered with the debris of an
army in flight: fire-blackened tanks, shell holes, barbed-wire
entanglements, minefields and trenches filled with bodies.
And an unusual sight: thousands of cars standing end on
with their noses buried in the sand, a hedgehog deterrent

---

[20] The author was in this first group to visit the battlefield.

to an assault by airborne troops. There was still sporadic firing from the last pockets of resistance. The city itself was a jumble of bombed, burned, shattered rubble, an awesome demonstration of what a battle to the death will produce. A damp breeze from the Shatt-el-Arab carried the stench of death; now and then a stray dog wandered by, sniffing the air and howling. Near the great bridge, a marvel of engineering now cut in half by an explosion, lay heaps of crumpled forms, corpses swelling in the heat. It was here that the Iraqis had made their final stand. Half hanging from a foxhole was the body of a machine gunner, with three cartridge belts around his neck and a large hole where his stomach had been. Nearby sat three Iranians with their automatic rifles across their knees and a thousand-yard stare in their eyes. Blood-splattered Iraqi prisoners, tied up and blindfolded, leaned against a wall. Everywhere lay spent shells, discarded helmets, and pairs of boots. 'They run faster barefoot,' joked the accompanying officer. Judging by the piles of corpses, it was obvious that not many had managed to run away. A black slash indicated where a firebomb had incinerated houses and men; their burned corpses were hairless. Nearby sat a group of Iranians with a flame-thrower. One of the soldiers pointed at the corpses floating in the water. 'They tried to get away and we shot them, one by one.'

This war between Iraqi Sunnis and Iranian Shi'ites turned into a 'holy crusade' that went on for years and claimed hundreds of thousand of victims. Finally the Gulf Arabs switched sides. Much too late they found out that the shah had been the lesser evil.

And what became of the mullahs and their revolutionary helpers who inspired the crowd? Ayatollah Morteza Motahhari, theologian of the School of Islam in Qum and protagonist of ideas for reform of the entire religious Shi'ite system, became the principal theologian of the Islamic Revolution. He was assassinated by a group of mujahedin calling themselves 'Keeper of the Faith of the Koran'. A bomb blew up Ayatollah Behesti. Sadegh Ghotbzadeh, who tried to have the shah assassinated, was hanged by order of his ayatollah. The hanging judge Assadollah Ladjevardi was gunned down in a tailor's shop. Ayatollah Sadegh Khalkali, who ordered the assassination of Princess Ashraf's son and the extermination of the Turkomans and Kurds, was interned in a psychiatric ward. Abdol-Hassan Bani Sadr, the republic's first president, escaped into exile. Mehdi Bazargan, who resigned as Khomeini's prime minister, died of old age. Shapour Bakhtiar, the interim prime minister who wanted to settle the crisis by peaceful means, was assassinated in Paris. And the Ayatollah Khomeini outlived the shah by nine years. He died of old age in June 1989. He had no peace in life, and he was to have no peace in death; an explosion destroyed his mausoleum.

And then . . .

History will record that Mohammad Reza II Pahlevi, shahinshah of Iran, was the last of the mighty dynastic monarchs who assigned themselves the divine right to wield absolute power. The collapse of the Iranian empire and its ricochet effect on other royal dynasties may not spell the end for constitutional monarchies. They will remain in the head-of-state business as long as they follow the principal rules: they must be born to it; they must be non-political; and they must simply be there. But it certainly marks the end of an era. The shah committed a capital error when he inflated his own power and underrated the prestige of a religious imam because of his irremovable prejudice against a religious revival. But people who are neglected and downtrodden have but one escape: their faith.

The tragedy of Iran lay in two principal opposites: an

arrogant, flamboyant, irresolute monarch, who hated blood-shed, yet was responsible for the shedding of a great deal of it. And a scholarly mullah, who found himself at the centre of a confrontation and so who used religion to indict a social system that had outlived its time. He toppled a sovereign, and then assumed the title of imam, which in the Shi'ite religion is exclusively reserved for the original twelve Imams of the Prophet. The Imam Khomeini went on to transform the *passive* Shi'ites into *active* Shi'ites. He politicised Islamic jurisprudence and installed an absolute and totalitarian regime in the name of Allah, the prophet and his twelve imams, and the disinherited. In doing so, Khomeini launched his country on an Islamic renaissance and initiated a veritable theoretic and political revolution that rapidly spread abroad. Islamic fundamentalism was exported to its neighbouring countries and was the catalyst for a series of civil wars throughout the Islamic Crescent and way beyond. Planes were hijacked, opponents assassinated. Sunni clashed with Shi'ite. The Syrian town of Hama was wiped off the map by artillery after the Muslim Brotherhood staged an uprising against the regime of Hafez-el-Assad. Twenty-five thousand were systematically butchered in one bloody weekend. Iraq cashed in on the turmoil of its neighbour and invaded Iran. Saddam Hussein was driven to this step by the justifiable fear of a Shi'ite uprising in Iraq. In the invasion, he was financially supported by his Sunni neighbours in the Gulf. While this war heated up, a most unlikely alliance was formed between Iran, the 'defender of the true faith,' and 'Satan' Israel. After eight terrible years the war ended in a stalemate. When the Gulf Arabs refused to continue their funding of Iraq's military effort, Saddam Hussein invaded Kuwait and set off the Gulf War, which ended in a cloud of noxious fumes from burning oil wells. The Islamic menace had become a reality. The USA worried about its oil reserves, and the Soviet Union, within its territorial limits, had to deal with 55 million Muslims. It was in the interests of both superpowers to put a lid on the mullahs. And thus it was that on a summer's day in 1990 the world got drawn into a conflict that began on a cold winter's day in Tehran eleven years before.

As for Iran, it will go its own way as it has done for thousands of years.

'*Allah akbar* – God is great – and everyone must obey *His* will.'

Epilogue

'More alive dead'

> When bad men combine, the good must associate;
>   else they will fall,
> one by one, an unpitied sacrifice in a contemptible
>   struggle.
>
> Edmund Burke, 1729–1797

We adopt lost causes with a certain ease, weeping over the fate of the irresolute Louis XVI more than over that of the decisive Danton. But let us not be blinded by sentiment; the monarchs ousted by the revolutionaries no longer deserved their kingdoms. They wore the sad masks of discarded potentates; their weak personalities had been a magnet for intrigue and corruption. Until their monarchical vessels struck a rock, and sank.

But in the same way the bloody policies of the great revolutionaries added much to the misery of the people; with contemptible cynicism the insurrectionists made use of any villainy in order to seize power from a deposed ruler. Their use of capital punishment violated the only indisputable human kinship – solidarity in the fact of death – which could be legitimised only by a principle higher than man. To achieve their end, the new leaders stopped at nothing. And what did the people demand in exchange? Flags, victories, and deaths. They got it all. As long as the unity of the nation was at stake, everything was permitted, including crimes against humanity. The revolutionaries' plans were sound, but their methods often damnable. It is a fact that a democracy cannot be born in a single day. So, if morally they were wrong, historically they were proved right. Morality and History make for an incompatible marriage. There lies the real tragedy of revolution.

The convulsions of the past two centuries have brought about the disappearance of the great empires as the anchors of internal and international order. The spread of nationalism, coinciding with the industrial revolution which brought ease of travel and communication has led to their demise as much as revolution itself. Loose federations or republics replaced the indigenous kings who achieved equilibrium sometimes by brutal means; the end result was global instability, the fragmentation of nations into mini-states, forcing many smaller countries to join larger federations in order to survive.

As centuries go, this one began better than did the last one, when revolutions were shaking Russia and Mexico, the Boers were rebelling in South Africa and the Boxers in China. But the twenty-first century rings in a new phenomenon, that of monetary globalisation. It is a powerful vehicle that increases economic growth, spreads new technologies, and drives up living standards in rich and (some) poor countries alike. For the time being, the aim of most countries around the world is directed at achieving affluence, and that in turn reduces the chances of political upheavals or revolts. The quest for greater happiness holds a tight grip on the human imagination. We live in a Revolution of Well-Being. A comfortable lifestyle is considered the solution to most people's difficulties. As technology brings this goal within reach, the inequalities it produces threaten its realisation. Technology has fuelled a rise of mass industrialisation; it has shrunk the globe through modern travel and a virtual presence, and it has put unprecedented knowledge and power into the hands of individuals. These fundamental changes pose many problems: they create an acute risk to national sovereignty; they erode local culture; and they threaten social stability. The main question remains as to whether nations will be able to control such upheavals or whether the upheavals will come to control the nations.

In the recent 'Economic Revolution of Europe', its member nations see the antidote to their eternal pernicious nationalism in economic unification, where technology complements politics. Major companies already disregard national borders; exports rise; investment decisions are no longer based on national interests. Multinationals organise their production in global terms. Rapid economic growth and trade expansion has sharply cut the numbers of the desperately poor. Joining the better-off classes takes the ammunition out of the revolutionaries' guns. Yet there is always the danger of economic world instability; globalisation opens the way to total dependence on commercial superpowers. Smaller nations will feel threatened by any kind of change from abroad, which menaces their own political, cultural, and social structure. What has always been local and familiar is suddenly being replaced by something that is utterly foreign. For the moment, the people of most countries feel that they have more to gain than to lose. But this does not preclude the possibility of a powerful backlash, with unpredictable consequences. Advanced technology has widened the gap between the haves and have-nots. The ballooning global population will sharply increase its demand for food, shelter, and everything else. Including comfort. There is the risk of revolt if one class or society feels excluded from the benefits of the kind of technology that leads to general well-being. This could drive them to using revolutionary means to solve their frustrations. The ease with which the repressed can subvert their subjugators and the expansion of regional conflicts into major wars will speed up in the future. People often talk about consciously choosing their future, but historically it is clear that only rarely has such a choice been available, and then mostly under authoritarian leadership. Such leaders make a deliberate choice which sets their course and afterwards they use their power to manipulate their fellow man. It is more difficult today to leave a permanent imprint on history, and rebellions led by one or two agitators, such as those produced in Paris, Petrograd, or Tehran, seem arcane to us. Modern telecommunications accelerate events, but so do the counter-measures for sudden, violent repression. Automated observers watch us and Big Brother has become a reality. Well-being is important, but so is personal liberty.

Man is a strange animal. He needs friends, but he also needs enemies. Of that there will always be enough although with the fall of Communism, the West has lost a certain amount. However, over the last few years we have recovered a few. The Muslim Integrists, the Russian Mafia, the affair-conscious politician – not forgetting one or two mighty economic organisations. With them, we have the right to ask ourselves some serious questions. It is today as it was throughout history. Men appear with sinister intentions, ready to devastate our economies and destroy our culture. The questions of class distinction or religion serve them well as their Trojan Horse. In countries where individual freedom is continuously abused, its absence does become an issue. But freedom as we know it today can be a dangerous concept, as it can raise hopes that can never be realised. Modern ideas spread easily across political boundaries by means of the global media and can quickly lead to tragedy. Castro's Cuba has already passed through one electronic upheaval, a 'Fax and Television Revolution'. The promise of a better life, piped in by satellite from Miami, has led to the drama of the Cuban boat people. Thousands perished, eaten by sharks or swept by storms from their inflated rubber rafts. Their next attempt to reach freedom will certainly not repeat the errors of the past. They will not flee across a raging sea; they will turn on their fossilised leaders. Cuba-sized revolutions are a problem that the modern world can handle. But there are also 1 billion Indians and (soon) 2 billion Chinese who look for betterment. The present leadership is likely to discover that size and military might do not equal internal strength. The restless masses of Asia will rise and throw off the yoke of concentration camps, gulags, and the terror of their secret police, and they will press to be freed from whatever prevents them from becoming whatever they want to be.

In 1930, a 'half-naked fakir' (in Churchill's words) gave the world its first taste of freedom when he successfully demonstrated a new version of revolution by peaceful change. Fifty-nine years later, an unknown Chinese with a briefcase blocked a line of tanks that were rumbling into Tianammen square to put down a rebellion in the world's most populous nation. This single act of purpose and courage electrified the world. It also set off warning bells. Yes, the notion of freedom is spreading fast to the great majority of humanity. The new millennium will offer for many a New Order to replace *l'ancien régime*. This could well be danger in disguise, since any notion of a newly independent republic is always so ill defined. More often than not, it leads to social disorder. The day when Asia and its billions of 'starving masses rise from slumber',[1] that day will be the all-devouring Big Bang. Sure as day follows night, that day will come. At the change of one millennium into the next, the world has a much better idea of what it is leaving behind than of what lies ahead.

History is man, and every man has his personality, ambitions, passions. Nobody can escape his natural environment, his

---

[1] The first line of the Socialist hymn, 'The Internationale'.

upbringing, or his basic character. Of all those who lived through the centuries, many were called, but few were chosen. By their example they inspired followers and determined the fate of us all. Every one of their acts could be justified, provided it was perpetrated in the name of patriotism, God – or, best of all, an ideal.

Our lives are built on the sum total of the people who came before us. 'In all countries death is an end. It comes, and the curtain goes down. Not here. Here, a dead person is more alive dead . . .' Thus wrote the poet Federico García Lorca the night before he faced a firing squad. How true. A man is alive as long as he is remembered. He is killed only by forgetfulness. Perhaps a revolutionary's greatest legacy to all of us is not his military skill, nor his political achievements, but the fact that his spirit never dies. This is the ultimate monument to a legendary man.

He is *more alive dead*.

Bibliography

Chapter 1: 10 August 1794

Anecdotes peu connues sur Danton, Paris, 1793.
Bailly, A.D., *Anecdotes sur la mort de Louis XVI*, Paris, 1804.
Beaucourt, Marquis, *Captivité et derniers moments de Louis XVI*, Paris, 1892.
Behrens, A., *The Ancien Régime*, London, 1967.
Bonnet, J., *La Mort de Marat*, Paris, 1986.
Bressand, J., *Récit des Temps Révolutionnaires*, Paris, 1984.
Campan, A., *Mémoires*, Paris, 1821.
Castelot, A., *Louis XVII*, Paris, 1960.
Convention Nationale sur le jugement Citoyen Capet par J. Fouchet, 1793.
Crapelet, *Portrait de Marat*, 1794.
Decaux, A., *Face à face de l'histoire*, Paris, 1977.
Desessarts, *La crime de Robespierre et ses complices, la mort de Marat*, 1797.
Detremau, N., *Trois jours pour détruire la monarchie*, Paris, 1988.
Dumineray, H., *La Peste Rouge*, Paris, 1851.
Dunn, S., *Death of Louis XVI*, Princeton, 1994.
Firemont, Abbé, *Mémoires*, Paris, 1815.
Furneaux, R., *The Bourbon Tragedy*, London, 1968.
Hampton, D., *Danton*, London, 1978.
Hue, F., *The Last Years of Louis XVI*, London, 1866.
Jugement du citoyen Capet et sa femme, Marie Antoinette, Paris, 1796.
La mort et la résurrection de Louis XVI, 1792.
Lenôtre, G., *The Dauphin: Louis XVII*, London, 1911.
Letter of M. Burke, member of parliament, London, 1790.
Marat, J.P., *L'ami du peuple*, 1790.
Mathiez, A., *Le dix août*, Paris, 1931.
Morris, G., *A Diary of the French Revolution 1789–93*, London, 1939.
Nodier, C., *Le 21 janvier*, Paris, 1816.
Révélation sur la procédure et exécution de Charlotte Corday, 1794.
Roederer, P., *Chronique des cinquante jours du 20 juin au 10 août*, Paris, 1832.
Romartin, *Les géants de '89*, Paris, 1977.
Schama, S., *Citizens: a chronicle of the French revolution*, London, 1989.
Seward, D., *The Bourbon Kings of France*, London, 1976.
Speech by Mr Pitt before the House of Commons, 1793.
Sutherland, D.M.G., *France 1789–1815*, London, 1985.
Thompson, S., *Leaders of the French Revolution*, London, 1988.
Tocqueville, A. de, *L'ancien régime et la révolution*, Paris, 1877.

Turgy, F., *Les quatre jours de la Terreur*, Paris, 1814
Yalom, M., *Les Temps des Orages*, Paris, 1989.

Archival sources
The Archives Nationales, Paris (especially the eyewitness accounts of trials and executions).

Chapter 2: 13 August 1809

Bartsch, R., *Der Volkskried in Tirol*, 1905.
Frankl, L.A., *Andreas Hofer im Liede*, 1884.
Hirn, J., *Tirol's Erhebung im Jahre 1809*, 1909.
Magenschab, H., *Andreas Hofer*, 1984.
Paulin, K., *Das Leben des Andreas Hofer*, 1935.

Archival sources
The Archives Nationales, Paris; the Bibliothèque Centre Culturelle d'Autriche, Paris; Oesterreichische Staatsbibliothek, Vienna.

Chapter 3: 18 November 1910

Alba, V., *The Mexicans*,
Atkins, R., *Revolution*,
Blasco Ibanez, V., *Mexico in Revolution*,
Cline, H.F., *The United States and Mexico*,
Harris, L.A., *Pancho Villa and the Columbus Raid*,
Pinchon, E., *Viva Villa*,
Tuchmann, B., *The Zimmerman Telegram*,

Chapter 4: 7 November 1917

Conquest, R., *The Great Terror*, London, 1990.
Denikin, A., *The Russian Turmoil*, London, 1922.
Djilus, M., *Conversations with Stalin*, London, 1962.
Golovine, N., *The Russian Army in the World War*, New Haven, 1932.
Kerenski, A., *The Crucifixion of Liberty*, New York, 1934.
Mourousy, P., *Lenin: autopsie d'un dictateur*, Paris, 1992.
Moynahan, B., *Comrades*, London, 1992.
Müller, A., *Gespräche zur Weltgeschichte*, Stuttgart, 1965.
Pares, B., *The Fall of the Russian Monarchy*, London, 1939.
Plowman, S., *My Kingdom for a Grave*, London, 1970.
Radzinsky, E., *The Last Tsar*, London, 1992.
Reed, J., *Ten Days that Shook the World*, New York, 1919.
Serge (Kibaltshish), V., *L'an 1 de la Révolution Russe*, Paris, 1971.
Sokolov, N., *Enquête Judiciaire sur l'assassinat de la Famille Impériale Russe*, Paris, 1929.
Souvarine, B., *Stalin*, London, 1939.
Trotsky, L., *The History of the Russian Revolution*, New York, 1932.

Additional sources
Conversation with Father B. Chukov of the Russian Orthodox Church in Paris.

Chapter 5: 9 January 1919

Akademie Wissenschaft, *Revolutionaere Ereignisse 17/18*, 1957.
Badia, G., *Rosa Luxemburg,*
Beda, S., *The Spartakist Uprising*, 1958.
Bernstein, E., *Die Deutsche Revolution*, 1921.
Braubach, M., *Aufstieg Brandenburgs 1640–1815*, 1933.
Bulow, H.D. von, *Der Geist des neuer Kriegssystems*, 1799.
Cowles, V., *Wilhelm der Kaiser*, 1963.
Ebda, C., *The Spartakist Uprising*, 1958.
Feldman, G., *Army, Industry, Labor in Germany,1966.*
Freiheit Verlag, *Der Mord an Karl Liebknecht und Rosa Luxemburg*, 1920.
Froehlich, P., *Rosa Luxemburg,1939.*
Ilsemann, S., *Der Kaiser in Holland,1967.*
Liebknecht, K. *Antimilitarismus,*
Luxemburg, R., *Die Akkumulation des Kapitals,1912.*
Luxemburg, R., *Junius Brochure,1916.*
Macartney, C., *Hapsburg and Hohenzollern Dynasties*, London, 1970.
Mommsen, H., *Die Verspielte Freiheit,1989.*
Nettl, P., *Rosa Luxemburg,*
Quack, S., *Geistig frei, niemandes Knecht*, 1983.
Reiners, L., *In Europa gehen die Lichter aus*, 1954.
Runkel, F., *Die Deutsche Revolution,*
Waldman, E., *Spartakus*, 1967.
Ziegler, W., *Volk Ohne Fuehrung*, 1938.

Archival sources
Deutsches Historisches Institut, Paris.

Chapter 6: 20 July 1944

Bullock, A., *Hitler*, 1954.
Guenther, H., *Geschichte des 2. Weltkriegs*, 1965.
Hauner, M., *Hitler: a chronology*, London, 1983.
Heyde, von der, *Der 20, Juli 1944 in OKW-AHA,*
Maser, W., *Adolf Hitler*, 1971.
Page, H.P., *General Friedrick Olbricht*, 1992.
Pridun, K., *20 Juli 1944, Stellungsnahme,*

Archival and additional sources
The Deutsches Historiches Institut, Paris; interview by the author with Albert Speer and Otto Skorzeny, both now deceased.

Chapter 7: 15 August 1945

Akamatsu, P., *Meiji 1868*, Paris, 1968.

Bergamini, D., *The Conspiracy of Hirohito*, Paris, 1974.
Churchill, W., *The History of the Second World War,*
Fuller, J.F.C., *The Decisive Battles of the Western World*, vol. II, London, 1970.
Guillain, R., *Le peuple japonais et la guerre*, Paris, 1947.
Leonard, J.N., *Medieval Japan*, 1969.
Okasaki, A., *Histoire de Japon*, Paris, 1958.
Pacific War Research Group, *Japan's Longest Day*, 1965.

Additional sources
The author's research in Japan with survivors.

Chapter 8: 8 October 1967

Kalfon, P., *Che*, 1997.
Maspero, F. and Guevara, C., *Journal de Bolivie*, 1968.
Ramirez, D.A., *Le Che en Bolivie*, 1997.
Stage, J., *Revolution*, 1968.
Taibo, P., *Guevara*, 1997.

Archival and additional sources
The Cuban Archives, Havana; the author's personal notes and interviews with eyewitnesses.

Chapter 9: 16 January 1979

Ajomand, S.A., *The Turban for the Crown*, London, 1988.
Harney, D., *The Priest and the King*, London, 1998.
Holloway, (Admiral) J.L., III, et al, *Rescue Mission Report*, 1982.
Hoveyda, F., *The Fall of the Shah*, London, 1980.
Huyser, R., *Mission to Tehran*, London, 1986.
Jordan, H., *The Last Year of the Carter Presidency*, New York, 1982.
Legrand, J., *Le Chah d'Iran*, Paris, 1998.
Moreau, ., *R-comme racket pétrolier*, Paris, 1976.
Mozaffari, M., *Pouvoir Shiite*, Paris, 1998.
Naraghi, E., *Du Palis du Chah aux prisons de la Révolution*, Paris, 1991.
Pahlevi, R. (Shah of Iran), *Answer to History*, New York, 1980.
Parsons, A., *The Pride and the Fall*, London, 1984.
Powell, J., *The Other Side of the Story*, New York, 1984.
Samson, A., *The Seven Sisters*, London, 1975.
Scholl-Latour, P., *Allah ist mit den Standhaften*, Stuttgart, 1983.
Scott, C.W., *Pieces of the Game*, Atlanta, 1984.
Shawcross, W., *The Shah's Last Ride*, New York, 1988.
Sick, G., *All Fall Down*, London, 1985.
Taheri, A., *The Unknown Life of the Shah*, London, 1991.

Additional sources
Much is based on the author's personal observations as a journalist during visits to Iran, starting in 1960, including an interview with the shah in 1972, and interview with Prime Minister Freydoun Hoveyda, and a visit to the Ayatollah Khomeini's residence outside Paris in 1978. The author was present in Tehran during the revolution and the hostage crisis, and was given a guided tour of Evin prison in 1982. He covered the Iran–Iraq war both from Tehran and Baghdad.

Index